Fuji X Secrets

Rico Pfirstinger studied communications and has been working as a journalist, publicist, and photographer since the mid-'80s. He has written numerous books on a diverse range of topics, from computing technology to digital desktop publishing to sled dog racing. He worked as the department head of special assignments for Hubert Burda Media in Munich, Germany, and he later also served as chief editor for a winter sports website.

After eight years as a freelance film critic in Los Angeles, Rico now lives in Germany and devotes his time to digital photography and compact camera systems.

Rico writes the popular X-Pert Corner blog and leads workshops called Fuji X Secrets where he offers tips and tricks on using the Fujifilm X series cameras.

Rico Pfirstinger

Fuji X Secrets

142 Ways to Make the Most of Your
Fujifilm X Series Camera

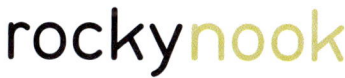

Fuji X Secrets
142 Ways to Make the Most of Your Fujifilm X Series Camera
Rico Pfirstinger
www.fuji-x-secrets.net

Project editor: Maggie Yates
Project manager: Lisa Brazieal
Marketing manager: Mercedes Murray
Copyeditor: Maggie Yates
Layout and type: Petra Strauch
Front cover design: Rebecca Cowlin
Cover production: WolfsonDesign
Indexer: Maggie Yates

ISBN: 978-1-68198-416-2
1st Edition (1st printing, February, 2019)
© 2019 Rico Pfirstinger
All images © Rico Pfirstinger unless otherwise noted

Rocky Nook, Inc.
1010 B Street, Suite 350
San Rafael, CA 94901
U.S.A.

www.rockynook.com

Distributed in the UK and Europe by Publishers Group UK
Distributed in the U.S. and all other territories by Ingram Publisher Services

Library of Congress Control Number: 2018937562

Printed in the U.S.A.

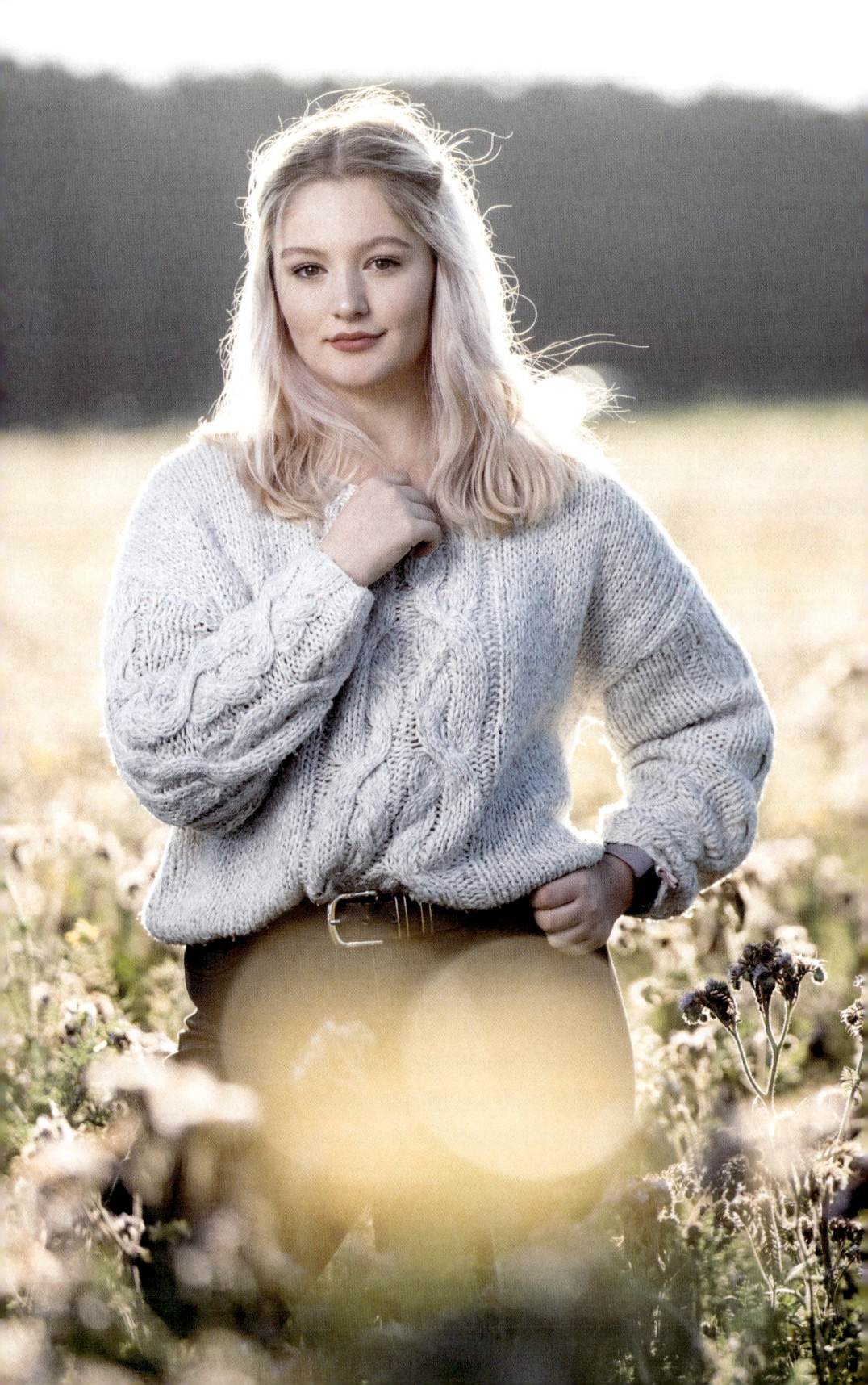

1. YOUR FUJIFILM X SYSTEM

Fujifilm's mirrorless X series consists of more than 30 different cameras with either fixed (FL) or interchangeable lenses
(IL). They can be categorized into several families that share
the same CMOS sensors and processing engines:

■ X100 Classic (FL): 12 MP APS-C Bayer CMOS sensor (Fuji-
film/Sony design with CDAF), EXR I engine

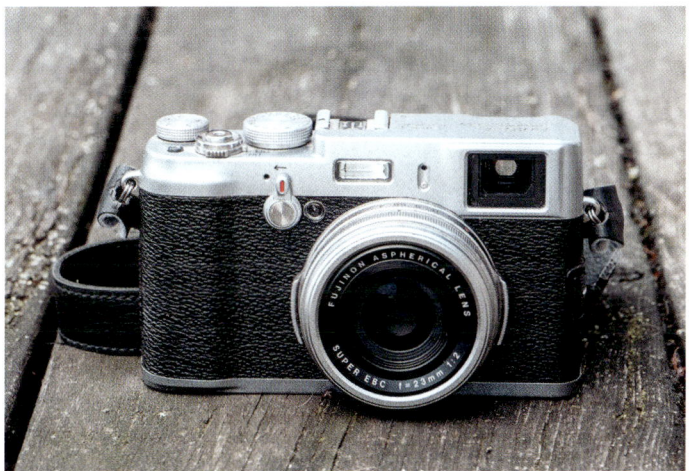

Fig. 1: The original **X100** was Fujifilm's first X series camera. It
features a trademark retro design with pseudo-analog controls,
dedicated dials for aperture and shutter speed, and a hybrid viewfinder that can fill a dual role as EVF (electronic viewfinder) or OVF
(optical viewfinder). Its Sony-based 12 MP sensor was already a little outdated when the camera launched in spring 2011, but thanks
to competent image processing and a 23mmF2 leaf-shutter lens
with almost "magic" qualities, the X100 earned plenty of praise,
which led to three evenly successful follow-ups: the X100S(econd),
the X100T(hird), and the X100F(ourth).

- X10, XF1, X-S1 (FL): 12 MP 2/3" Bayer EXR CMOS sensor (Fujifilm/Toshiba design with CDAF), EXR I engine

- X20, X30, XQ1, XQ2 (FL): 12 MP 2/3" X-Trans CMOS II sensor (Fujifilm/Toshiba design with hybrid CDAF/PDAF), EXR II engine

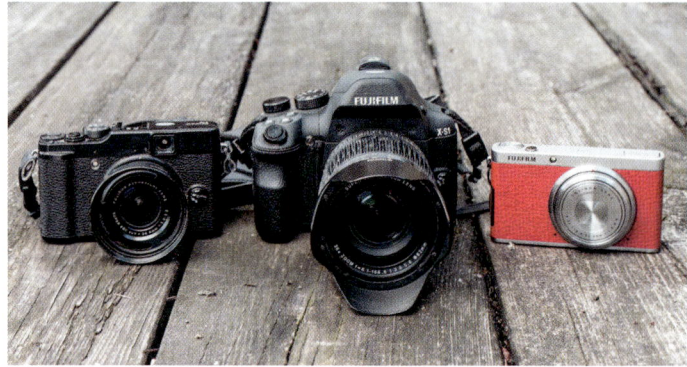

Fig. 2: Soon after launching the X100, Fujifilm added the **X10** to the lineup. This little brother to the X100 features a zoom lens and a smaller 2/3" EXR sensor with 12 MP. It was later complemented by the more elegant **XF1** and the rugged **X-S1** bridge camera. While they all share sensors and processors with the X10, each model has a different design, user interface, and lens.

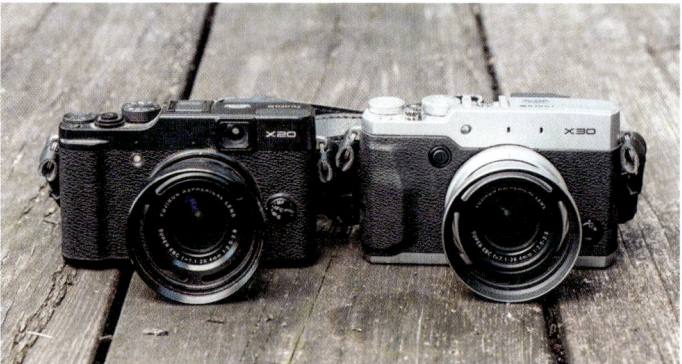

Fig. 3: The **X20, X30,** and **XQ1/2** can be considered modernized versions of the X10 and XF1, featuring a 12 MP 2/3" X-Trans sensor with hybrid-AF (CDAF/PDAF) and a faster EXR II processor. With its built-in high-resolution EVF, faster autofocus and a more complete feature set, the X30 was the most mature camera of Fuji's now discontinued 2/3" sensor lineup.

- X-Pro1, X-E1 (IL): 16 MP APS-C X-Trans CMOS I sensor (Fujifilm/Sony design with CDAF), EXR I engine

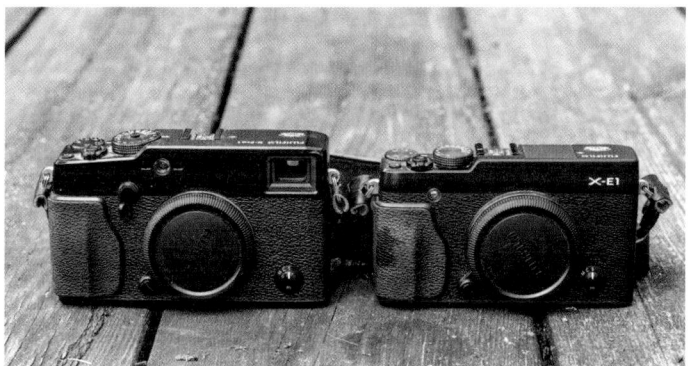

Fig. 4: The **X-Pro1** and **X-E1** both feature a 16 MP X-Trans CMOS I sensor, EXR I processor, and an almost identical set of functions. The main difference? While the X-Pro1 incorporated a hybrid viewfinder similar to the X100 line, the smaller and cheaper X-E1 offered a regular EVF, but with a higher resolution. And while the X-Pro1 was tailored toward compact X-mount prime lenses (18mm, 35mm, and 60mm), the X-E1 was offered with a high-quality 18–55mmF2.8–4 "kit zoom" featuring an optical image stabilizer (OIS).

- X-A1, X-A2 (IL): 16 MP APS-C Bayer CMOS sensor (Fujifilm/Sony design with CDAF), EXR II engine

- X-M1 (IL): 16 MP APS-C X-Trans CMOS I sensor (Fujifilm/Sony design with CDAF), EXR II engine

- X-A10, X-A20 (IL): 16 MP APS-C Bayer CMOS sensor (Fujifilm/Sony design with CDAF); the cameras are built by Xacti in Jakarta/Indonesia

- X-A3 (IL): 24 MP APS-C Bayer CMOS sensor (Fujifilm/Sony design with CDAF); the camera is made by Xacti in Jakarta/Indonesia

- XF10 (FL) and X-A5, X-T100 (IL): 24 MP APS-C Bayer CMOS sensor (Fujifilm/Sony design with hybrid CDAF/PDAF); the cameras are manufactured by Xacti in Jakarta/Indonesia

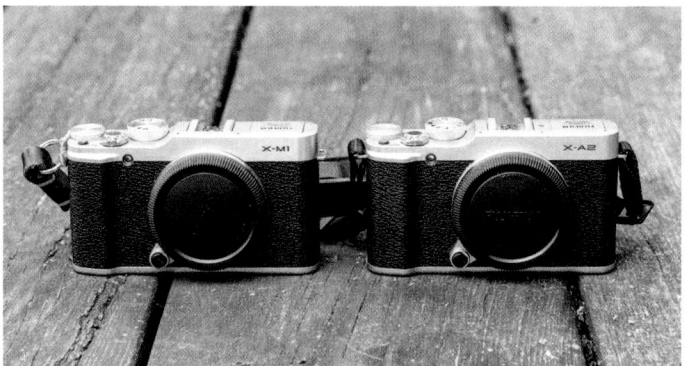

Fig. 5: The X-A1 and **X-M1** were Fujifilm's first entry-level offerings for the interchangeable X-mount system. They lack an EVF, so users have to rely on a tiltable rear LCD display to frame their shots. The two cameras look identical from the outside and offer the same feature set, but they use different sensor designs. The X-A1 incorporates a 16 MP Bayer sensor with an anti-aliasing (AA) filter, whereas the more expensive X-M1 features a 16 MP X-Trans sensor without an AA filter. While there was never a successor to the X-M1, the X-A1 was very popular—particularly in East Asian markets—prompting the release of the **X-A2**, which looked just like its predecessor. Beginning with the X-A3, the series was outsourced to contract manufacturer Xacti in Indonesia.

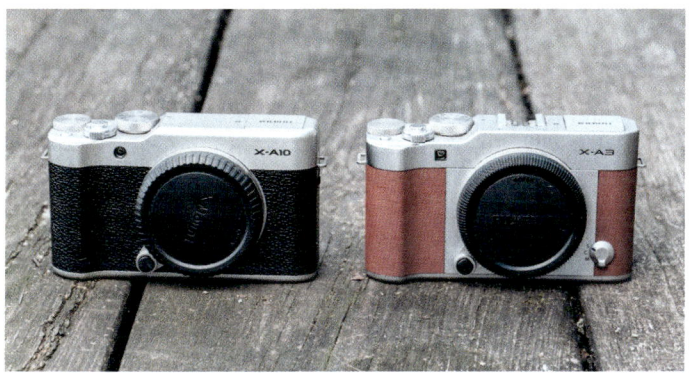

Fig. 6: While the **X-A10** and X-A20 are little-known, low-cost mod-els for specific markets, the more fully featured **X-A3** has been available all over the world, specifically targeting customers in Asia. Despite its 24 MP sensor, many considered the X-A3 to be a marginal improvement over the X-A2, citing Fujifilm's decision to outsource development and production of the camera to contract manufacturer Xacti.

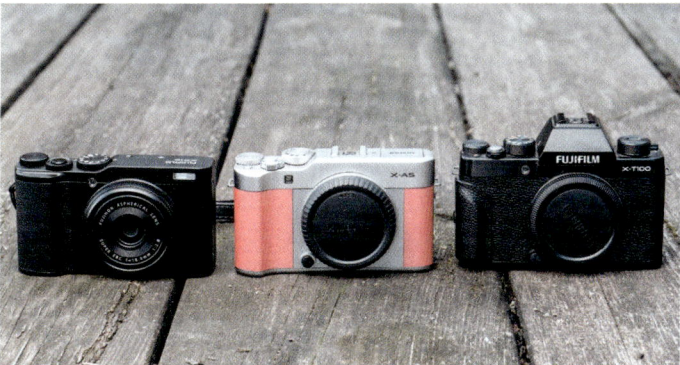

Fig. 7: The **XF10**, **X-A5**, and **X-T100** attract customers with faster hybrid-AF, plenty of features, and improved overall performance. Of particular interest is the X-T100, which serves as a stepping stone between the entry-level X-A lineup and the more sophis-ticated X-T20. With its high-resolution EVF and a 24 MP Bayer sensor without AA filter, the X-T100 also serves enthusiast users as a second body.

- X100S, X100T, X70 (FL), and X-E2, X-E2S, X-T1, X-T10 (IL): 16 MP APS-C X-Trans CMOS II sensor (Fujifilm/Sony design with hybrid CDAF/PDAF), EXR II engine

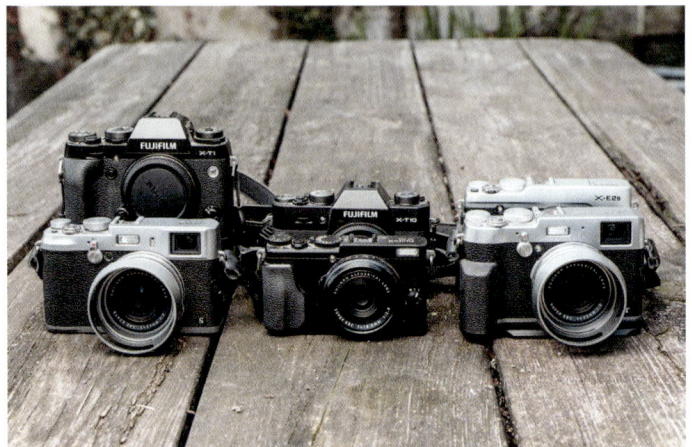

Fig. 8: Popular second-generation workhorses like the **X-T1, X-T10, X-E2(S), X70** and **X100T** not only feature the same APS-C sensor and EXR II processor, but also a common set of features. Be careful if you have an **X100S,** though: Despite its similar hardware, it functions more like the older X-Pro1 or X-E1.

- X-Pro2, X-T2, X-T20, X-E3, X-H1 (IL), and X100F (FL): 24 MP APS-C X-Trans CMOS III sensor (Fujifilm/Sony design with hybrid CDAF/PDAF), X-Processor Pro engine

- GFX 50S, GFX 50R (IL): 51 MP medium-format (44×33mm) Bayer CMOS sensor (Fujifilm/Sony design with CDAF), X-Processor Pro engine

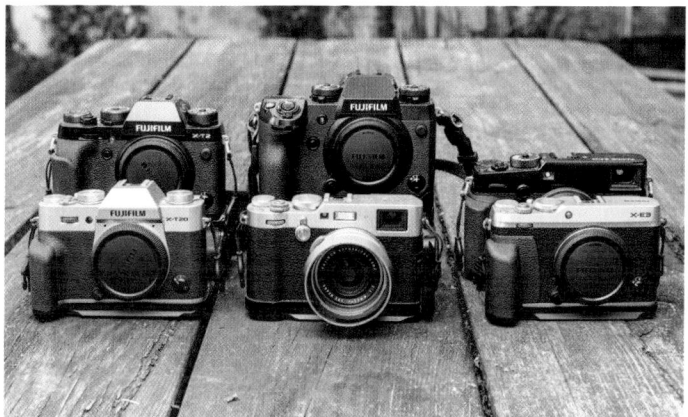

Fig. 9: Fuji's third-generation APS-C lineup with X-Trans CMOS III and X-Processor Pro was launched in early 2016 with the **X-Pro2** and culminates in the high-performance **X-H1** from spring 2018. Along with the **X-T2, X-T20, X-E3,** and **X100F,** these powerful cameras not only share a common sensor and processing engine, they also feature a very similar feature set which has been continuously expanded by numerous firmware updates. The Japanese call this Kaizen.

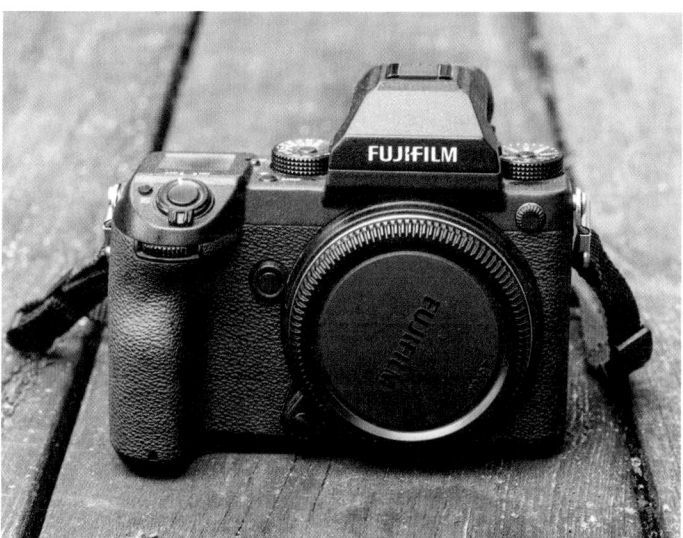

Fig. 10: With the **GFX 50S,** Fujifilm has launched a second lineup of interchangeable lens cameras, adding the medium-format G-mount to the APS-C-sized X-mount. Despite its impressive specs and image quality that surpasses all "full-frame" offerings on the market (44×33mm Bayer sensor with 51 MP, no AA filter), the GFX 50S and GFX 50R are just a beginning. The next GFX generation features more than 100 megapixels.

- X-T3 (IL): 26 MP APS-C X-Trans CMOS 4 sensor (Fujifilm/ Sony design with hybrid CDAF/PDAF), X-Processor 4 engine

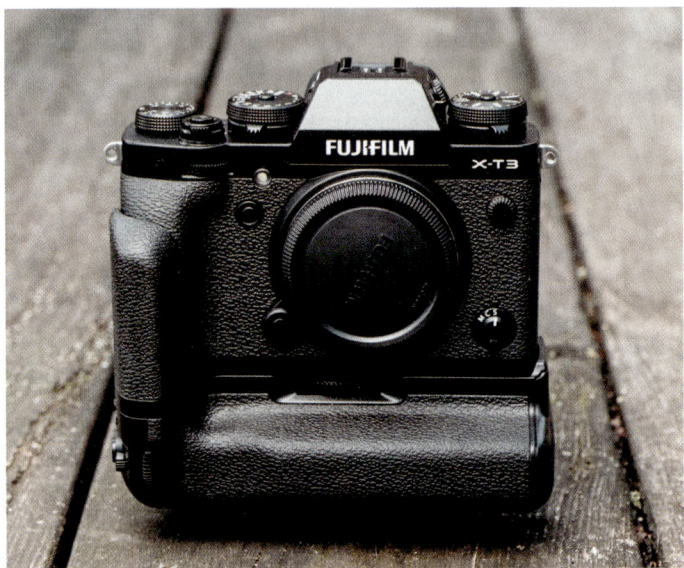

Fig. 11: The **X-T3** is the original fourth-generation model in Fujifilm's system camera lineup. It's not hard to imagine that its backside-illuminated 26 MP X-Trans CMOS 4 sensor and X-Processor 4 will also appear in future cameras, like a potential X-T30, X-E4, or X-Pro3.

All X series models contain sensors that were manufactured by either Toshiba (2/3") or Sony (APS-C & medium format). They feature on-sensor autofocus with either contrast detection autofocus (CDAF) or hybrid-AF. The latter combines CDAF with phase detection autofocus (PDAF).

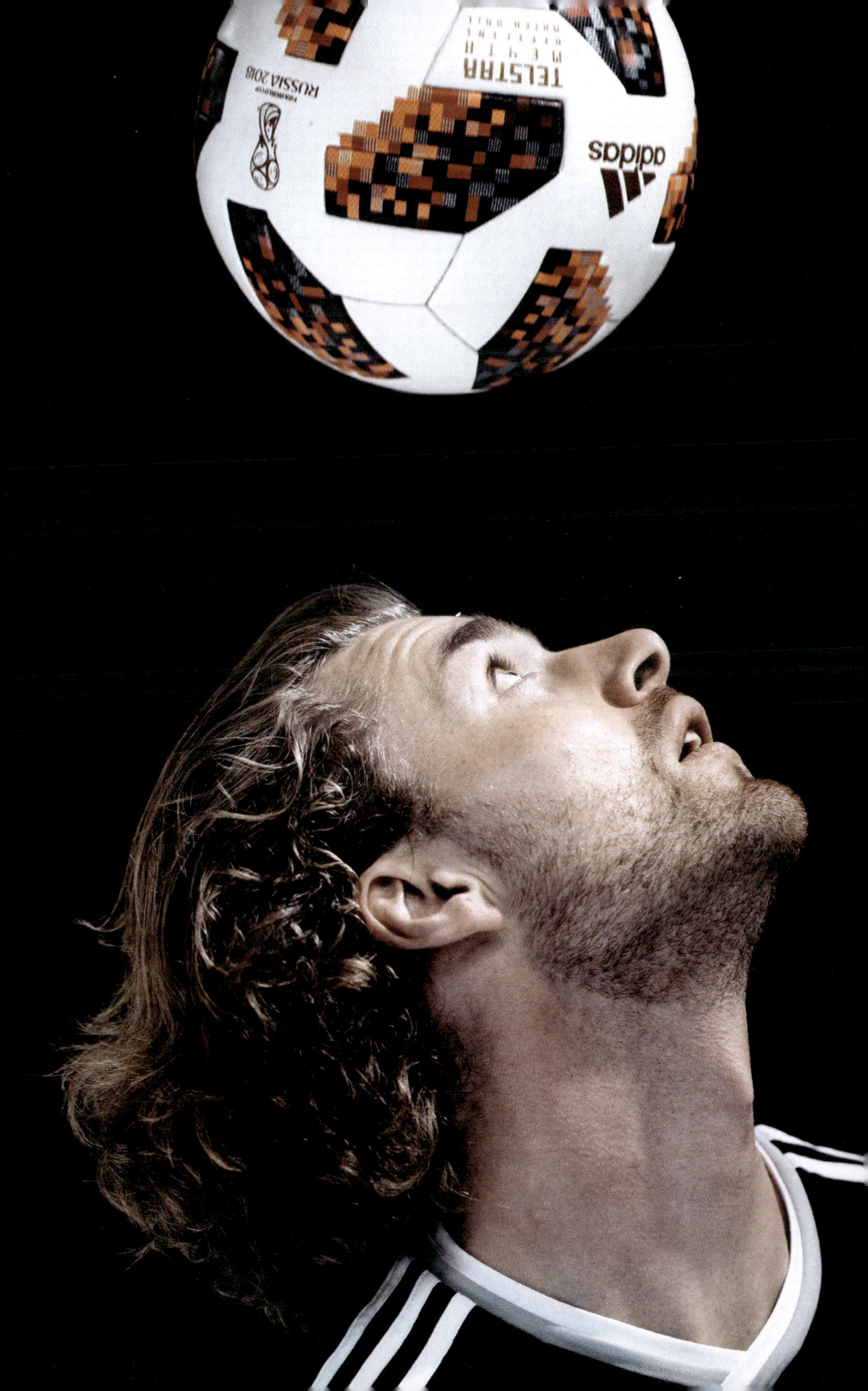

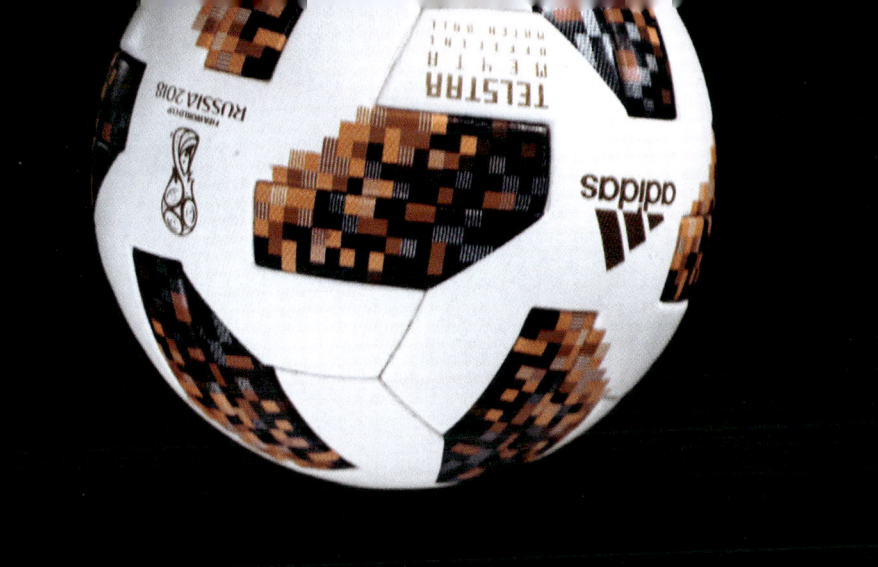

BAYER OR X-TRANS?

Another useful X camera categorization is the use of either a Bayer or an X-Trans color filter array (CFA) on the sensor. Cameras from most manufacturers use Bayer sensors (with a simple 2×2 CFA). However, Bayer sensors are quite susceptible to unpleasant moiré effects. That's why cameras with Bayer sensors typically use an anti-aliasing (AA) filter in front of the sensor to mitigate moiré, but at a cost of detail resolution.

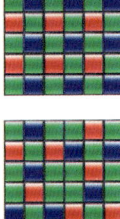

Fig. 12:

Bayer vs. X-Trans: Most cameras use Bayer sensors with a simple repetitive 2×2 color matrix that consists of two green, one blue, and one red pixel (top). Fujifilm's custom X-Trans sensor matrix (bottom) is built upon a more complex 6×6 matrix that mitigates moiré even without an anti-aliasing (AA) filter.

Fujifilm's "exotic" X-Trans color filter array was designed as a better Bayer alternative. X-Trans works without anti-aliasing filters, but thanks to its larger and more complex 6×6 color pattern, it is still quite moiré-proof.

However, not all X series cameras use Fujifilm's X-Trans design. For example, models like the classic X100, the X10, XF1, or X-S1, and the entry-level X-A line all use Bayer sensors with anti-aliasing (AA) filters. The X-T100 and the high-end GFX 50S and GFX 50R even use Bayer sensors without an AA filter.

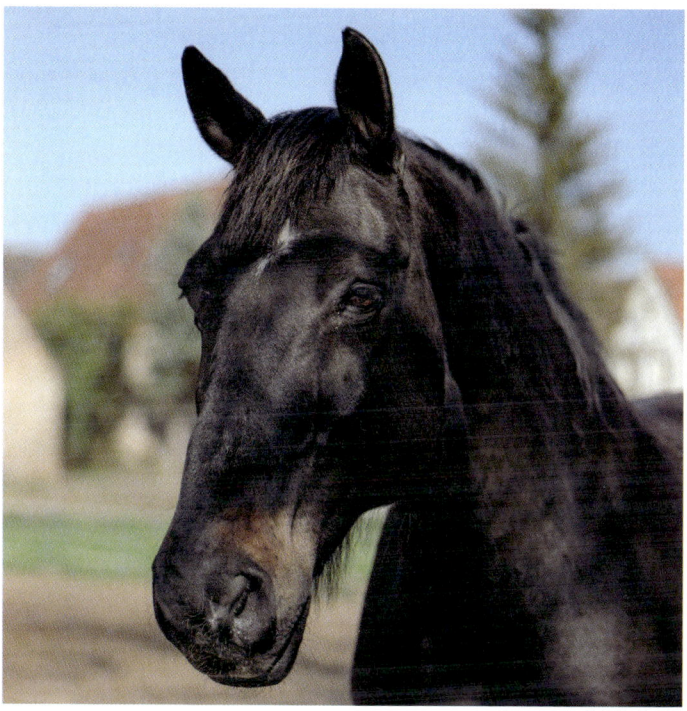

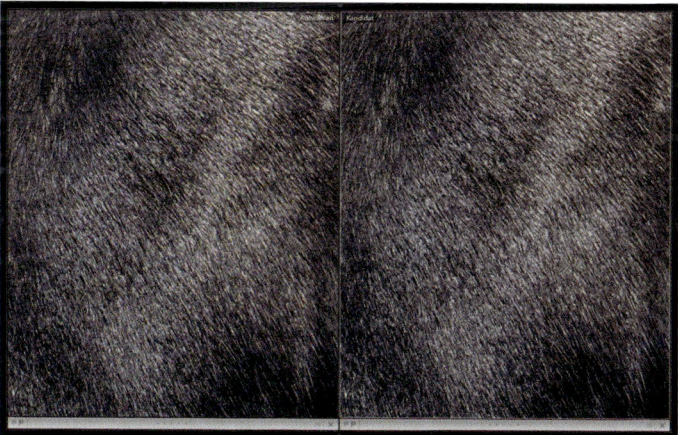

Fig. 13: Using **Bayer sensors without AA filters** can lead to un-pleasant moiré effects, especially in the fine structures of textiles, hair, or foliage. This example was taken with the GFX 50S (top). Below you can see a magnified portion with visible moiré (left) in Adobe Lightroom Classic CC. On the right, you can see the same portion of the image after applying Lightroom's anti-moiré brush: the moiré is gone.

Why did Fujifilm deploy Bayer and not X-Trans in the GFX?

■ *Reason 1:* X-Trans requires more processing power than Bayer, so it's reasonable to use a Bayer sensor without an AA filter in cameras with a very high pixel count. After all, the GFX 50S and GFX 50R already feature 51 MP, and future models are offering more than 100 MP.

■ *Reason 2:* Moiré can be digitally removed by powerful processing engines or state-of-the-art RAW conversion software.

MAIN CATEGORIES

For the purpose of this book, we can categorize all X cameras into the following main categories:

■ Models with the X-Processor 4 engine (as of December 2018, only the X-T3 fits this category).

■ Models featuring the still current X-Processor Pro engine (e.g., X-H1, X-T2, X-T20, X-Pro2, X-E3, X100F, GFX 50S, GFX 50R).

■ Models with the older but still popular EXR II engine (e.g., X-T1, X-T10, X-E2(S), X100T, X70, X30).

■ Models that have been outsourced to the Xacti factory in Jakarta (e.g., XF10, X-T100, X-A5, X-A3, X-A10, X-A20).

■ Models with the original EXR I engine from 2011/2012 (e.g., X100, X-Pro1, X-E1).

While this book is dedicated to all X camera users, it is particularly useful to those using a camera with the current X-Processor 4 and X-Processor Pro engines. That said, users of EXR II cameras and Xacti-built models will also benefit due to the similarities of many features, and even users of older EXR I cameras will find plenty of useful information.

Fuji X Secrets is based on my popular Fuji X Secrets Camera and RAW workshops that I have been offering in Europe, Asia, and North America since 2014. Like my workshops, this book targets Fujifilm enthusiasts from all around the world who thrive to make the best out of their X cameras.

Important: *If not indicated otherwise, specific menu path descriptions such as* SHOOTING MENU > IMAGE QUALITY SETTING > IMAGE QUALITY > FINE+RAW *refer to current X camera models with the X-Processor 4 and X-Processor Pro menu structure, such as the X-T3, X-Pro2, X-H1, X-T2, X-T20, X-E3, X100F, GFX 50S, and GFX 50R. I may also put parts of a menu path in brackets, for example:* SHOOTING MENU > (IMAGE QUALITY SETTING >) IMAGE QUALITY > FINE+RAW. *In many cases of older X models (like the X-T1, X-T10, X-E2, or X100T) or in entry-level cameras (like the X-T100 or X-A5), you can still locate a specific menu function by ignoring the part of the menu path in brackets.*

1.1 THE BASICS (1):
THINGS YOU SHOULD KNOW
ABOUT YOUR CAMERA

> **TIP 1**　**RTFM! Read The Fuji Manual!** Versions in different languages, updates, and supplements are available online.

In case you have misplaced your user manual, or if you want to update to a newer edition of the manual, you can obtain downloadable PDF versions [1] in all supported languages from Fujifilm. You will also find updates and supplementary material that cover new features and changes based on firmware updates.

Please do yourself a big favor and thoroughly study the manuals to get acquainted with the different functions of your cameras, and don't forget that your lenses come with user manuals, as well. This book doesn't replace a camera manual; it serves as an *enhancement* to the manual and offers valuable tips and background information about how to use the various features and functions to make the most of your equipment.

> **TIP 2**　Things you should know about spare batteries and third-party knock-offs.

In most X series cameras, the rechargeable battery is rather small. Depending on how you use your camera, a fully charged battery will last for 250 to 400 shots, sometimes more.

If available, I recommend setting the camera to High Performance Mode or Boost Mode to secure the best autofocus and overall performance (such as a high frame rate in the viewfinder).

This means that you will most likely require a few spare batteries to get comfortably through a typical day of shooting.

Please note:

■ Unlike older models, the current X series generations with X-Processor Pro and X-Processor 4 feature an accurate battery indicator with five bars and a percentage display.

■ In shooting mode, this percentage display is available in the INFO display of the LCD monitor. To activate the INFO display, (repeatedly) press the DISP/BACK button until the INFO display appears on the monitor. In playback mode, the percentage indicator is also available in the INFO display.

■ When the battery indicator shows one remaining red bar, it's almost time to replace the battery.

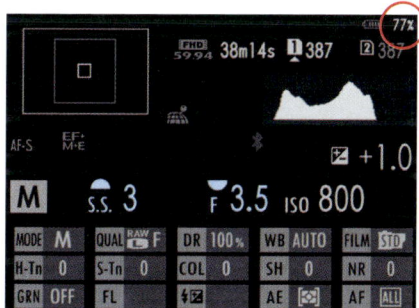

Fig. 14: The **INFO display** of X series cameras with an X-Processor Pro or X-Processor 4 engine features an accurate battery life indicator with a percentage display. You can access the INFO display with the DISP/BACK button.

Most X series cameras use NP-W126(S) rechargeable batteries. As of December 2018, this type of battery is used in Fujifilm's X-Pro1, X-Pro2, X-E1, X-E2, X-E2S, X-E3, X-H1, X-T1, X-T2, X-T3, X-T10, X-T20, X-T100, X-M1, X-A1, X-A2, X-A3, X-A5, X-A10, X-A20, and X100F models. It can be interchanged between these cameras.

The difference between the regular and the newer S-type battery is the latter's improved ability to manage heat. For high-performance applications such as long 4K video recordings in a hot environment, the newer NP-W126S type is favorable, if not mandatory. However, if you already own a bunch of older NP-W126 batteries, you can still use them in your cameras.

There are a few exceptions: The X-H1 and X-T3 demand the newer S-type batteries and will issue a warning when they detect the older type or third-party batteries. These cameras will still work with non-S-type batteries, but there's an increased chance for malfunctions such as freezes as well as compromised performance.

You can obtain NP-W126S batteries from Fujifilm, or you can try compatible products from a variety of third-party vendors. A word of caution: Despite their vendors claiming otherwise, pretty much none of the aftermarket batteries offer the same quality, safety, and capacity as the more expensive Fujifilm batteries. You are likely to experience inaccurate battery life displays with third-party offerings, and the camera may unexpectedly switch off with an empty battery even though the indicator shows there was some power left. To avoid such trouble, use original Fujifilm NP-W126S batteries.

If you store your camera for an extended period without a charged battery, the body's built-in emergency power source may run out of juice, and all camera and user set-tings will reset to factory conditions.

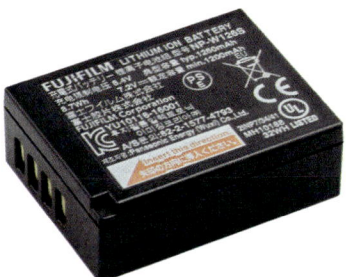

Fig. 15:
Fujifilm's original **NP-W126S** battery is without doubt the safest and best-performing choice. It's also more expensive than third-party knock-offs.

Fujifilm's GFX medium format cameras use larger **NP-T125** batteries. As of December 2018, I'm not aware of any third-party alternatives for this rather expensive battery.

Several (mostly older) X series cameras use batteries that are smaller than the standard NP-W126(S): The X100, X100S, X100T, X30, X70, XF10, and X-S1 all require **NP-95** batteries. The X10, X20, and XF1 use even smaller **NP-50** batteries, and the XQ1 and XQ2 require tiny **NP-48** batteries. You can get third-party alternatives for all three types. However, the same reservations as for the NP-W126 knock-offs do apply.

Battery chargers and travel adapters	TIP 3

Along with spare batteries, the aftermarket also offers chargers that work with regular power outlets, USB ports, or a car's cigarette lighter jack. This way, you can charge your batteries not only at home or in your hotel room, but also on your computer's USB port or when you are traveling in a car or plane.

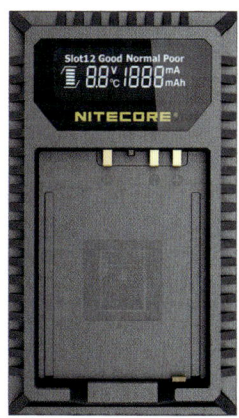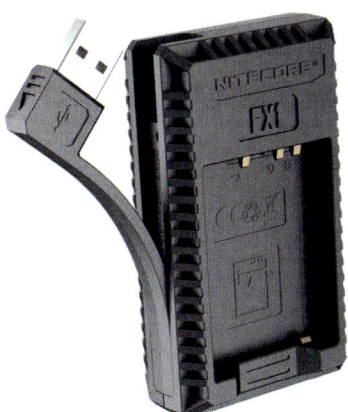

Fig. 16: My personal travel charger is the **Nitecore FX1** [2] with dual slots and a status display (left). This charger connects to any USB-A port (right) and can smart-charge original Fujifilm NP-W126 and NP-W126S batteries with temperature monitoring.

While traveling, don't forget that different countries use different formats for power outlets, so you may want to carry a suitable travel adapter.

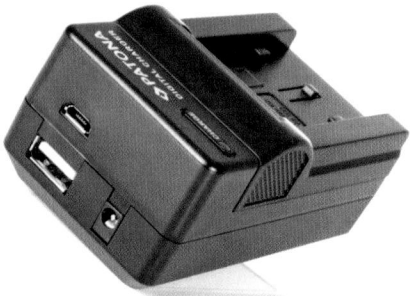

Fig. 17:
Some **third-party chargers** can get their power from more than one source, such as power outlets, USB ports, and car ciga-rette lighter jacks.

As an alternative to external battery chargers, the battery can also be charged inside the camera via the camera's built-in USB port. Use a USB 2 micro cable to connect the camera to pretty much any power source with a USB port, such as your laptop or your cell phone charger. With the X-T2 and X-H1, you can also use a USB 3 micro cable. The X-T3 uses USB-C with Power Delivery support, so you can speed-up charging by using a USB-C power supply with at least 30W and cables that support Power Delivery.

As of December 2018, the X series models that support USB charging are the XQ1, XQ2, X30, X70, XF10, X100T, X100F, X-A3, X-A5, X-A10, X-A20, X-T3, X-T2, X-T20, X-T100, X-E3, and X-H1.

USB chargers and mobile power banks can not only charge X cameras with USB charging capability, they can also power some models while they are switched on and in use. You can find more information on compatible cameras and batteries in a support document on Fujifilm's web-site [3].

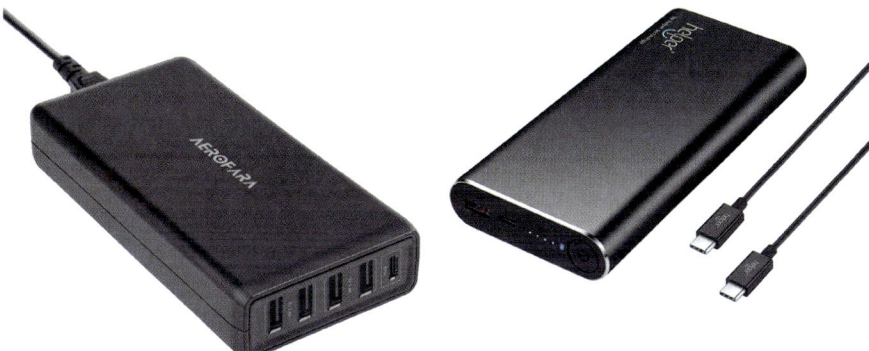

Fig. 18: **USB chargers** (left) and **power banks** (right) are useful accessories for road warriors and users who want to power the camera externally for long exposures, video, timelapse, and interval shooting.

Where to find the latest firmware	TIP 4

Fujifilm keeps improving the firmware of your cameras and lenses.

■ To check which firmware version is installed in your camera and lens, switch the camera on while pressing and holding the DISP/BACK button.

■ You can and should download the latest firmware versions for your cameras and lenses online [4]. While you are there, you can also download current versions of Fuji's application software, such as RAW File Converter EX, Fujifilm X RAW Studio, and Fujifilm X Acquire.

■ A step-by-step video guide illustrating the firmware upgrade process is available online [5]. At this Fujifilm support website, macOS [6] and Windows [7] users can also find detailed firmware download instructions for their operating systems.

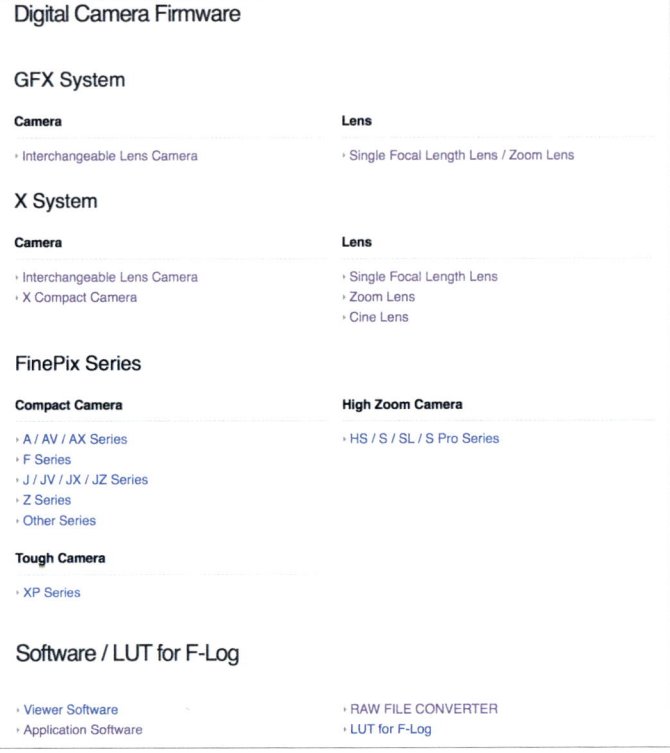

Digital Camera Firmware

GFX System

Camera	Lens
› Interchangeable Lens Camera	› Single Focal Length Lens / Zoom Lens

X System

Camera	Lens
› Interchangeable Lens Camera	› Single Focal Length Lens
› X Compact Camera	› Zoom Lens
	› Cine Lens

FinePix Series

Compact Camera	High Zoom Camera
› A / AV / AX Series	› HS / S / SL / S Pro Series
› F Series	
› J / JV / JX / JZ Series	
› Z Series	
› Other Series	

Tough Camera

› XP Series	

Software / LUT for F-Log

› Viewer Software	› RAW FILE CONVERTER
› Application Software	› LUT for F-Log

Fig. 19: Fujifilm's **Download Software and Firmware** webpage is your hub to obtain firmware updates for your Fuji X cameras and lenses as well as current versions of supplementary software such as X RAW Studio and RAW File Converter EX.

TIP 5	Tips for updating your firmware

■ If you know about a new firmware release but can't find it on Fuji's firmware update page, there's a good chance that your web browser is still caching an older version of that page. In this case, either delete your browser cache or force your browser to reload the webpage from the server.

■ Make sure that your computer doesn't change the name of firmware files you download due to naming conflicts caused by previous firmware versions that are still residing in your download folder. For example, the correct file name of the camera firmware for an X-H1 is always FWUP0015.DAT., while firmware updates for the X-T2 are always named FWUP0010.DAT.

- The same scheme applies to lenses, so each X-mount or G-mount lens uses a unique file name. For example, firmware updates for the popular XF18–55mmF2.8–4 R LM OIS are always named XFUP0004.DAT.

- Confusingly, fixed-lens X series cameras (X100 series, X70, X10/20/30, XF series, XQ series, and X-S1) all share the same file name for their firmware updates: FPUP-DATE.DAT.

- If your camera features dual memory card slots, always use slot 1 for firmware updates.

- Make sure your battery is fully charged when updating your firmware.

- Only use memory cards with a capacity of up to 32 GB for firmware updates.

- Copy new firmware files for your camera or lenses into the top directory of your SD memory card, and always use cards that have been freshly formatted in your camera. After you have copied the firmware to the card, make sure to properly unmount the card from your computer before removing it.

- If you want to update the firmware for a specific lens, make sure the lens is attached to the camera when you initiate the update process.

- To start the update process for your camera or a lens, switch the camera on while pressing and holding the DISP/BACK button and follow the instructions on the screen.

- Never switch the camera off during the update process. The camera will tell you when the update is complete. Only then can you safely switch it off.

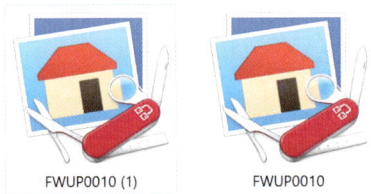

FWUP0010 (1)   FWUP0010

Fig. 20: The **most common mistake in concert with Fujifilm firm-ware updates** is users downloading new firmware into a folder on their PC that already contains older firmware for the same camera model or lens. In this example, the folder already contained an earlier firmware for the X-T2 with the name FWUP0010.DAT. Down-loading a newer FWUP0010.DAT firmware file from the Fujifilm webpage lead to a name conflict which was automatically resolved by the PC's operating system: It changed the name of the newer file to FWUP0010 (1).DAT. However, FWUP0010 (1).DAT will not be recognized by the X-T2, because the camera is only looking for firmware update files with the name FWUP0010.DAT.

If the firmware in your camera or lens needs to be updated due to compatibility issues, the camera may alert you of this problem when you switch it on. If that's the case, download the new firmware from the website links provided in tip 4 and update your camera and/or lens.

TIP 6	Wireless firmware updates using Bluetooth and Wi-Fi

If your camera supports Bluetooth, you can perform wire-less firmware updates using your smartphone or tablet and Fujifilm's Camera Remote app, which is available for iOS and Android. As of December 2018, only the X-E3, X-H1, X-T3, and GFX 50R supported this feature—and only for body firmware, not for lenses or accessories. However, it's clear that upcoming X series cameras will support wireless updates, as well, and there's also a chance of firmware enhancements that might bring wireless updates to other Bluetooth-enabled models like the X-A5, X-T100, and XF10.

To use wireless firmware updates, your camera needs a Bluetooth connection to a tablet or smartphone via the Camera Remote app. This app is a free download for iOS and

Android, and there's a useful online manual explaining its various functions [8].

When your Bluetooth-enabled camera is paired with your wireless device, the Camera Remote App will announce the availability of new camera firmware and offer to download it to your smartphone or tablet. From there, the firmware file is transferred to the camera via the camera's Wi-Fi hotspot.

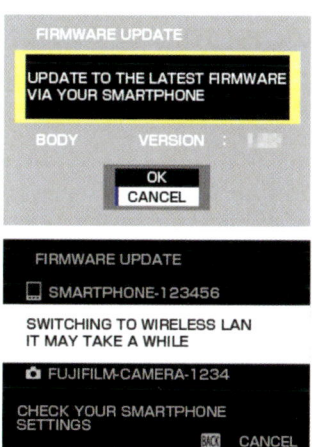

Fig. 21:
Wireless firmware updates:
After the Camera Remote app on your smartphone or tablet has finished downloading a new camera firmware, its Wi-Fi network must be switched to the camera's own hotspot to transfer the firmware file to the camera.

Using Camera Remote is a good alternative for users who want to install new firmware without access to a personal computer. You can find step-by-step instructions for wireless firmware updates online [9].

Which memory cards to use	TIP 7

Turbo-charge your camera and its built-in buffer memory by using the fastest and most reliable UHS-I and UHS-II memory cards:

■ For cameras with a superfast UHS-II slot, which offers transmission speeds of up to 300 MB/s, I highly recommend **Sony SF-G** cards with write speeds up to 299 MB/s.

These cards are also known to be particularly reliable and freeze-resistant when used with higher-end camera models like the X-T2, X-H1, X-T3, and GFX. As of December 2018, X series cameras that support UHS-II are the X-T1, X-Pro2 (slot 1 only), X-T2 (both slots), X-H1 (both slots), X-T3 (both slots), GFX 50S (both slots), and GFX 50R (both slots).

■ All remaining X series cameras support speeds up to the slower UHS-I standard with transfer rates of 95 MB/s or less. For these cameras (and for slot 2 of the X-Pro2), I recommend **SanDisk Extreme Pro 95 MB/s** cards.

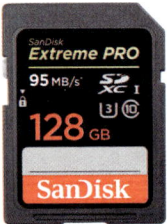

Fig. 22: Fast **SanDisk Extreme Pro 95 MB/s** SD memory cards are popular workhorses for many serious X series users. They are the perfect choice for cameras with UHS-I support, such as the X-T10, X-E2(S), X-T20, X-E3, X70, and the X100 family. They are also recommended for slot 2 of the X-Pro2 and older models such as the X-Pro1 and X-E1, entry-level cameras like the X-A series and X-M1, the X-T100, and all X series compact cameras.

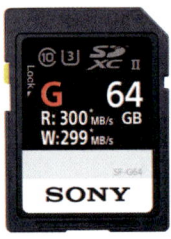

Fig. 23: For maximum UHS-II performance and compatibility, I recommend superfast **Sony SF-G** cards. Please note that these cards only make sense in cameras that explicitly support UHS-II, such as the X-T1, X-Pro2 (only slot 1), X-T2, X-H1, X-T3, and GFX. If your camera or card slot doesn't support UHS-II, you are better off using a fast UHS-I card like the SanDisk Extreme Pro 95 MB/s.

Important: Look out for fakes! Sadly, there's a fair share of fake SD cards on the market. High-end brands and models are particularly affected, so make sure to buy your fast UHS-I and UHS-II cards from reputable sources. Fake cards aren't just slower and less reliable than the originals, they also tend to lie about their actual capacity. A fake 64 GB card could, in reality, contain a cheap 8 GB chip with a manipulated controller that simulates 64 GB to the camera, resulting in severe data loss.

Working with dual card slots	TIP 8

Some X cameras, such as the X-Pro2, X-T2, X-T3, X-H1, and GFX, offer two SD card slots numbered "1" and "2". This means that you can use two SD cards at the same time.

Please note:

- The primary SD card slot of your dual-slot camera is always slot 1. If you are working with a single SD card, always put it in this slot.

- Firmware upgrades are only supported in slot 1.

- In the X-Pro2, only slot 1 supports UHS-II. The secondary slot only supports UHS-I.

- In the X-T2, X-T3, X-H1, and GFX 50, both slots support UHS-II, making them both suitable for very fast memory cards like the Sony SF-G series. However, it is my experience that the second UHS-II card slot works a little bit slower than the primary slot.

Using two memory cards at the same time gives you three different options to configure how image data is transferred to your SD cards. To do so, select SET UP > SAVE DATA SET-UP > CARD SLOT SETTING (STILL IMAGE) and pick one of the following options:

- **SEQUENTIAL:** In this default mode, the camera saves all image data (RAW and JPEG) to a manually selected card slot. You can change the slot for sequential image recording in the SET UP > SAVE DATA SET-UP menu. When the card in the active slot is full, the camera automatically switches to the card in the other slot.

- **BACKUP:** In this mode, the camera is sending all image data (RAW and JPEG) to both slots at the same time, creating a backup copy that can be useful if one of the cards gets lost or suffers data loss. In this mode, the overall data transfer rate is limited by the slower of the two cards (and slots) that are in use. This can become a performance issue in situations that require many images being taken with high burst rates while shooting FINE+RAW, so make sure that the cards in both slots are equally fast.

■ **RAW/JPEG:** This setting splits the image data up by saving RAW files to slot 1 and JPEGs to slot 2, so this setting is only useful when you are shooting FINE+RAW or NORMAL+RAW. If you shoot RAW-only or JPEG-only, RAW/JPEG mode turns into BACKUP mode, saving your RAW or JPEG data to both cards at the same time.

I always recommend shooting FINE+RAW (or NORMAL+RAW). If you follow this advice, selecting RAW/JPEG mode (and using the fastest compatible cards in slots 1 and 2, respectively) will give you the best camera performance in terms of continuous burst rates.

However, RAW/JPEG data save mode also has its quirks:

■ Splitting up RAW and JPEG image data to slots 1 and 2 only works in regular shooting mode (i.e., when you take a fresh picture), not when you are using the camera's built-in RAW converter to create a JPEG from an existing RAW file on card 1. JPEGs generated from RAWs on card 1 are also saved on card 1 (the RAW card) instead of card 2 (the JPEG card).

■ In playback mode, the camera will display smaller-sized JPEG images that are embedded in the RAW files on card 1 instead of showing the full-resolution JPEGs on card 2. To access the full-resolution JPEGs (e.g., in order to zoom in and check critical focus), you have to manually switch slots in playback mode by pressing and holding the playback button until the camera confirms the switch. Sadly, the camera will revert playback mode back to card 1 after you take another picture, so you have to go through the motions of switching slots in playback mode each time you take another shot.

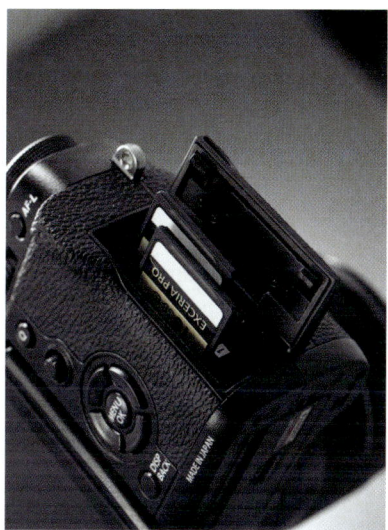

Fig. 24: Dual-slot cameras like the X-T2 can work with **two SD memory cards at the same time**. For maximum performance, you should use fast UHS-II cards (such as the Sony SF-G with 300 MB/s).

Resetting the frame counter and assigning a new image starting number	TIP 9

Follow these steps to reset the image counter to zero (if you have a dual-slot camera, make sure that you only use a single SD card in slot 1):

■ Select SET UP > SAVE DATA SET-UP > FRAME NO. > RENEW, then format the SD card with SET UP > (USER SETTING >) FORMAT and take a picture. The frame counter will start from zero.

■ To avoid another automatic image counter reset when you are reformatting an SD card, select SET UP > SAVE DATA SET-UP > FRAME NO. > CONTINUOUS.

You can assign pretty much any number as the camera's new frame-counter starting number. The method is similar, but involves an extra step in your computer:

■ Select SET UP > SAVE DATA SET-UP > FRAME NO. > RENEW, then format the SD card with SET UP > (USER SETTING >) FORMAT and take a picture. The frame counter will start from zero.

■ Remove the SD card from your camera and insert it in your computer. Locate your image (for example DSCF0001. JPG or DSCF0001.RAF) in the DCIM folder and change the frame-number portion of the file name (0001) to the number you'd like to use as your new starting point. For example, you can change the file name to DSCF2000.JPG.

■ Properly unmount and remove the SD card from your computer and put the card back into your camera. Now take another picture. The camera will use the modified frame number as a starting point. In our example, the new image file's name would be DSCF2001.

■ To avoid another automatic frame-counter reset when you are reformatting an SD card, select SET UP > SAVE DATA SET-UP > FRAME NO. > CONTINUOUS.

| TIP 10 | Use High Performance or Boost mode! |

In their default setting, most X cameras operate with reduced performance to conserve power. To enjoy your camera's full capabilities, it's necessary to select HIGH PER-FORMANCE or BOOST (X-T2, X-T3, and X-H1) in the POWER MANAGEMENT menu.

Since the camera consumes more power in High Perfor-mance or Boost mode, it's even more important to always have replacement batteries at hand.

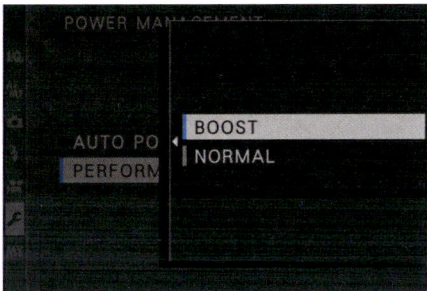 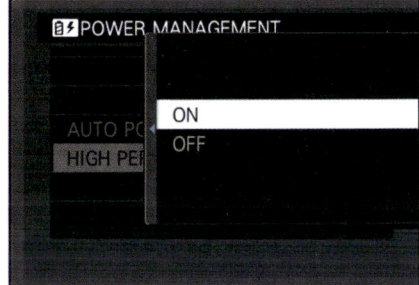

Fig. 25: Activating **High Performance or Boost mode** is a good idea if you are interested in fast autofocus and a responsive live view image. These examples show the respective menu items in an X-H1 (left) and X-T100 (right).

If you have a battery grip attached to your X-T2, X-T3, or X-H1, Boost mode is set with the switch on the back of that grip. You can learn more about the Vertical Power Booster Grip's benefits for the X-T2 and X-H1 online [10].

Please note that Boost mode in the X-T3 doesn't require the battery grip to achieve maximum performance, because the new energy-saving X-Processor 4 can draw all its power from a single battery.

Important: When Boost mode is off, the X-T2, X-T3, and X-H1 will enter an energy saving mode after approximately 10 seconds of user inactivity. This results in a dramatic reduction of the live view's frame rate. As soon as a button is pressed or a dial is turned, the live view goes back to normal.

Keeping the camera sensor clean	TIP 11

Sooner or later, all cameras with interchangeable lenses get dust or dirt on the sensor. This manifests as spots on your image, especially in photos taken at small apertures. You can prevent this from happening by taking measures to avoid sensor dust as much as possible. You can also clean dust by using your camera's built-in cleaning mechanism:

- Select SET UP > (USER SETTING >) SENSOR CLEANING > OK to activate the built-in cleaning mechanism that helps loosen dust particles. By default, this mechanism will be automatically employed when you switch *off* the camera. I recommend setting the camera to also activate this mechanism when it is switched *on:* to do this, select SET UP > (USER SETTING >) SENSOR CLEANING > WHEN SWITCHED ON > ON.

In addition to that, it's sensible to adhere to a regiment that avoids exposing the camera to dust and dirt:

- Never leave the camera without a lens or its protective body cap.

- Don't exchange lenses in dusty environments.

- When exchanging lenses, always hold the camera with the open lens mount pointed downward—never upward.

- When you attach a new lens, make sure the rear glass of the lens is clean and free of dust particles. Otherwise, dust from the lens could travel to the sensor.

- Never touch the sensor!

Fig. 26: **Dust spots** on the sensor made visible: this sensor badly needs cleaning.

Do-it-yourself sensor cleaning   TIP 12

When the built-in sensor-cleaning function doesn't do a proper job, you have
three basic options for cleaning the
sensor by yourself:

- Touchless cleaning
- Dry cleaning
- Wet cleaning

Touchless cleaning involves using a
blower, like the *Giottos Rocket Air Blaster*,
to rid the sensor of dust particles. An
important feature of such devices is a
filter in the intake valve that prevents
contaminated (dusty) air from being
blown against the sensor.

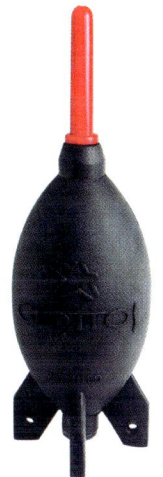

Fig. 27:
Touchless
sensor cleaning:
**Giottos Rocket
Air Blaster**.

*Important: Don't use compressed air
from aerosol cans that contain propel-
lants. Particles could hit the sensor like
tiny projectiles and damage the protective surface!*

A popular means to **dry clean** the sensor is the *Pentax Sensor
Cleaning Kit*. The sticky head of this funny-looking cleaning
device picks up dust and dirt from the sensor surface and
transfers it to sticky paper sheets that are included with
the product.

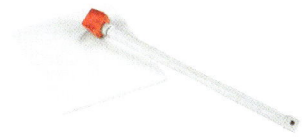

Fig. 28:
Dry cleaning: **Pentax Sensor
Cleaning Kit**

Tough sensor dirt (like water or oil stains) requires **wet
cleaning** with a *sensor swab*. Suitable products are offered

by companies likes *Photographic Solutions* and *Visible Dust*. They consist of wipers that are wetted with special cleaning fluids (such as *Eclipse*). Wipe one side of the swab from left to right over the full width of the sensor, and then from right to left with the other side of the swab. Your X-mount camera requires swabs that match APS-C-sized sensors. At Photographic Solutions, this translates into product size number 2.

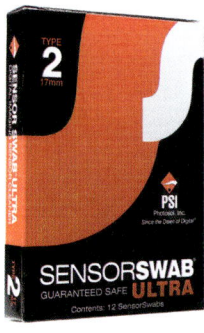

Fig. 29:
Wet cleaning: **sensor swabs** from Photographic Solutions.

Inexpensive and effective alternatives to products from Visible Dust or Photographic Solutions are APS-C-sized swabs from the Asian brand VSGO.

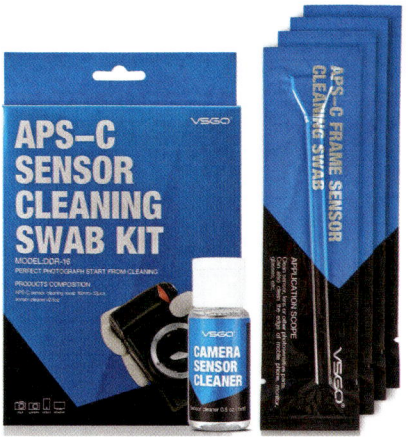

Fig. 30:
My personal sensor cleaning choice for X-mount cameras: **VSGO** swabs and cleaning fluid.

Sadly, VSGO swabs aren't available for medium format sensors. GFX users can use swabs and solutions from Visible Dust as an alternative [11].

*Important: There's a small chance that sensor spots are caused by dust particles enclosed **behind** the protective surface of the sensor. If some spots simply won't go away, the camera needs to be serviced by Fujifilm.*

Sensor cleaning and IBIS	TIP 13

If your X camera features in-body image stabilization (IBIS), DIY sensor cleaning is a little bit trickier. As of December 2018, IBIS was only available in the X-H1, but upcoming models like the GFX 100 are supposed to offer this useful feature, too.

Here are step-by-step instructions on how to prepare an X-H1 for wet and dry sensor cleaning:

- Make sure that the IBIS is turned off by selecting SHOOTING MENU > SHOOTING SETTING > IS MODE > OFF. This setting locks the sensor in place while you are cleaning it.

- Select SET UP > BUTTON/DIAL SETTING > SHOOT WITHOUT LENS > OFF. This makes sure that you don't accidently release the shutter while you are cleaning the sensor (which could have disastrous consequences).

- Select SET UP > POWER MANAGEMENT > AUTO POWER OFF > OFF. This makes sure that the camera doesn't automatically power down while you are still cleaning the sensor.

- Remove the lens or body cap and clean the sensor as usual. Make sure that the camera is switched ON during the cleaning process.

■ When you are finished cleaning the sensor, don't forget to revert the Power Management, Shoot Without Lens, and IBIS settings to their previous operational states.

Please note that keeping the camera turned on during sensor cleaning is an exception that we only make for cameras with IBIS. All other cameras should always be powered down during sensor cleaning.

TIP 14	Pixel mapping

Cameras with X-Processor Pro and X-Processor 4 offer an automatic pixel mapping feature. To use it, select SHOOTING MENU > IMAGE QUALITY SETTING > PIXEL MAPPING. Pixel mapping detects defective pixels on your sensor and maps them out, meaning they are interpolated with the information of surrounding pixels. Since the number of hot pixels increases with sensor temperature, pixel mapping is only available when the camera hasn't already heated up.

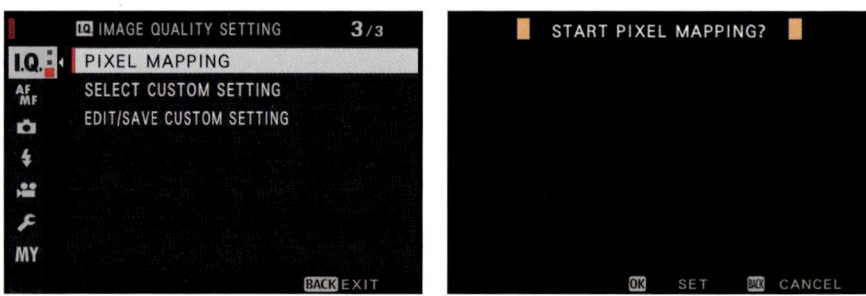

Fig. 31: **Pixel mapping** is a very useful function that is unjustly overlooked by many users. To avoid unpleasant pixel malfunctions in your images, it's best to apply it on a regular basis.

Please note that a few defective pixels are perfectly normal in every digital camera. As the sensor ages (even when the camera is not in use), the number of dead pixels increases along with it. In addition to the manufacturing process, defective pixels are also caused by cosmic radiation. For example, frequently taking your camera on long-haul flights will increase the risk.

Knowing all this, it's a good idea to regularly use the pixel mapping function in order to keep the defective pixel map inside your camera up-to-date. It only takes a few seconds.

If you are experiencing an unhealthy number of defective pixels, but your X camera doesn't offer pixel mapping, you can still have the camera remapped by Fujifilm's service department.

1.2 THE BASICS (2): THINGS YOU SHOULD KNOW ABOUT YOUR LENSES

Your camera is compatible with the following native X-mount (APS-C) or G-mount (44×33mm medium format) lenses:

■ Fujinon XF lenses (X-mount prime and zoom lenses)

■ Fujinon XC lenses (compact, affordable X-mount lenses)

■ Zeiss Touit X-mount lenses (prime lenses)

■ Fujinon GF lenses (G-mount medium format prime and zoom lenses)

In addition to native X-mount and G-mount lenses, you can also attach a host of current and older lenses from other manufacturers via suitable adapters. Remember that by using a "dumb" mechanical adapter, adapted lenses will always operate at the set working aperture. Autofocus, program AE, and shutter priority AE will not be available, either. Third-party *smart* adapters (which are mostly available to adapt Canon EF lenses to the X-mount or G-mount) are more expensive and can overcome these limitations.

TIP 15 X-mount compatible **Samyang lenses** are just like adapted lenses!

Manual focus lenses from Samyang/Rokinon/Walimex and similar brands aren't native X-mount lenses. They simply come with a compatible mechanical mount, so you don't have to buy an additional adapter. These lenses behave like other adapted third-party lenses: they don't communicate with the camera (there's no data transmission because there aren't any electronic contacts), there's no autofocus, the live view [12] operates with the currently set working aperture, and you can only use AE modes **A** and **M**.

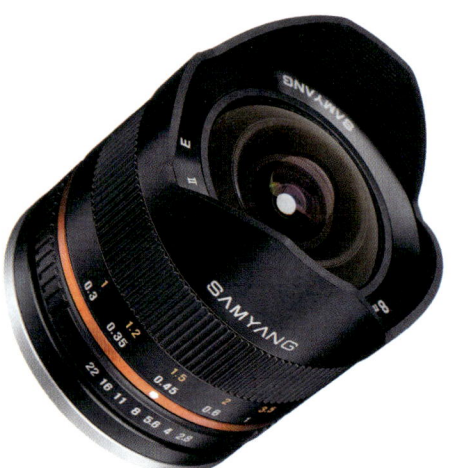

Fig. 32: The affordable **Samyang 8mmF2.8 Fisheye II** manual focus lens for Fujifilm X-mount is a popular choice to record images with extreme angles.

TIP 16 Zeiss Touit lenses

Even though Touit lenses with native X-mount compatibility offer great image quality and work like Fujinon XF lenses, Zeiss tends to be hesitant to support new camera features with lens firmware updates. It took Zeiss about half a year longer than Fuji to offer PDAF support, and there is still no LMO support. There's also no indication that Zeiss wants to continue with the Touit line of lenses.

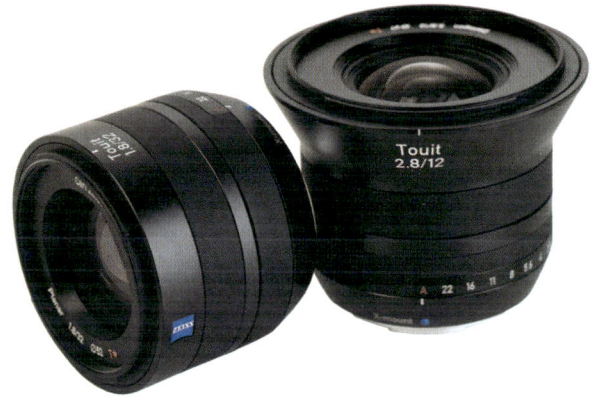

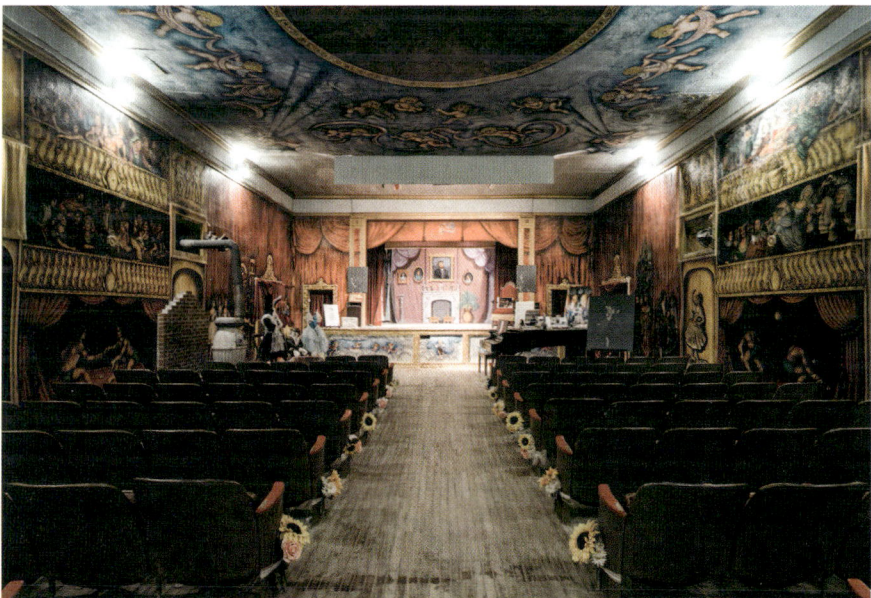

Fig. 33: **Zeiss Touit** 1.8/32mm and 2.8/12mm are autofocus lenses with native X-mount compatibility (above). The wide field of view of the Touit 2.8/12mm lens makes it ideal for landscape or interior shots (below).

TIP 17	Decoding XF18–135mmF3.5–5.6 R LM OIS WR

This tip is of the "what you always wanted to know but never dared to ask" variety:

- **XF:** "X" means X-mount or X series; "F" means Fine, designating Fuji's premium line of lenses. There's also the smaller, more affordable XC line ("C" stands for Compact or Casual). And let's not forget GF lenses for GFX medium format cameras (G-mount).

- **18–135mm:** This is the focal length range of the zoom lens. To translate the numbers to their full-frame equivalents, you must multiply them by the APS-C crop factor [13] of 1.5. Hence, the field of view (FOV) of an 18–135mm zoom on your X-mount camera is identical to the FOV of a 27–202mm zoom lens on a full-frame (35mm format) camera. GF lenses have a crop factor of 0.79. Mounted on a GFX camera, a GF63mmF2.8 R lens offers the same FOV as a 50mm lens on a "full-frame" (a.k.a. 35mm format) camera.

- **F3.5–5.6:** This range describes the maximum aperture opening at the low and high end of the focal length range. In this case, the lens offers a maximum aperture of f/3.5 at 18mm and f/5.6 at 135mm.

- **R:** This stands for Ring and means that the lens features an aperture ring. This is a standard feature of all Fujinon XF lenses except the XF27mmF2.8 pancake lens. XC zooms don't offer an aperture ring, either. With ringless lenses, the aperture setting is controlled with the command dial when you are using exposure modes **A** or **M**.

- **LM:** This stands for Linear Motor, which ensures quick and silent autofocus operation.

- **OIS:** This is the Optical Image Stabilizer [14]. This feature allows you to perform handheld shots at up to five stops slower of a shutter speed than you would usually need to eliminate camera shake. For example, in situations that would normally require a shutter speed of 1/16os to ensure a clear image, you could shoot with 1/8s and still get usable results. It's important to remember that motion blur often plays a role at slower shutter speeds since many subjects tend to move. Obviously the OIS cannot reduce motion blur [15]—only blurring that occurs due to camera shake (i.e., the shaky hands of the photographer).

- **WR** denotes weather resistant lenses.

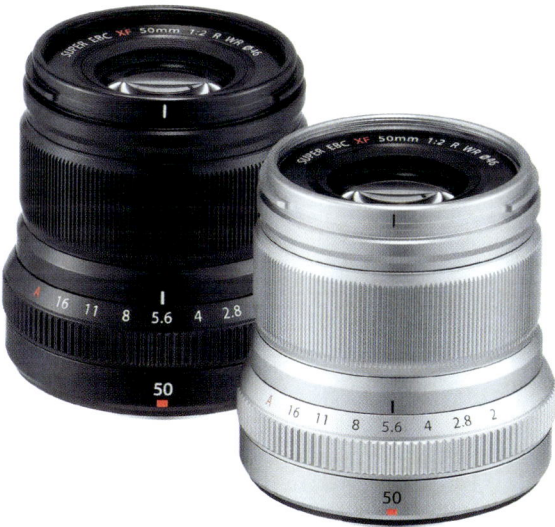

Fig. 34: Along with the XF35mmF2 R WR and XF23mmF2 R WR, the affordable **XF50mmF2 R WR** is one of Fujifilm's popular compact prime lenses for the X series. These lenses are weather resistant, and their lean design doesn't obscure the optical viewfinder of the X-Pro1 and X-Pro2. Due to their compact size, terrific performance, and excellent image quality, they are my favorite prime lenses for smaller X cameras like the X-T20, X-E3, or X-T100. You can get these lenses in two different colors, and a new XF16mmF2.8 R WR has already been placed on Fujifilm's lens roadmap for 2019.

TIP 18 | OIS and IBIS

Many XF, XC, and GF lenses feature built-in Optical Image Stabilization (OIS). In addition to that, the X-H1 and the upcoming GFX 100 offer In Body Image Stabilization (IBIS), which works with all lenses, even manually adapted third-party lenses.

OIS and IBIS perform the same task: they prevent camera shake and blurry images in situations that require you to take handheld shots at a slower-than-usual shutter speed.

To control the OIS/IBIS, XF and GF lenses offer a dedicated OIS on/off switch on the lens barrel. The OIS in XC lenses is controlled through the camera menu. The same applies to the IBIS of the X-H1 with lenses (native or adapted) that don't have built-in OIS.

For handheld shots, an old rule of thumb recommends using shutter speeds that are at least as fast as the reciprocal of the full-frame-equivalent focal length that is in use. For example, with a 50mm lens and an APS-C crop factor of 1.5, the minimum safe shutter speed for handheld shooting would be $[1/(50 \times 1.5)]\,s = 1/75s$. In other words, when you are shooting handheld with a 50mm lens and don't want shaky images, you should use shutter speeds at least as fast as 1/75s. Or you can use the OIS to add a few more stops.

Of course, rules of thumb don't apply to everybody. Some users have quite steady hands, while others have a shaky grip. The settings and equipment that work for me may not work for you. However, the OIS will always give you a few extra stops of shutter-speed headroom.

In SHOOTING MENU > (SHOOTING SETTING >) IS MODE, you can choose between two basic OIS modes:

■ **OIS mode 1** (CONTINUOUS) is the default setting. It's always stabilizing the image, even when you are just looking through the viewfinder before you press the shutter button.

■ **OIS mode 2** (SHOOTING ONLY) engages only when you fully depress the shutter button to take an image (or half-press it in AF-C mode).

Please note that the OIS can also *introduce* camera shake, especially at faster shutter speeds. This adverse effect is more likely to occur in OIS mode 1 than in mode 2. However, OIS mode 1 is more effective when used at very slow shutter speeds, such as 1/15s, 1/8s, or even 1/4s.

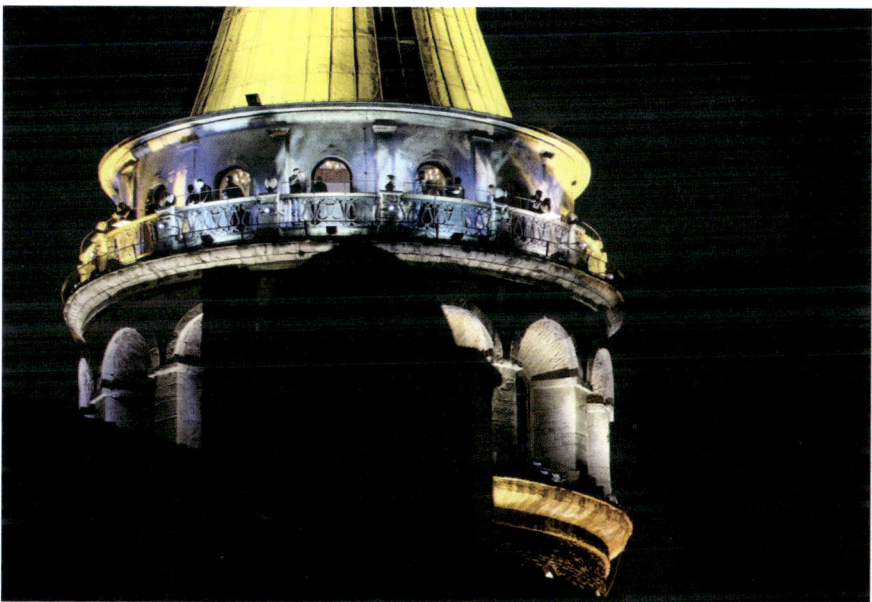

Fig. 35: The **optical image stabilizer** of the XF50–140mm in action: Thanks to a slow shutter speed of 1/6s, I could still use ISO 800 for this handheld night shot. Even at a full-frame equivalent of 210mm, the OIS could successfully compensate for any camera shake.

These are my recommendations for using OIS and IBIS:

■ Only use (switch on) OIS/IBIS when necessary. When you are using fast shutter speeds that don't require image stabilization, you can safely turn the OIS off to eliminate it as a potential interference. That said, I found the OIS useful even at shutter speed of 1/2000s and 1/4000s when I was shooting with an XF18–55mm lens from a small helicopter with extreme high-frequency vibration.

■ I generally prefer to use the OIS in mode 2 ("shooting only"). However, mode 1 is more useful at very slow shutter speeds and when you are using telephoto lenses, because in mode 1, the OIS and IBIS will also stabilize the live view image, making it easier to compose and focus a shot.

■ Consider turning off the OIS/IBIS when you are working from a good tripod or with shutter speeds that are slower than a second. Of course, this decision very much depends on the sturdiness of the tripod, prevailing wind conditions, and vibrations caused by traffic. Shooting in "vibrant" cities, one encounters many situations where leaving OIS/IBIS on is a good idea even with the sturdiest of tripods.

■ Depending on the lens, you might also want to switch OIS/IBIS off for panning [16] shots in case you find it difficult to smoothly track your subject with the OIS turned on.

By the way, OIS and IBIS both emit a soft humming sound, even when the function is turned off. Don't worry about the noise—it's perfectly normal.

Important: If you are using manually adapted third-party lenses on an X-H1, its IBIS can only perform correctly if you have entered and selected the focal length of the attached lens in SHOOTING MENU > SHOOTING SETTING > MOUNT ADAPTOR SETTING.

TIP 19	OIS and motion detection: what's going on?

When Auto-ISO is active, and you are shooting in either aperture priority **A** or program AE **P**, most entry and enthusiast level models (e.g. X-E3, X-E2S, X-T20, X-T10, X-T100, X-M1,

X-A series, etc.) offer another OIS option: *motion detection.* When the camera detects subject movement at the time of shooting, this feature increases the shutter speed by one or two stops to reduce unwanted motion blur. To compensate for the reduced exposure time, the camera will increase the ISO value of the shot accordingly.

Motion detection reacts on either subject movement or camera movement, both of which can't be compensated by the OIS. This makes it possible to select a slower minimum shutter speed in the Auto-ISO settings (which would be suitable for static subjects). However, when the motion detection registers subject or camera movement while the shutter button is half or fully depressed, it will temporarily increase the minimum shutter speed by one or two stops. It's a smart way of adapting to a quickly changing scene.

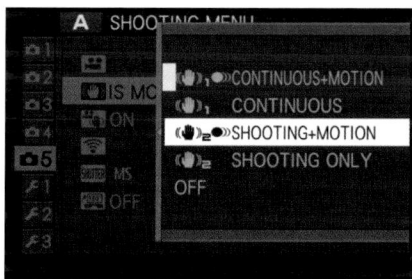

Fig. 36: **OIS motion detection** automatically increases the shutter speed by one or two stops when the camera detects movement while the shutter button is half or fully depressed. This feature is only available in aperture priority or program AE mode, and it also requires Auto-ISO. When all these prerequisites are met, the IS MODE menu (here from the X-T100) displays two additional "+MOTION" options that are otherwise invisible.

Motion detection can be combined with both OIS modes (1 and 2). You can find these options in the OIS menu as CON-TINUOUS+MOTION (OIS mode 1 with motion detection) and SHOOTING+MOTION (OIS mode 2 with motion detection).

Don't forget that these two additional OIS options are only available when Auto-ISO is active, and the camera is set to either aperture priority **A** or program AE **P**. To grant motion detection sufficient operating room, the Auto-ISO ceiling (MAX. SENSITIVITY) should be set to a reasonably high value, such as 6400 or 12800 (if available).

Important: Higher-end models like the X-Pro2, X-T1, X-T2, X-T3, X-H1, and GFX 50 don't offer motion detection OIS options because these cameras are lacking automatic scene recognition (SR+) functionality, which is a prerequisite of motion detection.

TIP 20	How the **XF23mmF1.4 R, XF16mmF1.4 R WR,** and **XF14mmF2.8 R** are different

Unlike standard X-mount lenses, the wide-angle primes XF14mmF2.8 R, XF16mmF1.4 R WR, and XF23mmF1.4 R feature a more traditional manual focus ring with a clutch mechanism.

■ Pull the focus ring towards the camera to set the lens to manual focus.

■ Push the focus ring away from the camera to set the lens to autofocus.

■ Alternatively, you can use the camera's own focus mode selector to set it to manual focus mode. In this case, the lens remains in autofocus mode, and you can only use Instant AF (usually assigned to the AF-L button) to change the focus. This also means that you cannot manually adjust focus on the lens after focusing with Instant AF.

■ You cannot use Instant AF (AF-L button) to focus when the focus ring of the lens is set to manual focus. In this case, you can only use the manual focus ring to change or adjust focus.

■ The analog depth-of-field (DOF) markers on the lens barrel are less conservative (and in my opinion less useful) than the camera's pixel-based scale. This is because the pixel-based scale is using a much smaller circle of con-fusion [17] to display DOF ranges for pixel-sharp results at 100% magnification, whereas the engraved scale on the lens uses a value that's based on looking at typically sized prints from a typical distance with typical eyesight. Some photographers regard the engraved scale (which equals the electronic film format-based scale in cameras with X-Processor Pro and 4) as more practical. Person-ally, I prefer the pixel-based scale. In any case, the actual difference between the two scales is about 3.5 aperture stops.

■ It's not possible to reverse the focusing direction of the manual focus ring with the 14mm, 16mm, or 23mm lenses.

■ If you set your camera to AF+MF mode (SHOOTING MENU > AF/MF SETTING > AF+MF > ON), you can only use this feature when the lens clutch is set to MF and the camera is set to AF-S. In this configuration, you can autofocus by half-pressing the shutter button, and then manually adjusting the focus with the focus ring (while keeping the shutter button half-pressed).

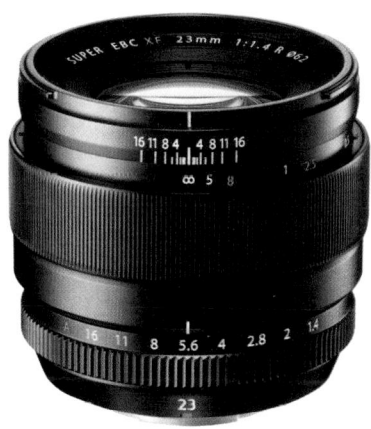

Fig. 37:
Fujinon XF23mmF1.4 R with engraved dis-tance and DOF mark-ers. It's a nice retro touch, but you lose some state-of-the-art digital functionality.

TIP 21	XF56mmF1.2 R: APD or not?

Fujifilm offers two versions of the XF56mmF1.2 R portrait lens: a regular version and an APD version. Please note that the newer and more expensive APD version is not replacing or succeeding the classic XF56mmF1.2 R lens. It's not even per se considered an overall improvement. It's just *different*. APD presents itself as another option for photographers who shoot portraits at a wide-open aperture and want very smooth bokeh.

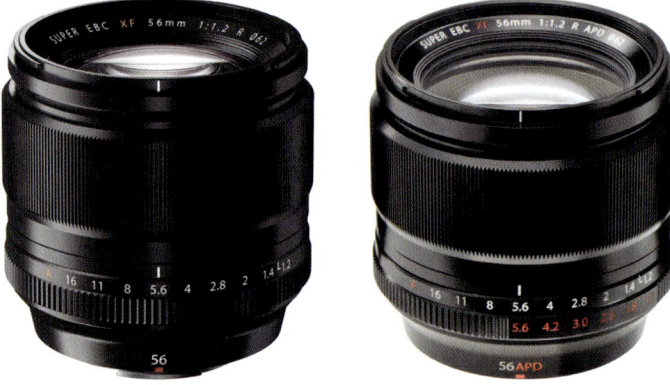

Fig. 38: The **XF56mmF1.2 R** lens is available in a regular (left) and in a special APD version (right).

Let's first establish what the APD (apodization) filter is actually doing. This non-removable filter sits in the same optical plane as the aperture, and its effect is actually quite similar: It reduces the amount of light that reaches the sensor.

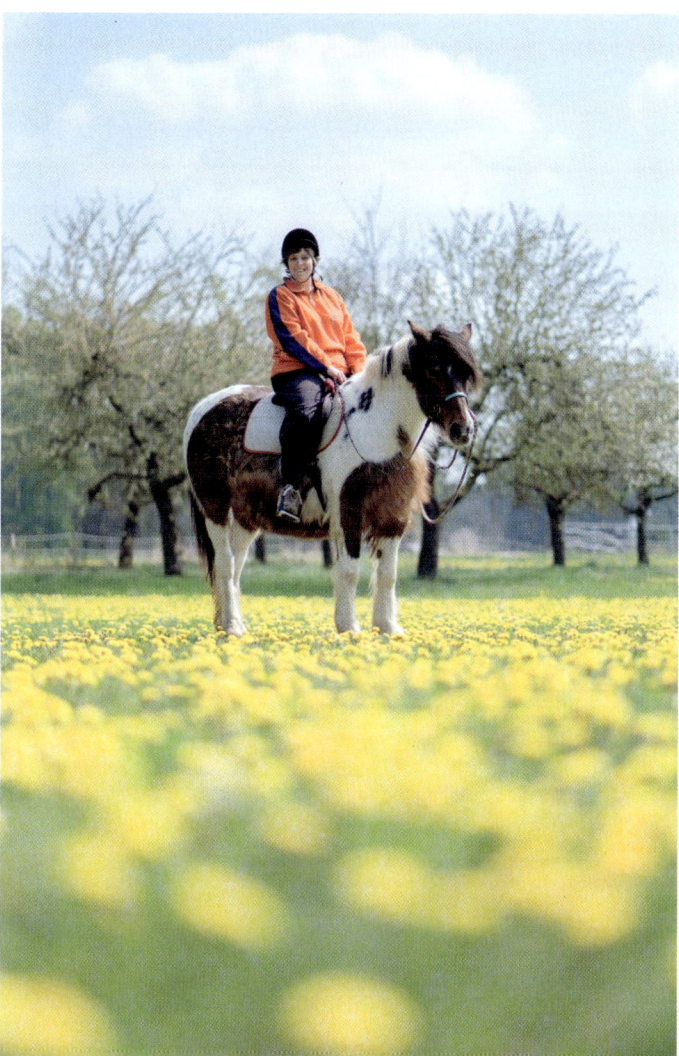

Fig. 39: The regular **XF56mmF1.2 R** lens is a popular choice for smooth portraits with pleasant bokeh and great subject separation.

Here's the difference from regular aperture blades: Normal blades feature hard edges, whereas the APD filter works with a smooth gradient (like a radial neutral density filter) that gets increasingly translucent from edge to center of the image circle.

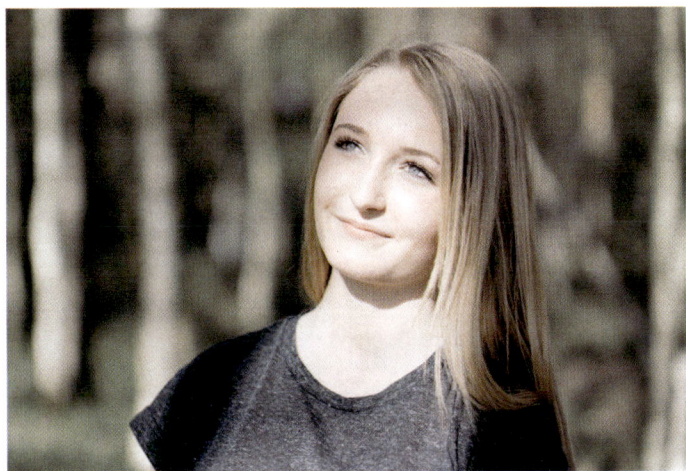

Fig. 40: The **XF56mmF1.2 R APD** is a specialty lens that can further smoothen already blurry backgrounds by filing off the edges
of blur discs.

The gradient of the APD filter has an additional softening
effect on out-of-focus areas: the hard and defined edges of
blur discs are literally filed off. The effect decreases as the
lens is stopped down, and at apertures of f/5.6 and smaller,
the APD filter has no effect at all. That's why Fujifilm recommends using the XF56mmF1.2 R APD between f/1.2 and f/2.

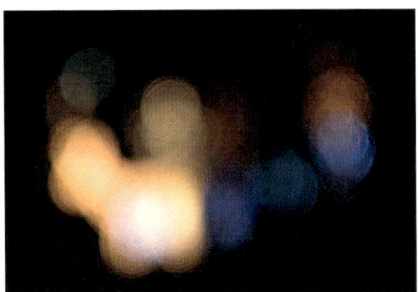 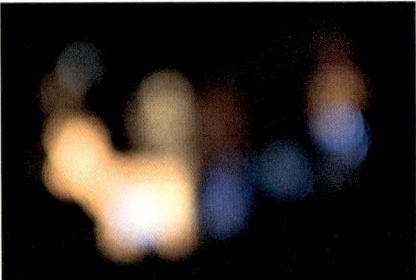

Fig. 41: To understand the **difference between a regular 56mm
lens and one with a built-in apodization filter,** it's best to take a
picture that consists of nothing else but blur discs. The example
on the left shows how such a scenario looks with a regular 56mm
lens at f/1.2. The example on the right shows the same subject shot
using the APD version. It clearly illustrates how the apodization
filter is shaving the hard edges off blur discs.

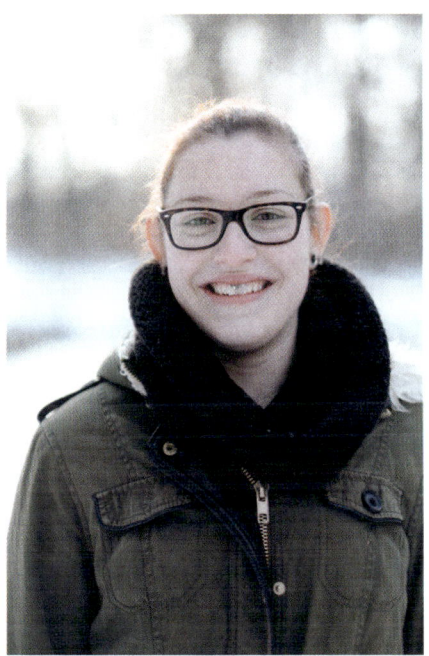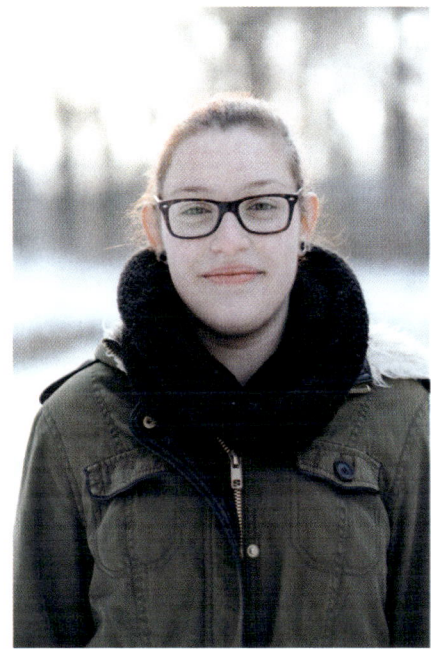

Fig. 42: Here's a more life-like example that demonstrates the **effect of the APD filter:** The image on the left was taken with a regular XF56mmF1.2 R lens, while the image on the right displays the APD version.

So why not dump the regular XF56mm lens and replace it with the APD version? It's because the APD filter introduces shortcomings of its own:

- The brightness of the APD lens is reduced between f/1.2 and f/5.6. For example, setting the APD lens to f/1.2 results in an *effective* lens speed of f/1.7. Since the APD lens is slower, shooting wide-open in poor light requires slower shutter speeds and/or higher ISO settings. At least you don't have to guess, because the *effective* aperture is shown by red markings on the aperture ring.

- The APD filter has a negative impact on autofocus performance. Fast PDAF (phase detection AF) is not available at all, and CDAF (contrast detection AF) performance is reduced in poor light along with the decreased lens brightness.

The APD version is significantly more expensive than the regular version, so you basically have to pay more for less performance. For the APD version to be a reasonable choice, you really have to love its softened, out-of-focus blur when shooting wide-open.

| TIP 22 | Using the Lens Modulation Optimizer (LMO) |

Most enthusiast and pro-level camera models support the Lens Modulation Optimizer or LMO. This feature premiered in the X100S and X20 fixed-lens cameras (where it can't be switched off). It counteracts common optical phenomena (like diffraction [18] and corner softness) when the camera converts the RAW data into JPEG images. To make it work, the firmware of the attached lens sends its LMO correction data to the camera as hidden metadata with every image.

■ Neither Fujinon XC lenses nor Zeiss Touit lenses support the LMO.

■ LMO data is proprietary and not available to external RAW converters.

If your lens supports the LMO (all Fujinon XF and GF lenses do), you should enable the function by selecting SHOOTING MENU > (IMAGE QUALITY SETTING >) LENS MODULATION OPTIMIZER > ON.

You can also use the built-in RAW converter of your camera (PLAYBACK MENU > RAW CONVERSION) to enable or disable the LMO for a specific JPEG result. With this method, it's easy to create and compare versions of a shot with and without LMO enhancements.

The LMO takes care of the following optical effects:

- **Diffraction softness:** This effect increasingly occurs when the lens is stopped down beyond a certain point. APS-C cameras with 24 MP typically exhibit diffraction at apertures of 10 and smaller. While stopping down increases the overall depth of field (DOF), it also reduces the maximum resolution of the lens/camera combination. The LMO counteracts this effect and reconstructs some of the lost detail.

- **Corner softness:** Even the best lenses aren't as sharp in the corners as they are in the center. The LMO can digitally compensate for that loss of quality.

LMO corrections are based on complex deconvolution [19] algorithms. Currently, this is only supported in-camera with the built-in RAW converter. External converters such as Adobe Lightroom, Adobe Camera Raw, Capture One Pro, Silkypix, Iridient Developer, or Photo Ninja can't process LMO data. This means that LMO corrections are only visible in JPEGs that have been generated by the camera.

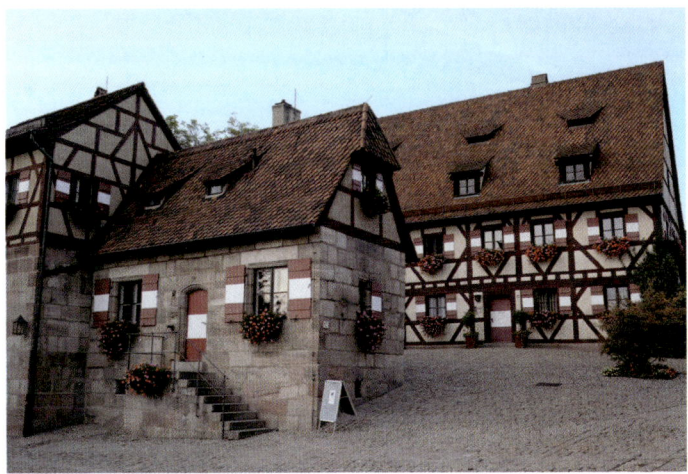

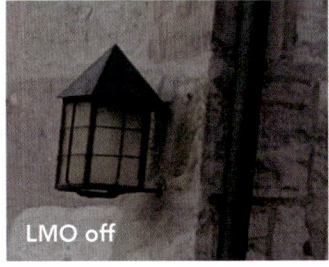
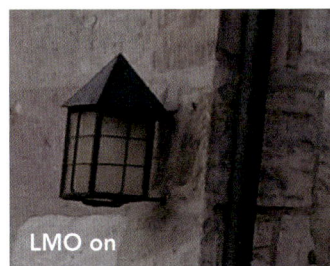

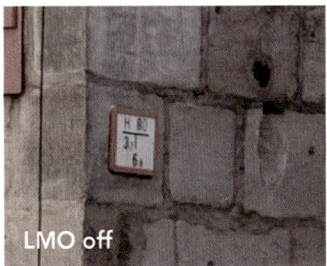
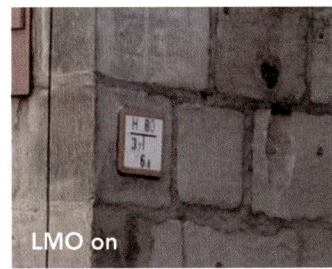

Fig. 43: This example illustrates how the **Lens Modulation Optimizer (LMO)** improves the edge and corner sharpness of Fujifilm's native XF and GF lenses. It was shot with an X-E2 and an XF23mmF1.4 R WR lens at f/8. Let's have a closer look at the lantern situated near the left edge of the scene: The two crops in the center row show the lantern with LMO OFF (left crop) and LMO ON (right crop). There's a small visible improvement in the version with the active LMO. However, if you compare crops of the sign taken from the center of the scene (bottom row), there's no visible difference between the versions with and without LMO. That's no surprise: Lenses achieve their maximum resolution around the image center, so the LMO's job is to only compensate the inevitable loss of resolution near the edges of the frame.

Things you should know about digital lens corrections:	TIP 23

Most modern lenses achieve their optimal image quality through a combination of optical and digital corrections. Corrections are mostly applied to the three following phenomena:

- **Vignetting:** This effect results in a loss of brightness from center to corner. Vignetting [20] is more pronounced at large (open) apertures.

- **Distortion:** There are pincushion- and barrel-type distortions [21], both of which make straight lines seem curved. Several premium primes like the XF14mm, XF23mm (F1.4 and F2), XF35mmF1.4, XF56mm, and XF90mm are fully optically corrected for distortion. Others (such as the Zeiss Touit range, compact pancake lenses, the XF35mmF2, or zoom lenses) require a combination of optical and digital distortion correction.

- **Chromatic aberration:** Chromatic aberration [22] results in color fringing. This effect can be corrected (or mitigated) with apochromatic lenses, or digitally corrected during RAW conversion.

Some camera makers rely on dedicated correction profiles that must be provided by each RAW converter maker. Fujifilm isn't one of these companies: all current Fujifilm cameras save digital corrections as metadata in the RAW file. RAW converters can access this lens-specific metadata and use it to apply appropriate corrections. This way, the built-in RAW converter and external RAW conversion software, such as Adobe Lightroom, Silkypix, Iridient Developer, or Capture One, can use the metadata in the RAW file to correct or mitigate vignetting, distortion, and chromatic aberration.

A major benefit of this method is that many RAW converters automatically support new lenses since Fujifilm delivers the correction data via the RAW metadata. However, there's also a drawback: some RAW converters (such as

Lightroom, Adobe Camera Raw, and Silkypix) don't give you the option to switch off metadata-based digital lens correc- tions, even if you're convinced they aren't necessary. Since digital distortion correction always results in some loss of image sharpness and detail due to the required stretching and interpolation of pixels, this can be a headache for some users. Obviously, not all subjects or images require the same amount of digital correction (it can also be a simple matter of taste), so full user control over the application of digital lens corrections is a very nice feature.

Luckily, software like Iridient Developer and Capture One offer control over how much digital metadata distortion (or vignetting) correction should be applied. Other programs (like Photo Ninja and AccuRaw) simply ignore lens-correc- tion metadata. With such programs, all corrections must be applied either manually or by using a dedicated profile.

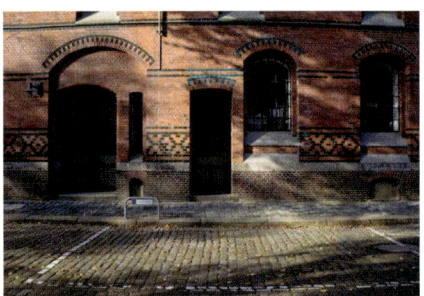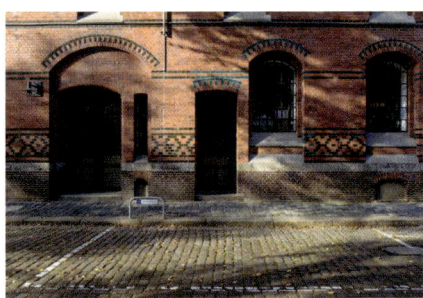

Fig. 44: This example was taken with an X100F and WCL-X100 conversion lens. In the image on the left, **digital lens-correction metadata** was ignored. As a result, there's visible barrel distortion caused by the WCL. The image on the right shows the same shot, but this time with digital lens-correction metadata, which is auto- matically applied by compatible RAW converters such as Adobe Lightroom.

Important: *Adobe Lightroom and Adobe Camera RAW offer additional lens-correction profiles for X100 series cameras that (if you choose to activate them) are applied on top of any correction that is already applied based on the RAW meta-data. The combination of metadata-based and profile-based correction is designed to render perfectly corrected X100/S/T/F results. However, in the real world, "clinically perfect" is often too much, so it will depend on the subject and your personal preference if (or to what degree) you want to apply these ad-ditional correction profiles.*

X100 series and X70: Using wide-angle and tele conversion lenses	TIP 24

The X100 series is famous for its built-in 23mmF2 lens. Many things changed and improved during the journey from the X100 Classic to the X100F, but the lens (which corresponds to a 35mm field of view in full-frame terms) remained mostly the same.

For added flexibility, you can attach wide (WCL-X100 & WCL-X100II) or tele conversion lenses (TCL-X100 & TCL-X100II) to your X100/S/T/F. The WCLs convert the focal length of the camera's built-in lens to 19mm, and the TCLs turn it into a 33mm outfit. In full-frame equivalency terms, this corresponds to 28mm and 50mm lenses. Adding a WCL or TCL doesn't impact the speed of the resulting lens, so the aperture numbers on your camera remain valid.

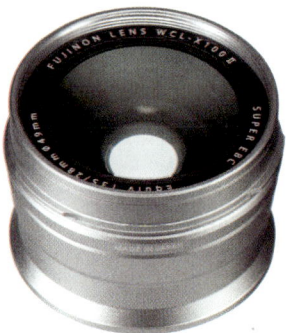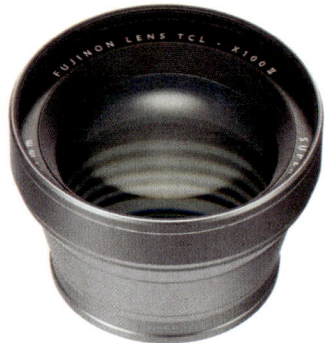

Fig. 45: The **WCL-X100(II) and TCL-X100(II) conversion lenses** are screw-mount adapters that connect directly to the built-in 23mmF2 lens of your X100 series camera.

Optically, there is *no* difference between the older and the newer "type II" versions of the wide and tele conversion adapters. It's just a matter of convenience—the newer versions are automatically recognized by the X100F when you attach and remove them from the camera's lens, but the older are not. Instead, you have to go to the SHOOTING MENU > (SHOOTING SETTING >) CONVERSION LENS menu and tell the camera when you attach or remove an older conversion lens (WIDE, TELE, or OFF).

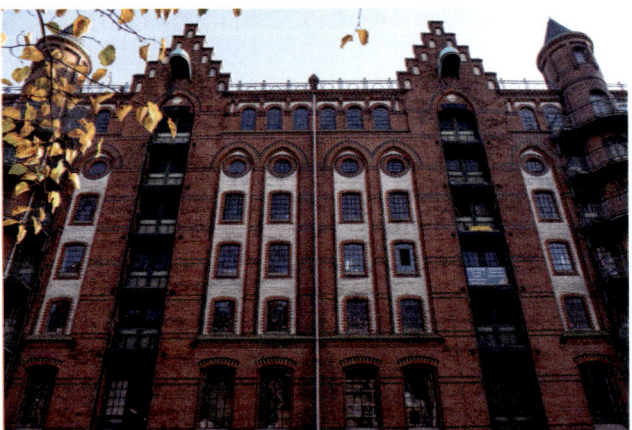

Fig. 46: The **WCL-X100(II)** turns the fixed 23mmF2 lens of your X100 series camera into a 19mmF2 wide-angle lens with an expanded field of view.

If you already own a legacy WCL-X100 or TCL-X100 converter from a previous X100, X100S, or X100T camera, you can keep using it on your X100F. Just don't forget to tell the camera when a conversion lens has been attached or removed. Here's why:

■ The WCL and TCL conversion lenses require custom digital lens correction for distortion, vignetting, and chromatic aberration. These corrections can only be properly applied (or stored in the RAW metadata) if the camera knows that a WCL or TCL has been attached.

■ When you attach a first-generation WCL or TCL and forget to tell the camera, it will apply the wrong correction data, and image quality will suffer.

■ The same happens when you remove a first-generation WCL and TCL and forget to tell the camera. The camera still believes that a conversion lens is attached and acts accordingly; the wrong lens-correction data will be used, and image quality will suffer.

■ Telling the camera about a WCL or TCL corrects the size and position of the bright frame and AF frames in the optical viewfinder (OVF). It also adjusts the electronic distance and depth-of-field scales in the viewfinder or LCD monitor.

The newer type-II conversion lenses can save you from forgetting to tell the X100F about attaching or removing WCLs and TCLs. If you are a frequent user of a first-generation WCL or TCL, I recommend adding the CONVERSION LENS menu option to the MY MENU of the X100F for quick and easy access. You can edit the MY MENU with SET UP > USER SETTING > MY MENU SETTING.

*Important: Since the X100, X100S, and X100T do not feature automatic WCL or TCL recognition, it doesn't matter if you attach older type-I or newer type-II conversion lenses to any of these cameras. You **always** have to manually tell these cameras when you are use a conversion lens.*

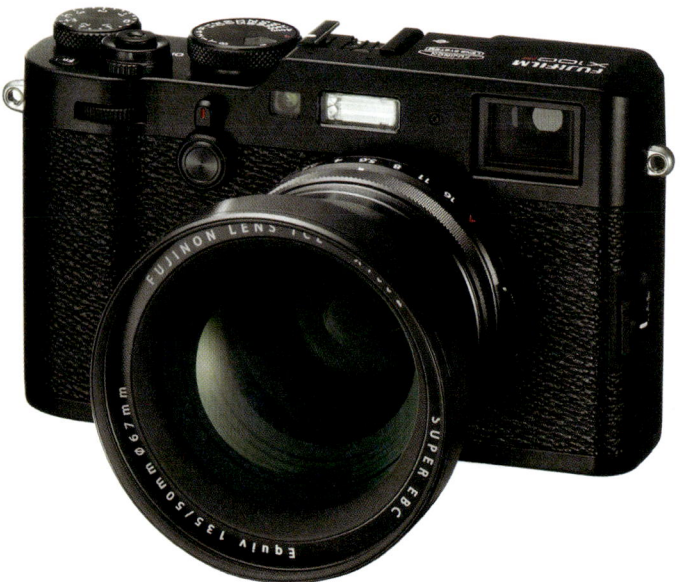

Fig. 47: A black X100F with a corresponding **TCL-X100II** tele conversion lens.

Analog to the X100 series, you can turn the 18.5mmF2.8 lens
of the compact X70 into a 14mmF2.8 lens by attaching the
WCL-X70 wide-angle conversion lens, resulting in a 21mm
"full-frame" equivalent. Again, you have to manually inform
the camera (SHOOTING MENU > WIDE CONVERSION LENS
> ON) in order to avoid unwanted distortion and vignett-
ing. Don't forget to switch this option off again when you
remove the conversion lens.

TIP 25	Using teleconverters

Teleconverters are installed between the camera body and
an XF or GF lens, where they extend the effective focal
length of the lens by a factor of either 1.4 or 2. This leads to
losing either one or two aperture stops of brightness, and it
puts a (small) toll on image resolution. Hence, teleconverters
should be used in concert with premium lenses that offer a

resolution reserve that's big enough to render the inevitable toll on image quality practically invisible.

As of December 2018, there are four teleconverters available from Fujifilm:

- The **XF1.4x TC WR** and **XF2x TC WR** for X-mount are mechanically compatible with the XF50–140mmF2.8 R LM OIS WR, the XF100–400mmF4.5–5.6 R LM OIS WR, and the XF80mmF2.8 R LM OIS WR Macro. It is *not* recommended to use them with the XF200mmF2 R LM OIS WR.

- The **XF1.4x TC F2 WR** is compatible and included with the XF200mmF2 R LM OIS WR high-end telephoto prime. After applying lens firmware updates that were released in late December of 2018, it can also be used with the XF50–140mmF2.8 R LM OIS WR, XF100–400mmF4.5–5.6 R LM OIS WR, and XF80mmF2.8 R LM OIS WR Macro lenses.

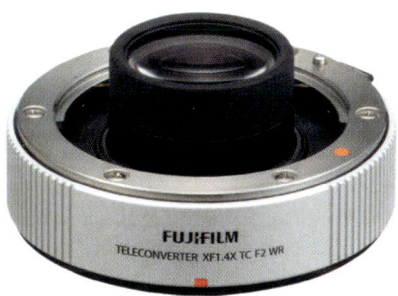

Fig. 48:
The XF1.4x TC F2 WR turns the XF200mmF2 R LM OIS WR telephoto prime effectively into an XF280mmF2.8 R LM OIS WR.

- The **GF1.4x TC WR** for G-mount is mechanically compatible with the GF250mmF4 R LM OIS WR, effectively turning it into a GF350mmF5.6 R LM OIS WR. Additional compatible lenses will follow in the future.

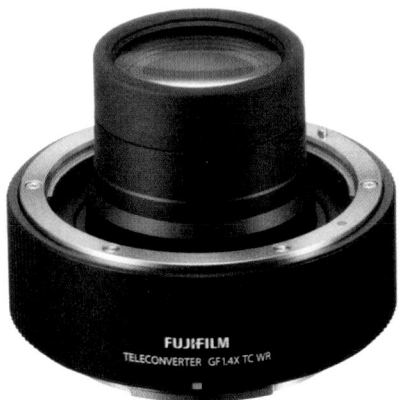
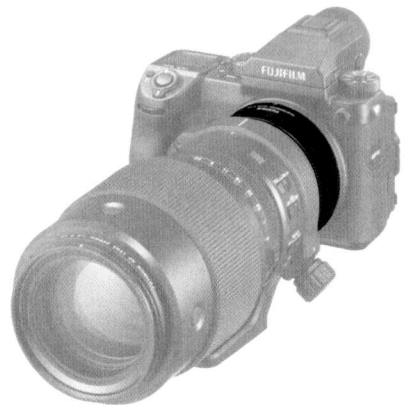

Fig. 49: Like its smaller X-mount siblings, the **GF1.4x TC WR** (left) protrudes deeply into the rear barrel of the host lens, disguising much of its actual size when it's sandwiched between the camera and lens (right).

Unlike screw-on conversion lenses for the X70 and X100 series, XF and GF teleconverters have an impact on the speed (maximum brightness) of the resulting lens package.

To give you an example, the XF2x TC WR effectively turns the ultra-sharp XF80mmF2.8 R LM OIS WR Macro lens into an XF160mmF5.6 R LM OIS WR Macro. Setting the aperture of this combo to f/2.8 actually means setting an effective aperture of f/5.6. Using a 2x teleconverter, the light loss comprises two stops, whereas 1.4x converters take away one stop of light.

Luckily, all this is recognized and handled by the camera and lens firmware (as long as you have kept them up to date). The firmware will automatically adjust the on-screen displays and the EXIF [23] data to reflect the *effective* aperture values. It will also change the lens-correction metadata (factoring in updated values for distortion, vignetting, and chromatic aberration) and include the presence of the teleconverter in the EXIF lens description. For example, a GF250mmF4 R LM OIS WR becomes a GF250mmF4 R LM OIS WR +1.4x.

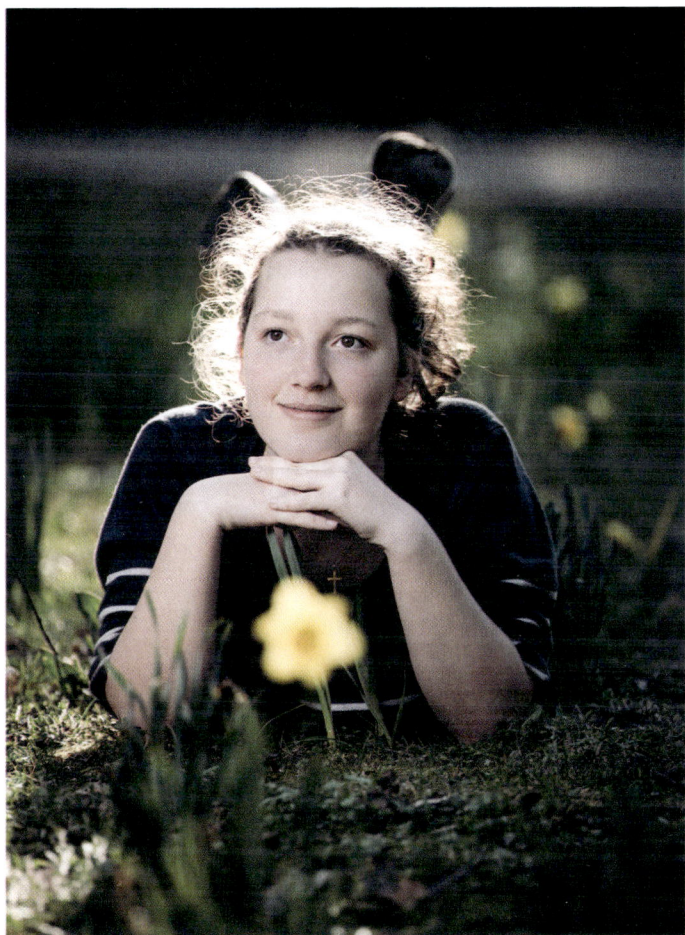

Fig. 50: The **GF1.4x TC WR** in action. It was attached to a GF250mmF4 R LM OIS WR, effectively turning it into a GF350mmF5.6 R LM OIS WR lens.

Depending on the quality of your individual lens copy, using the XF100–400mmF4.5–5.6 R LM OIS WR in concert with an XF2x TC WR tends to stretch things thin with regards to performance and image quality, particularly at the long end of the lens. At effectively an 800mm focal length (that's a full-frame equivalent of 1200mm), the wide-open aperture of this combo is f/11, which can make it hard for your camera's autofocus to gather enough light to operate quickly and precisely. There's also some loss of resolution—not only because of the optics involved, but also often due to atmospheric effects when you are capturing far-away subjects.

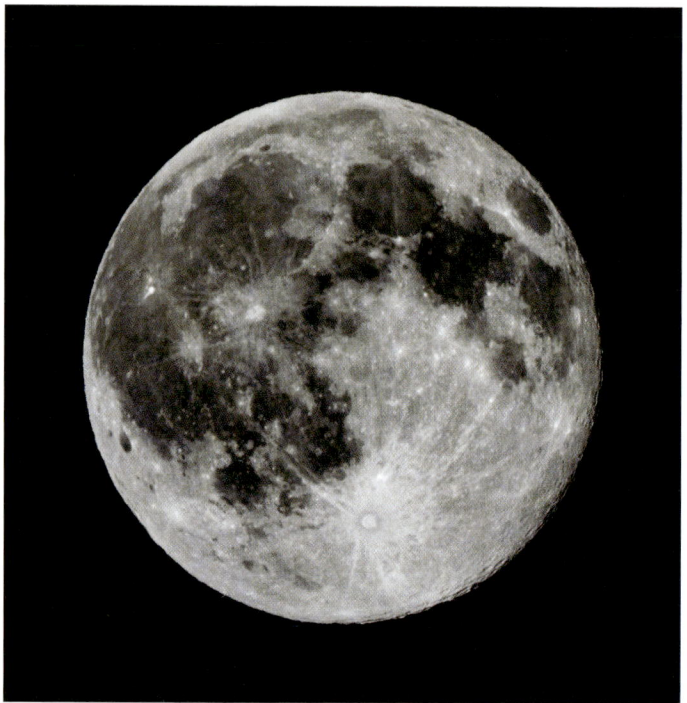

Fig. 51: XF100–400mmF4.5–5.6 R LM OIS WR & XF2x TC WR: Shooting the moon with effectively 800mm (or 1200mm in full-frame terms) during a warm summer night resulted in some unwelcome atmospheric effects. That's why astronomic telescopes are usually placed on mountains or in space. This example is based on a square 5 MP crop.

TIP 26	Macro extension tubes

You can add macro capability to many of your GF, XF, and XC lenses by using Fujifilm's electronic macro extension tubes: MCEX-11 or MCEX-16 for X-mount, and MCEX-18G WR or MCEX-45G WR for G-mount.

You can download PDF files ([24] and [25]) from Fujifilm's website that show how the different extension tubes enhance the magnification factor of each X-mount or G-mount lens. Please note that the camera's electronic depth-of-field/distance scale doesn't reflect the use of macro extension tubes.

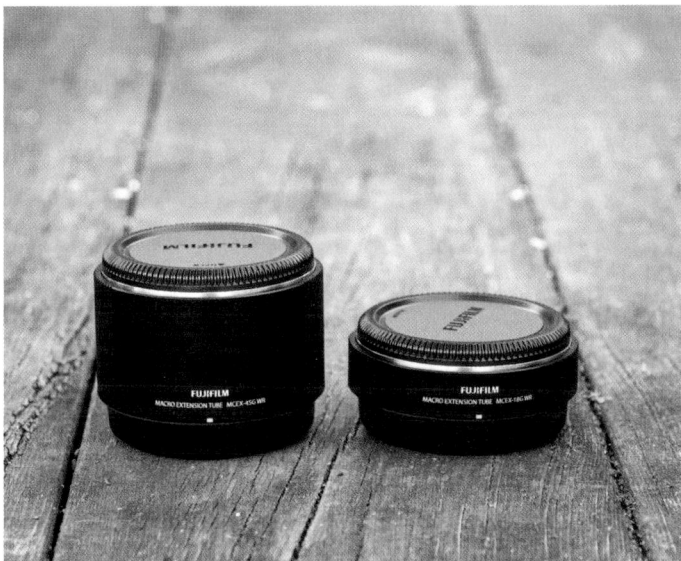

Fig. 52: The **MCEX-18G WR** and **MCEX-45G WR** macro extension tubes for the GFX can be combined with most GF lenses. According to Fujifilm, the 18mm version is the smallest possible size that meets the structural requirements, while the 45mm tube was designed to add 1:1 magnification to the GF120mmF4 R LM OIS WR Macro lens.

A word of caution: Stay away from cheap third-party macro extension tubes with electronic contacts. Some of them turned out to be a bad fit, damaging cameras and lenses.

It's also not recommended to stack more than one macro extension tube on your camera.

TIP 27 | Use the included lens hood!

Most Fujifilm XC, XF, and GF lenses come with a fitted lens hood, which should be used whenever possible. Apart from its optical benefits, the hood protects the lens and the front glass element from damage.

Lens hoods can pose problems, too: they make the lens appear bigger than it is, and they can shade the in-camera/on-camera flash or the autofocus assist light. They also use up extra space in your bag, although most hoods can be reverse-mounted on the lens for transport purposes.

When you shoot with a small shoe-mounted flash, or when you depend on using the AF assist lamp, it's best to remove the lens hood.

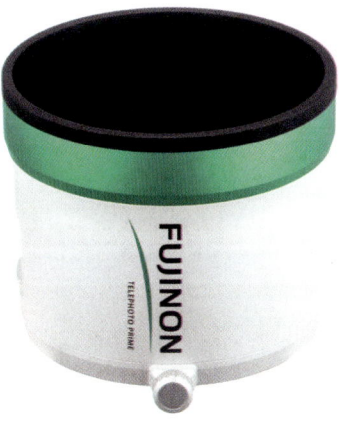

Fig. 53:
Lens hoods like this large attachment for the **XF200mmF2 R LM OIS WR** offer optical benefits and robust lens protection in one package.

Sadly, X100 series cameras don't come with an included lens hood. However, there are offerings from Fujifilm and aftermarket manufacturers. My personal choice is the original Fujifilm LH-X100. This hood comes with an AR-X100 adapter ring and is compatible with the WCL-X100 and WCL-X100II wide-angle conversion lenses.

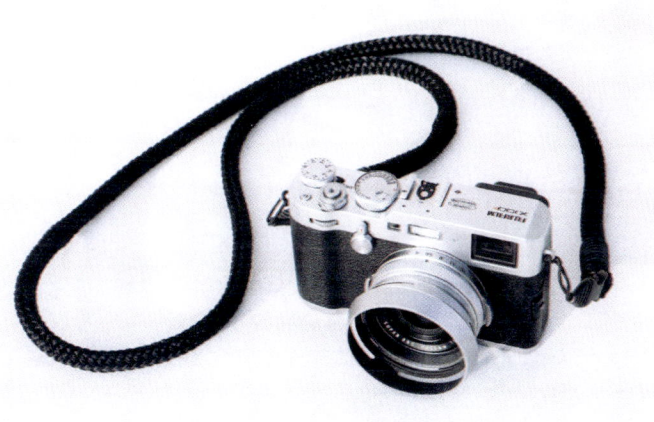

Fig. 54: My X100F with an installed **LH-X100 lens hood**.

The 23mmF2 lens in the X100F is susceptible to lens flare, especially when you shoot against a bright light source like the sun. This can result in a decrease of contrast, which can add a "dreamy" look to a scene. If you don't like that, try to shade the lens from the light source with your hand, or add contrast during post-processing.

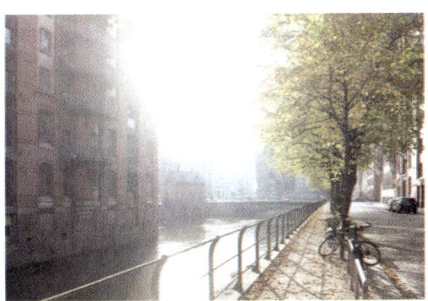
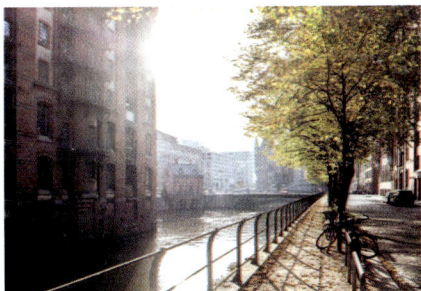

Fig. 55: Shooting against the sun with an attached WCL-X100 can cause the image to lack contrast (left). To compensate, you can add contrast and darken shadow tones in RAW post-processing (right).

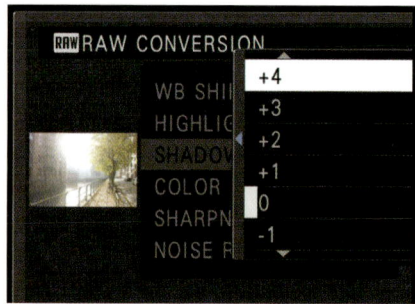

Fig. 56: You can also **add shadow contrast in-camera** by increasing the SHADOW TONE setting in the IMAGE QUALITY SETTING
menu before shooting—or later during playback in the RAW CON-
VERSION menu.

*Important: Don't use screw-in lens hoods with lenses that
feature a retractable inner tube, such as the XF27mmF2.8,
XF60mmF2.4 R Macro, or XF35mmF1.4 R. The inner tube
doesn't respond well to shocks and pressure. By using a
screw-in hood, you'd directly transfer pressure or shocks from
the lens hood to the delicate inner lens tube. It's a recipe for
disaster.*

TIP 28	Lens protection filters—yes or no?

Digital cameras don't require the UV or skylight filters that
used to be very popular in the days of analog film photography. This means that a permanently affixed filter has no
optical purpose, and only serves as protective glass. This
additional glass can have a negative effect on image quality,
especially at night or when you shoot against a bright light
source. Filters increase the chance of ghosting, unwanted
reflections, or a loss of contrast.

I recommend using protective filters only in situations
that require this additional protective layer. In most situations, the lens hood should provide sufficient protection.
If you still decide to use a filter, make sure to choose a
high-quality product. For example, Fujifilm offers protective

filters that feature the same Super EBC coating used on their GF/XF/XC lenses. Be prepared to pay a premium, though.

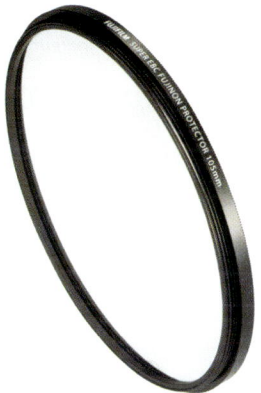

Fig. 57:
With a diameter of 105mm, the **PRF-105** for the XF200mmF2 is (so far) the largest lens protection filter for the X series.

39mm filters can be tricky!	TIP 29

The **XF60mmF2.4 R** and **XF27mmF2.8** lenses require filters with a 39mm thread. Those filters are designed to allow the inner lens barrel freely retract into the outer barrel while the filter is attached. If this isn't possible (for example, because a thin step-up ring is directly attached to the lens or because the filter's overall diameter is too large), the lens can be damaged when the filter or step-up ring collides with the outer barrel of the lens.

A typical indicator for this and other mechanical lens problems is a message alerting you that the camera needs to be switched off and on again. A possible solution is putting a spacer (a suitable 39mm filter, for example) between the lens and the step-up ring. You should remove the glass from the spacer. You can refit a cheap, old, or unused 39mm filter to do the job as long as it doesn't interfere with the outer lens barrel when the inner barrel is retracting.

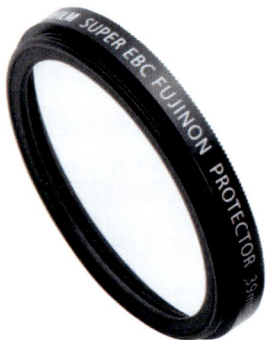

Fig. 58:
A **39mm protection filter** by
Fujifilm. A filter like this can also
be used as a spacer between the
lens (XF60mm or XF27mm) and a
step-up ring.

Don't forget that screw-in lens hoods are an absolute no-go
for a lens with retractable inner barrels like the XF27mmF2.8.

| TIP 30 | Switch off the camera when exchanging lenses! |

The user manual of your system camera asks you to switch
off the camera before exchanging lenses. Then again, who
cares, right? In the heat of the moment, many of us forget
(or simply don't have the time) to follow this advice, and so
far, nothing terrible has happened.

However, instead of making a bad habit out of this, we
should consider why Fujifilm is actually asking us to exchange lenses only when the camera is turned off:

■ Several lenses (like the XF60mmF2.4 R Macro or the
XF27mmF2.8) have moving inner barrels. During focusing, the inner barrel can protrude way outside the
protective edge of the outer barrel. The secure storage
and transport state for these lenses is always with a fully
retracted inner barrel, and this secure state is automatically entered when you turn off the camera *before* you
remove the lens.

■ The same applies to lenses like the new XC15-45mm
F3.5–5.6 OIS PZ power zoom: Switch off the camera while
the lens is still attached, and the power zoom will safely
retract to its compact transport and storage position. On
the other hand, if you remove the lens before turning off

the camera, your lens may end up in a less compact and more vulnerable state.

■ When the camera/lens is powering off, a lock mechanism holds the linear motor driven inner-focusing element of the GF250mmF4 R LM OIS WR and XF200mmF2 R LM OIS WR in place. This suppresses "clacking" noises (caused by the loose lens group) when you carry the lens around off-camera. If you remove the lens while the camera power is still on, this lock mechanism isn't activated. By the way: "Clacking" is perfectly normal for other lenses with inner-focusing mechanisms, such as the XF90mmF2 R LM or XF50–140mmF2.8 R LM OIS WR, so don't worry: nothing is broken. Off-camera, there's simply no camera-powered magnetic field to hold the rear element in place, so it is loosely moving in the barrel when you shake the lens.

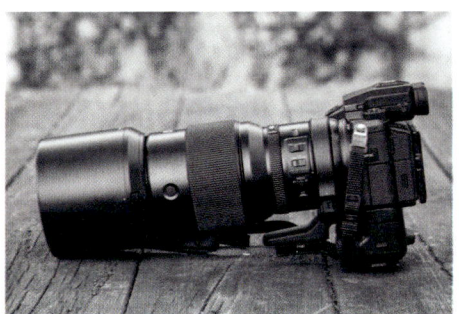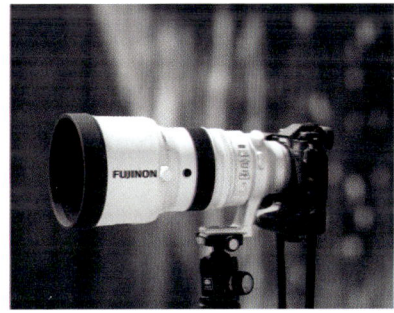

Fig. 59: The GF250mmF4 R LM OIS WR (left) and the XF200mmF2 R LM OIS WR (right) are lenses with a **lock mechanism** to hold the inner focusing element in place when the lens is off-camera. However, this mechanical lock is only activated when you switch off the camera *before* you remove the lens.

Lens sample variation and how to deal with it	TIP 31

It's true: Not all copies of a specific lens type are the same. Some copies are better than others, often also depending on what you shoot, what settings you use and what you look at in the end result. This applies to all lenses from all well-known manufacturers, so it's not Fujifilm-specific.

That said, most of us are using Fujinon lenses, and as somebody who has tested, owns or has owned at least one copy of every GF, XF, XC, and Zeiss Touit lens model, I am happy to report that quality issues with individual samples are quite rare. Yes, each lens copy is unique, but the differences in image quality are usually negligible in practical use. You could measure them, but you can't see them in a normal shot.

Thanks to their less complex construction, prime lenses rarely exhibit sample variation issues. Real problems are more common with complex zoom lenses, and they are typically related to decentered lens elements, which results in visible corner softness affecting one or several image quadrants. In my experience, the most likely candidates for this issue are the XF10–24mmF4 R OIS and the XF18–135mmF3.5–5-6 R LM OIS WR.

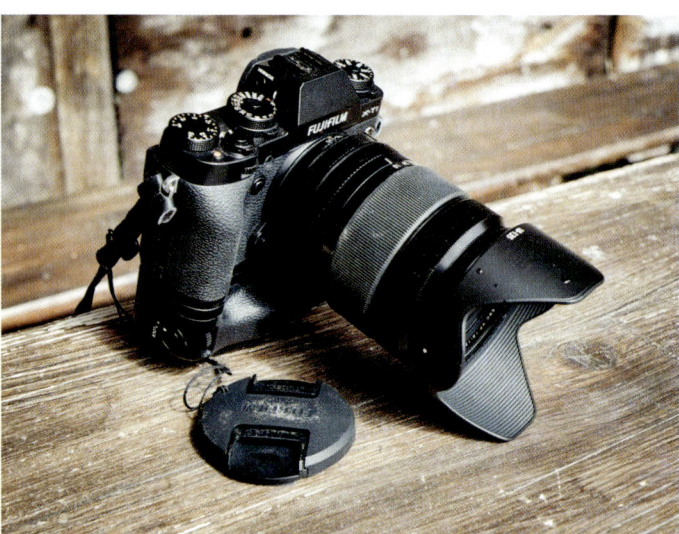

Fig. 60: The highly versatile **XF18–135mmF3.5–5-6 R LM OIS WR** appears to be more vulnerable for sample variation than other lenses of the GF/XF/XC lineup. On the bright side, the recently announced XF16–80mmF4 R OIS WR promises to be a more consistent alternative. It is supposed to be available in 2019.

Decentered lenses can be realigned and calibrated by Fuji-film (this service should be free within the warranty pe-riod), and I recommend that you document the problem for the service technician if you are confident that one exists. Testing for a decentered lens can be performed at home in several ways. One simple but effective method is suggested by Lensrentals [26], another one by the German website Onzesi [27] (English Google translation here: [28]).

1.3 THE BASICS (3): USEFUL ACCESSORIES

There's a rich selection of accessories for X series cameras. I'll cover a few select items that can, in my opinion and experience, improve the functionality of your camera.

Optional handgrips	TIP 32

An optional handgrip can improve the ergonomics of your camera when you are using heavy lenses or if you have large hands.

Fujifilm offers handgrips for many X series cameras that provide full access to the battery compartment and are compatible with Arca-Swiss-type tripod heads, so you don't need a dedicated quick release plate. The handgrip *is* the quick release plate.

Fig. 61: The optional **handgrip MHG-XT10** provides direct access to the battery compartment of the X-T10 and X-T20 and can be mounted on an Arca-Swiss-type tripod head. Similar grips are available for the X-T1, X-T2, X-T3, X-Pro2, X-E3, X-E2(S), and X100T.

A **Vertical Power (Booster) Grip** is another useful option to enhance both the ergonomics and the performance of your X-T1, X-T2, X-T3, X-H1, or GFX 50 S. Vertical power grips can fit one or two additional batteries to increase the maximum number of shots per charge.

For improved upright shooting, vertical power grips mirror many of the respective camera body's controls. The tripod-mounting socket is aligned with the camera's optical axis, and the grip is resistant to dust and water. Vertical grips for the X-T2, X-T3, X-H1 and GFX 50S also offer their own direct battery-charging functionality via an external power supply.

The Vertical Power Grips for the X-T2 and X-H1 are actually Vertical Power Booster Grips, since they both feature a dedicated Boost mode switch that improves AF speed and the EVF refresh rate. When fitted with the grip, these cameras can use multiple batteries simultaneously to improve performance on aspects such as 4K video recording, continuous shooting, shooting interval, shutter release time lag, and blackout time.

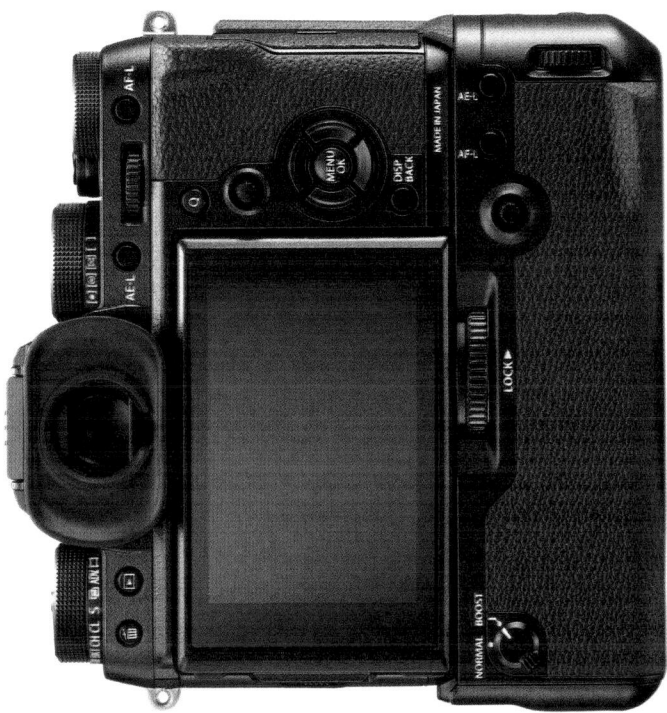

Fig. 62: A **Vertical Power Booster Grip** is a useful companion for the X-T2 and X-H1. Personally, I almost never take it off. It enhances the camera's usability with large and heavy lenses, offers improved ergonomics for vertical shooting, and features a headphone output for videographers. Its most important features are the addition of up to two batteries and its performance-boosting capabilities. With a total of three batteries in the camera body and the grip, users can spend a day of intense shooting without changing or charging batteries. When they are empty, the two extra batteries can be simultaneously recharged in the grip with an external power supply.

The GFX 50S and the new X-T3 can achieve their maximum performance without adding vertical power grips.

| TIP 33 | Off-camera TTL flash with a Canon OC-E3 TTL extension cord |

X series cameras with a hot shoe can be combined with most third-party flashes, as long as the flash output is controlled manually. However, Fuji's automated TTL flash exposure only works with Fujifilm compatible TTL flash units like the **EF-20, EF-X20,** and **EF-42,** or the great **Metz M400.** In late 2016, Fujifilm also added the professional **EF-X500** flash unit to the lineup. The EF-X500 allows wireless TTL and FP high-speed-sync (HSS).

TTL is an abbreviation for "Through The Lens," which means that the camera determines the appropriate flash output by measuring a scene through the lens with a weak pre-flash. To work in TTL mode, compatible flash units must be connected with the camera's hot shoe, and strangely enough, there's still no Fujifilm-branded TTL extension cable on the market that allows you to use a TTL flash off-camera.

A simple solution for this dilemma is using a **Canon OC-E3** extension cable, which is pin-compatible with Fuji's flash contacts. With such a cable (or an equivalent third-party product), it is possible to use an EF-20, EF-X20, EF-42, EF-X500, or any other Fuji TTL-compatible flash off-camera in TTL mode.

Please note that Canon OC-E3 cables are only compatible with Fuji's TTL flash *connectors,* not with Fuji's TTL flash *protocol.* This means that it isn't possible to use Canon TTL flash devices with your X camera in TTL mode.

Fujifilm's compact (and retro-styled) EF-X20 flash features an optical slave mode and can be wirelessly triggered by another flash unit. However, this is no automated TTL mode, so the output of the EF-X20 must be manually controlled while in slave mode.

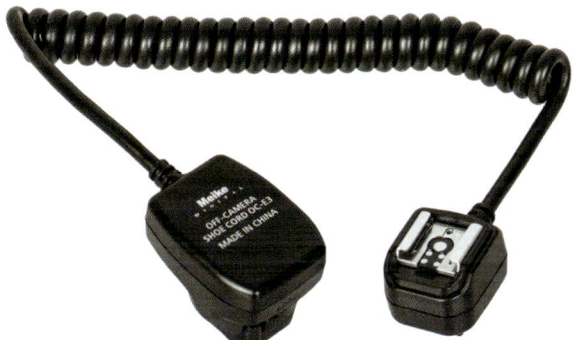

Fig. 63: A **Canon-compatible TTL extension cord** also works with Fujifilm X series cameras.

Possible issues regarding Canon TTL flash devices	TIP 34

When Fujifilm introduced its previous generation of X cam-eras with the X-Pro2 in early 2016, using Canon-compatible flash devices (e.g., flash units or radio transmitters) on the hot shoe sometimes led to an overload of the camera's pro-cessor, which resulted in overheating (you'd see overheating warnings if this happened). It was caused by incompatible Canon/Fuji TTL flash protocols that are routed through compatible flash contacts, as described in the previous tip.

After several firmware upgrades, it's unlikely that this issue still persists. However, if it does, it can even occur when you are using your Canon-compatible flash gear in full manual mode without any expectation of TTL exposure control. You may only want a simple trigger signal, but what you get are colliding protocols with adverse side effects.

Should you encounter these problems with your gear, you have three basic choices:

■ Stop using your Canon-compatible TTL flash or transmit-ter and replace it with simpler devices that only use a central trigger contact.

■ Tape the TTL contacts of your flash devices, leaving only the central trigger contact. This ensures that the only electric connection between the camera and the flash or transmitter is the flash trigger contact.

■ Use an adapter that isolates the flash sync signal and blocks all other hot shoe pin connections to your flash device. This is like taping TTL pins, just more convenient. Suitable adapters are available for only a few dollars.

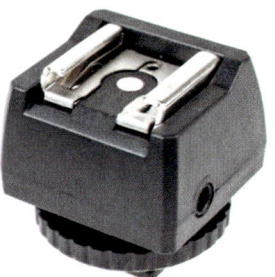 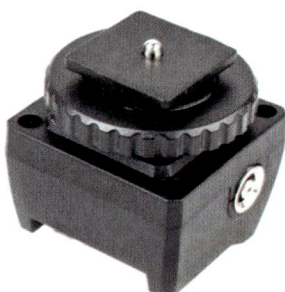

Fig. 64: Do you experience overheating warnings after connecting incompatible TTL flash units to your Fuji X camera? A cheap and simple **mid-contact hot shoe adapter** separates the trigger signal from undesirable TTL signals.

Please note that flawless flash operation is only guaranteed when you use devices that explicitly support the Fujifilm X flash system and protocol. Alternatively, you can also use simple, manual flash devices and transmitters that only use the camera's central trigger contact. Other flash devices (that were originally made for other camera brands and systems) may also work in full manual mode, but there's no guarantee for it. Proceed at your own risk.

| TIP 35 | Remote shutter release option |

From time to time you may encounter situations that require you to remotely release the shutter without vibration. A quick-and-dirty method is to use the camera's self-timer with a delay of either two or ten seconds, although a better way is using a remote shutter release. Most X cameras offer at least two of the following three port options to connect remote shutter releases:

- Some X cameras (especially the retro-branded ones) feature a **mechanical thread** in the shutter button that allows you to screw in a traditional mechanical cable release.

- Most models include either an **RR-80** (Mini-USB, older cameras) or **RR-90** (Micro-USB, more recent models) port that is compatible with a variety of electronic remote controls.

- You can connect Canon-compatible electronic remote shutter releases to the **Mic/remote release port** (a 2.5mm socket that exists in most X series cameras). Fujifilm is also now selling a Canon-style remote named **RR-100**.

Electronic shutter releases are available in tethered and wireless versions. Wireless options always consist of a transmitter and a receiver. The transmitter sends a trigger signal that is picked up by the receiver, which triggers the camera with an electronic cable that's connected to the RR-80, RR-90, or 2.5mm remote release port (RR-100).

Fujifilm offers basic RR-80, RR-90, and RR-100 (Canon-style) shutter release cables, but there are more sophisticated (both tethered and wireless) solutions from third parties, such as programmable intervalometers.

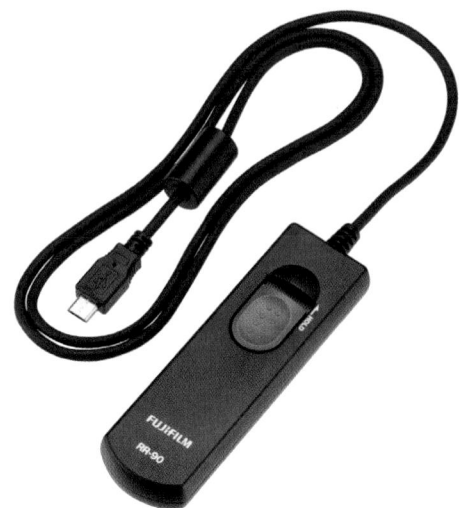

Fig. 65: Fujifilm's **RR-90** is a simple and reliable remote for most X camera models.

If you already own an older RR-80-type shutter release (which was the standard for the X-E1), you can buy a third-party adapter cable that lets you use RR-80 remote shutter releases with RR-90 cameras. Please note that a simple USB-Mini to USB-Micro adapter doesn't work; you have to ask for a dedicated RR-80 to RR-90 adapter.

The 2.5mm remote release port (RR-100) is compatible with a widely used Canon remote shutter release standard. Among others, it is compatible to the following camera models: Canon EOS Digital Rebel, Canon EOS 1000D, Canon EOS 100D, Canon EOS 1100D, Canon EOS 300D, Canon EOS 350D, Canon EOS 400D, Canon EOS 450D, Canon EOS 500D, Canon EOS 550D, Canon EOS 600D, Canon EOS 60D, Canon EOS 60Da, Canon EOS 650D, Canon EOS 700D, Canon EOS Kiss Digital, Canon EOS Kiss F, Canon EOS Kiss Digital N, Canon EOS Kiss X2, Canon EOS Kiss X3, Canon EOS Kiss X4, Canon EOS Kiss X5, Canon EOS Kiss X50, Canon EOS Kiss X6i, Canon PowerShot G1 X, Canon PowerShot G10, Canon PowerShot G11, Canon PowerShot G12, Canon PowerShot G15, Canon PowerShot SX50 HS, Canon EOS Rebel SL1, Canon

EOS Rebel T1i, Canon EOS Rebel 70 T2i, Canon EOS Rebel T3, Canon EOS Rebel T3i, Canon EOS Rebel T4i, Canon EOS Rebel XS, Canon EOS Rebel XSi, Canon EOS Rebel XT, Canon EOS Rebel XTi, Canon EOS Rebel T5i, Contax 645, Contax N, Contax N Digital, Contax N1, Contax NX, Hasselblad H1, Hasselblad H3D, Hasselblad H4D-200MS, Hasselblad H4D-31, Hasselblad H4D-40, Hasselblad H4D-50, Hasselblad H4D-50MS, Hasselblad H4D-60, Pentax 645D, Pentax *ist D, Pentax *ist DL, Pentax *ist DL2, Pentax *ist DS, Pentax *ist DS2, Pentax K-30, Pentax K-5, Pentax K-7, Pentax K-m, Pentax K10 Grand Prix, Pentax K100D, Pentax K100D Super, Pentax K10D, Pentax K110D, Pentax K200D, Pentax K20D, Pentax MZ-6, Pentax MZ-L, Pentax ZX-L, Samsung GX-1L, Samsung GX-1S, Samsung GX-20, Samsung NX10, Samsung NX100, Samsung NX11, Samsung NX5, Sigma SD1, Sigma SD1 Merrill, and Sigma SD15.

This list isn't complete, but it's a pretty good start. Remote shutter releases that are compatible with any of these listed cameras should also work with your X camera, as long as it features a 2.5mm remote release port.

Personally, I'm a big fan of Canon's simple yet effective **RS-60E3** electronic remote shutter release. It's small and affordable, and it shines with a nice attention to detail.

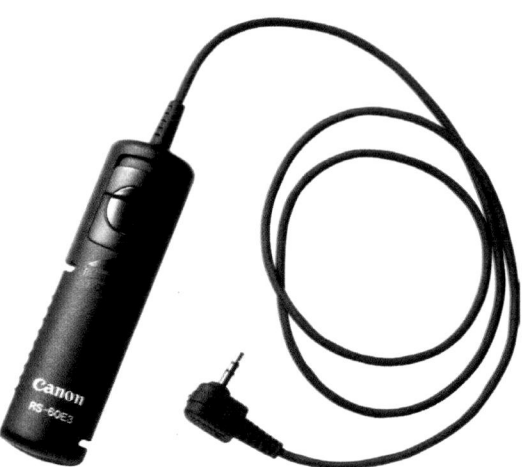

Fig. 66: The **Canon RS-60E3** is my favorite electronic cable release for Fujifilm X cameras—thanks to its attention to detail. For
example, the 90-degree angle of the plug ensures that the release
can be used in concert with L brackets when the camera is sitting upright on a tripod. Also, two carvings make it easy to neatly
spool the cable around the release after shooting. Finally, there's
a built-in socket for the 2.5mm plug that prevents the cable from
unspooling in the bag.

Alternatively, you can remotely control Wi-Fi-enabled
X cameras with the free Fujifilm Camera Remote app [29]
for iOS or Android devices. Step-by-step instructions are
available online [30].

If you own an X camera with Bluetooth, you can use that
semi-permanent connection to your smartphone or tablet
to remotely release the shutter [31].

2. USING YOUR X SERIES CAMERA

2.1 READY, SET, GO!

New users often ask about how to achieve the perfect settings for their camera. Short answer: there are no perfect settings. If they existed, Fuji could have saved us the trouble of navigating piles of menu options and simply implemented those ideal settings as the factory default. That said, allow me to suggest some basic settings that are meant to provide good overall performance and as much flexibility as possible.

- Many settings (such as film simulation modes, color saturation, contrast, sharpness, noise reduction, film grain effect, etc.) belong in the "JPEG settings" category. They don't affect the RAW files; only the out-of-camera JPEGs that are generated during RAW conversion. These settings aren't global or camera-specific—they are *image-specific,* and each image should be adjusted individually.

- In addition to the recommended standard settings, there are many shortcuts and key combinations that can make choosing the optimal camera settings for any situation much easier.

Recommended default settings for your X series camera	TIP 36

There is no perfect set of basic camera settings that could suit all users in all situations. However, the following settings will allow you to use current (and also many older) X camera models in a flexible manner with good overall performance.

- Select **FINE+RAW** or NORMAL+RAW under SHOOTING MENU > (IMAGE QUALITY SETTING >) IMAGE QUALITY. This will get you high-resolution out-of-camera JPEGs (digital prints) *and* flexible RAW files (digital negatives). Using the RAW files, you can create a variety of diverse JPEGs with different looks and settings using the camera's built-in RAW converter (PLAYBACK MENU > RAW CONVERSION). Specifically, you can adjust JPEG parameters such as white balance, film simulation, contrast, brightness, noise reduction, and color saturation. This enables you to create different versions of a shot from a single RAW file; for example, you can make color and black-and-white versions of the same image, including different contrast settings. You don't have to worry about finding the perfect JPEG settings prior to taking a shot because you can always change and optimize those settings afterward in the camera's internal RAW converter.

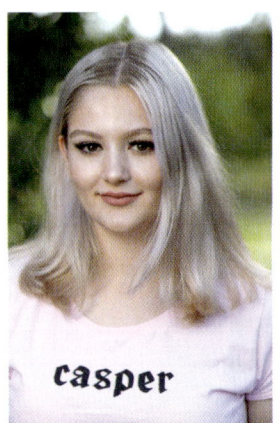 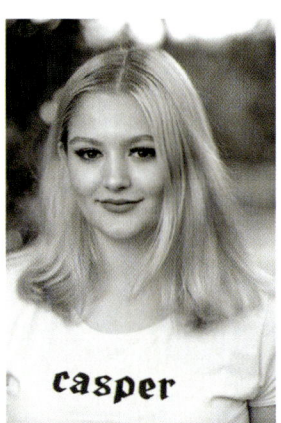 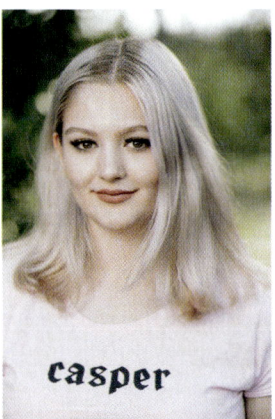

Fig. 67: Shooting **FINE+RAW** immediately gives you a ready-to-use JPEG (left), and the freedom to generate different or improved versions from the RAW file later, either in-camera (center) or with an external RAW converter like Adobe Lightroom (right).

- Make sure to use the camera's **mechanical shutter** as your default setting by selecting SHOOTING MENU > (SHOOTING SETTING >) SHUTTER TYPE > MS. Use of the electronic shutter (ES or MS+ES) can create all kinds of issues and should be limited to the rare cases where the ES is beneficial: shooting with a wide-open aperture (and without an ND filter) in bright daylight, or situations that require you to shoot in complete silence (with the alternative of not shooting at all). If your camera offers an electronic first curtain shutter (EFCS), feel free to set this option in order to eliminate shutter shock. Examples for X cameras with EFCS are the X-H1, X-T3, and GFX 50.

■ The most flexible and accurate AF-S setting is **Single Point AF** (SHOOTING MENU > AF/MF SETTING > AF MODE > SINGLE POINT). This mode allows you to select the area of the image where the camera should be focused. Even better, if your X camera supports the new AF mode **ALL** (several recent models do), select this mode as your default setting. That way, you can seamlessly cycle between Single-Point, Zone, and Wide/Tracking AF modes simply by changing the AF frame size. This is fast and convenient, and any Fn button that was previously used for changing the AF mode can now be reassigned to serve a different purpose.

■ Set SHOOTING MENU > AF/MF SETTING > RELEASE/FOCUS PRIORITY > FOCUS for both AF-S and AF-C. **Focus Priority** makes sure that the camera records a picture only when the autofocus thinks that it has locked onto a target. In RELEASE mode, the camera will take the shot even if the autofocus couldn't lock on a target. Please note that if you are using AF+MF mode, AF-S will always operate with release priority. That's why my recommended default setting for AF/MF SETTING > AF+MF is OFF.

■ If you want to quickly take a series of single shots, I recommend selecting SET UP > SCREEN SET-UP > IMAGE DISP. > OFF to not interrupt your flow. However, I *normally* set **Image Display** to the shortest available time span, which in most X cameras is 0.5 SEC. Why? I like to see a quick preview of the final image that represents the camera's exposure and dynamic range (DR) settings. To cancel an ongoing image preview and continue shooting, simply half-press the shutter button.

■ If available, use the VIEW MODE button to activate the **eye sensor,** which will allow the camera to automatically switch from LCD to electronic viewfinder when you look through the EVF.

■ For **exposure metering,** I recommend using MULTI metering as your default mode. Intelligent matrix metering usually delivers results that don't require a massive amount of exposure correction.

■ Set SHOOTING MENU > (IMAGE QUALITY SETTING >) WHITE BALANCE > AUTO to let the camera determine and set the correct **white balance** for a scene. Since you are shooting FINE+RAW, you can always adjust the white balance later, either with the camera's built-in RAW converter or with external RAW conversion software such as Adobe Lightroom. That said, AUTO will deliver very good results in most scenarios.

■ Select SHOOTING MENU > (IMAGE QUALITY SETTING >) DYNAMIC RANGE > DR100% as your default setting. If you require more **highlight dynamic range** (DR) for a specific subject in order to avoid blown highlights, you can manually set DR200% (for *one* extra stop of dynamic range in the highlights) or DR400% (for *two* extra stops of dynamic range in the highlights). Setting DYNAMIC RANGE to AUTO is *not* recommended. Extending the dynamic range can bring back texture to otherwise blown areas of your shot (such as white clouds on a sunny day).

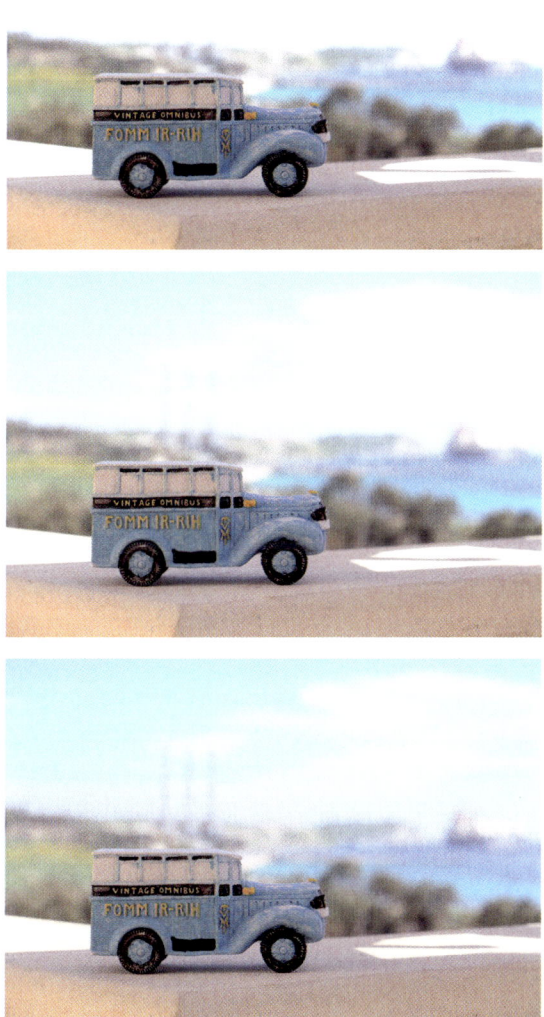

Fig. 68: All Fujifilm X cameras feature a powerful and often mis-understood **DR function** that can increase highlight dynamic range by up to two full stops (EV). The default setting is DR100% (top). Seeing blown highlights that you do not like? Increase dynamic range to DR200% (center) or DR400% (bottom) to get an extra one or two stops worth of highlight detail.

■ To use **adapted lenses** with your X-mount or G-mount camera, you need either Fujifilm's Leica M or Hasselblad H adapter, or a suitable third-party adapter. To make third-party adapters work, you must select SHOOT WITHOUT LENS > ON. Depending on your camera, you'll find this option either under SET UP > BUTTON/DIAL SETTING or in the SHOOTING MENU. This is necessary because adapted lenses (and mechanical third-party lens adapters) do not feature electronic X-mount/G-mount contacts, so the lens will not register as being connected to the camera. When you are working with a manually adapted lens, you should also enter its focal length in SHOOTING MENU > (SHOOTING SETTING >) MOUNT ADAPTOR SETTING. This ensures that the EXIF [32] data will reflect the proper focal length. In the X-Pro1 and X-Pro2, it will also determine the proper size and position of the bright frame in the optical viewfinder (OVF), and in the X-H1, entering the correct focal length is essential for the IBIS to work correctly with adapted lenses.

■ Do you sometimes shoot with very slow shutter speeds lasting several seconds? In this case, I recommend setting SHOOTING MENU > (IMAGE QUALITY SETTING >) LONG EXPOSURE NR > ON to improve the quality of your results. In this mode, the camera performs a so-called dark-frame subtraction [33] to reduce noise and eliminate hot pixels. With this process, the total exposure time is at least doubled because the camera is taking the shot twice: once normally and once with a closed shutter curtain. The second shot is then subtracted from the first to improve the overall result.

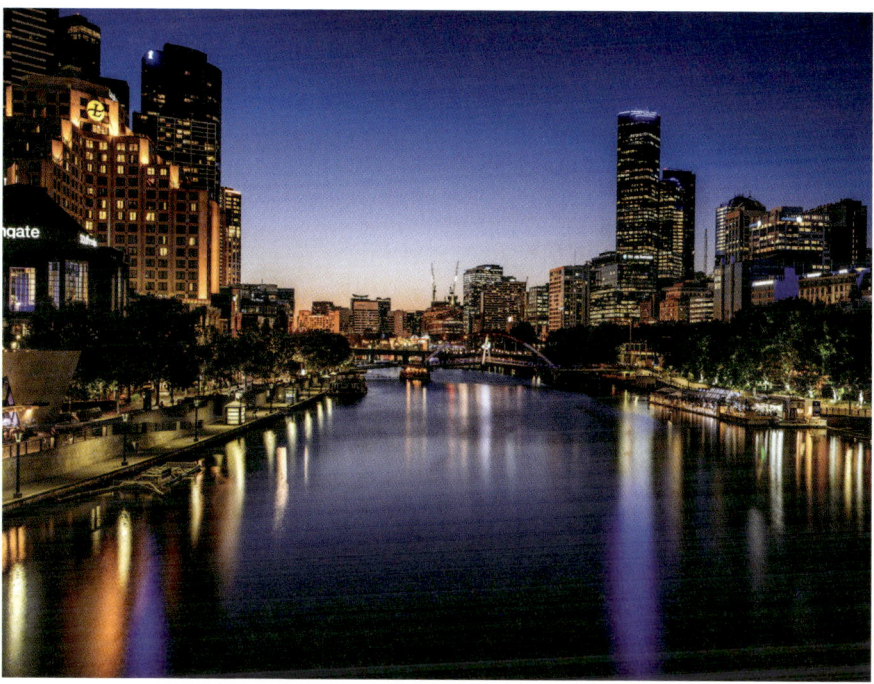

Fig. 69: Long exposures like this Melbourne cityscape benefit from the **dark-frame subtraction** that is automatically applied by the LONG EXPOSURE NR > ON setting.

■ I recommend *not* using the AUTO setting for the **bright-ness control for the EVF** because it tends to show an overly bright live view image in bright sunlight and a very subdued image when it's dark. Instead, I set SET UP > SCREEN SET-UP > EVF BRIGHTNESS > MANUAL > 0. I use the same setting for the rear LCD.

■ For the purpose of this book, we assume that SHUTTER AF and SHUTTER AE (in the SET UP > BUTTON DIAL SETTING menu) are both set to ON, which is also the factory default setting of those X series cameras that offer these options (several recent models do). This ensures that autofocus and exposure (including the working aperture) are locked when you half-press the shutter button in AF-S mode, so the camera is primed for the least possible shutter lag once you fully press the shutter button. In AF-C mode, SHUT-TER AF ON means that the AF keeps tracking a subject while the shutter button is half-pressed or pressed, and SHUTTER AE ON makes sure that the exposure is locked as long as you half-press or press the shutter button.

TIP 37	Avoiding the camera menus: practical shortcuts for your X camera

Shortcuts are timesavers. Here are a few that were primarily designed for the more recent line of X series cameras with an X-Processor Pro or X-Processor 4 engine. However, many will also work with other or older models.

■ Pull up the Quick menu with the Q button, then press and hold the Q button again for a few seconds to directly open the configuration menu for your custom user settings. Some background: Most X series cameras offer seven custom user settings (C1 through C7) that can hold groups of frequently used camera settings. You can select one of these groups (or profiles) via the Quick menu or an appropriately configured Fn button. Please understand that C1 through C7 aren't camera *modes;* they are memory locations. Each location conveniently stores a configured profile. You can use these profiles as shortcuts to instantly overwrite your current camera settings with another predefined set of options.

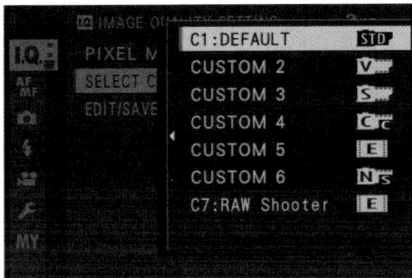

Fig. 70: **Custom settings** are memory locations that store mostly JPEG settings. Personally, I only need two profiles in my X series cameras: a DEFAULT profile on position C1 to quickly return to the factory settings, and a flat RAW SHOOTER profile on position C7 to maximize dynamic range in the live view and live histogram. Recent models also allow you to assign names to custom settings.

■ Press and hold the Q button while the Quick menu is *not* open to directly access the Quick menu configuration page. In this mode, you can customize the contents of the Quick menu to better meet your personal requirements. You can assign one of about two dozen different settings to any of the 16 available Quick menu tiles. If you don't need 16 shortcuts, you can even select NONE to reduce the size of the Quick menu and make it easier to navigate.

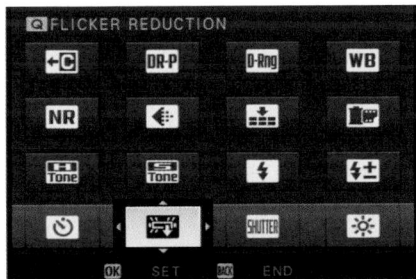

Fig. 71: I recommend **personalizing the Quick menu** of your X camera for better access to functions that you need the most. Luckily, this option is available in most X series cameras.

■ Press and hold the MENU/OK button to lock the selector keys and the Q button. Press and hold the MENU/OK button again to remove the key lock. This shortcut works with most X series cameras; however, it is *not* available in the X-H1 and X-T3.

■ To see where the Fn buttons are located and what's as-signed to each of them, press and hold the DISP/BACK button. When the configuration menu pops up, you can review and reassign all Fn button functions.

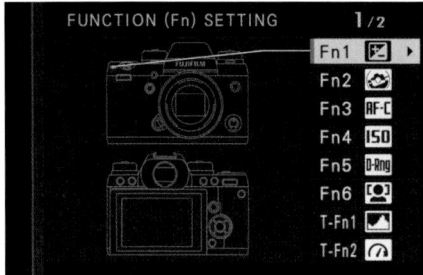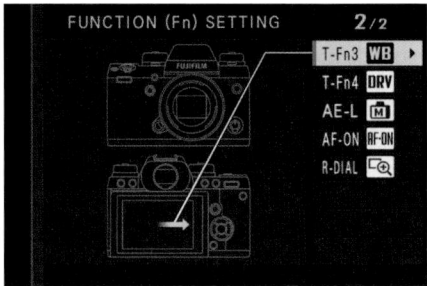

Fig. 72: Fn buttons are essential to provide direct and immediate access to important and frequently used camera functions. As Fujifilm X cameras grow in features and complexity, the number of available Fn buttons has been increased accordingly. In fact, there is a trend to make (almost) every physical button a user-configurable Fn button. Recent touchscreen models like the X-E3 and X-H1 take this idea even further with the addition of virtual Touch-Fn buttons that are activated by making a flicking gesture on the touchscreen. This illustration shows the two configuration pages for the 13 **Fn and Touch-Fn buttons** available in my X-H1 with firmware 1.20. In this camera, each of the 13 actual and virtual Fn buttons can perform one of 45 (Fn) or 40 (Touch-Fn) different functions.

■ To confirm a new menu selection in shooting mode, you can either press the MENU/OK button or half-press the shutter button.

■ Half-press the shutter button to switch from playback mode back to shooting mode.

■ Half-press the shutter button during an ongoing image preview (SET UP > SCREEN SET-UP > IMAGE DISP.) to immediately cancel that preview.

- Half-press the shutter button for a few seconds to wake up the camera from sleep mode.

- In AF-S shooting mode (with Single Point AF) or MF mode, press the rear command dial to zoom into the currently active focus frame. When zoomed-in, you can select different magnification levels by turning the rear command dial. Please note that with cameras that allow the rear command dial to serve as an Fn button, this is the FOCUS CHECK default configuration for the rear command dial Fn button. If you assign a different function to the R-DIAL Fn button, this useful zoom shortcut won't be available.

- Press and hold the rear command dial in MF mode to cycle between the available manual focus assist modes, such as standard, focus peaking, and digital split image. The X-T3 also offers a new digital microprism mode.

- After selecting FOCUS AREA (usually after assigning this function to a Fn button if it isn't a hardwired button), you can move the focus frame or zone around with the four selector (arrow) keys. Press the DISP/BACK button to reset the position of the AF frame or AF zone to the center of the screen. You can change the size of the selected AF frame or zone by turning the command dial. To reset the size of the AF frame or zone to default, press the command dial.

- Recent cameras like the X-Pro2, X-T2, X-H1, X-E3, X100F, XF10, and GFX 50 feature a focus stick. It's a useful, tiny joystick that allows you to directly move the focus area or zone in eight directions. Press the focus stick in shooting mode to access the focus frame and AF zone selection screen (FOCUS AREA screen). Here, you can move the active focus frame or zone around with the focus stick and change its size by turning the command dial. In this selection screen, you can press the focus stick again to center the focus frame or AF zone.

- In shooting mode, you can directly move the focus stick in eight directions to change the position of the active focus frame or AF zone. However, you can't change their size before pressing the focus stick and entering the FOCUS AREA screen.

- Press and hold the focus stick in shooting mode to access the focus stick options menu. You can select to deactivate the stick completely, to activate the stick by pressing it, or to keep it permanently activated. For this book, we choose the latter option (ON) to ensure that the focus stick is always directly available.

- In playback mode (while viewing an image), use the front command dial to browse through the images that are on file.

- During image playback, you can turn the rear command dial to zoom in and out. By pressing the DISP/BACK button, you can always directly return to the standard-size view. Press the rear command dial to zoom in to a 100% view of a shot. When you are zoomed in, pressing the dial again returns the camera to its regular view, displaying the full image.

- While displaying an image with RAW data in playback mode, you can press the Q button to directly access the built-in RAW converter. This function allows you to create new JPEG versions of your image with different settings.

- In playback mode, press the upper selector button (or move the focus stick in the up direction) to view the first of several information pages that show additional shooting parameters and the position of the focus point.

- For direct access to the format menu, press and hold the DELETE ("trash") button for about three seconds. Then keep the DELETE button depressed while you press the rear command dial. As of December 2018, this function was only available in cameras with X-Processor Pro and X-Processor 4.

Suggested Fn button assignment	TIP 38

A smart assignment of your Fn buttons can save you cumbersome trips to the camera menu. While this book cannot provide specific Fn-button guides for each of the more than 30 different X series cameras that Fujifilm has introduced between 2011 and 2018, there are several cross-model functions and controls that should always be available at your fingertip:

- **AF MODE.** Please don't confuse this setting with FOCUS MODE. Focus Mode is either AF-S(ingle), AF-C(ontinuous) or MF (manual focus), and it's usually controlled with a switch at the front or side of your camera, or with a virtual button on the touchscreen. No, this is about AF MODE, which is combining AF-S or AF-C with either SINGLE POINT, ZONE, or WIDE/TRACKING autofocus. To quickly switch between these options, it's useful to assign the AF MODE selection to one of the Fn buttons. There's one exception, though: if your camera supports the new AF mode ALL, you should most definitely set ALL as your permanent AF mode default. ALL is ingenious, because you can seamlessly change AF modes between SINGLE POINT, ZONE, and WIDE/TRACKING simply by changing the size of the focus frame while you are in the FOCUS AREA screen.

- **FOCUS AREA.** The FOCUS AREA screen allows you to move around the active focus point or AF zone within the image frame. You can also change its size. FOCUS AREA can be activated by pressing the focus stick, or by pressing a dedicated button (usually labeled "AF"). If your camera has neither, it's your turn to make sure that FOCUS AREA is assigned to one of your Fn buttons.

■ **ISO.** Since ISO signal amplification is an important and frequently used setting, it should be directly accessible. That's why some of the more advanced X cameras offer a dedicated ISO dial. For the rest of us, it's useful to assign ISO to one of the Fn buttons instead of accessing it via the regular or Quick menu. There's another reason beyond speed and convenience: accessing ISO through an Fn button opens a *transparent* menu, so in manual exposure mode **M**, you can immediately see the effect of any ISO change in the live view image. This results in a more intuitive user experience than blindly changing ISO in the Quick menu or shooting menu.

■ **DYNAMIC RANGE.** Fujifilm cameras offer a very powerful DR function to extend the highlight dynamic range of an image, so it's a very good idea to keep this function right at your fingertips.

■ **FACE DETECTION.** Face Detection is another function that should be at your disposal when it's required (and only then), so putting it on an Fn button makes perfect sense.

■ **AF-L & AE-L: AF-ON and PREVIEW EXP. IN MANUAL MODE.** In several X cameras (the X-T2, X-T3, X-T20, X-E3, and X-H1 come to mind), dedicated AF-L and AE-L buttons can also serve as Fn keys, so you can repurpose them as needed. That said, I don't tend to *radically* change their assignment. Instead, I turn the AF-L button into the AF-ON (a.k.a. "back-button focusing") function. And since I shoot more than 95% of my images in manual exposure mode (where AE-Lock is meaningless), I assign the PREVIEW EXP./WB IN MANUAL MODE toggle to the AE-L button.

■ **R-DIAL: FOCUS CHECK.** In several recent X models, pressing the rear command dial also serves as an Fn button. The factory default setting is FOCUS CHECK, which allows you to zoom into the live view image on the electronic viewfinder or LCD monitor. Since this is an important and convenient function, I do not recommend changing this default assignment. Please note that all related tips in this book assume that FOCUS CHECK is assigned (or hardwired) to the rear command dial button.

■ **HISTOGRAM.** With the exception of the X100F, all cameras with X-Processor Pro and X-Processor 4 feature a color RGB live histogram with live overexposure warning, also known as "blinkies." The only way to access this essential feature is via an Fn or a Touch-Fn button, so please make sure that it's assigned to one.

■ **ELECTRONIC LEVEL.** The GFX 50, X-H1, and X-T3 are the first models to offer a dual-axis electronic level display, as opposed to the regular single-axis indicator that can be found in pretty much all X series cameras. The dual-axis indicator helps you correctly align the camera to avoid non-parallel vertical lines, especially in city and architecture shots. Like the RGB histogram, this feature is only accessible via an Fn or a Touch-Fn button.

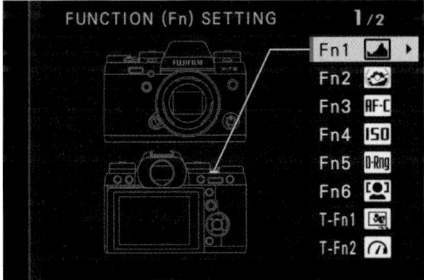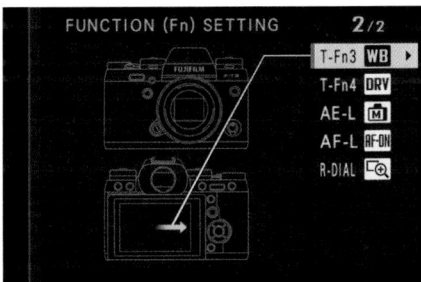

Fig. 73: This is the **Fn button assignment of my X-T3**. To edit the Fn button of your camera, press and hold the DISP/BACK button until the configuration page appears.

| TIP 39 | Recommended My Menu and Quick menu configuration |

To keep the shooting process effortless and free of interruptions, it's vital to assign frequently used functions to Fn buttons that are immediately accessible. However, the number of available buttons is often limited, especially since Touch-Fn still isn't universally available.

Luckily, we have My Menu and the Quick menu (Q button) to quickly access frequently used functions and menus that didn't fit into the Fn button lineup. My Menu is available in all cameras with X-Processor Pro and X-Processor 4, and most X cameras also offer a configurable Quick menu page.

■ To configure **My Menu,** select SET UP > USER SETTING > MY MENU SETTING, where you can add new items, rank existing items (= change their position in My Menu), or remove items from the menu.

■ To configure the **Quick menu,** press and hold the Q button until the Quick menu configuration page appears, where you can change each of the 16 items and assign them either a new function or no function at all (NONE).

The following figures illustrate the My Menu and Quick menu settings in my X-H1. Neither is set in stone.

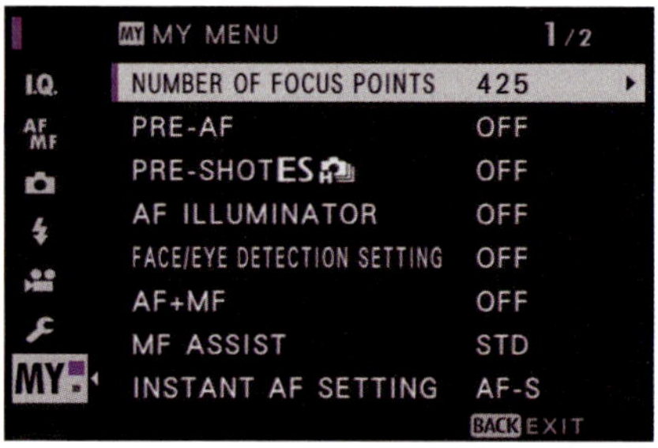

Fig. 74: **My Menu** in my X-T3 and other current X-series cameras consists of two menu pages with a total of 16 possible entries. I use the first page to quickly change and review the autofocus configuration.

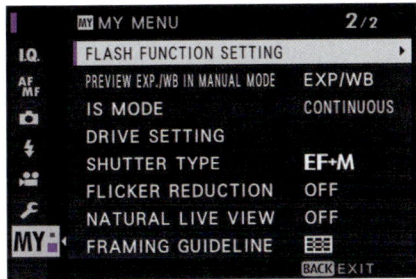

Fig. 75: The second **My Menu** page is reserved for exposure settings and general parameters such as OIS/IBIS mode, shutter type,
flash configuration, or the DRIVE mode.

Please note that in cameras without IBIS, the OIS mode
menu is only available when a lens with OIS has been attached. In a similar fashion, manual exposure mode **M** must
be enabled to access the PREVIEW EXP./WB IN MANUAL
MODE setting.

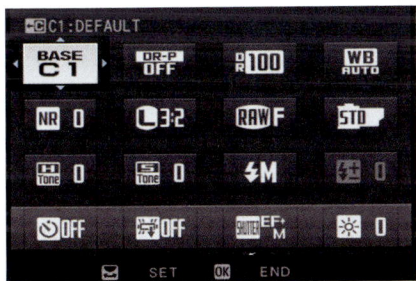

Fig. 76: The **Quick menu** page of my X-H1 and X-T3 isn't very
different from the factory default setting. I always make sure that I
can access the flash mode and the flash exposure compensation
directly from this menu, and I like to have direct access to the
shutter-type setting and flicker reduction. Since I don't need quick
access to the COLOR and SHARPNESS items, I replaced them with
the flash configuration items.

Always shoot FINE+RAW or NORMAL+RAW!	TIP 40

Should you shoot RAW [34] or JPEG [35]? The best option is
using both formats by setting SHOOTING MENU > (IMAGE
QUALITY SETTING >) IMAGE QUALITY > FINE+RAW (or

NORMAL+RAW). It doesn't matter if you consider yourself a diehard RAW shooter or a JPEG shooter.

This is how **RAW shooters** benefit from shooting FINE+RAW or NORMAL+RAW:

■ During external RAW processing, the camera-made JPEG can be used as a (sometimes hard-to-beat) reference image.

■ Checking critical focus is only possible at 100% magnification, which only a full-size JPEG can provide. The JPEG that's embedded in the RAW file for preview purposes is too small. Make sure you select one of the available L (Large) options under SHOOTING MENU > (IMAGE QUALITY SETTING >) IMAGE SIZE.

■ The IMAGE SIZE menu isn't available in RAW-only mode. Different image formats, such as 1:1 or 16:9, are only available in JPEG-only mode or FINE+RAW (NORMAL+RAW) mode. Autofocus and exposure metering adapt to the currently selected format (aspect ratio) and deliver more accurate readings when you are shooting with odd formats like 1:1. No worries, though: the RAW is always recorded in the sensor's native format (3:2 or 4:3, depending on your camera model), so you don't lose any image information.

This is how **JPEG shooters** benefit from shooting FINE+RAW or NORMAL+RAW:

■ Nobody is capable of always setting the *perfect* shooting parameters (exposure, white balance, and dynamic range, as well as JPEG parameters such as film simulation, color, sharpness, noise reduction, shadow and highlight contrast, grain effect, etc.) in advance. FINE+RAW solves this problem by allowing you to change and adjust those settings *after* the fact, either with the built-in RAW converter or external RAW conversion software. This means you can worry about those JPEG settings later and concentrate on more important factors of your shot, such as focus, framing, and timing.

■ Even if you chose the perfect settings in advance, it's possible that you'd like to have more than one version of a shot, such as a color version and a black-and-white version, or versions with different color film simulations. Again, FINE+RAW does the trick because you can use the built-in RAW converter to create (and compare) different JPEG versions of a shot.

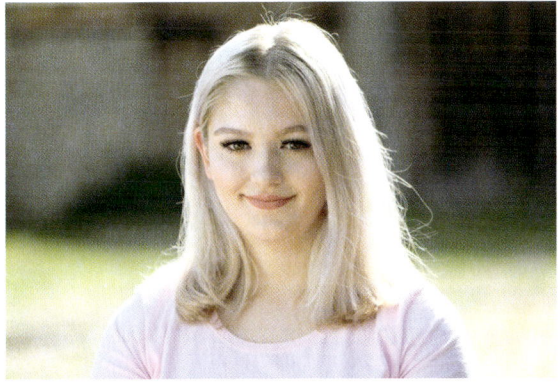

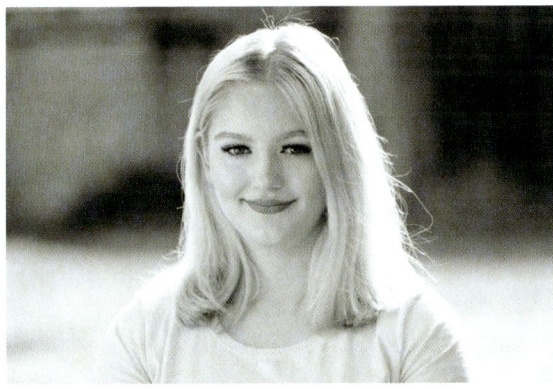

Fig. 77: All X cameras feature a **built-in RAW converter** that allows users to quickly create different JPEG versions of a shot. It only takes a few seconds to modify exposure, contrast settings, and noise reduction of a color image (above), or to create a black-and-white version (below). All you need is the shot's RAW file.

■ There's always progress in the digital domain. Things that appear impossible today may be a reality in just a few years. It's perfectly feasible that future RAW convert-ers will be able to extract much better image quality from your RAW files than today's cameras and RAW proces-sors. It pays to be prepared by archiving the RAW files of your valuable shots. Storage space is cheap; some of your images may be priceless.

■ Your skills may improve as well! Several months or a few years from now, you may be much more comfort-able using post-processing software than you are today. Wouldn't it be sad if you couldn't revisit great shots of the past and process them in a better way? Don't forget: only RAW files contain the full potential of an image. JPEGs are a processed and compressed subset with lim-ited latitude for post-processing. RAW files feature much better tonality and dynamic range. By the way, using the built-in RAW converter of your X camera isn't more complex or complicated than using the camera's JPEG settings in the shooting menu (which should be familiar to you as a JPEG shooter).

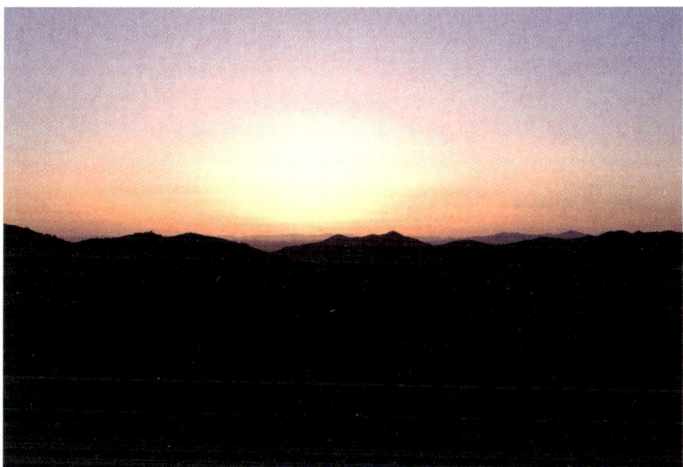

Fig. 78: X series cameras feature competent JPEG engines with terrific film simulations, but that doesn't mean that **JPEG-only shooting** is the way to go. This JPEG of a moody sunset was processed with the Velvia film simulation in my X-T20, and while this result may be exactly what you're looking for, it clearly illustrates the limited dynamic range of straight-out-of-camera JPEGs, which often render high-contrast scenes with blown highlights or blocked shadows (or both). There is no meaningful way to restore what has been lost in processing the JPEG. Instead, you must process the RAW file of this shot.

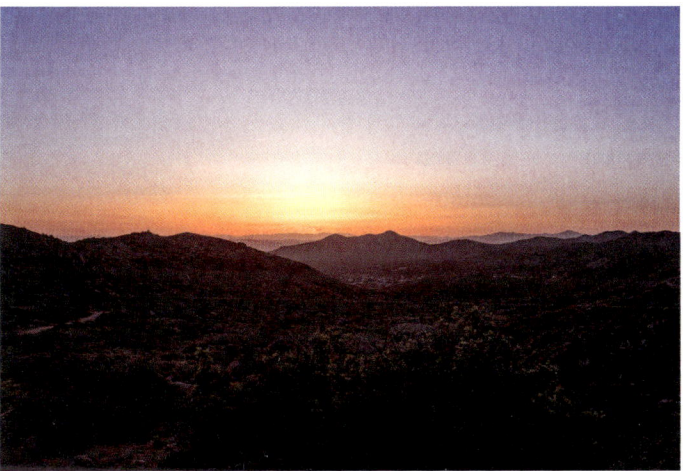

Fig. 79: This sample is a **Lightroom-processed version** of the RAW file of the previous shot, showcasing the superior dynamic range of the camera's original sensor data. Despite their small size and affordable price, all Fujifilm APS-C cameras offer a dynamic range that rivals or even surpasses that of several current full-frame cameras from Canon and Leica, but you need the RAW file to unlock their huge potential.

As you can see, FINE+RAW is the best and most flexible choice. The one detrimental aspect of using FINE+RAW (or NORMAL+RAW) is that it results in larger amounts of data being recorded. This doesn't matter much in practical terms, since modern X cameras can quickly transfer large amounts of data to the memory card. Just make sure to use a fast card.

Let me use this opportunity to address a widespread misconception: RAW files aren't images that you can directly look at. RAWs contain image *data* that still must be *interpreted* or *processed* into an actual image—either in-camera or with external software. Every digital image (including the live view on the monitor, JPEGs from the camera, or TIFF files from Adobe Lightroom) is the result of such a translation.

A JPEG shooter who doesn't keep RAW files must settle for only one of the many possible interpretations of RAW data into an image, and it's very unlikely that this single JPEG from the camera is the best of all possible versions of the image. Basically, discarding the RAW file turns your X camera into an instant camera: you only get one (most likely not the best) image per shot.

Please note that in the context of this book, the recommended FINE+RAW setting is my preferred alternative to the NORMAL+RAW setting. NORMAL JPEGs apply more JPEG compression, are smaller in size than FINE JPEGs, and contain more artifacts and less information. If memory space is a concern and you don't plan on using the camera's JPEGs for more than checking critical focus, you can just as well set your camera to NORMAL+RAW instead of FINE+RAW.

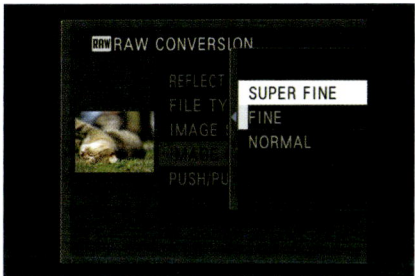

Fig. 80: With the GFX 50S, Fujifilm has introduced an additional **SUPER FINE** format for JPEGs. It's safe to assume that this option will also be available in future GFX camera models. However, I don't recommend selecting SUPER FINE+RAW as your default setting. Instead, keep shooting FINE+RAW or NORMAL+RAW and create individual SUPER FINE versions of those rare shots that may actually require SUEPR FINE image quality. You can easily do this with the camera's built-in RAW converter.

Compressed or uncompressed RAW files?	TIP 41

X cameras with X-Processor Pro and X-Processor 4 offer a choice of uncompressed and compressed RAW files (SHOOTING MENU > IMAGE QUALITY SETTING > RAW RECORDING). Compression cuts the size of RAW files roughly in half, so you can store twice as many of them on a memory card or your computer. The compression also helps speed up camera processes: smaller files take longer to overflow the fast camera buffer, and they take less time to transfer to the memory card.

It's important to note that Fujifilm's RAW compression is lossless, so there's no difference in image quality between uncompressed and compressed RAWs. However, not all external RAW converters may be able to process Fuji's compressed RAWs, because the compression format is proprietary. RAW converter manufacturers can obtain a free SDK from Fujifilm to support the compressed RAW file format.

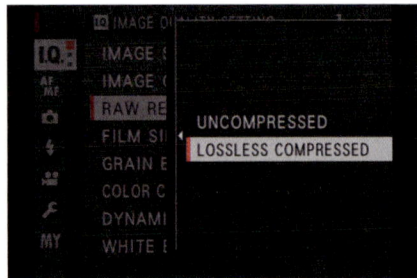

Fig. 81: To save space and improve speed and performance, I recommend shooting RAW in the LOSSLESS COMPRESSED format.
The image quality remains the same.

Windows user should always install the latest version of
RAW FILE CONVERTER EX, even if you don't intend to ever
use it. This software is available as a free download [94]. It
installs a codec that allows Windows to display thumbnail
images of lossless compressed Fuji RAW files anywhere on
your PC. Sadly, a similar tool isn't available for macOS.

TIP 42	Picking a suitable image format

The full resolution of your X camera is only available in its
native image format (3:2 or 4:3, depending on the sensor).
However, using a different image format (such as 1:1 or 16:9)
can still be reasonable. For example, some people prefer to
view their images on a 16:9 4K television, while others are
fans of the classic (square) medium-format look.

No matter what format (aspect ratio) and resolution you
choose in SHOOTING MENU > (IMAGE QUALITY SETTING >)
IMAGE SIZE, it will only affect the JPEGs coming from your
camera. With the exceptions of deliberate sensor crop
modes in the GFX and X-T3, RAW files are always recorded
in full resolution in the native sensor format. This means
that as long as you kept your RAW files, you can generate
new full-size (native format) JPEGs with the built-in RAW
converter or an external RAW processor.

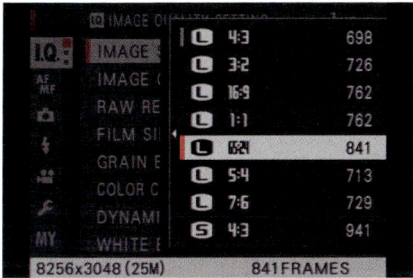

Fig. 82: Apart from its native 4:3 sensor format, the medium-format GFX 50 offers plenty of **non-native JPEG image formats** (above). It even features a **35mm FORMAT MODE** for adapting smaller "full-frame" lenses. In this sensor crop mode, the camera is only using a cropped 3:2 "full-frame" portion of its sensor, reducing the size of RAW and JPEG files accordingly. In a similar fashion, the X-T3 offers a so-called **Sports Finder Mode** with a crop factor of 1.25x in relation to the native sensor format.

If you want to compose shots in non-native formats like 1:1 or 16:9, you should select the desired format in the shooting menu. Here's why:

- The live view in the viewfinder or on the LCD will automatically adjust to the new format, making it easier to compose an image.

- The camera's autofocus frames will adapt to the selected image format.

- Your camera's exposure metering and live histogram are based on what's displayed in the live view. Changing the live view to 16:9 or 1:1 will enhance metering accuracy for the respective format.

The magical half-press	TIP 43

A basic rule for successfully using mirrorless X series cameras is minimizing the delay between pressing the shutter button and the camera taking the image. It's about not missing the decisive moment due to shutter lag.

It's up to you to anticipate these decisive moments. By half-pressing the shutter button, you are preparing the camera: exposure and autofocus (unless you are using AF-C) will be set and locked, and the lens aperture will move to its working position. The camera is now ready to record an image with minimal shutter lag—all that's left to do is to fully depress the already half-pressed shutter button at the right instant.

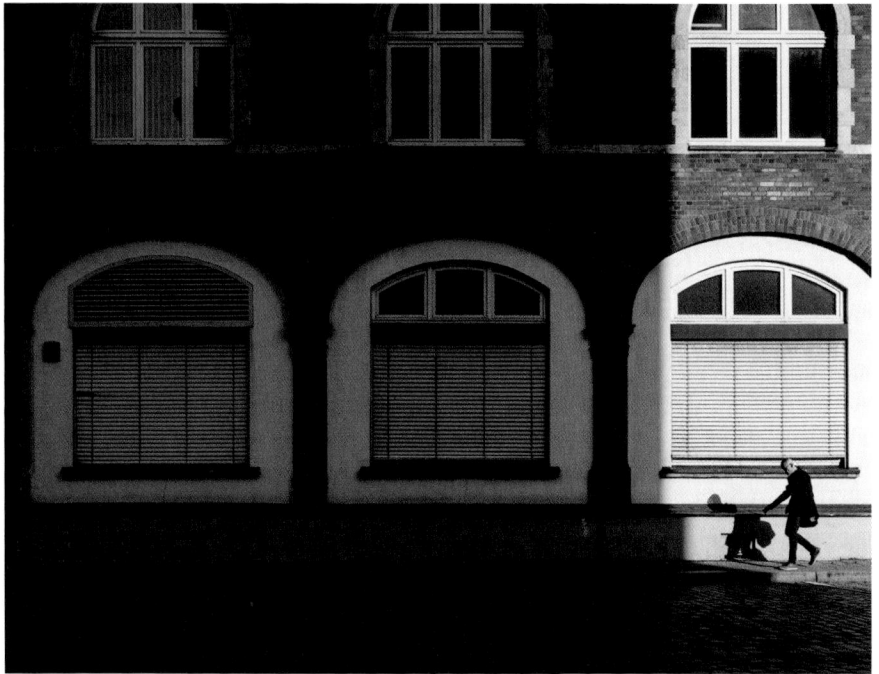

Fig. 83: To make sure that your camera is ready when you are, it's useful to prime the camera by **half-pressing the shutter button**. This shot was taken with an X100F.

Don't forget that priming the camera by half-pressing the shutter only works if SHUTTER AE and SHUTTER AF are both set to ON in the SET UP > BUTTON DIAL SETTING menu. This option is available in several recent X camera models, such as the X-H1, X-T2, X-T3, X-T20, X-E3, and GFX 50. The

X-T2, X-T3, and X-H1 even offer separate SHUTTER AE and SHUTTER AF settings for AF-S and AF-C mode, in which case all four options should be set to ON.

2.2 MONITOR AND VIEWFINDER

Many recent X camera models feature a high-resolution electronic viewfinder (EVF) along with an LCD touchscreen. Both can be used for image composition and playback.

Make use of the eye sensor!	TIP 44

If your camera has an electronic viewfinder (EVF), use the VIEW MODE button to activate the built-in eye sensor. The camera will now automatically switch to whichever view (viewfinder or LCD touchscreen) is in use when you are taking or reviewing images (or making changes to the camera menu).

When you are working with a tripod or holding the LCD display close to your body, the eye sensor can get confused. In such cases, use the VIEW MODE button to set the camera to LCD ONLY.

Instant review	TIP 45

To instantly review an image right after you have taken it, you can select SET UP > SCREEN SET-UP > IMAGE DISP. and then set a display period (most models offer a selection of 0.5 SEC, 1.5 SEC, or CONTINUOUS). The image will always be displayed in the currently active view (LCD or viewfinder). Personally, I like to work with the shortest available time setting.

You can immediately cancel an ongoing image review and continue shooting by half-pressing the shutter button. With the CONTINUOUS option, you can also zoom into the image: pressing the rear command dial will directly zoom to the highest available magnification.

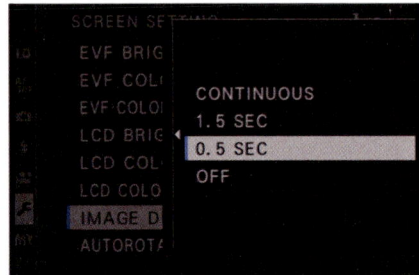

Fig. 84: I generally set IMAGE DISP. to **0.5 SEC**. in order to get a glimpse at the final JPEG image result of each shot, including all JPEG, dynamic range, and exposure settings.

In situations that require you to take a series of shots in quick succession, it may be advisable to switch image re-view off. To do so, select SET UP > SCREEN SET-UP > IMAGE DISP. > OFF. You can still check your latest shot by pressing the playback button.

Please don't forget that the maximum magnification (to check critical focus) is only available when the camera is set to record RAW *and* JPEG files in size L (with dual-slot models operating in sequential data save mode).

| TIP 46 | The DISP/BACK button can be tricky! |

The DISP/BACK button serves two different purposes:

■ As a BACK button, it returns the camera to a higher menu or selection level without saving changes you may have made in the menu sub-level.

■ As a DISPLAY button, it changes the display mode of the currently active view (LCD monitor or viewfinder).

Please keep in mind that changing the display mode only affects the currently active view. For example, to change the display mode of the EVF, the EVF must be in use when you press the DISP/BACK button. When you are using the eye sensor, you must look through the EVF while you are pressing the DISP/BACK button. If you don't, you will only change the display mode of the (then active) LCD monitor.

When the camera is in shooting mode, the viewfinder and the LCD monitor can each use different display modes at the same time.

If you select a display with information overlays in shooting mode, you can choose which elements should appear in the viewfinder or on the LCD monitor. Select SET UP > SCREEN SET-UP > DISP. CUSTOM SETTING, and then check the items that you want displayed in the EVF and on the LCD.

WYSIWYG—What You See Is What You Get!	TIP 47

The EVF and LCD monitor of mirrorless cameras normally operate in WYSIWYG mode [36]: What You See Is What You Get. This means that the viewfinder and monitor are always trying to display a live view [37] image that closely resembles how the resulting JPEG will look. The live view simulates exposure, colors, contrast, and white balance. When you half-press the shutter button, the camera will set the selected working aperture, so the live view will also display a preview of the depth of field.

The live view's exposure simulation is quite helpful because it allows you to recognize exposure errors *before* you take the picture. Please note that the live histogram is always based on the current live view image.

The live view's WYSIWYG simulation is available in all four of the camera's exposure modes: program AE **P**, aperture priority **A**, shutter priority **S**, and manual exposure mode **M**.

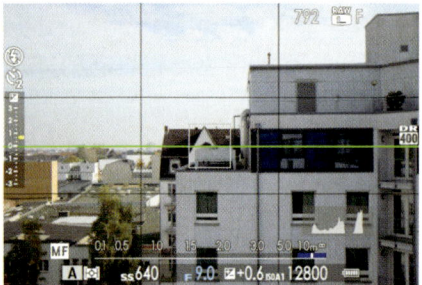 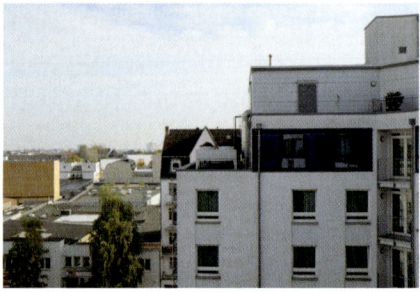

Fig. 85: **WYSIWYG:** This X100F example illustrates how closely the live view (left) represents the actually taken JPEG from the camera (right). The live view doesn't just simulate exposure, white balance, film simulation, and other JPEG settings, it also previews fixed dynamic range settings like DR400%.

In manual exposure mode M, most X cameras allow you to switch off the exposure simulation by selecting SET UP > SCREEN SET-UP > PREVIEW EXP./WB IN MANUAL MODE > OFF. That way, the camera will always display a bright live view image in manual mode, regardless of the actually selected exposure parameters (shutter speed, aperture, and ISO). This can be useful in a studio setting with flash photography. For example, you may want to eliminate the surrounding-light component by stopping down the aperture and fully illuminating your subject with strobes.

Please note that in this mode, both the live view and the live histogram aren't representing the actual exposure of your image, so don't forget to switch the exposure simulation back on if you want to work with a proper exposure simulation and live histogram in manual mode M.

The live view's exposure simulation may be restricted in situations with very low light and slow shutter speeds of several seconds—the live view and the live histogram may appear darker than the actual result. In such scenarios, you should first take a test shot and review it in playback mode. The information display (which you can select with the DISP/BACK button) will show you a playback histogram of the recorded JPEG image. This includes a preview with "blinkies," which indicate blown (overexposed) highlights.

Using the Natural Live View   TIP 48

The so-called Natural Live View is a display mode that's available in most X series cameras. It disables the WYSIWYG simulation of JPEG settings such as Film Simulation, Highlight Tone, Shadow Tone, or Color. Instead, it will display a rather flat live view image with increased dynamic range in the highlights and shadows, and with colors that are supposed to resemble what our eyes would see through an optical viewfinder. It will also set the live view to Auto white balance, so there will be no simulation of any white balance custom settings or presets. However, all current JPEG and white balance settings will still be applied to the *actual image* that's recorded.

Depending on your camera, select either SET UP > SCREEN SET-UP > PREVIEW PIC. EFFECT > OFF or SET UP > SCREEN SET-UP > NATURAL LIVE VIEW > ON to set the camera to Natural Live View mode. This setting enables generic-looking previews for color, black-and-white, and sepia shots that do *not* reflect the look of the actual JPEG results. This makes Natural Live View particularly useful: you can see what's going on in the dark parts of a high-contrast scene while composing the shot.

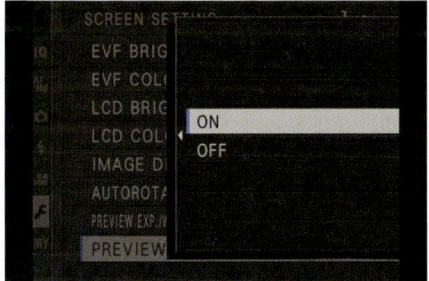 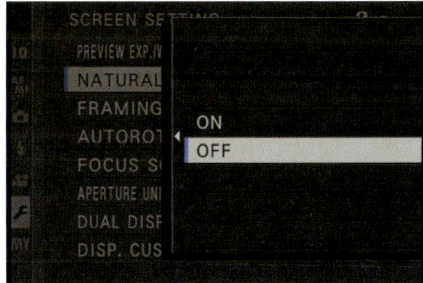

Fig. 86: PREVIEW PIC. EFFECT **ON** (left) equals NATURAL LIVE VIEW **OFF** (right). They are the same setting. With the X-H1 and X-T3, Fujifilm has changed the name of the function in the menu.

*Important: The Natural Live View of the X30, X100T, X100F, X-Pro2, X-H1, X-T2, X-T3, X-T20, X-E3, GFX 50S, and GFX 50R extends highlight dynamic range by two stops in the live view image (but not in the final RAW or JPEG), rendering the live histogram inaccurate when shooting with DR100%, DR200%, or DR-Auto dynamic range settings. Do **not** set PREVIEW PIC. EFFECT to OFF (or NATURAL LIVE VIEW to ON) if you want to use the live view and/or live histogram to determine the correct exposure of a shot.*

TIP 49	Using the LCD touchscreen

All recent X cameras feature a touchscreen that can perform several functions in shooting mode and playback mode. To use the touchscreen, make sure that SET UP > (BUTTON/ DIAL SETTING >) TOUCH SCREEN SETTING > ON is selected.

In *shooting mode,* you can use the touchscreen to pick a focus frame or zone; to autofocus with the selected focus frame or zone; or to autofocus and shoot with the selected focus frame or zone.

- **AREA:** Select a focus frame or zone by tapping once on the LCD touchscreen.

- **AF:** Tap on the LCD touchscreen to pick a focus frame or zone and trigger the autofocus. In MF mode, this option will focus the camera using Instant-AF.

- **SHOT:** Tap on the touchscreen to select a focus area or zone, trigger the autofocus through this frame or zone, and take a picture without further delay. In MF mode, this option will immediately take a shot without (re-) focusing.

- **OFF:** Temporarily disable shooting with the touchscreen. This prevents you from accidentally triggering any of the three other touchscreen functions.

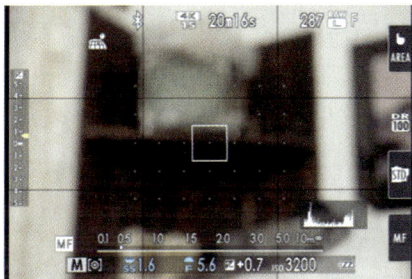

Fig. 87: This screenshot of the **X-T100** LCD monitor illustrates how Fujifilm increasingly moves functions to the touchscreen. At the top right, there's a touch button for controlling the touchscreen focus mode (here set to AREA). Below, there's another touch button to change the film simulation mode (here set to STD Provia). In the lower-right corner, you can see a touch button to set the focus mode (here set to MF). In addition to that, you can double-tap to magnify the live view image or flick your finger in all four directions to access the four Touch-Fn buttons.

In *playback mode,* you can use the touchscreen like a smartphone to browse through images. You can also zoom in and out of an image by double-tapping, or by pinching the image with two fingers.

2.3 EXPOSING RIGHT

It's not the job of the camera to find and set the right exposure; it's your job as the photographer. That said, all X series cameras feature the usual set of AE (auto exposure) modes: aperture priority **A**, shutter priority **S**, and program AE **P**.

- **Aperture priority A** will automatically set a suitable shutter speed to match a preset aperture based on your exposure.

- **Shutter priority S** will automatically set a suitable aperture to match a preset shutter speed based on your exposure.

- **Program AE** 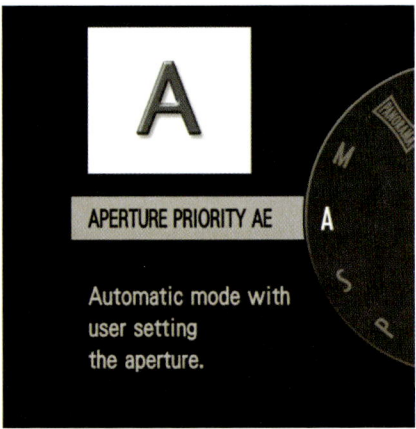 will automatically set a suitable aperture and shutter speed combination based on your exposure.

- **Auto-ISO** can contribute a suitable ISO setting (within predefined limits). In digital cameras, ISO is the level of signal amplification applied to an image that has been recorded by the camera's sensor. ISO always refers to the brightness of the final image product (JPEG) from the camera, and not necessarily to the RAW data.

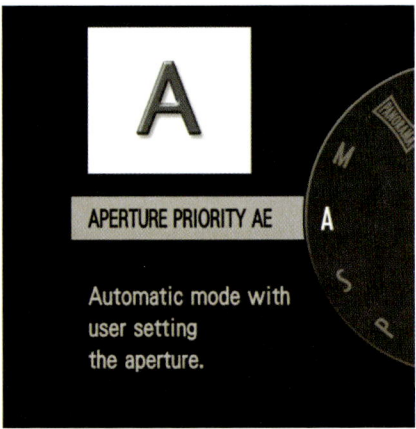

APERTURE PRIORITY AE   A

Automatic mode with
user setting
the aperture.

Fig. 88: In most X series cameras, auto exposure modes are set with the aperture ring on the lens and the shutter speed dial on the camera body: Pre-selecting an aperture and setting the shutter speed dial to "A" activates *aperture priority* mode. Selecting "A" on the aperture ring or lens in concert with a specific shutter speed activates *shutter priority* mode. Finally, selecting "A" on both the lens and the shutter speed dial selects *program AE*. However, compact and entry-level models like the X-T100 feature **dedicated mode dials** for selecting the exposure mode.

It is important to understand that auto exposure (AE) modes (including Auto-ISO) are not responsible for correctly exposing images; exposure is *always* the responsibility of the photographer. AE modes automatically fill variables (such as the shutter speed in aperture priority **A**) in a way that matches the exposure you've set yourself. Auto exposure will only deliver good results if the photographer is exposing correctly.

EXPOSING CORRECTLY—HOW DOES THIS WORK?

Don't panic! Unlike conventional DSLR cameras, mirrorless cameras make things easy. Up to four different metering modes (multi, spot, center-weighted, and average), the WYSIWYG live view, and the live (RGB) histogram help you find the correct exposure for any given scene. If you shoot in one of the three AE modes, the most important tool is the exposure compensation dial, which allows you to correct the metered exposure up to ±3 EV in convenient steps of 1/3 EV. EV means Exposure Value, and 1 EV is equivalent to one full aperture stop. The correct exposure isn't what the camera is metering; it's what *you* make of the metering by adjusting the exposure compensation dial or manual exposure settings.

Choosing the right metering method	TIP 50

There are up to four different metering methods available to measure the amount of light that goes through the lens and hits the image sensor:

- **Average** metering calculates an unweighted average of the total light that hits the entire sensor area.

- **Spot** metering only considers two percent of the sensor area. The metering area covers a medium-sized focus frame in the center of the image. Alternatively, you can link spot metering to the size and position of the active focus frame (in SINGLE POINT AF and MF mode).

- **Center-weighted** metering is available in cameras with X-Processor Pro and X-Processor 4. It is a crossbreed between average and spot metering. While it encompasses the entire image area, it puts special emphasis on the image center.

- **Multi** or **matrix** metering calculates a weighted average of the total light that hits the sensor. The weight is a result of 256 metering areas (the matrix) that the camera evaluates and compares to typical scenarios, which is why multi metering is considered "smarter" than the other methods. For example, multi metering is designed to recognize when you are shooting against the sun.

Average, spot, and center-weighted metering return exposure recommendations based on middle gray. In other words, when you take a picture of a black wall and then a picture of a white wall with auto exposure (AE), the results will both look middle gray. This means:

- If you want the black wall to look black in the resulting image, you must manually adjust the exposure downward.

- If you want the white wall to look bright white in the resulting image, you must manually adjust the exposure upward.

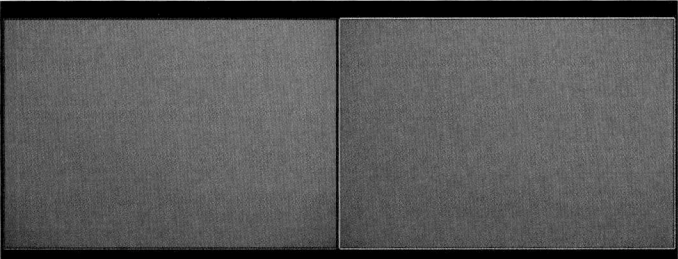

Fig. 89: This illustration shows a black sheet of paper and a white sheet of paper. Both were photographed with the camera's spot metering without any exposure correction. As you can see, the camera delivered a **middle-gray exposure** in both cases. To get an image that reflects the actual brightness of the subject, the metered exposure must be adjusted.

Fujifilm recommends a correction of +1 EV when you are shooting in snowfields, or −2/3 EV when you are shooting subjects in spotlight. Instead of these rules, I recommend a more precise and methodical course of action using the live view and the live histogram. To minimize corrective adjustments, it's best to select a metering method that fits the subject and the job at hand:

- **Multi** metering is a general-purpose method. Since it is supposed to be "smarter" than the other methods, there's a good chance that you won't have to apply (m)any corrective adjustments to the proposed exposure.

- **Average** and, to a lesser degree, **center-weighted** metering are rather neutral metering methods that will likely stay more consistent despite small changes in composition (or framing) than multi metering and spot metering. I recommend average metering if you want to take a series of shots of the same subjects under similar conditions. In such cases, average metering will help you keep the exposure consistent.

- **Spot** metering bases its measurements on one spot of the overall image. This means you must work very precisely to make sure you are metering the appropriate part (spot) of the scene. The resulting exposure recommendation will expose this spot with middle-gray brightness. For example, if you spot meter a backlit face against the sun, the metered exposure will display the face with middle-gray brightness (or zone 5 in the famous Ansel Adams zone system [38]). If that's too dark for your taste, you can use the exposure compensation dial to lift the exposure by +1/3 EV or +2/3 EV. On the other hand, if the person has dark skin, you may want to reduce the exposure with a correction in the opposite direction. It's up to you to choose the zone (brightness) of the spot-metered part of the image.

Spot metering is the most powerful and challenging metering method. It's useful when the light is very difficult—too difficult for multi and average metering. Typical examples are isolated bright objects in front of a dark background (and vice versa), such as a musician or an actor on a stage, or strongly backlit subjects. Whenever your exposure must be spot on, spot metering is your friend.

With that said, it's obvious that spot metering requires you to meter very precisely. Even small changes in the camera's direction can lead to dramatic changes in the metered result. Therefore, it can be useful to combine spot metering with the camera's AE-L function. AE-L will lock your exposure to prevent it from changing when you alter your composition, or when your subject starts to move away from your metering spot.

The best way to use spot metering is in manual mode **M**. In this mode, metering doesn't affect the exposure because you are setting all the exposure parameters (shutter speed, aperture, and ISO) manually. Spot metering in manual mode helps you determine the brightness level of any part of your image for any set exposure. The exposure scale in the viewfinder or LCD tells you exactly how much brighter or darker than middle gray (zone 5) the spot metered object would appear in your shot (either ±3 EV or ±5 EV, depending on your camera).

Don't forget to *disable* Auto-ISO in manual mode **M**. If you don't, the camera will still operate in some kind of AE mode (I call it "misomatic"); in this mode, the ISO setting will be the exposure variable that's automatically adjusted.

TIP 51	Linking spot metering to focus frames

Traditionally, spot metering covers the center of the frame with an area that's about as large as a medium-sized (standard) focus frame. However, by selecting SHOOTING MENU > (AF/MF SETTING >) INTERLOCK SPOT AE & FOCUS AREA > ON, you can link the spot metering area to the position and size(!) of the active focus frame in Single Point AF and MF mode.

This is a very useful feature if you are using one of the camera's many off-center AF frames, since it's likely that your focus area covers the same part of your subject that is also relevant for exposure metering (such as the brightly lit face of a stage actor who is standing in front of a dark background).

If you want to decouple spot metering from the AF area and limit it to the very center of the frame, make sure to select SHOOTING MENU > (AF/MF SETTING >) INTERLOCK SPOT AE & FOCUS AREA > OFF.

Please remember that the camera will not interlock spot metering with the focus area if you set it to either Zone AF or Wide/Tracking AF. Interlocking only works in concert with Single Point AF or manual focus (MF) mode.

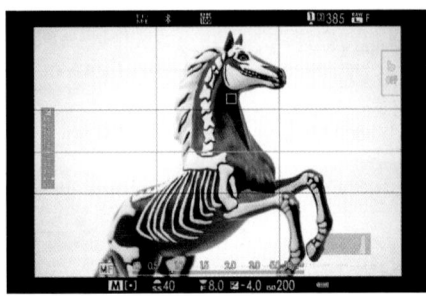

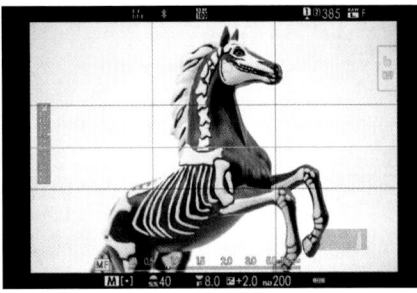

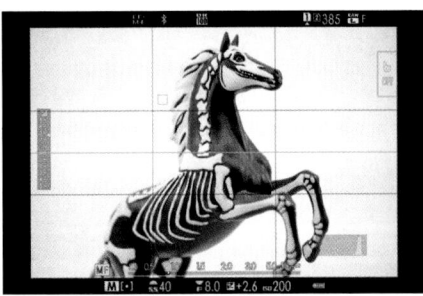

Fig. 90: **Spot metering and manual exposure mode:** Metering different parts of an image is easy with spot metering. Simply set an exposure (aperture, shutter speed, and ISO), then point the small spot-metering area at different parts of the scene. The exposure scale at the left or bottom of your live view tells you the brightness of any metered spot, with 0 representing middle gray (= zone 5 in the Ansel Adams zone system). To make things easier and most effective, interlock spot metering with the size and position of the currently active focus frame and select the smallest available focus frame size in AF-S or MF mode.

In this example, I spot-metered the darkest part of the model horse at −4 EV (top), its brightest part at +2 EV (center), and the brightest overall part of the scene at +2.66 EV (bottom). This means that the dynamic range of this scene comprises less than 7 EV (2.66 + 4 = 6.66), a range that fits neatly into a regular DR100% JPEG image.

Using the live view and live histogram

Unlike optical viewfinders in DSLRs, the electronic live view of modern mirrorless cameras provides an accurate simulation of the resulting JPEG image. The live preview encompasses color, contrast, exposure, and effect settings.

In standard display mode, this WYSIWYG preview is complemented by a live histogram [39]. I strongly recommend using the live histogram because it provides a useful overview of the brightness distribution in your scene. It also helps you identify areas of over- and underexposure in advance, so you can take corrective measures:

■ If bars are piling up like a bell curve at the right end of the histogram, but cut off mid-peak, parts of your shot will be overexposed with blown highlights. If this affects important parts of your image, you should correct the exposure downward. Alternately, you can expand the shot's dynamic range by selecting DR200% or DR400% in the respective menu.

■ If the histogram leans to the left, leaving plenty of unused space on the right, the shot might end up underexposed. In this case, you can adjust the exposure upward.

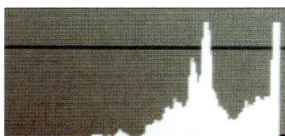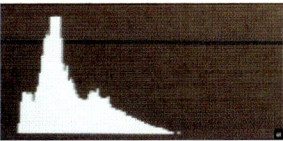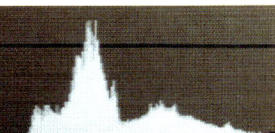

Fig. 91: Different **live histograms** showing a tendency for over-exposure, underexposure, and a balanced exposure of the same scene.

The histogram provides a technical representation of the live view simulation. When the Natural Live View is turned off, both the live view and the live histogram will reflect the current JPEG settings of the camera (white balance, film simulation, color, and highlight and shadow contrast). For example, the VELVIA film simulation delivers more contrast and more saturated colors than PRO NEG. STD, and this is reflected in the live view and the live histogram.

It's important to note that in many recent X camera models, the live view and live histogram now also represent (simulate) the effect of manual DR200% or DR400% dynamic range settings. However, if you set the camera to DR-Auto, the live view and live histogram will always display a DR100% preview.

When you half-press the shutter button, the camera's live view will also try to give you an accurate representation of the resulting image's dynamic range. That said, there is no live histogram when you half-press the shutter button, so you'll have to fully rely on the visual impression provided by the live view image.

With the exception of the X100F, all cameras with X-Processor Pro or X-Processor 4 also offer an **RGB histogram** [40], which is only available by assigning it to an Fn or Touch-Fn button. The RGB histogram is once again based on the current live view image, so it represents the resulting JPEG image. In fact, the color histogram displays four different histograms at once: overall luminance distribution (a larger version of the standard histogram) and separate histograms for the three color channels: red, green, and blue. That way, you can immediately recognize clipping of individual color channels in your JPEG. For example, shooting a red rose, the red channel is the first to clip and, thus, lose texture.

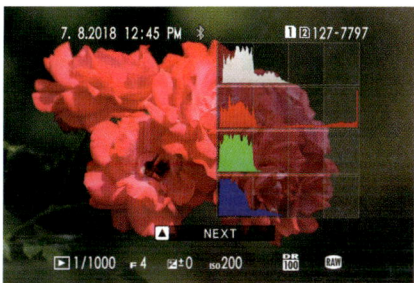

Fig. 92: The **RGB histogram** of this image of a rose illustrates how the red channel is already clipping (indicated by the peaking line at the right edge of the red channel histogram), while green, blue, and overall luminance are barely touching the right half of the histogram. Please note that as long as the Natural Live View is turned off, the histogram always reflects the current JPEG settings (film simulation, contrast settings, color saturation setting, etc.). This JPEG was created with the Provia factory settings of my X-H1.

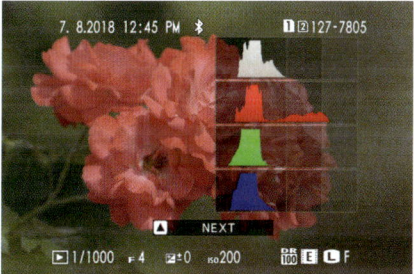

Fig. 93: This is the same RAW image, but this time processed with **flat JPEG settings:** Eterna film simulation, Shadow Tone −2, Highlight Tone −2, and Color −4. These settings reflect the flattest possible color profile that you can achieve in an X-H1, and there's now plenty of additional headroom in the shadows and highlights. Thanks to the much higher dynamic range of the flat JPEG, there's also no clipping of the red channel in the histogram. This flat JPEG reflects the dynamic range of the actual RAW file much better than the camera's default JPEG settings, and many RAW shooters use these or similar flat JPEG settings in concert with the RGB histogram because it makes it easier to determine the optimal exposure right at the sensor's saturation limit.

The RGB histogram also includes "blinkies," which are live overexposure or clipping warnings. If bright parts of your scene start to blink in RGB histogram mode, the blinking areas will be blown in the resulting JPEG (= losing texture and detail). The blinkies make it easy to set an exposure where important highlights are protected (= not blinking in the RGB histogram view).

| TIP 53 | Auto exposure (AE) with modes **P**, **A**, and **S** |

P (program AE), **A** (aperture priority), and **S** (shutter priority) are the three auto exposure modes of your X series camera.

A brief reminder:

- **Program AE P** will automatically set a suitable aperture and shutter-speed combination.

- **Aperture priority A** will automatically set a suitable shutter speed to match a preset aperture.

- **Shutter priority S** will automatically set a suitable aperture to match a preset shutter speed.

To take a picture in one of the AE modes, you can follow these steps:

- Meter the exposure with one of the available metering modes (usually either *multi* or *average* metering).

- After metering, adjust the exposure to taste using the exposure compensation dial. Use the live view and the live histogram to determine the best adjustment. Remember: it's not the camera that's setting the exposure; it's you. Don't blindly follow what the camera is proposing. Instead, always keep an eye on the live view and the live histogram. If available, you may also want to use the RGB histogram.

- When you half-press the shutter button, your exposure will be locked as long as you keep the button half-depressed. This means that while the shutter button is half-pressed, you can adjust the framing or composition of your shot without changing the exposure.

■ Instead of half-pressing the shutter button, you can also use the AE-L function to meter a scene and lock the exposure. You can configure the AE-L button to either lock the exposure as long as you press the AE-L button (SET UP > BUTTON/DIAL SETTING > AE/AF LOCK MODE > AE&AF ON WHEN PRESSING), or use the button as a toggle to lock and unlock the exposure (SET UP > BUTTON/DIAL SETTING > AE/AF LOCK MODE > AE&AF ON/OFF SWITCH). When the exposure is locked with AE-L, you can still correct it with the exposure compensation dial.

■ To take the shot, fully depress the shutter button.

Metering and exposure are two different things. After metering a scene, the photographer sets the actual auto exposure with the exposure compensation dial:

■ **Metering** is performed using either multi, center-weighted, average, or spot metering.

■ Use the **exposure compensation dial** to adjust the metering result. Use the information from the live view and live histogram to adjust your settings. Of course, there are many instances where the initial metering is already spot-on, so you won't have to apply any further correction.

■ **Expose** the image using one of three AE modes: aperture priority, shutter priority, or program AE.

While most X cameras feature dedicated exposure compensation dials, a few models (such as the X-H1, GFX 50S, and several entry-level models) don't. In those cameras, exposure compensation is assumed by one of the command or multi-purpose dials.

TIP 54   Using manual exposure **M**

In manual exposure mode, you manually specify all three exposure parameters: aperture, shutter speed, and ISO amplification. For this to work, Auto-ISO must be turned off. Otherwise, ISO would become an exposure variable that the camera would automatically fill.

For the live view and live histogram to correctly display the set exposure in manual mode, make sure that SET UP > SCREEN SET-UP > PREVIEW EXP./WB IN MANUAL MODE > PREVIEW EXP./WB is set. I recommend setting the metering to spot metering.

Here's how you can expose in manual mode:

■ Select and set an aperture and shutter speed that suits your subject and image idea. Aperture controls the depth of field [41]; shutter speed controls the amount of motion blur [42] and camera shake in your exposure.

■ Next, select an ISO value that will yield the desired brightness in your shot. You can (and should) use the live view and live histogram to find a suitable setting. As usual, try not to blow out important highlights. The live histogram is your friend.

■ You can check specific parts of your scene by spot metering them. The exposure scale in the live view screen tells you how much above or below middle gray (zone 5) the spot-metered selection will be exposed. This tool helps you ensure that important parts of your image (such as skin tones or snow) will be exposed exactly like you want them to be.

■ Finally, you may want to readjust or fine-tune aperture, shutter speed, and ISO according to your metering. Once everything is set, you can take the shot(s).

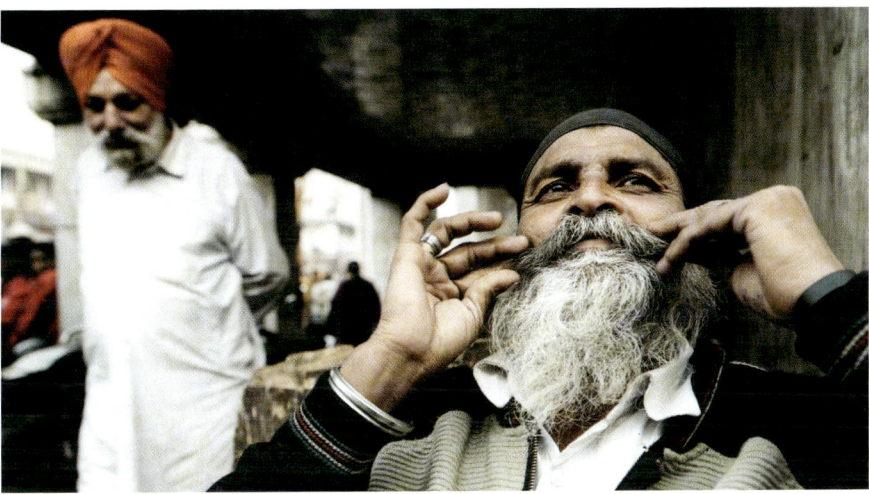

Fig. 94: Here's a confession: I shoot in **manual exposure mode** most of the time. And maybe you should, too. Not only can the camera make fewer mistakes when you are in charge, but manual mode also gives you full control over aperture (depth of field), shutter speed (motion blur, camera shake), and ISO (noise level, effective dynamic range). Manual mode also ensures that multiple shots of a scene have the same constant exposure, because the exposure doesn't change unless *you* change it. It also forces you to think about your actual exposure parameters: Why are you using a particular setting for aperture, shutter speed, and ISO? Thanks to the WYSIWYG nature of mirrorless cameras, manual exposure mode can help you avoid unpleasant surprises: You *set* the exposure, you *see* the exposure in the live view, and you *get* the exposure that you set and saw in your JPEG.

Using aperture priority A	TIP 55

In aperture priority AE [43], you manually set the aperture [44] and the camera automatically selects a suitable shutter speed based on your chosen exposure (as set with the exposure compensation dial). Which aperture should you select? Let's look at some basics:

- As the aperture gets smaller (= the aperture number gets higher), your depth of field (DOF) [45] increases. DOF is the zone in front of and behind the focus plane that appears in perfect focus when you look at the finished image. In standard display mode, the viewfinder and LCD offer a focus and DOF scale that displays the focus distance as well as the calculated depth-of-field zone that surrounds it.

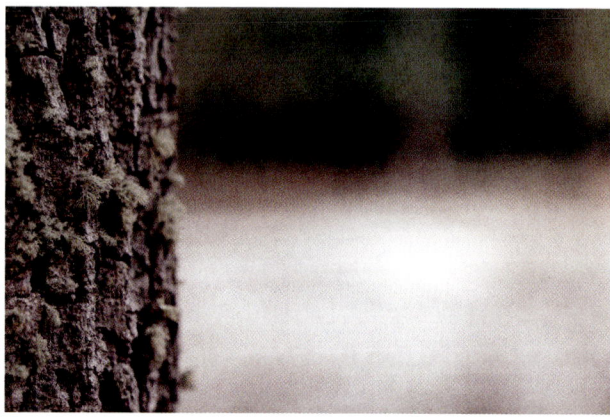

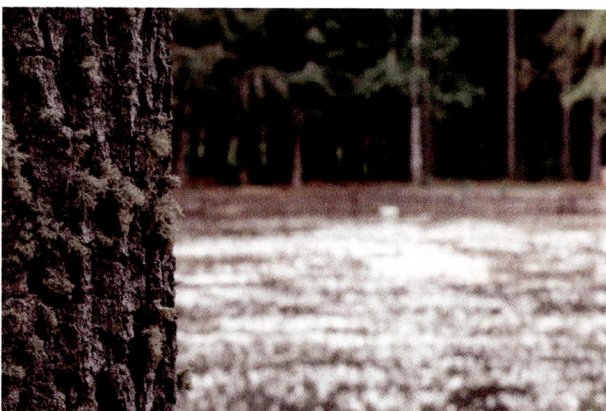

Fig. 95: This example shows the same scene shot twice with an X-T1 and the XF90mmF2 R LM WR lens. The image above was shot wide open at f/2; the image below was stopped-down to the maximum of f/16. While stopping down clearly increases the depth of field, the look of the remaining out-of-focus area (also known as **bokeh**) is still smooth and silky, which is a trademark of the XF90mmF2 lens. Within the Fujifilm X-mount universe, I consider this the "perfect lens" because it doesn't show relevant weaknesses in any field of use.

- Fast lenses like the XF56mmF1.2 R or the XF35mmF1.4 R often exhibit a tight DOF of less than an inch when used wide open, so in a portrait shot, only one of the subject's eyes may be perfectly in focus. If that's the case, you can stop down the lens or change the position of your subject so that both eyes are the same distance from the camera.

- Stopping down a lens beyond f/10 (using 24 MP APS-C cameras) leads to increased diffraction blur [46] across the image area. While increasing the depth of field enlarges the in-focus zone, maximum detail within that zone is reduced. In other words, when you shoot with f/22 using a wide-angle lens, there's a good chance that your scene will be in focus from front to infinity. However, its overall crispness will be significantly lower than it would be at f/8. The Lens Modulation Optimizer (LMO) in your camera can compensate for diffraction blur to a degree, but its effect only extends to JPEGs created in-camera by the built-in RAW converter. External RAW converters can't support the LMO.

- When you shoot wide open or with a high ISO setting, it's possible that the suitable shutter speed is faster than the camera's maximum mechanical shutter speed (usually 1/4000s or 1/8000s). If that's the case, the shutter speed will be displayed in red (overexposure warning). You can use shutter speeds beyond the mechanical threshold by activating the camera's electronic shutter.

Using shutter priority S	TIP 56

Shutter priority AE [47] works like aperture priority, except you are manually setting a shutter speed [48], and the camera automatically selects a fitting aperture value based on your exposure. Shutter priority is only available when you're using native X-mount lenses with electronic contacts. Adapted lenses (at least those with "dumb" adapters) can only be used with aperture priority or in manual mode.

Setting the right shutter speed depends on two factors:

■ Motion blur [49]: The faster your subject is moving, the faster your shutter speed must be to avoid shots with motion blur. This doesn't mean that motion blur is always bad; it can be used as a conscious choice to add dynamic punch to your image. For instance, panning [50] the camera blurs the background behind a sharp main subject. Motion blur can be a benefit of long exposures [51]–exposure times of several seconds or minutes can smoothen water surfaces, blur cloudy skies, or add star trails.

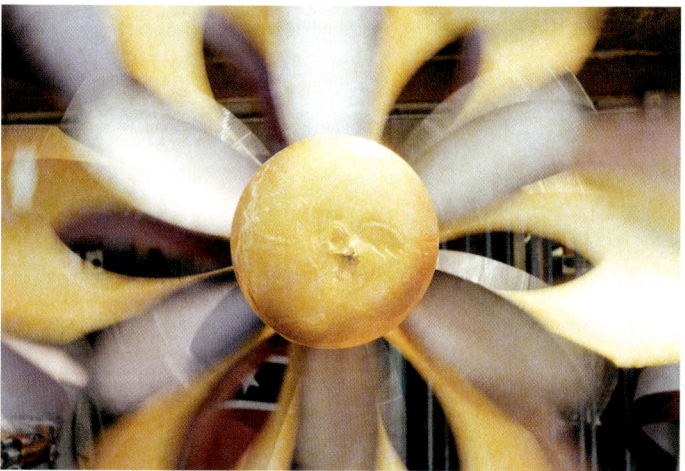

Fig. 96: In this handheld shot of a spinning wind wheel, **motion blur** was a conscious choice. Shot with an X-T20 and the versatile XF27mmF2.8 pancake lens at f/13, the selected shutter speed of 1/30s at base ISO 200 was slow enough to illustrate the motion of the propellers around the stationary (and thus unblurred) node. At the same time, it was fast enough to avoid camera shake which would have blurred the non-moving parts, as well.

■ Blur due to camera shake [52]: if you don't hold the camera steady when you take a shot, the resulting image can be blurred. The optical image stabilizer [53] (OIS) and In Body Image Stabilization (IBIS) can help, or you can put the camera on a tripod or a solid surface and use the self-timer or a remote shutter release to take the shot. A rule of thumb suggests using at least the reciprocal of the "full-frame" equivalent focal length as your shutter speed. For example, if you are using a 200mm lens on your APS-C camera (and the OIS has been switched off), your minimum shutter speed should be 1/300s, since you must multiply the focal length with the APS-C crop factor [54] of 1.5. Of course, rules of thumb don't apply to everyone in every situation. It really depends on your technique and whether you're blessed with steady hands.

If you set a very slow shutter speed or choose a high ISO setting in shutter priority mode, it's possible that even the smallest aperture opening of your lens will still be too large to avoid overexposure. In this case, the aperture value will be displayed in red.

If your X camera features a dedicated shutter speed dial, you can use it to quickly change the shutter speed in full-stop increments. You can also use the command dial to fine-tune your selection in 1/3 EV intermediate steps.

*Hint: Setting the shutter speed dial of current X series cameras to **T** (Time) allows you to select the **full** range of available shutter speeds (in 1/3 EV steps) by turning a command dial. If your camera has multiple command dials, you can assign shutter speed control to one of them in SET UP > BUTTON/ DIAL SETTING > COMMAND DIAL SETTING. Personally, I always assign shutter speed to the front command dial.*

Using program AE **P** and program shift   TIP 57

In program AE, the camera will automatically pick a combination of aperture *and* shutter speed settings that correspond to your set exposure. This mode can be useful for inexperienced photographers or in situations when you don't have the time to manually adjust the aperture or shutter speed.

In program AE, the slowest possible shutter speed is limited. In several recent models, the maximum duration is 4 seconds. When this (in concert with an already wide-open aperture) is not sufficiently slow to achieve the set exposure, the camera will display a red underexposure warning.

Even in program AE, you can influence shutter speed and aperture to a degree by using program shift [55]. Program shift allows you to select more suitable combinations of aperture and shutter speed compared to the one originally proposed by the camera's program AE. You can cycle through different combinations of apertures and shutter speeds that all result in the same exposure. When the camera is in program AE mode, you can activate program shift by turning the command dial that is otherwise responsible for adjusting the shutter speed.

Let's say you are shooting a portrait with the XF16–55mmF2.8 R LM WR zoom lens. It's a bright day, so program AE offers a shutter speed of 1/500s with an aperture of f/5.6. However, you prefer to shoot the portrait wide open at f/2.8 to achieve a blurrier background. In this situation, you have two choices: You can either switch to aperture priority mode by manually setting an aperture of f/2.8, or you can use program shift by turning the command dial until the aperture display shows f/2.8. Opening the aperture two stops from f/5.6 to f/2.8 won't change the original exposure because program shift will automatically adjust the shutter speed two stops from 1/500s to 1/2000s.

Important: Program shift is **not** available if Dynamic Range is set to AUTO or if a TTL flash unit is in use.

TIP 58	Playing it safe with auto exposure bracketing

As you know by now, the automatic exposure (AE) modes **P**, **A**, and **S** are merely responsible for automatically filling exposure variables. The exposure itself is the responsibility of the photographer. You can use metering (multi, center-weighted, average, or spot), the live view, and the live histogram to determine the correct exposure.

Nobody is perfect! If you want to play it safe, auto exposure bracketing [56] can be a helpful feature. In this mode, the camera takes a series of at least two shots in quick succession, each with a different exposure. Mostly it's one shot with normal exposure, one underexposed shot, and one overexposed shot.

Exposure bracketing is especially useful with subjects that don't move. After you've taken the shot, you can decide which of the differently exposed versions you want to keep.

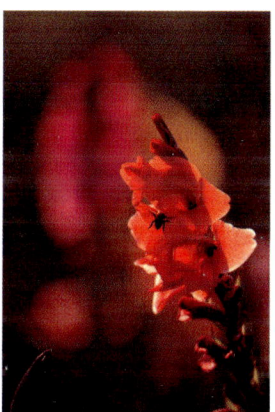 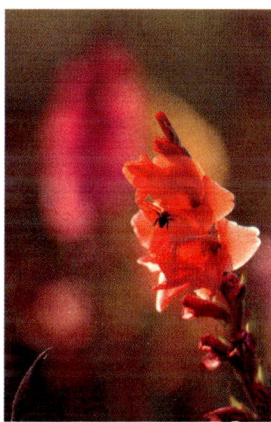 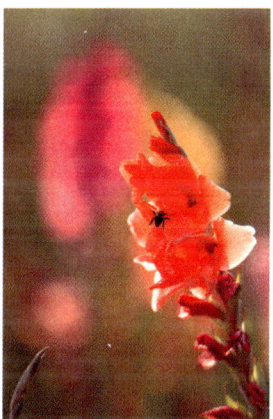

Fig. 97: **Auto exposure bracketing** automatically takes two or more images with varying exposure. Contrary to its name, AE bracketing even works in manual exposure mode, so you can manually set an exposure (aperture, shutter speed, ISO) that you think is right, and AE bracketing will give you additional options with different shutter speeds that are brighter and/or darker than your original exposure. In this example, the image in the middle shows the originally set exposure. The image to the left was bracketed 2/3 EV darker, and the one on the right was bracketed 2/3 EV brighter.

Depending on your X camera model, you can find AE BKT in the DRIVE menu or by selecting BKT on the DRIVE dial. In the latter case, you also have to make sure that AE bracketing is selected in the BKT settings of the shooting menu. There, you can also configure your AE bracketing parameters (such as the exposure distance between images).

TIP 59 | Long exposures

Long exposures can lead to impressive results. Fireworks, night shots, interesting water surfaces, stars, or clouds: exposure times of several seconds or even minutes capture the course of time in a single photograph. Of course, this only works if you put the camera on a tripod or a solid, non-vibrating surface.

You have two basic options:

■ Set the shutter-speed dial to **T** (Time) and then use the command dial to set the shutter speed. To avoid camera shake, use a remote shutter release or the self-timer to take the shot.

■ Set the shutter speed dial to **B** (Bulb), then press and hold the shutter button for as long as you want the camera to expose. Obviously, it makes sense to use a remote shutter release that can be locked for the duration of the shot.

■ If your camera has a mode dial instead of a shutter speed dial (like the recent X-T100), set exposure mode **M** or **S** and select a shutter speed or **Bulb** with the command dial that is responsible for changing the shutter speed.

For good-quality results, make sure to set SHOOTING MENU > (IMAGE QUALITY SETTING >) LONG EXPOSURE NR > ON. By doing so, the camera will perform a dark-frame subtraction [57] depending on what ISO and exposure time you used. Dark-frame subtraction doubles the effective exposure duration, so be patient.

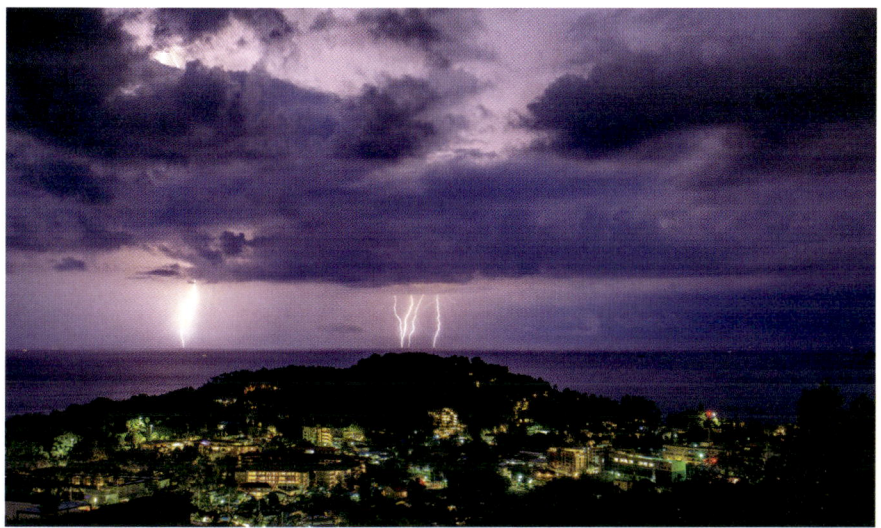

Fig. 98: A **long exposure** of 30 seconds taken in T mode. Make sure to use a tripod for these kinds of shots.

Long exposures in bright daylight	TIP 60

To achieve long exposure times under normal daylight conditions, you can't just stop down the lens. Even at f/22, your shutter speed would still be too fast. Besides, diffraction blur is kicking it beyond f/10 (assuming a 24 MP APS-C model), so stopping down beyond this point is only recommended when it cannot be avoided.

To realize long shutter speeds in good light, it's best to use a so-called ND filter [58], or neutral density filter. This is a fancy name for a gray filter that you can put in front of the lens to block a portion of the light from reaching the sensor.

For example, a filter with an ND 3.0 specification will extend your exposure time by a factor of about 1000 (or 10 f-stops). This means that by using such a filter, a scene that would normally require a shutter speed of 1/50s at f/8 can be shot at the same aperture with an exposure time of 20 seconds.

However, there's a catch: since X series cameras are equipped with a rather weak infrared (IR) cut filter in front of their sensors, long exposures (typically one minute or longer) in bright daylight should be performed with a regular neutral density (ND) filter *and* a dedicated IR cut filter in front of the lens. This will help you avoid false colors. A few ND filters already include an IR cut filter.

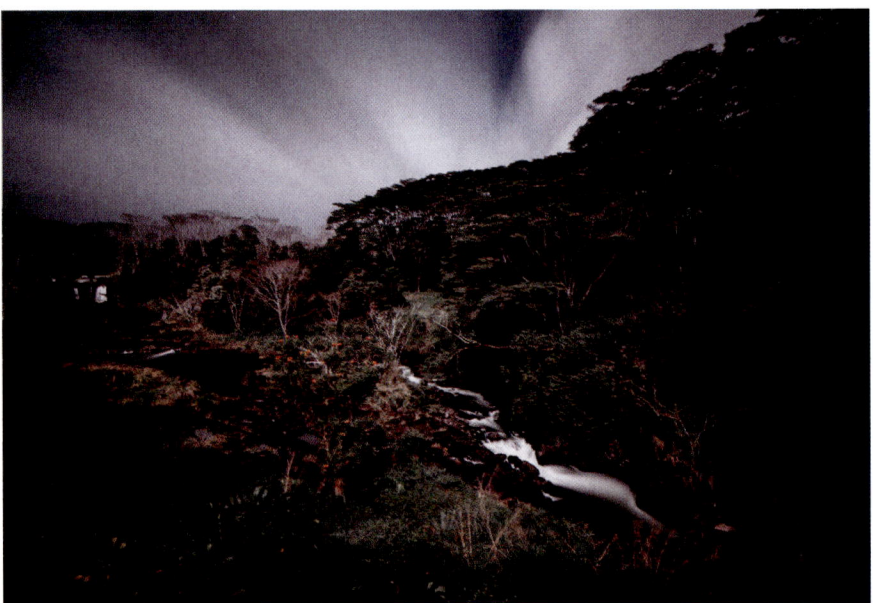

Fig. 99: This **long daylight exposure** lasted almost 4 minutes and was made possible by using a strong ND filter.

TIP 61	ISO settings—what's the deal?

The meaning of ISO in the digital realm is often misunderstood. Unlike film, higher ISO settings *don't* increase the sensor's sensitivity. For example, the sensors in Fujifilm's APS-C cameras before the X-T3 are all calibrated to a native ISO 200 (based on the popular SOS standard) [59], and this remains the same no matter what ISO you set in these cameras.

To be clear, there's no difference between taking a shot with f/5.6 and 1/60s at either ISO L (100) or at ISO H (25600). In both cases, the sensor is exposed to the exact same amount of light (or photons) due to the fixed f/5.6 and 1/60s setting. The amount of light (the actual exposure) is solely determined by aperture and shutter speed.

So, what exactly is ISO doing? ISO determines the amount of *signal amplification* that's applied to the image. ISO 200, the APS-C sensor's native setting in our example, is equivalent to the camera's basic calibration. At ISO 400, the signal (or sensor data) is amplified by one aperture stop (1 EV) to brighten the image and increase its exposure. At ISO 800, the amplification amounts to two stops (2 EV), and so on. At ISO 25600, the additional amplification of the light recorded by the sensor amounts to seven stops or 7 EV. It's not surprising that image quality decreases when ISO amplification increases, because noise and artifacts are amplified along with the actual image data.

The amplification we are talking about means brightening the image by increasing its exposure. If you are familiar with RAW converters such as Adobe Lightroom, you know there's an exposure slider. Moving this slider to the left or right changes the exposure (and hence the ISO) of an image after the fact. The concept of ISO amplification isn't limited to the camera itself—it's part of the entire workflow from in-camera exposure via RAW file (digital negative) to the final JPEG or TIFF file (digital print).

If you take a shot with an ISO 800 setting, you're telling the camera's Auto-exposure (AE) to expose the image two stops darker than it would at its base ISO of 200, then amplify (brighten) that image two stops to compensate for the underexposure.

Regarding image quality and ISO, there's a basic rule: lower ISO settings lead to higher-quality results—hence the general recommendation to keep the ISO settings as low as possible. However, we obviously can't shoot with base ISO all the time, especially in low-light situations.

There are two basic methods to amplify a digital image:

- **Analog/digital hybrid amplification** *prior* **to writing the RAW file:** This method applies a mix of analog and digital signal processing to amplify or push the image to the brightness level that corresponds to the ISO setting. The digitized result of this process is then saved as a RAW file.

- **Digital amplification (push)** *after* **writing the RAW file:** This method changes the brightness of an image during RAW processing, *after* the RAW file has been written. The metadata (a.k.a. instructions) in the RAW file will tell the RAW converter what to do. You can also use your X camera's built-in RAW converter to adjust the effective brightness (and hence, ISO) of an image after it has been recorded, or by moving your external RAW converter's exposure slider.

Digital amplification during RAW processing is beneficial because it's reversible. If the digital amplification (exposure) was too strong, you can always take it back. If it was too weak, you can push it up. ISO (a.k.a. exposure amplification) is a volatile aspect of the photography process because it can be changed anytime: in-camera, prior to writing the RAW file, or later during RAW processing.

The sensor in your X series camera is a so-called ISOless sensor. This means there's no relevant quality difference between conventional signal amplification prior to writing a RAW file and digital amplification later during RAW conversion. This is great, because it allows you to digitally increase the ISO (a.k.a. brightness/exposure) of your shots during RAW processing, either in-camera or with external software such as Lightroom. Pushing the exposure up later in Lightroom won't look much different from choosing a higher ISO setting when you take the shot.

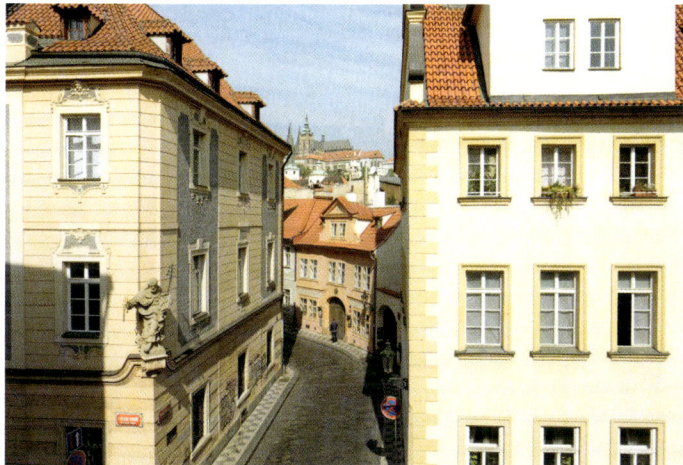

Fig. 100: **ISOless sensor (1):** This shot was taken with an X-Pro2 at ISO 1600, with classic analog/digital in-camera amplification from base-ISO 200 to ISO 1600. The ISO 1600 result was then burned into the RAW file.

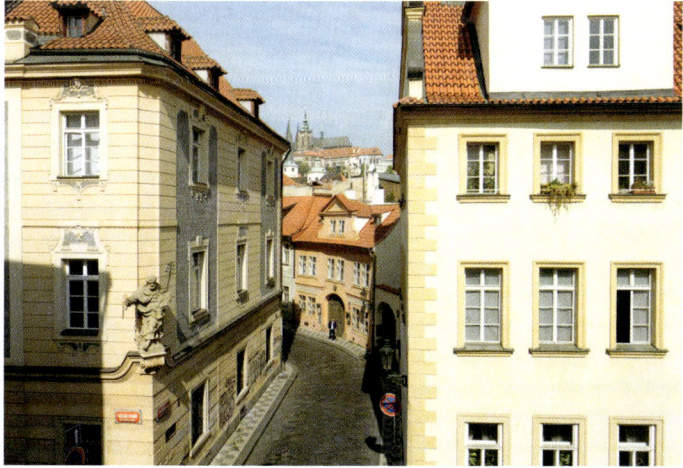

Fig. 101: **ISOless sensor (2):** This shot was also *effectively* taken at ISO 1600. However, it was shot with an ISO 200 base-ISO setting, using the same aperture and shutter speed as the previous shot, effectively underexposing it three stops (3 EV). The amplification from ISO 200 to ISO 1600 took place digitally during RAW conversion, simply by moving the exposure slider 3 EV to the right, compensating for the underexposure. You won't be able to see any quality difference between the two shots in this book, so I invite you to look at full-size samples that are uploaded to Flickr [60].

While the sensors of all X series APS-C cameras from the classic X100 up to the X-H1 are calibrated to base ISO 200, X cameras with a medium format (GFX 50) or 2/3" sensor (X10, X20, X30, X-S1, XF1, XQ1, and XQ2) use a base ISO setting of 100. Please note that the new X-T3 uses a base ISO setting of 160.

TIP 62	What you should know about extended ISO

You will probably have noticed that in addition to the standard ISO settings (usually ISO 200 to ISO 12800), your X cameras offer additional settings. In most APS-C models, these settings are L (100), H (25600), and H (51200).

- **H means High:** In these modes, image data is further digitally amplified. This enormous amplification leads to a visible decrease in quality. While ISO 25600 is still quite usable (especially for black-and-white JPEGs using the ACROS film simulation), ISO 51200 is only for emergencies.

- **L means LOW:** In ISO L (100) mode, an ISO 200 RAW is overexposed by one stop. During RAW conversion, the JPEG is pulled down one stop and saved, resulting in ISO 100 JPEG file. A digital pull is the direct opposite of a digital push operation: digital pull decreases the exposure of the resulting image. The ISO 100 RAW and JPEG files contain one stop *less* dynamic range than normal ISO 200 files. This means that bright areas like clouds in the sky can easily appear blown out. On the other hand, ISO 100 can add contrast and punch to scenes with dull lighting and little contrast.

As of December 2018, RAW shooting and extended ISO settings can only be combined in cameras with an X-Processor Pro and X-Processor 4 engines. With all other X models, extended ISO settings are only available in concert with JPEG-only shooting. If you are using a medium-format camera like the GFX 50S, don't forget that its base ISO is already 100, so its extended ISO L is ISO 50. The same applies to the X-T3 with base ISO 160: here, the lowest extended ISO L is 80.

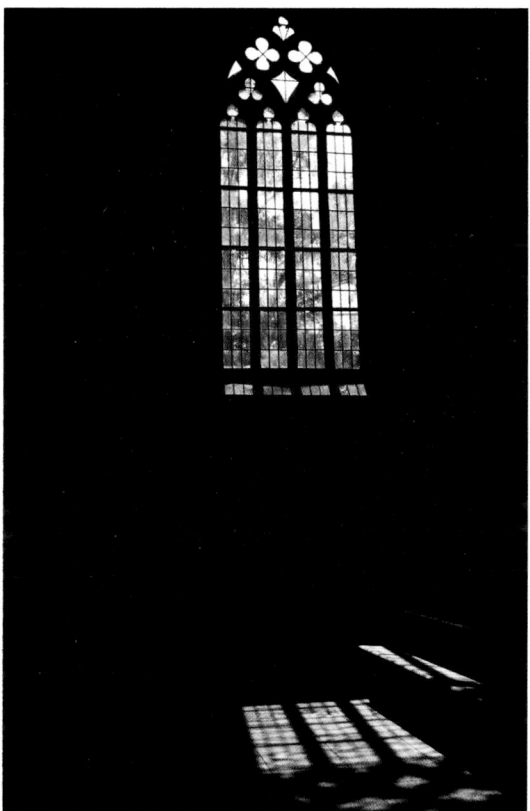

Fig. 102: **Extended ISO L (100)** can add punch thanks to its decreased dynamic range. To pull it off, set your APS-C camera to manual exposure mode, select base ISO 200, and expose the scene to the highlights using the live view and live histogram. Exposing to the highlights means that the brightest important parts of the scene are exposed as bright as possible, but without clipping (= losing highlight detail). After the exposure to the highlights is manually set, change the ISO setting from 200 to L (100) without changing aperture or shutter speed. This will increase the contrast of the image by darkening the shadows and midtones one stop, while bright highlights remain where they were.

If you have an X-T3, you can perform the same procedure with ISO 160 and ISO L (80). GFX shooters use ISO 100 and ISO L (50).

Important: Extended ISO settings are not available when the electronic shutter (ES) is selected.

While shooting in extended ISO L diminishes highlight dynamic range, this fact is *not* reflected in the live view and live histogram. This means that the live view and live histogram become pretty much useless for determining the correct exposure to the highlights when you are using ISO L. Only when you half-press and hold the shutter button to lock the exposure, the live view will adapt, but at that stage, there is no histogram available.

Practically, this means that it's not recommended that you use extended ISO in one of the auto exposure (AE) modes: **P**, **A**, and **S**. Assuming that you are using an X series camera with base ISO 200, you should instead first set the correct exposure to the highlights in manual mode **M** at ISO 200 using the live view and live histogram, and then change the ISO setting to ISO L (100) without further adjustments to shutter speed and aperture. This will keep your highlights intact and add contrast to the image by lowering the midtones and shadows to the new ISO 100 settings.

If you are using a camera with a base ISO of 100 (like the GFX 50S), manually set the highlight exposure at base ISO 100, then change ISO to L (50) without touching aperture or shutter speed. If you use an X-T3, manually expose at ISO 160 and then switch to ISO L (80).

A few X series cameras (like the X-Pro2, X-T2, or X-H1) also offer extended ISO L (160) and L (125) settings, which are derived from ISO 320 and ISO 250 by overexposing the shot one stop, then pulling it back down one stop during RAW conversion to match the brightness of the selected ISO L setting of 160 or 125. Doing so takes away one stop of dynamic range. *I strongly recommend not using these two additional extended ISO L settings at all.*

In the X-T3, the additional ISO L settings are 125 and 100. Again, do not use them at all.

Auto-ISO and minimum shutter speed	TIP 63

You can automate the task of selecting the best (or lowest) ISO setting possible for any given shooting situation. Auto-ISO is an option with up to three configurable presets (AUTO1, AUTO2, and AUTO3) that can be configured in the ISO menu of your camera:

- DEFAULT SENSITIVITY: This is the lower ISO limit. The camera will always try to use this ISO setting as long as the other parameters permit it.

- MAX. SENSITIVITY: This is the upper ISO limit. The camera's Auto-ISO will never go beyond this level.

- MIN. SHUTTER SPEED: Auto-ISO will automatically increase the ISO setting (up to the MAX. SENSITIVITY threshold) when the minimum shutter speed cannot be realized. Some APS-C cameras also offer a new AUTO setting here: If you set MIN. SHUTTER SPEED to AUTO, the camera will adjust the minimum shutter speed depending on the current focal length, using the formula *Minimum Shutter Speed = [1/(Focal Length × 1.5)] s*.

Obviously, MIN. SHUTTER SPEED is only relevant in auto exposure (AE) modes **A** and **P**, because the shutter speed is already set manually in modes **M** and **S**. Auto-ISO minimum shutter speed makes sure that within the lower and upper ISO limits, the camera will always use a shutter speed that is at least as fast as the set minimum shutter speed.

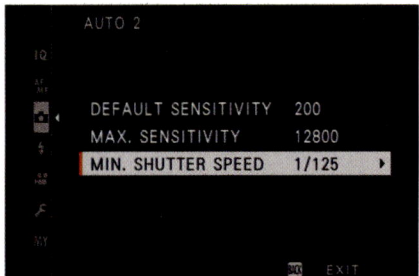

Fig. 103: **Auto-ISO** works with an ISO range between DEFAULT SENSITIVITY (the bottom) and MAX. SENSITIVITY (the ceiling). It will always try to keep ISO as close to the bottom as possible, but only as long as the resulting shutter speed isn't slower as the set MIN. SHUTTER SPEED.

Here's an example: Let's say you are shooting in mode **A** (aperture priority) in bright light conditions using f/5.6. Auto-ISO is set to ISO 200 as the lower limit and ISO 12800 as the upper limit. You have set 1/125s as your minimum shutter speed, because you want to avoid motion blur while taking pictures of people walking in the street.

As long as the scene is brightly lit, there is no problem. The camera will use ISO 200 with shutter speeds at least as fast as 1/125s. However, as the sun sets and it becomes impossible to successfully use 1/125s at f/5.6 and ISO 200, Auto-ISO will increase the ISO to ensure that the shutter speed doesn't drop below 1/125s. This continues as the light conditions deteriorate until Auto-ISO reaches the upper ISO limit (in our case, ISO 12800). What now? Since the camera can't increase the ISO any further, it will start to reduce the shutter speed to values slower than 1/125s to still ensure a correct exposure.

In mode **S** (shutter priority), the photographer sets the shutter speed. In this mode, Auto-ISO will increase the ISO setting only when the aperture is already wide open and can't be opened further. This can be a problem with fast lenses like the XF56mmF1.2, XF35mmF1.4, or XF23mmF1.4. When shot wide open, the depth of field of these lenses is quite limited (to say the least). That's why Auto-ISO is better used in modes **P** or **A**, at least in concert with fast lenses.

Auto-ISO in manual mode **M**: the "misomatic."	TIP 64

Manual mode in concert with Auto-**ISO** turns into another auto**MATIC** exposure mode: the so-called "**misomatic.**" In this mode, you preselect the aperture and shutter speed, and the camera automatically selects a suitable ISO setting that matches the exposure that has been determined by the currently active metering mode.

To be useful in a misomatic setup, Auto-ISO should be able to use the full ISO bandwidth, so you should configure it with the camera's base ISO as the lower limit (ISO 100, 160, or 200, depending on your camera) and the highest possible upper limit (ISO 12800 in most X cameras).

Misomatic gives you full manual control over aperture (depth of field) and shutter speed (motion blur and camera shake). You can tailor shutter speed and aperture to the requirements of the task at hand; there will be no surprises. At the same time, you still enjoy the comfort of automatic exposure (AE).

Misomatic also allows you to adjust the camera-metered exposure with the exposure compensation dial. For this to be effective, it's even more important to set the Auto-ISO DEFAULT SENSITIVITY as low as possible and the MAX. SENSITIVITY as high as possible.

If you don't want to spend time with exposure compensation while you are in misomatic mode, you can use Fuji's DR function as a workaround by selecting DR200% in concert with the misomatic. This setting is your insurance against accidental overexposure by the camera's AE, because it gives you at least one stop of extra latitude for after-the-fact overexposure corrections with the internal or an external RAW converter. To correct a bad auto-exposure after the fact, you can use the PUSH or PULL commands of the camera's internal RAW converter or move the exposure slider of your external RAW processing software.

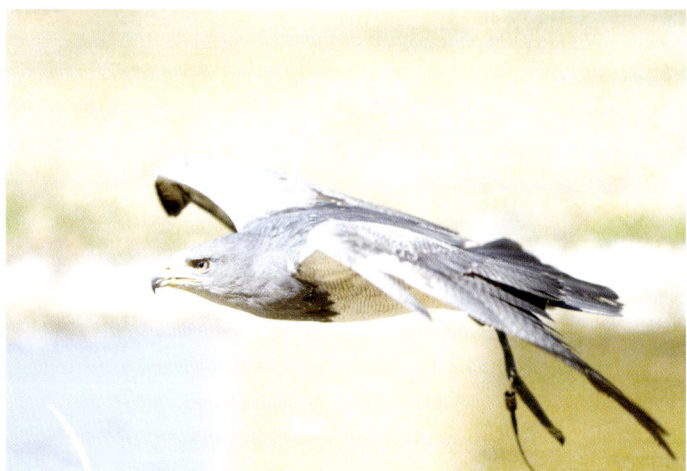

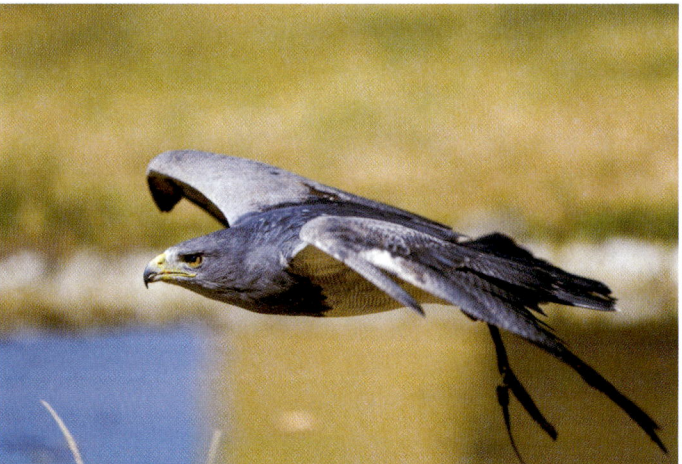

Fig. 104: **Misomatic** combines manual exposure with Auto-ISO. It can be helpful in situations with quickly and suddenly changing light conditions, such as concerts and other stage events, sporting events, action shots, or street photography. Basically, it's about situations that don't leave us enough time to manually adjust the exposure, and where catching the decisive moment is our priority. In misomatic mode, we can set the desired depth-of-field (aperture) and motion blur (shutter speed), while the camera auto-exposes the images by applying the right amount of ISO amplification. To protect against accidental overexposure (top image), we can buy "insurance" by setting the camera to DR200% in misomatic mode. That way, overexposures can be corrected during RAW conversion (bottom image).

Don't forget: ISO is just an amplification of the image signal. Using the misomatic, the amount of light that reaches the sensor is solely determined by your manual aperture and shutter speed settings. It always stays the same, regardless of the automatic ISO setting chosen by the camera. In misomatic mode, the only exposure variable is the amount of signal amplification (a.k.a. ISO), and with an ISOless sensor, this variable can also be adjusted later during RAW conversion. In this context, choosing DR200% ensures that there's ample leeway for after-the-fact exposure corrections of at least ±1 EV.

Extending the dynamic range	TIP 65

If the dynamic range of a subject is larger than the dynamic range of the camera's sensor or image processing, one of the following phenomena occurs:

- The highlights of the image are blown out or appear too bright (overexposed).

- Midtones appear too dark (underexposed) and shadows lose detail in the blackness.

In both cases, the shot's exposure is out of balance. Sadly, it's very difficult (if not impossible) to restore blown highlights. It's much easier to lift underexposed midtones and blocked shadows. This procedure is called tone-mapping, and it's the only way to access a camera's full dynamic range potential. Certain tonal values of the original exposure are reassigned and changed, either by employing a tone curve or by using a more complex procedure known as adaptive tone-mapping.

To record the full tonal range of a high-contrast subject, it's best to expose the image in a way that preserves the color and texture of the important bright parts of the scene. Of course, doing so can lead to an image with underexposed midtones and blocked shadows that need further processing to look natural, realistic, and pleasing. You can correct these issues with most external RAW converters.

While every RAW converter is different, most programs offer functions to selectively manipulate the exposure of a shot after the fact. For example, you can change the overall exposure with the exposure slider, and you can restore blown highlights with a highlight recovery slider. Most converters also offer sliders that only target shadow tones.

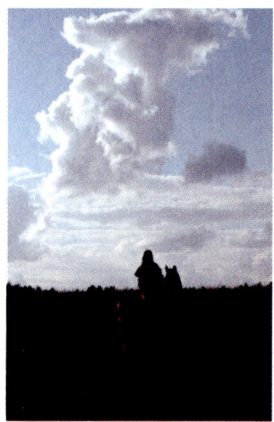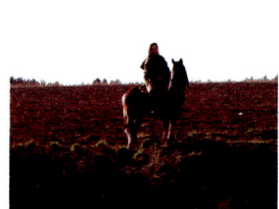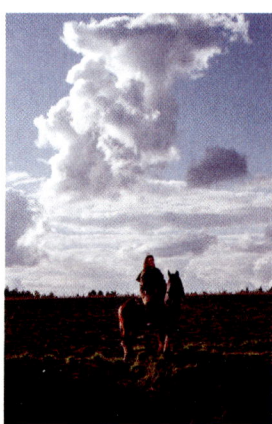

Fig. 105: In many instances, the **dynamic range** of a JPEG is often smaller than the dynamic range of the scene, so no matter how you expose it in your camera, some parts of the result will end up either too dark or too bright (or both). Here's a practical example using an X-E1 with Astia film simulation.

The image on the left was exposed to the highlights, showing color and texture in the blue sky and white clouds. However, the darker foreground is clearly underexposed, resulting in blocked shadows. Horse and rider are almost reduced to a silhouette.

The image in the middle depicts the same scene, but this time it was exposed about two stops (EV) brighter, removing blocked shadows and adding detail to the main subject. However, the cloudy blue sky is now overexposed and has all but disappeared.

This is a catch-22, because no matter how you expose this scene, the JPEG from the camera will always display essential parts either too dark or too bright. Quite obviously, different parts of this scene require different exposures. To pull this off, we use the RAW file of the image on the left, which was exposed to preserve the clouds and the sky. By applying tone-mapping in a state-of-the-art RAW converter, we selectively push (brighten) shadows and midtones without brightening the highlights of the clouds and sky. We can even add additional contrast to the clouds and darken the sky a bit. The example on the right shows the result out of Adobe Lightroom Classic CC, where different pixels received different levels of (after-the-fact) amplification.

The built-in DR function of your X camera can help you automate the tone-mapping procedure. It works in two stages:

■ The RAW file is exposed one (DR200%) or two (DR400%) stops darker than indicated in order to preserve bright highlights of a scene.

■ During the RAW conversion in the camera, the under-exposed shadows and midtones are digitally amplified by one (DR200%) or two (DR400%) stops to restore their natural brightness, while the (already correctly exposed) highlights are mostly left alone in order to preserve them.

The resulting JPEG from the camera has undergone a selective exposure correction. The DR function restores the shadows and midtones of a shot that was initially exposed one or two stops darker to preserve the highlights of the scene. Looking at the resulting JPEGs, this leads to an effective gain in dynamic range (DR): one additional stop of highlight DR at DR200%, and two stops of additional highlight DR at DR400%.

In DR-Auto mode, the camera will automatically select a suitable DR setting. Please note that in this mode, all but the very first X series models will only choose either DR100% (no highlight DR expansion) or DR200% (one stop of highlight DR expansion). DR400% (two stops of highlight DR expansion) is only available when it is manually selected.

You can change the DR settings of your camera in the Quick menu or by selecting SHOOTING MENU > (IMAGE QUALITY SETTING >) DYNAMIC RANGE and then either AUTO, DR100%, DR200%, or DR400%.

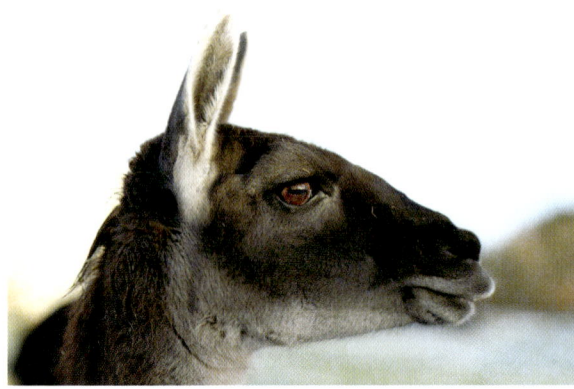

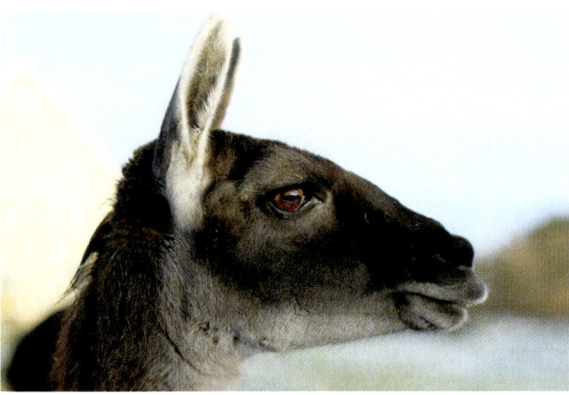

Fig. 106: These examples show the same shot with **DR100%** (above) and **DR400%** (below). At DR100%, the darker llama (our main subject) is correctly exposed in the foreground, but the much brighter colors in the sunny background are almost completely blown because they were outside of the camera's dynamic range. In the DR400% version of the shot, the exposure (brightness) of the llama didn't change. However, the bright background is now perfectly colored and textured. To pull this off, the camera exposed the RAW file of the scene two stops (EV) darker than indicated, then boosted shadows and midtones two stops brighter during RAW conversion. The result is a DR400% JPEG with 2 EV of extended dynamic range.

TIP 66	Extending the dynamic range for RAW shooters

RAW shooters typically set the camera to DR100% and perform the tone-mapping of their shots later during RAW processing. DR100% provides a realistic live view and live histogram (WYSIWYG).

The normal strategy of a RAW shooter is to expose toward the essential highlights of a high-contrast scene, making sure that there's sufficient color texture in the bright parts of the shot. This can result in an image with dark midtones and blocked shadows. However, while blown highlights are hard or even impossible to restore, blocked shadows can be lifted (pushed) later. Balanced results from scenes with a very high dynamic range can be achieved in almost any good external RAW conversion software.

Here's what to do:

■ Use the live view and live histogram to adjust the exposure in a way that ensures that the important highlights of your scene don't blow. This will preserve the highlights, but it may also lead to darkened midtones and blocked shadows that you must deal with later during the RAW conversion of your shot.

■ After taking the shot, enhance darkened shadows and midtones by selectively lifting their exposure in your RAW conversion software. For example, you could first lift the overall exposure and then restore the highlights with a highlight-recovery slider, or you could lift only the shadow tones with a shadow-tone slider. You can also combine both methods; many RAW converters are quite flexible and offer several sliders to selectively change the exposure. Lightroom and Adobe Camera RAW (ACR), for example, feature five different controls (exposure, whites, blacks, shadows, and highlights) to perform this task. Whenever you change an exposure slider, you are effectively changing the ISO of any part of the image that is affected by this slider. However, in the digital domain of the RAW conversion stage, nothing is lost, and everything is fully reversible. *Selectively* changing the exposure of an image is known as tone-mapping.

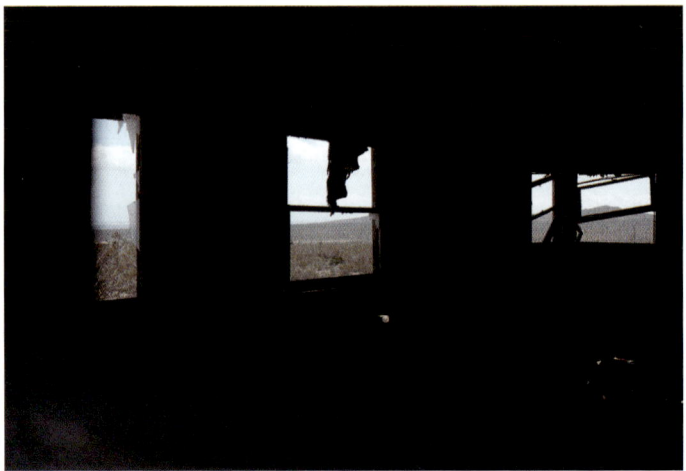

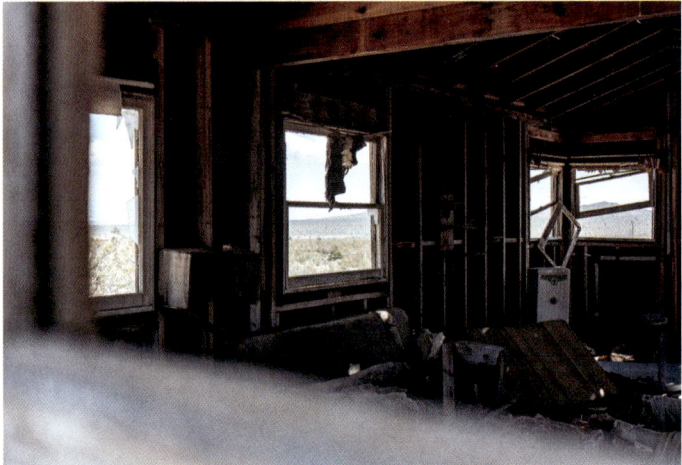

Fig. 107: The example above shows an image that has been **exposed to the highlights**. The exterior is perfectly exposed, but this means that the interior is literally left in the dark. If that's what you want, great! If not, you must apply some tone-mapping to the RAW file.

The example below shows the same image after tone-mapping in Adobe Lightroom. The dark shadow regions have been lifted, revealing plenty of detail where the previous image only displayed a dark patch. This method is also known as applying adaptive ISO, because different parts of the image received a different degree of exposure-push amplification. While the shadows were pushed up (ISO increase), the highlights mostly remained as they were.

JPEG settings for RAW shooters TIP 67

The previous tip explained the procedure to capture, compress, and later decompress scenes with high dynamic range. Since our exposure relies on the live view and the live histogram, it's useful to find camera settings that force the live histogram and live view to display as much dynamic range as possible. After all, we are shooting RAW and aren't really interested in the JPEGs from the camera, so we want the live view and live histogram to closely represent the data that will be recorded in the RAW files. This goal can be achieved by choosing JPEG parameters in the IMAGE QUALITY SETTING menu that display as much dynamic range as possible:

- Set FILM SIMULATION to ETERNA. This setting results in JPEGs with less contrast than the other film simulation modes.

- If ETERNA isn't available in your X camera, set PRO NEG. STD.

- If PRO NEG. STD isn't available either, or if you are using a first-generation EXR I engine camera like the X-Pro1 or X-E1, select PROVIA.

- Set HIGHLIGHT TONE to −2. This setting reduces the highlight contrast of the JPEG in the live view and in the live histogram.

- Set SHADOW TONE to −2. This setting reduces the shadow contrast of the JPEG in the live view and the live histogram.

- If you are shooting scenes with bright and saturated tones of red, blue, or green, you can also dial back the COLOR setting.

The above JPEG settings give you a live view and live histogram with maximum dynamic range. JPEGs that are generated with these settings may look flat, but we usually don't intend to keep them, anyway. We are only interested in the RAW file, which isn't affected by JPEG settings at all. However, the live view and live histogram *are* affected, and a flat live view image with a correspondingly flat live histogram is exactly what we want. It helps us to better fine-tune our exposure to preserve important highlights.

You can save your "JPEG settings for RAW shooters" in a custom profile (C1 to C7) so you can quickly retrieve them to set your camera to "RAW shooter mode." Select SHOOTING MENU > (IMAGE QUALITY SETTING >) EDIT/SAVE CUSTOM SETTING to edit your custom settings.

Fig. 108: These examples were all taken with an X-H1 using the same exposure settings (ISO, aperture, and shutter speed). The exposure was geared towards the highlights of the sunlit parts behind the much darker tunnel, where the camera was positioned on a tripod.

The top image shows how the live view (or JPEG) of the correctly exposed scene looks with the camera's Provia factory setting. While the sunny background is nicely lit, the dark parts of the tunnel are impossible to make out. It is really hard to frame this shot if all you can see is (literally) the light at the end of the tunnel.

The image in the middle depicts the same scene with the same exposure settings, but this time I used "JPEG settings for RAW shooters" (Eterna, Shadow Tone −2, Highlight Tone −2). These settings deliver a flat live view image (or JPEG) with less contrast and significantly more dynamic range than the camera's default settings. Using flat JPEG settings can be very helpful when you compose high-contrast scenes. Expose to preserve important highlights but still see what you are actually shooting. Remember: JPEG settings don't affect the RAW data—they only affect how the RAW data is processed in the live view and the resulting JPEG image.

The bottom image is the final result after processing (tone-mapping) the RAW file in Lightroom Classic CC.

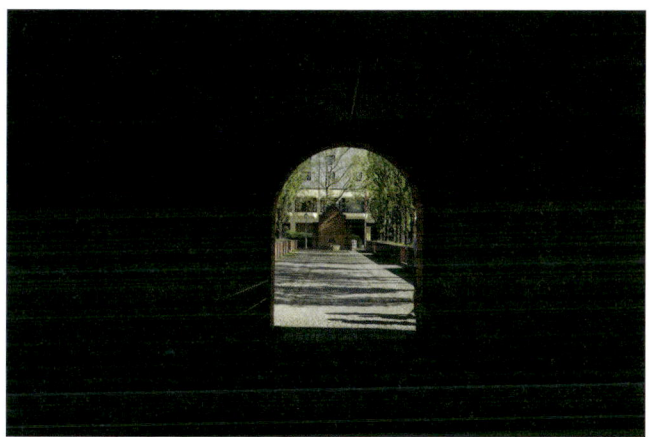

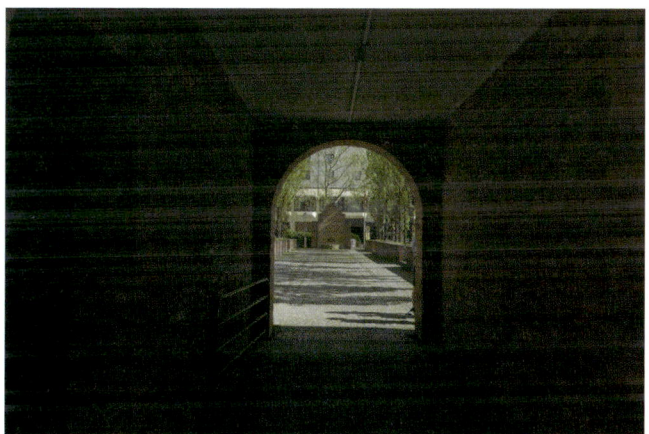

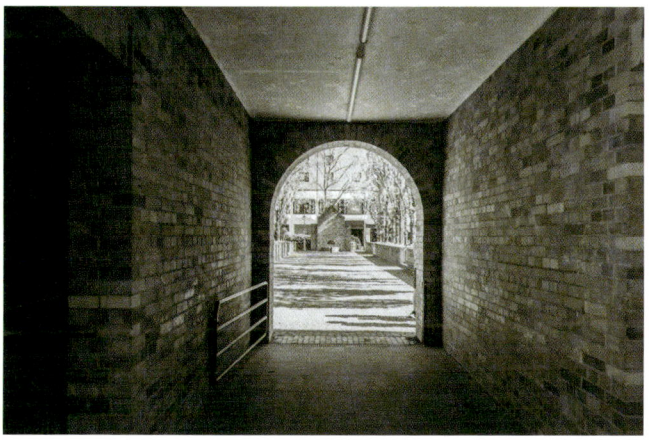

TIP 68   Extending the dynamic range for JPEG shooters

If you prefer to work with JPEGs that come directly from your camera (or want to shoot and keep RAWs *and* JPEGs), you can use Fuji's powerful DR function to capture scenes with high dynamic range. As you know, the DR function employs a two-stage process: reducing the exposure to capture critical highlights, and then lifting dark shadows and midtones to restore their brightness (exposure) back to realistic-looking levels.

You can simply set the camera to DR-Auto (not recommended), or manually set DR200% or DR400% (recommended) when you take pictures of high-contrast scenes. Remember that DR200% requires a minimum ISO setting of one stop (1 EV) above your X camera's base ISO, while DR400% requires a minimum ISO setting of two stops (2 EV) above base ISO. That's because the shadows and midtones in your scene will eventually be amplified by one (DR200%) or two (DR400%) ISO stops when the JPEG is created during RAW conversion.

What if we don't want to just *guess* what DR setting is optimal for any given scene? Can't we use the camera's metering to determine *exactly* how much DR expansion is required? Yes, we can!

■ To begin with, let's set the camera to DR100% and expose toward the critical highlights of a scene, just like a RAW shooter would do. Assuming that you are shooting in one of the AE modes, this will often require you to turn the exposure compensation dial in the negative direction until the live view and live histogram display the scene without blown highlights.

■ Next, turn the exposure compensation dial in the opposite (positive) direction until the shadows and midtones are displayed as bright as you want them to appear in the final image. Here's the important part: when you turn the exposure compensation dial up again, count the number of clicks it takes to reach the target brightness of your scene. One, two, or three clicks mean you should set the camera from DR100% to DR200% for one stop of additional highlight dynamic range. More than three clicks mean you should use DR400%. More than six clicks mean that highlights may be blown even when you set DR400%, so you might want to avoid overcompensating beyond six clicks. As you know, each click of the exposure compensation dial equals 1/3 EV (or a third of a stop).

The above describes the procedure for any of your camera's auto exposure (AE) modes **P**, **A**, and **S**, including *miso-matic* mode.

If you prefer to shoot in **manual exposure mode M**, make sure that the exposure preview for manual mode is enabled. Set DR100% and expose toward the critical highlights of your scene by manually setting aperture, shutter speed, and ISO. As usual, use the live view and the live histogram.

Now that your highlights are protected, the live view (aka JPEG) of your high-contrast scene may look too dark. To compensate this effect, manually raise the ISO in 1/3 EV steps until the brightness of the shadows and midtones in your live view image appear pleasing to your eye. Make sure to count the number of the 1/3 EV ISO compensation steps you took, then apply DR200% if you compensated 1, 2, or 3 steps, or set DR400% if you compensated either 4, 5, or 6 clicks.

Don't change aperture or shutter speed and don't compensate with more than six 1/3 EV ISO clicks (that's a total of 2 EV), or your resulting JPEG will be overexposed in the very highlights that you were trying to protect. Instead, try to reduce the shadow contrast by setting SHADOW TONE −1 or SHADOW TONE −2. You can also try a film simulation with less contrast, such as Pro Neg. Std or Eterna.

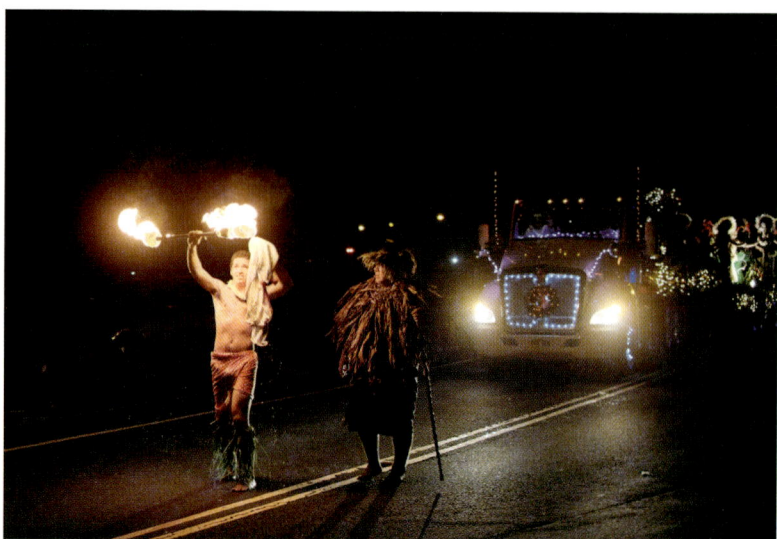

Fig. 109: **Night scenes** with bright lights and high contrast can benefit from a fixed DR400% setting to preserve color and texture in the highlights (Classic Chrome, DR400%).

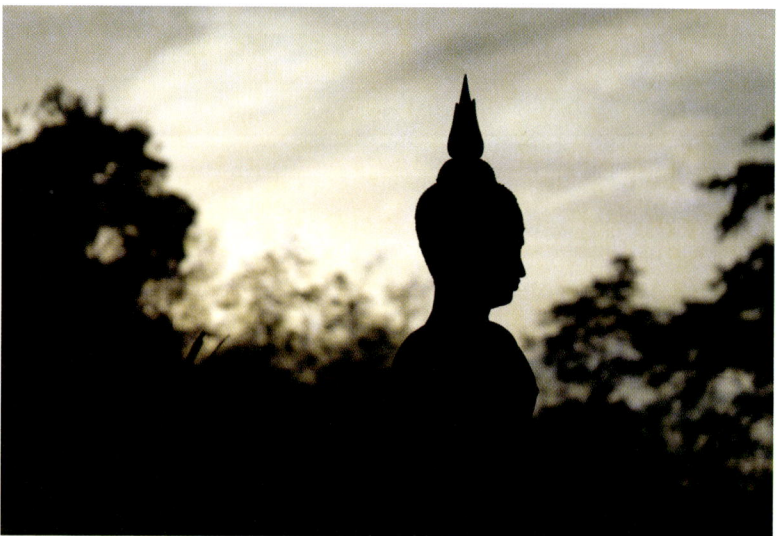

Fig. 110: On the other hand, there are instances where you may want to **maintain maximum contrast** and concentrate on the bright parts of a high-contrast scene. In such cases, a fixed DR100% setting is in order while you are exposing to the highlights (Provia, DR100%).

The two examples illustrate that DR-Auto is not a "smart" setting; it cannot predict what the photographer has in mind. In both cases, DR-Auto would have picked DR200%—not an optimal setting in either case.

*Important: The X30, X100T, and all cameras with X-Processor Pro (like the X-T2 or GFX 50) and X-Processor 4 (such as the X-T3) simulate the effect of manually selected DR200% and DR400% dynamic range settings in the live view and live histogram. However, automatic DR expansion via DR-Auto is **not** simulated in the live view. Instead, the live view and live histogram will display a DR100% simulation, even when DR-Auto eventually decides to take the shot at DR200%.*

In extended ISO L settings, the live view and live histogram wrongly show the dynamic range of a regular ISO setting, giving you the false impression of one stop more highlight dynamic range than what is actually available. Only when you lock the exposure by half-pressing the shutter button will the live view change to display the actually recorded dynamic range. However, at this stage, there's no live histogram available.

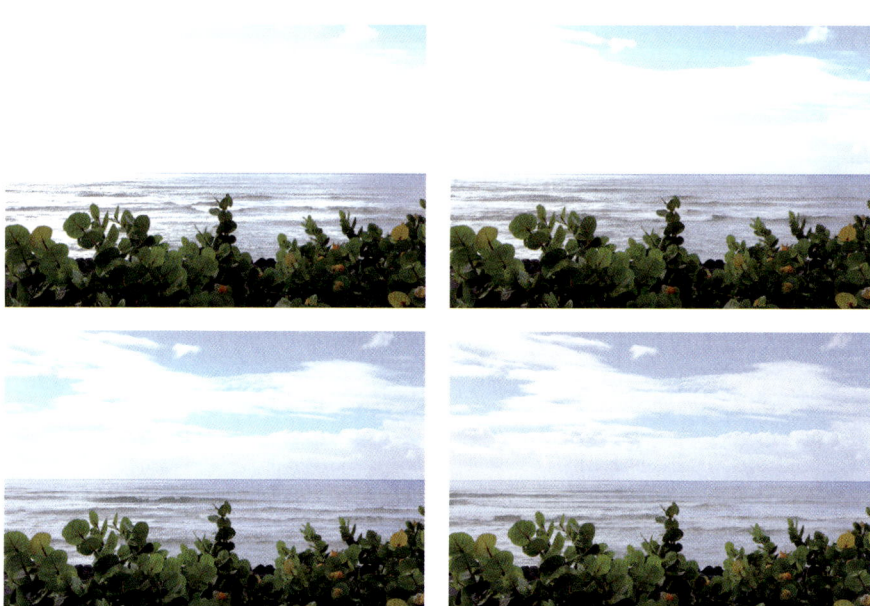

Fig. 111: **Comparing dynamic range settings in an X-Pro2:** The upper-left image shows our scene taken with extended ISO L (100), f/13, 1/50s, which is basically the missing DR50% setting. Highlight dynamic range is very poor; most bright parts of the image are blown.

The upper-right image shows the same subject shot with the camera's base ISO 200 (DR100%), f/13, 1/100s. Many parts of the shot are still without texture.

On the lower left, you can see an ISO 400 (DR200%), f/13, 1/200s version of the scene, which gives us another stop of highlight dynamic range. In this example, the clouds and the sky are already looking much better.

The lower-right example is an ISO 800 (DR400%), f/13, 1/400s version of our scene, which has two added stops of highlight dynamic range compared to a standard ISO 200 (DR100%) shot. Here, everything is smooth and shiny, with plenty of texture in the clouds and no discoloration of the sky.

All four images were captured with an X-Pro2 in AE mode **A**.

High-contrast scenes: Using the DR function to the benefit of RAW shooters

Fujifilm's DR function works by reducing the indicated ISO level of the RAW file by one (DR200%) or two (DR400%) stops. If you set ISO 800 and DR400% and take a picture, the RAW file of the image will be actually recorded with ISO 200—two stops darker than it appears in the live view or in the camera's resulting JPEG. Underexposing an image by one or two stops means that one or two stops of additional bright highlights are protected.

In other words: When the DR function is active, the camera's built-in RAW converter (which is also known as the JPEG engine) pushes the shadows and midtones of the underexposed RAW data one (DR200%) or two (DR400%) stops up to ensure that the live view and the resulting JPEG match the indicated ISO setting. It won't push the brightest highlights, though.

Example: If you set ISO 800 and DR400%, the RAW data will be recorded with ISO 200 (to protect two stops of highlights), but the built-in JPEG engine of the camera will make sure that the shadows and midtones of the live view and the resulting JPEG image are pushed back up two stops to ISO 800 to compensate for the RAW file's underexposure. The brightest highlights of the JPEG will remain at ISO 200, though.

That's why the minimum ISO settings for DR200% and DR400% in cameras with a base ISO of 200 are ISO 400 and ISO 800, respectively. In the same fashion, cameras with a base ISO of 100 require a minimum ISO setting of 200 for DR200% and ISO 400 for DR400%. Finally, the X-T3 features a base ISO level of 160, so DR200% requires at least ISO 320, while DR400% can't operate below ISO 640. Remember that per definition and convention, *ISO settings only apply to the JPEGs* generated in the camera, not to the RAW files. It's perfectly normal for the RAW data to be recorded lower or higher than the indicated ISO level, because all ISO settings only apply to JPEGs and the live view, not to RAW data.

Understanding this, it becomes clear that in cameras with base ISO 200, extended ISO L (100) is doing just the opposite of the DR function: it records RAW data one stop brighter at ISO 200, while the JPEG engine pulls down (darkens) the live view and the resulting JPEG one stop to simulate and match the indicated ISO 100 setting. Overexposing an image one stop brighter in the RAW than it appears in the live view and JPEG also means that one stop of highlight dynamic range is cut off and lost, so selecting ISO L (100) has the same effect as a DR50% setting would have (if that setting existed).

In cameras with base ISO 100 (like the GFX 50), the equivalent setting for "DR50%" is ISO L (50), and in the X-T3 (with base ISO 160), it's ISO L (80).

In many practical situations, correctly exposing to the important highlights of a scene results in a live view image that looks very dark in the midtones and shadows, which makes it hard to compose and focus the shot. Using "JPEG settings for RAW shooters" can mitigate this issue, but sometimes it's just not enough. If that's the case, using an equivalent ISO/DR setting can help us out.

For example, the following three exposure settings are perfectly equivalent at the RAW level:

- f/8, 1/400s, ISO 200/DR100%
- f/8, 1/400s, ISO 400/DR200%
- f/8, 1/400s, ISO 800/DR400%

The RAW data for these three shots is the same, only the JPEGs (and hence the live view) look quite different from each other: For example, the live view and JPEG of a f/8, 1/400s, ISO 800/DR400% shot looks two stops brighter than the equivalent f/8, 1/400s, ISO 200/DR100% version. However, the RAW data of these two shots is the same.

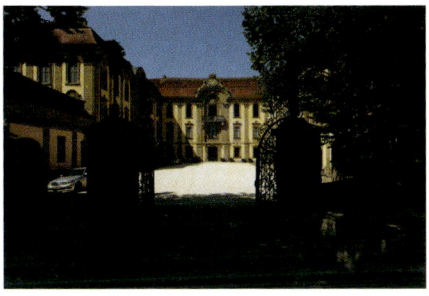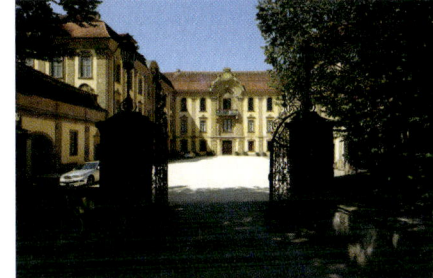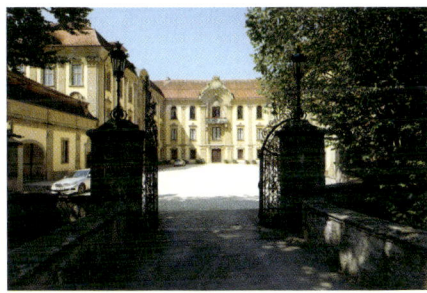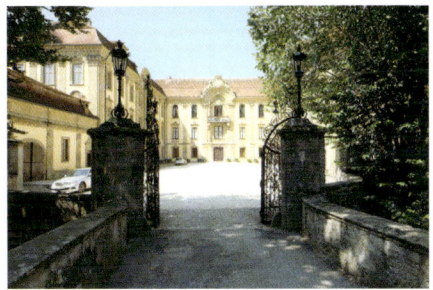

Fig. 112: In this X-H1 example, I took four images with the same exposure settings: aperture f/8 and shutter speed 1/400s. The only difference were four **equivalent ISO and DR settings** that neutralized each other at the RAW level: The upper-left image shows the JPEG that resulted from ISO L (100) a.k.a. DR50%, while the upper-right image shows ISO 200/DR100%. The lower-left JPEG is the ISO 400/DR200% version, and in the lower right, there's the image taken with ISO 800/DR400%.

The four JPEGs are clearly different with regards to shadow and midtone brightness, because they all have to match their respective indicated ISO settings. Obviously, a JPEG taken at ISO 800, f/8, 1/400s (lower right) must look brighter than one taken at ISO 100, f/8, 1/400s (upper left). However, the underlying RAW data is the same in all four instances.

This gives you additional options: For example, you can *manually* expose your scene to its important highlights at ISO 200/DR100% and then raise ISO one or two stops to 400 or 800, while at the same time changing the DR setting to DR200% or DR400%. *Increasing* RAW and JPEG ISO two stops from 200 to 800 and *decreasing* RAW ISO two stops by selecting DR400% leaves the RAW data unchanged: +2−2=0. The only thing that has become brighter is the live view and the JPEG from the camera.

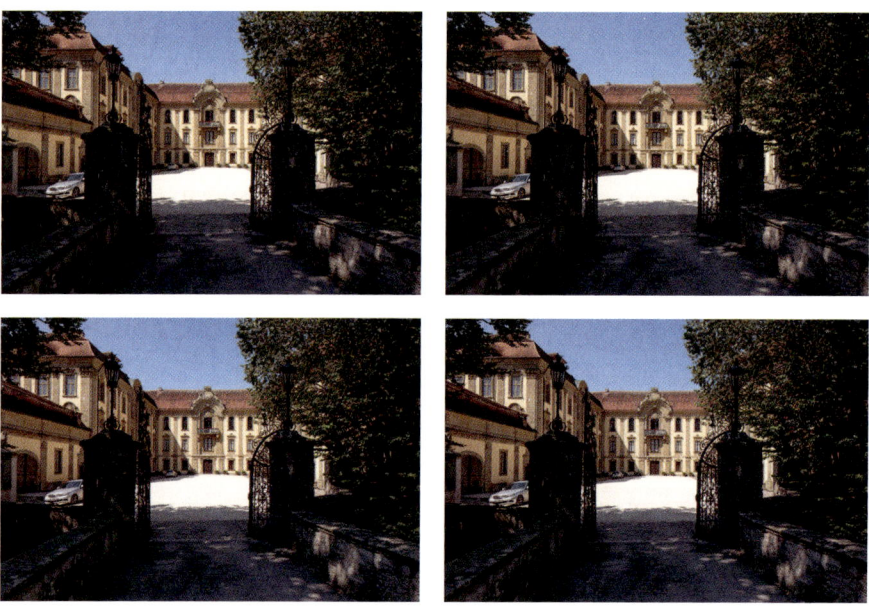

Fig. 113: This example shows the four shots from our previous illustration, all taken with the same exposure settings: aperture f/8 and shutter speed 1/400s. This time, however, I processed the RAW files of the four images in Lightroom Classic CC and applied the same development settings to all of them—with the exception of the exposure slider, which was adjusted to compensate Lightroom's import exposure pull or push that is automatically applied to the RAW data based on the indicated ISO/DR setting.

The Lightroom-processed results from the shots taken with ISO L (100)/DR50% (upper left, Lightroom exposure slider +1 EV), ISO 200/DR100% (upper right, exposure slider 0 EV), ISO 400/DR200% (lower left, exposure slider −1 EV) and ISO 800/DR400% (lower right, exposure slider −2 EV) look perfectly the same. This isn't at all surprising, because the RAW data *is* indeed the same.

This discovery can be of tremendous practical benefit if you intend to make the most of your camera's ISOless sensor and push its dynamic range capabilities to the limits.

The best way to use the DR function for shooting scenes with very high dynamic range is to expose in manual mode M. Here's how to proceed:

- Set manual mode M and make sure that the exposure preview for manual mode is enabled.

- Deploy "JPEG settings for RAW shooters" by selecting film simulation Eterna (or Pro Neg. Std), Highlight Tone −2, and Shadow Tone −2.

- Set DR100% and manually expose the high-contrast scene to protect important highlights. If available, use the RGB histogram with the live overexposure warning ("blinkies") and set an exposure that is just rich enough that some of the important highlights in your scene begin to blink. Remember that this is about protecting the *important* highlights. Feel free to overexpose parts of your scene that aren't worth saving, like the ball of the sun in a backlit daylight scene.

- Now that your exposure to the scene's important highlights is manually set and locked, the live view may look too dark to comfortably frame the scene. So, let's add the DR function to the mix: First, increase ISO as needed by either one or two full stops (1 or 2 EV). Then neutralize this ISO change by also increasing DR by the same amount (either DR200% or DR400%). For example, you can raise ISO from 200 to 800 (= a two-stop ISO *increase* applied to the RAW, the live view, and the JPEG) while also raising DR from DR100% to DR400% (= a two-stop ISO *decrease* that is applied only to the RAW file, but not to the live view and the JPEG).

- Having completed the previous step, the RAW remains as it was, but the live view looks either one or two stops brighter than before. That's great for demanding, high-contrast scenes, because not only can we perfectly expose to their important highlights, we can also still see what's going on in those really dark parts of the scene.

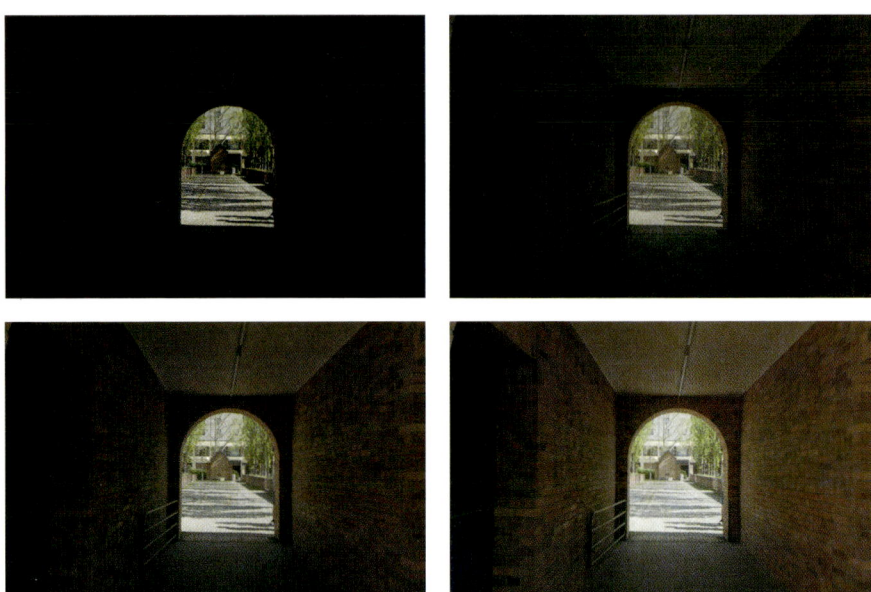

Fig. 114: Let's revisit this example that I shot with an X-H1 at f/11 and 1/125s. The upper-left image shows the scene as it looks with Provia factory settings and base ISO 200. The upper-right example shows the same image, but now with "JPEG settings for RAW shooters": film simulation Eterna, Shadow Tone –2, and Highlight Tone –2. While these are perfect settings for *exposing* a high-contrast scene toward its important highlights, the live view still looks a tad too dark to comfortably *frame* the scene. Luckily, we now know what to do: We can increase ISO/DR by one or two stops to ISO 400/DR200% (lower-left image) or ISO 800/DR400% (lower-right image) to get a brighter live view (and brighter JPEGs) without affecting the perfect RAW exposure that was determined and locked using the ISO 200/DR100% live view from the upper-left image.

Using manual mode **M** to expose high-contrast scenes is highly recommended because you can easily split the process into two stages: First, you determine and set the correct exposure to protect important highlights of the scene using DR100% and "JPEG settings for RAW shooters." When the exposure is set, you can concentrate on brightening the live view to a more useable level by increasing ISO one or two stops while also raising DR to either DR200% or DR400%.

With the brighter live view, you can easily compose the scene, focus it, and take the shot in the right moment. Not only can you now see what's going on in the shadows and midtones of the scene, the camera's auto white balance will also do a better job when it's not fishing in the dark. This is an accurate, reliable, and straightforward process, and I personally use it all the time with great success.

That said, a few older X models like the classic X100 or the X-A1 and X-M1 don't offer exposure preview in manual mode **M**, meaning you can't use the live view and live histogram in manual mode to determine the correct exposure to the important highlights of a scene. So, here's an alternative procedure to expose and shoot high-contrast scenes in either of the AE modes **P**, **A**, or **S**:

- Set the camera to one of the three AE modes. Select Auto-ISO and make sure that DR100% is set. I also recommend setting either matrix or average metering.

- Use "JPEG settings for RAW shooters" by selecting film simulation Eterna (or Pro Neg. Std), Highlight Tone –2, and Shadow Tone –2.

- Turn the exposure dial in the negative (–) direction to expose your high-contrast scene to protect important highlights. Use the live view and live histogram to determine the proper exposure that doesn't blow critical highlights.

- If the live view appears too dark after the exposure has been set to protect important highlights, you can brighten the image by turning the exposure dial (based on its current position) either three 1/3 EV clicks (= 1 EV) or six 1/3 EV clicks (= 2 EV) in the positive (+) direction, then immediately neutralize your change on the RAW-file level by selecting either DR200% or DR400%.

- If available, you can now use AE-Lock to lock the exposure setting, then take your shot(s).

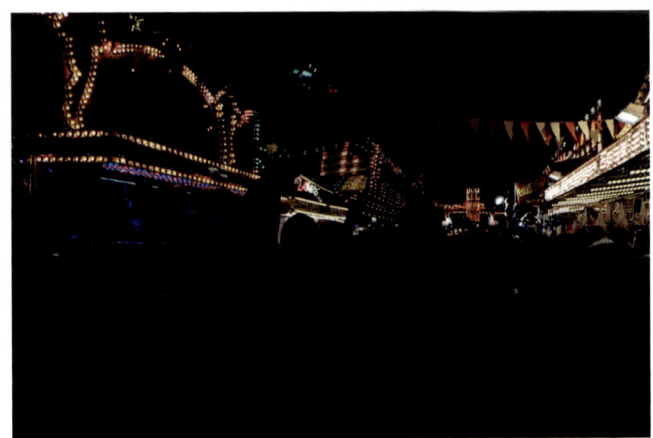

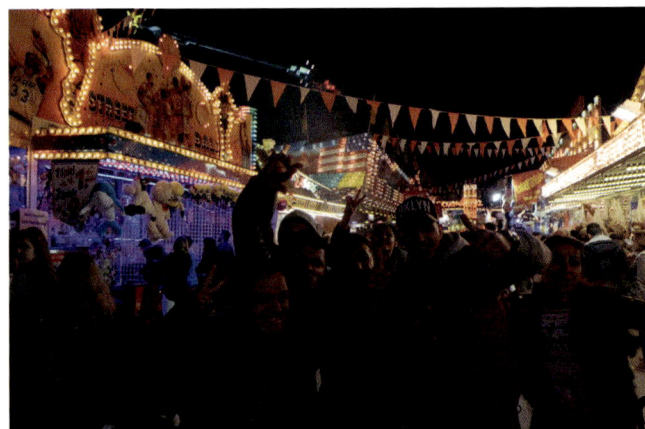

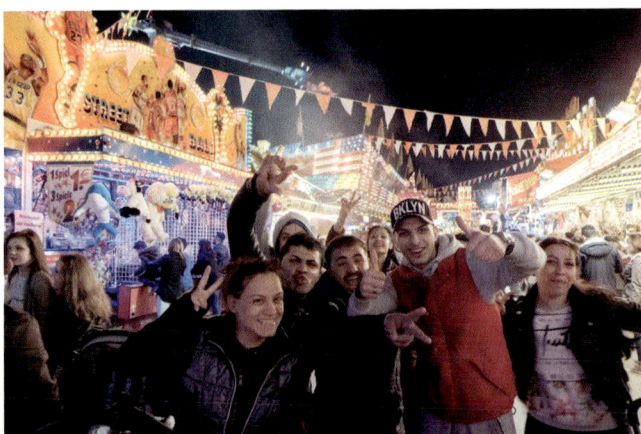

Fig. 115: This X-T1 example illustrates how using the DR function along with "JPEG settings for RAW shooters" can help you see in the darkness caused by scenes with extreme contrast. This exposure was limited by several factors: I couldn't go slower than 1/60s, because there were moving persons in the scene and I wanted to avoid motion blur. I also couldn't open up the aperture wider than f/4 due to depth-of-field requirements: the entire group of people was supposed to be in focus. Like all X series cameras, the X-T1 is ISOless, so I set the camera to base ISO 200 to preserve as many of the bright and colorful lights in the background as possible.

The image above shows the original exposure using Classic Chrome and otherwise standard JPEG settings at the camera's base ISO 200/DR100%, f/4, and 1/60s. While these settings perfectly protect the bright lights in the background, our main subjects are very much invisible. This makes framing the image and focusing on our actual subjects practically impossible. It's a catch-22: Even though the exposure is spot-on to record as much dynamic range as possible, we still can't practically use it.

The image in the middle shows how I resolved the problem by using "JPEG settings for RAW shooters" and the DR function. In the case of the X-T1, the settings were Pro Neg. Std, Shadow Tone −2, and Highlight Tone −2. However, these settings alone weren't sufficient, so I also increased ISO from 200 to 800, and DR from DR100% to DR400%, all while keeping f/4 and 1/60s. These settings didn't change the RAW data, but they allowed me to finally see what's going on. I could now compose the shot, and the camera's face detection was able to detect three faces and automatically focus on the face closest to the center of the frame.

The image below is the final result after processing the RAW file in Adobe Lightroom, again using the Classic Chrome film-simulation preset. I find the amount of dynamic range that can be extracted even from older sensors like the X-Trans CMOS II quite impressive.

As an alternative to raising ISO and DR in tandem (which brightens the live view without affecting the RAW exposure), you can also expose high-contrast scenes in manual mode **M** and then turn off the exposure preview after determining the correct exposure. Here's how it works:

■ Set manual mode **M**, DR100% and turn *on* exposure preview.

- Like before, expose toward the important highlights of your scene and set a suitable exposure (ISO, aperture, and shutter speed).

- If the live view appears too dark, turn *off* exposure preview in manual mode and take your shots. The easiest way to do this is by assigning the exposure preview function to an Fn button (most newer X cameras allow this). Personally, I have assigned the exposure preview toggle to the AE-L button of my X-T2, X-T3, and X-H1, because I'm mostly shooting in manual mode, where the classic AE-Lock function is not available.

Turning off exposure preview in manual mode forces the live view to behave like it was in one of the three auto-exposure (AE) modes **P**, **A**, or **S**: The live view image will automatically change its brightness toward a middle-gray exposure (depending on the scene and the selected exposure metering method), but without affecting the actual exposure of the shot.

Using this rather simple procedure may sound quite appealing, but it has one major drawback: The JPEGs of your shots are still recorded rather dark (exposed to the highlights), making it hard or impossible to immediately check critical focus and other details. You'd first have to push each image in the built-in or an external RAW converter. If you take a large number of images with this method, it can become quite a chore to browse through all your dark images and select the keepers.

TIP 70	Using the DR function for high-key and portrait photography

High-key photography [61] delivers images with tones that mostly occupy the right half of the histogram. High-key images can be achieved by lighting a scene brightly and uniformly with little difference in contrast, and then overexposing the scene by one or two stops. This results in images with a bright, clean, and joyful look. High-key is often used for product shots, portraits, and advertising.

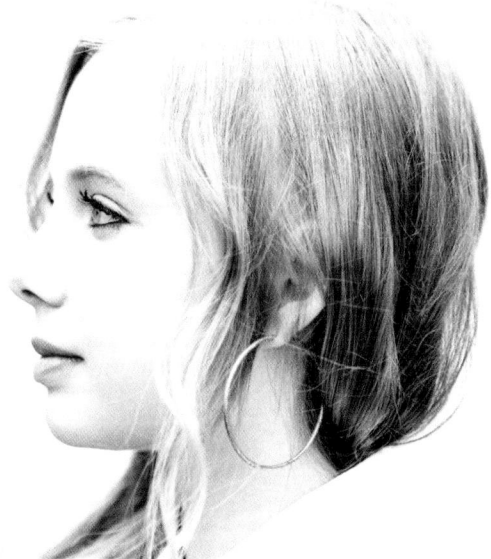

Fig. 116: I took this **high-key sample** under an overcast sky with soft, uniform natural lighting. I placed the model in front of a bright wall. Thanks to the resulting low contrast, the scene could be shot with a bright exposure at ISO 200 (DR100%) without blowing critical highlights.

Normally, high-key photographs require suitable low-contrast lighting. If the contrast is too big, a bright exposure of the darker tones would lead to blown highlights.

To be suitable for high-key, most of your scene should fit into the right half of the histogram. If that's not the case, there are two options: you can either reduce the contrast of the scene by applying fill light (like installing a flash or utilizing a lighting setup), or you can apply appropriate tone-mapping (pushing the shadows and midtones while protecting the highlights) during RAW conversion.

Thanks to Fuji's DR function, the second option is also available in-camera. You can use it to directly generate JPEGs with a high-key look. Here's how:

■ Set the camera to manual exposure mode **M** and turn off Auto-ISO, so aperture, shutter speed, and ISO can be set manually. Set the dynamic range to DR100% and make sure exposure preview in manual mode is turned on.

■ Expose the scene as usual to protect critical highlights that you do not want to blow. The live view and live histogram are your friends. Set aperture, shutter speed, and ISO accordingly. Take a test shot to be sure that the scene is exposed as brightly as possible without any blown critical highlights.

■ Now double your ISO setting (for example, from ISO 200 to ISO 400) and change the dynamic range setting from DR100% to DR200%. Don't change your aperture and shutter speed, though!

■ In the live view and live histogram, your scene will be looking brighter. Take another shot with these new settings and inspect the resulting high-key JPEG in your camera's playback mode.

As far as the RAW data is concerned, it makes no difference whether you shoot the same scene with ISO 200, DR100%, f/5.6, and 1/1000s, or with ISO 400, DR200%, f/5.6, and 1/1000s. Even ISO 800, DR400%, f/5.6, and 1/1000s would result in the same RAW data all over again. However, you will see a huge difference in the corresponding straight-out-of-camera JPEGs: shadows and midtones will appear increasingly bright (high-key), but the brightest highlights will be protected: this is your camera's built-in tone-mapping at work.

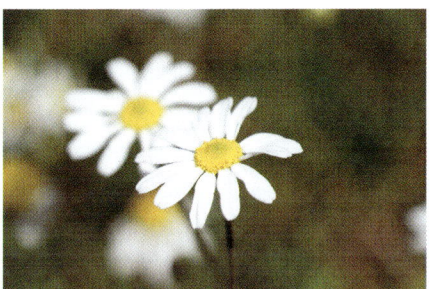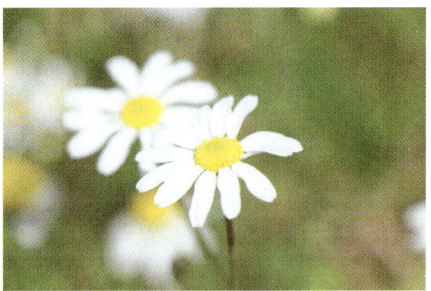

Fig. 117: Turning the DR function into a virtual high-key studio: The example on the left illustrates a regular exposure of a flower at ISO 200, DR100%, f/5.6, and 1/1000s. The exposure was designed to protect the structure of the white petals. The example on the right is the same scene shot at ISO 400, DR200%, f/5.6, and 1/1000s. This means that while the RAW data remains the same, only the JPEG from the ISO 400/DR200% version delivers the desired high-key look while leaving the structure of the petals intact. Doubling ISO and DR settings in tandem (leaving all other exposure parameters untouched) moves the histogram of the JPEG to the right, but without blowing bright highlights. Instead of cutting them off, the tonality of the bright highlights is compressed. You can fine-tune such results with the camera's built-in RAW converter, for example, by reducing the highlight contrast (HIGHLIGHT TONE setting). Additionally, you can revert a high-key shot that was taken (for example) at ISO 400/DR200% into a regular ISO 200/DR100% JPEG by reprocessing the RAW image in the built-in RAW converter using PULL −1 EV and DR100% settings.

Tone-mapping and tonality compression can also be used to improve portraits. It can reduce contrast and harsh shadows on faces that are illuminated by a single light source, such as the sun. With our high-key technique, dark eyes and shadows under the nose can be lifted without blowing the bright parts of the skin. At the same time, the tone-mapping and highlight tone compression makes skin blemishes almost disappear.

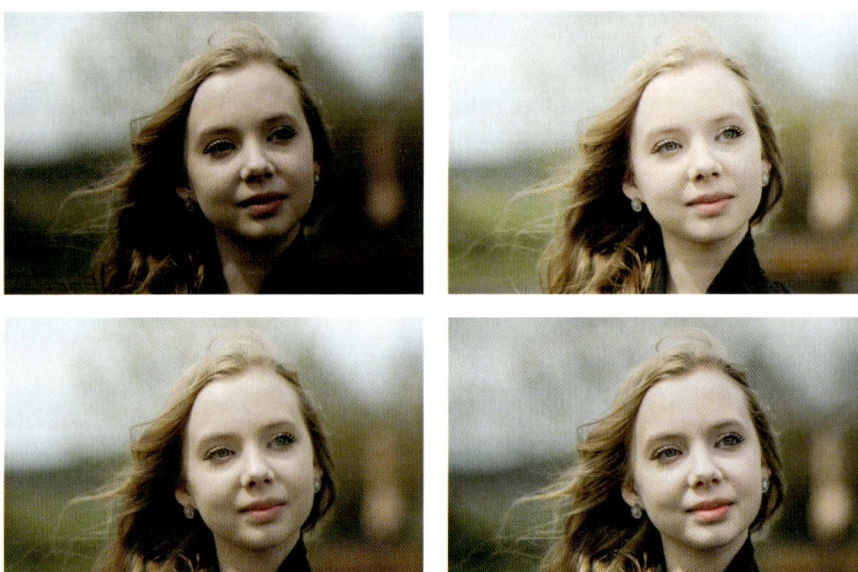

Fig. 118: **Using virtual high-key in a portrait:** This example illustrates a difficult lighting situation with strong contrast and harsh shadows on the face.

The upper-left sample shows a JPEG that was created by exposing for the highlights with the CLASSIC CHROME film simulation and ISO 200. This resulted in a rather dark face with strong contrast and shadows.

The upper-right image shows the same shot two ISO stops brighter, and with extended highlight dynamic range to protect the highlights. This means using ISO 800 and DR400% while maintaining the exposure (aperture and shutter speed) of the upper-left sample. Additionally, I set HIGHLIGHT TONE to −2 to pull back the brightest (skin) tones. As you can see, the eyes are now much brighter and the harsh contrasts are gone.

Too much? Don't worry! Using the camera's built-in RAW converter, you can always create more realistic versions of your high-key shots. In this case (lower-left image), I used PULL −1 (effectively pulling the shot from ISO 800 down to ISO 400) along with DR200% (to compensate for the pull), SHADOW TONE −2 (for more shadow detail), and HIGHLIGHT TONE −1 (to bring back the brightest skin tones).

Alternatively, you can also process the RAW file in any external RAW converter. In the case of the lower-right example, I used Adobe Lightroom.

Another useful application of the DR function is dealing with bright spots in an otherwise regular scene. With a normal exposure, these highlights can easily blow, which is particularly undesirable if they affect a human face.

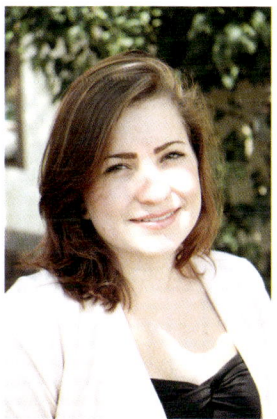 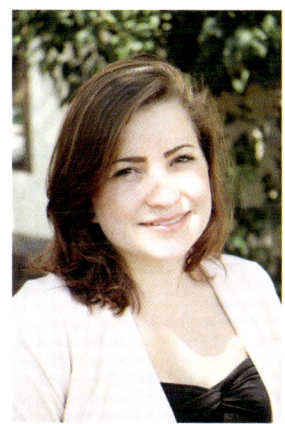 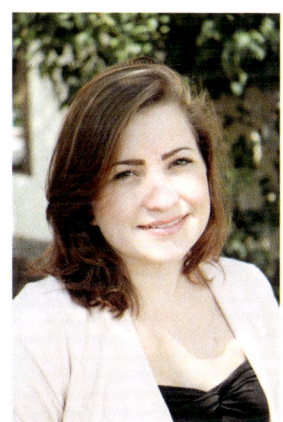

Fig. 119: This **skin-repair** example was taken in the shadow of a tree, with a few bright sunbeams making their way through the foliage onto our model's face. For the human eye, these bright spots look perfectly harmless. However, highlights like these can be a recipe for disaster for any digital camera if you decide to "correctly" expose the shot toward the darker parts of the face, like I did here.

The example on the left displays the JPEG with DR100%. While the shadow-parts of the skin are correctly exposed, the bright spots are clearly blown: there's no texture.

The image in the middle is the DR200% version, which brings the healing power of one extra stop of highlight dynamic range to the face.

The example on the right was processed with DR400%, which corresponds to two stops of additional highlight dynamic range. The previously "damaged" skin now looks perfectly okay.

DR versus DR-P	TIP 71

In addition to the DR function with its DR-Auto, DR100%, DR200%, and DR400% options, recent X series models like the X-H1 and X-T3 feature a function called DR-P, which stands for Dynamic Range Priority.

If you activate DR-P in the IMAGE QUALITY SETTING menu, it replaces the classic DR function, so you can't use both functions together. It's either the one or the other. Setting DR-P to anything but OFF automatically overrides and cancels your DR settings.

The AUTO, WEAK, and STRONG options of DR-P correspond to the DR-Auto, DR200%, and DR400% settings of the DR function, while OFF relays control back to whatever regular DR settings you have selected. This also means that DR-P WEAK and DR-P STRONG have the same minimum ISO requirements as DR200% and DR400%.

So, what exactly is the difference between DR-P and DR? It's rather mundane: DR-P *combines* regular DR settings with different contrast settings into a package that can't be untied later. For example, DR-P WEAK combines DR200% with HIGHLIGHT TONE −1 and SHADOW TONE −1. Correspondingly, DR-P STRONG results in a combination of DR400%, HIGHLIGHT TONE −2, and SHADOW TONE −2.

If this sounds like a neat shortcut to you, you might want to reconsider. In fact, I do not recommend using DR-P at all, because it is blocking you from changing Highlight Tone and Shadow Tone settings independently from DR settings in the camera's built-in RAW converter.

For example, if you take a picture with DR-P STRONG and later find that HIGHLIGHT TONE −2 and SHADOW TONE −2 look too shallow for your taste, you can't use the built-in RAW converter to create a new JPEG with more contrast by adjusting Shadow Tone and Highlight Tone. You would have to live with your mistake for good.

A much better alternative is to stay in control: Set DR-P to OFF and instead apply DR, Highlight Tone, and Shadow Tone settings independently from one another. By doing so, you can always revisit your RAW files later and create JPEGs with different contrast settings in your camera or with X RAW STUDIO.

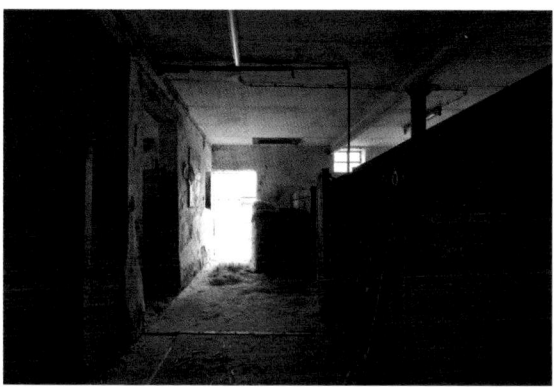

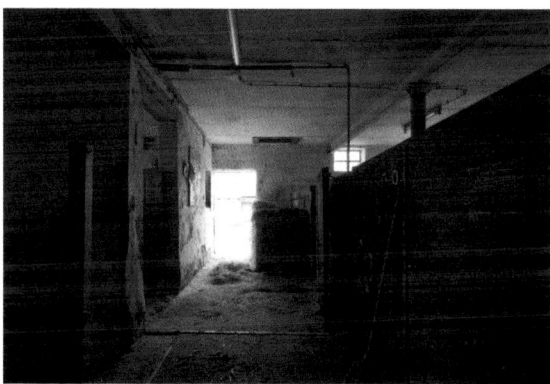

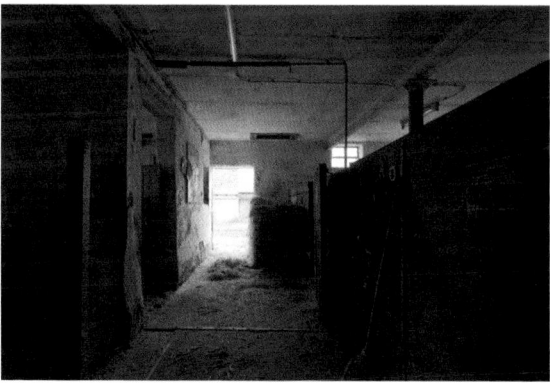

Fig. 120: This **Dynamic Range Priority** comparison shows JPEGs of the same high-contrast scene with DR-P OFF/DR100% (top), DR-P WEAK (center), and DR-P STRONG (bottom) settings. I set my X-H1 to ETERNA and fixed exposure settings of f/8, 1/8s and ISO 800.

| TIP 72 | Dual Conversion Gain and how to use it |

We already know that all cameras featuring the X-Trans CMOS III sensor use a base ISO of 200. Those cameras are the X-Pro2, X-H1, X-T2, X-T20, X-E3, and X100F. However, there's more: these cameras offer what's called "dual conversion gain"—a second (higher) base ISO level. In our case, this level is automatically activated when you set ISO 800 (or higher) at DR100%.

Dual conversion gain (DCG) reconfigures the sensor for low-light use: read noise is further reduced, which means that you can extract additional dynamic range in situations with very little light.

Normally, you wouldn't care about dual conversion gain, because the camera is performing everything automatically. There is no "on/off" switch or menu: simply set a minimum of ISO 800/DR100% (or ISO 1600/DR200%; or ISO 3200/DR400%) and dual conversion gain will be active.

You can make use of this second DCG ISO level in the same way that you use base ISO 200 to extract as much dynamic range from high-contrast scenes as possible. However, in this case, we are talking about situations with very little light; scenes that one would usually expose with really high ISO settings such as 6400, 12800, or even 25600.

Instead of setting these high ISO values, you can just as well set the camera to ISO 800/DR100% (or to equivalent ISO-level settings of ISO 1600/DR200% or ISO 3200/DR400%) and shoot away, while protecting as many highlights as possible.

Let me give you a practical example: During our Fuji X Secrets Bootcamp workshop in March 2018, we organized an evening get-together in an ancient wine cellar that was only illuminated by a few candles. I shot several candid portraits of the delegates with my X-H1 and an XF16–55mmF2.8 R LM WR lens in manual mode **M** with fixed settings of

ISO 800, f/2.8 (wide-open), and 1/20s (my slowest usable shutter speed for handheld shooting of living subjects). In order to see the image I was composing, I turned *off* the exposure preview in manual mode.

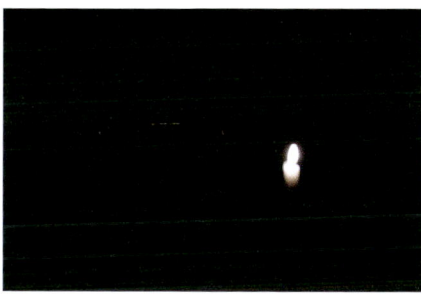 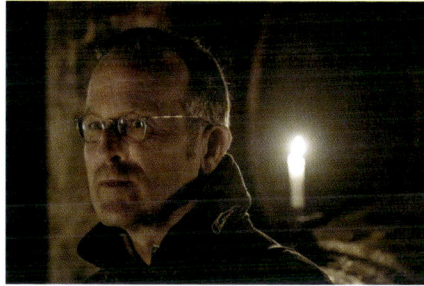

Fig. 121: This **dual conversion gain** example shows a low-light shot as it was taken with my X-H1 at 55mm focal length, f/2.8, 1/20s, and ISO 800/DR100% (the camera's additional "dual gain conversion" base ISO level). The unprocessed result on the left looks really, really dark. The only part that is clearly visible is one of the few candles that were lighting the scene.

On the right, you can see the same image after processing the RAW file in Lightroom Classic CC. Pushing the face of the person up from ISO 800 resulted in brightness equivalents of at least ISO 12800, while the already-bright parts of the candle remained at ISO 800 to protect as much of their texture and tones as possible. It's the usual tone-mapping procedure, and it gives you a glimpse of the dynamic range reserves that are available in Fuji's X cameras. You just have to be bold enough to unleash them.

In cameras with X-Trans CMOS III, dual conversion gain results in a noise advantage of approximately 1/3 EV. This doesn't sound like much (and it really isn't in normal situations), but it can be essential in situations where you have to push shadows up 4 or 5 stops during RAW processing (or need to take images at very high ISO levels like 12800 and above).

Important: Even though the X-T3 uses a new X-Trans CMOS 4 sensor with base ISO 160, its additional dual conversion gain ISO level is still ISO 800. This means that as far as DCG is concerned, the X-T3 behaves just like its older siblings.

| TIP 73 | Creating HDR images |

A popular method of capturing high-contrast scenes is HDR photography. HDR [62] means High Dynamic Range: multiple images of the scene are taken at different exposure levels and then merged into a single image with extended dynamic range. The merging process can be facilitated with specialized software, such as Photomatix Pro by HDRsoft.

Typically, HDR requires a minimum of two different exposures of a scene, but some photographers don't stop there. They take five, seven, or even nine different expo-sures, each separated from the other by (usually) one stop or 1 EV (exposure value).

Here's a procedure that you can use to quickly generate nine different exposures of a scene:

■ Put the camera on a tripod or a similar device.

■ Connect a remote shutter release or set the self-timer to 2 seconds to avoid camera shake.

■ Set the camera to aperture priority A.

■ Choose a low ISO setting (such as base ISO 200). Don't use extended ISO L, though!

■ Deactivate any DR expansion by setting the dynamic range to DR100%.

■ Select a suitable aperture for your shot and scene and use manual focus. This ensures that all nine images will be focused the same. If you like, you can also use adapted manual focus lenses.

■ Set AE BKT (auto exposure bracketing) to three shots with a variation of ±1 EV

■ Select AVERAGE exposure metering.

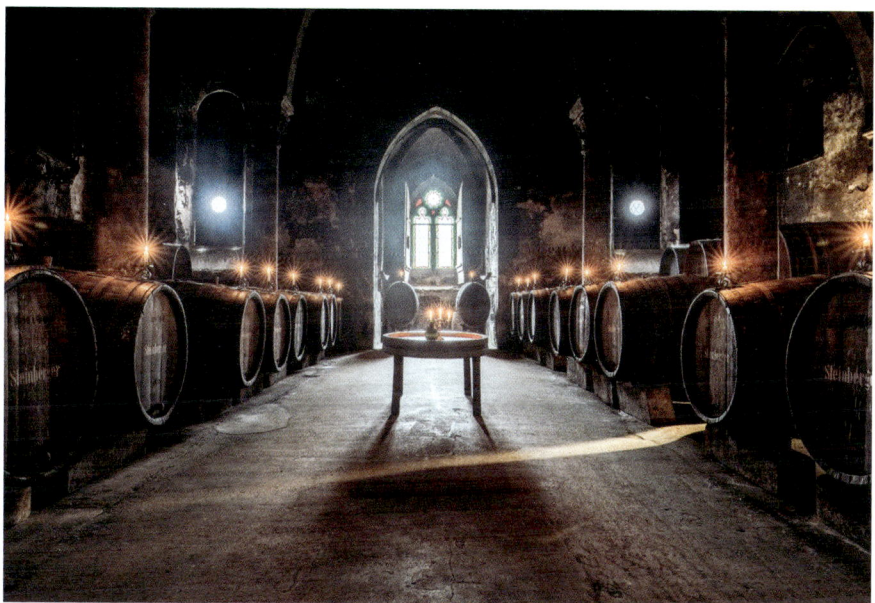

Fig. 122: This rather extreme **HDR image** consists of seven RAW shots , each taken with an exposure difference of 2 EV and merged in Adobe Lightroom.

Having prepared the camera for HDR, you can now follow these steps to capture the actual images:

- Set the exposure compensation dial to neutral (0) and press the shutter release. Make sure to either use a remote shutter release or the self-timer. The camera will now record the first three shots of the scene, with exposure levels of 0 EV, –1 EV, and +1 EV.

- Set the exposure compensation dial to –3 EV and press the shutter release. The camera is now recording three more images that deviate –4 EV, –3 EV, and –2 EV from the original exposure.

- Finally, set the exposure compensation dial to +3 EV. After releasing the shutter, you'll get three more exposures, this time with +2 EV, +3 EV, and +4 EV.

This procedure results in nine different exposures that you can merge using the HDR software of your choice. This will result in an image with an additional dynamic range of ±4 EV.

TIP 74	HDR: the handheld way

Thanks to the ISOless sensor in all X series cameras, you can effectively take handheld HDR shots by combining two vastly differently exposed RAW files into one HDR-DNG file in Adobe Lightroom or Adobe Camera RAW.

Let's start with preparing the camera for this endeavor:

■ Set the camera to aperture priority **A**.

■ Select a low ISO setting, such as ISO 200. Don't set extended ISO L.

■ Make sure the dynamic range is set to DR100%.

■ Pre-select a suitable aperture.

■ Set AE BKT to three shots with a variation of ±2 EV to activate the camera's auto exposure bracketing.

■ Select AVERAGE exposure metering.

■ Use "JPEG settings for RAW shooters": film simulation Eterna or Pro Neg. Std, Shadow Tone –2, and Highlight Tone –2.

Now let's take our HDR shots:

■ Expose to the highlights! Using the live view and live histogram, frame your scene, and turn the exposure compensation dial until critical highlights aren't blown.

■ Now correct the exposure by +2 EV using the exposure compensation dial (based on its current position): simply turn it six clicks in the plus direction. This will shift your locked exposure up by two stops. Don't recompose the scene.

- Focus and press the shutter button to take the shot. Hold the camera very steady while it takes a quick burst of three consecutive AE bracketing shots (each with a different exposure).

- Import the RAW files of the three bracketing shots into Adobe Lightroom or Adobe Camera RAW, where you can merge them into a single HDR-DNG file using the HDR function. You can process the HDR-DNG file in Lightroom like any normal RAW file.

By combining three shots with an exposure difference of 2 EV between each other, we dramatically enhance the overall dynamic range of the image. Since the shots were taken in a quick burst with maximum continuous drive speed, there's also little or no motion blur in the resulting DNG composite. This trick can even work for (slowly) moving subjects, especially since Lightroom's HDR merge tool includes automatic de-ghosting.

The darkest of the three shots is perfectly exposed to the highlights, while the other two bring 2 EV and 4 EV less shot noise to the table. Since our ISOless sensor provides very little sensor read noise, we can easily push the brightest of the three RAWs up another 3 EV without sacrificing too much image quality. This adds up to a whopping 7 EV of *additional* dynamic range, which should be enough to overcome almost every dynamic range challenge you may encounter in your photographic life. Even better, you can use this process for handheld shots—just make sure that the shutter speed of the brightest shot is still fast enough to prevent blurriness caused by camera shake.

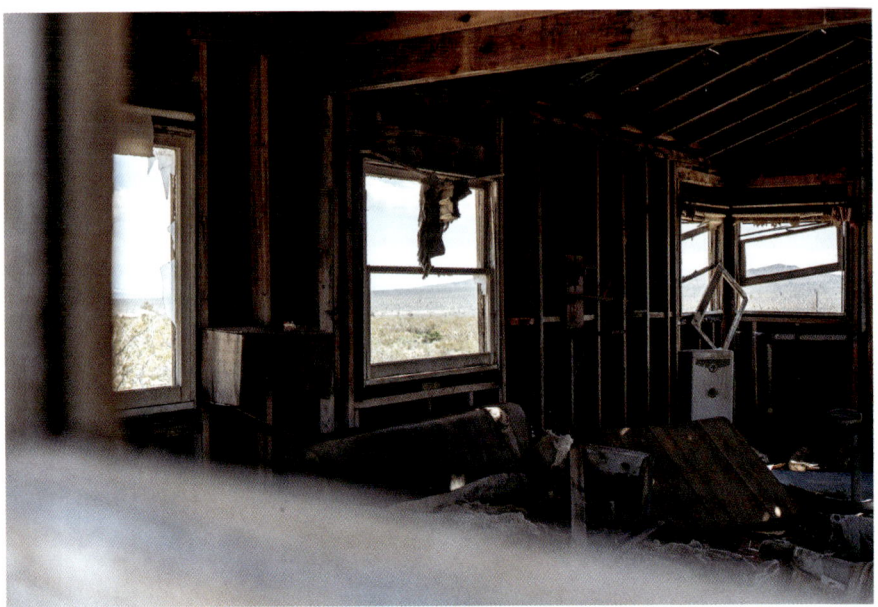

Fig. 123: This **handheld HDR** consists of the original "exposed-to-the-highlights" image, plus two additional shots that were exposed 2 EV and 4 EV brighter. Using Lightroom to merge the RAW files into a single HDR-DNG file, the result looks clean and noiseless in the shadows, with plenty of fine texture and no tonal gaps.

<table>
<tr><td>TIP 75</td><td>Electronic shutter (ES), electronic first curtain shutter (EFCS) and flicker reduction</td></tr>
</table>

Most X series cameras feature an electronic shutter (ES). It offers three advantages: it is completely silent, it eliminates vibrations from shutter shock, and it allows shutter speeds as fast as 1/32000s. That's great in situations where you want to be particularly stealthy, or when you want to use fast lenses (like the XF56mmF1.2 R) with a wide-open aperture in bright light and spare yourself the hassle of attaching an ND filter.

You can set which shutter type the camera is supposed to use in SHOOTIG MENU > (SHOOTING SETTING >) SHUTTER TYPE. There are at least three available options:

- **MS:** The camera is only using the mechanical shutter. This is the default setting and also my recommended standard setting.

- **ES:** This setting switches the camera to the electronic shutter with shutter speeds up to 1/32000s. Extended ISO settings aren't available in ES mode, and you cannot fire a flash when the ES is in use.

- **MS+ES:** In this mode, the camera combines both shutter types. It will automatically use the ES for shutter speeds faster than the maximum mechanical shutter speed. Flash photography is possible, but only within the envelope of the mechanical shutter. ISO may still be limited to the regular non-extended range.

To access shutter speeds beyond the camera's mechanical limit, you can set the shutter-speed dial to **T** and then browse through all available shutter speeds with the command dial in 1/3 EV steps.

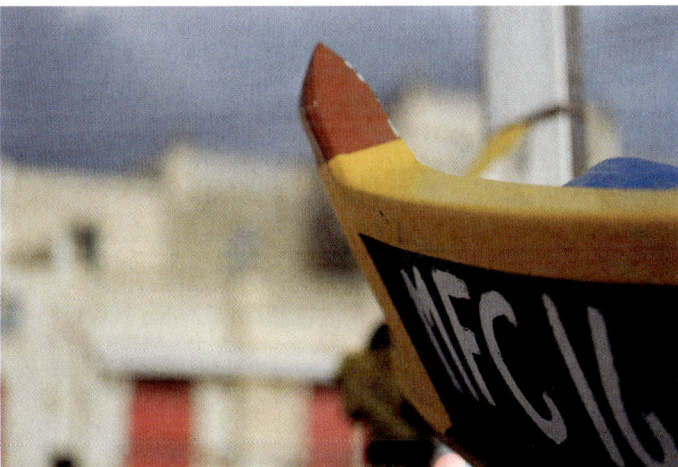

Fig. 124: The **electronic shutter** is a practical option for shots taken with fast lenses in bright light, when the maximum mechanical shutter speed simply isn't fast enough to avoid overexposure.

Please note that even at 1/32000s, the electronic shutter needs some time to capture all image contents. In most X camera models with ES, it takes the electronic shutter 1/20s to record all 24 megapixels of the sensor. This effect, known as Rolling Shutter [63], can lead to weird distortions when you are taking pictures of fast-moving subjects.

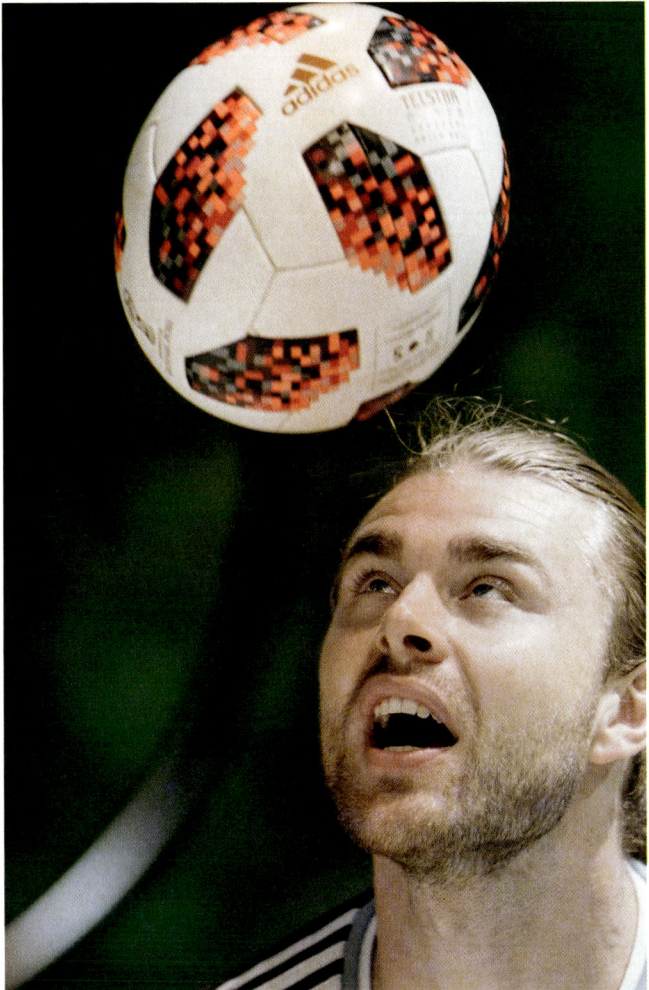

Fig. 125: The **distortion effect** of electronic rolling shutters becomes quite visible in scenes with fast-moving subjects like this football.

In addition, image quality will deteriorate when the ES is used in concert with pulsing or flickering artificial light sources. The long readout time and the rolling shutter are also responsible for the restrictions regarding flash photography.

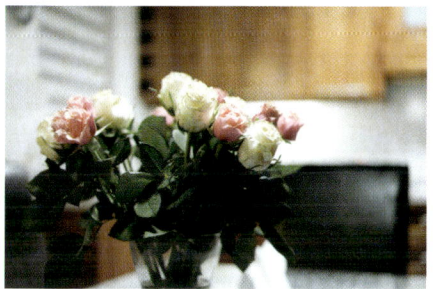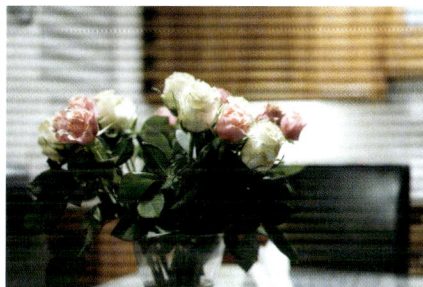

Fig. 126: **Pulsing light sources,** such as energy-saving lamps and LED lights, go on and off with the same frequency as the electric grid (50 Hz or 60 Hz). While the mechanical shutter can deal with this phenomenon, the electronic rolling shutter cannot. This example shows the same artificially lit scene taken with the mechanical shutter (left) and the electronic shutter (right) of my GFX 50S. The interference of the pulsing light with the rather slow line-by-line sensor readout of the large GFX sensor is hard to ignore.

With the GFX, Fujifilm introduced the option of an **electronic first curtain shutter (EFCS),** which is also available in the X-H1 and X-T3. The EFCS combines some advantages of the ES with some benefits of the MS: It reduces vibration and eliminates shutter shock by replacing the mechanical first shutter curtain with an electronic version. However, the second shutter curtain remains mechanical, thus avoiding issues caused by electronic rolling shutter. The EFCS also reduces the blackout period in the EVF and emits a softer mechanical shutter noise.

With very fast shutter speeds, using the EFCS can potentially be detrimental to image quality (especially the bokeh). That's why cameras with EFCS offer an EFCS+MS setting that automatically switches back to the MS when the shutter speed exceeds a certain threshold (1/2000s with

APS-C cameras and 1/640s in the GFX). If you choose to use the EFCS, I recommend the EFCS+MS option.

You may wonder: Is it safe to use the mechanical shutter or electronic first curtain shutter in situations with pulsing artificial light? The answer is yes *and* no, because pulsing light sources have the nasty habit of continuously going on and off, so the scene (your subject) is illuminated with varying amounts of light that fluctuate 50 or 60 times per second along with the phase frequency of the electric grid. Even in manual exposure mode **M**, shooting the same scene multiple times with exactly the same exposure settings can result in differently exposed images, depending on your shutter speed and how lucky you were to randomly catch a brighter or a darker portion of the AC phase.

While this flicker phenomenon is invisible to the human eye, your camera will experience it as soon as you select faster shutter speeds. In such cases, the camera can only record a random portion of the light's pulsating on/off cycle.

This is where **flicker reduction** comes into play. If you own one of the higher-end X camera models (such as the X-Pro2, X-T2, X-H1, X-T3, or GFX), you can find it under SHOOTING MENU > SHOOTING SETTING > FLICKER REDUCTION > ON. Additional X models may eventually obtain this function via firmware updates.

When you take a shot, flicker reduction [64] times your camera's exposure to coincide with cyclic peaks of the AC current phase. In other words, shots are delayed until the pulsating light happens to illuminate the scene with maximum brightness. Your series of exposures will look bright and uniform.

In a world of pulsing energy-saving light sources, flicker reduction is an essential feature. However, make sure to only use it in situations that actually require its magic. In natural daylight (or artificial light that doesn't pulse), flicker reduction is not only useless, it will also slow down your camera.

2.4 FOCUSING WITH YOUR X SERIES CAMERA

Most X series cameras use a hybrid autofocus system that combines CDAF and PDAF. CDAF, PDAF, hybrid AF? Let's clear it up:

- **CDAF** means **C**ontrast **D**etection **A**uto**F**ocus and is a standard in mirrorless cameras. CDAF is available throughout the entire sensor area. It works quite precisely but is not particularly fast.

- **PDAF** means **P**hase **D**etection **A**uto**F**ocus and is the standard AF in DSLRs. Since your X camera is mirrorless, its PDAF works directly on the sensor. With the exception of the X-T3, PDAF is only available throughout a central portion of the image frame. PDAF is fast and particularly good at tracking moving subjects. It can predict where a moving object will be a split second from now, a feature that can be quite useful when you shoot action in burst mode.

- **Hybrid AF** means that the camera automatically chooses and combines available AF methods (CDAF or PDAF) for the current subject and the current light conditions.

Note: Early X series compacts, the classic X100, X-Pro1, X-E1, X-M1, X-A1, X-A2, X-A3, GFX 50S, and GFX 50R are CDAF-only cameras that don't offer PDAF and hybrid autofocus. On the other hand, the new X-Trans CMOS 4 sensor in the X-T3 is Fuji's first sensor to offer PDAF and hybrid AF throughout the entire image area.

CDAF and PDAF: what's the difference?

Both AF methods offer distinct qualities that can be useful during your daily shooting:

■ CDAF focuses on surfaces and works best with areas that offer a lot of contrast. A solid white or black wall doesn't work well with CDAF, but a checkered wall works great. It's the same with clothes: unicolor may be tough, but patterned clothes work wonderfully. CDAF operates with a trial-and-error approach: it keeps adjusting the focus until it finds the distance setting with the utmost contrast. CDAF doesn't directly go to the optimal focus setting. This result is heightened autofocus motor activity and visible focus hunting while the AF iterates back and forth until it finds the optimal focus position.

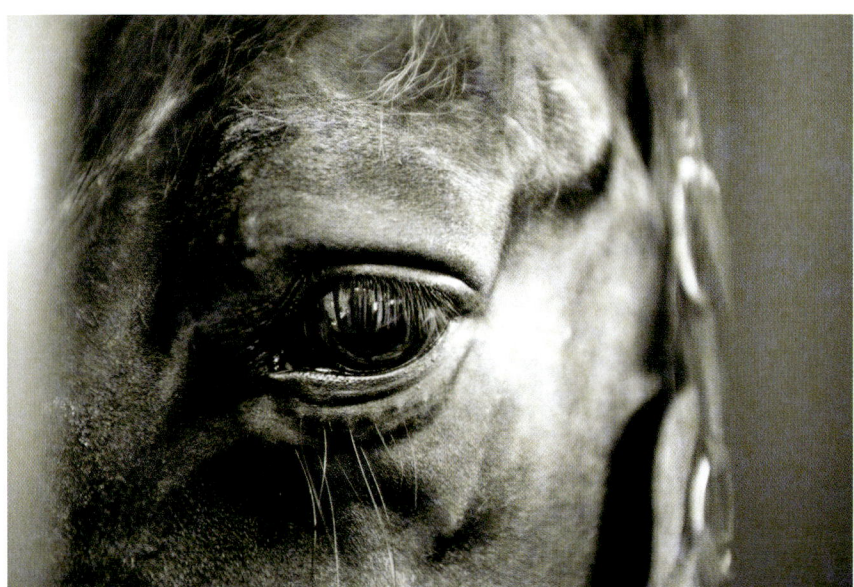

Fig. 127: The original X100 came to market in 2011. It was a CDAF-only camera with a rather slow **contrast detection autofocus** system. However, despite some people claiming otherwise, accurate autofocus was never an issue with this classic camera—as long as the subject didn't move too fast.

- PDAF loves focusing on edges, especially vertical edges (or horizontal ones if you hold the camera upright). Unlike CDAF, PDAF can directly determine the distance to an object, so there's no need for focus hunting. That's why PDAF is considerably faster.

- Both methods depend on sufficient light to work with maximum efficiency. The brighter a scene is and the more contrast it has, the better the AF will work. Bright lenses with large maximum aperture openings are beneficial because they allow the AF to work with more light and less depth of field, which helps increase the precision of the autofocus. It's worth noting that most lenses are less bright near their edges than they are at the center (this effect is called vignetting), so in poor light, the autofocus may work less efficiently with focus frames that are located far off center.

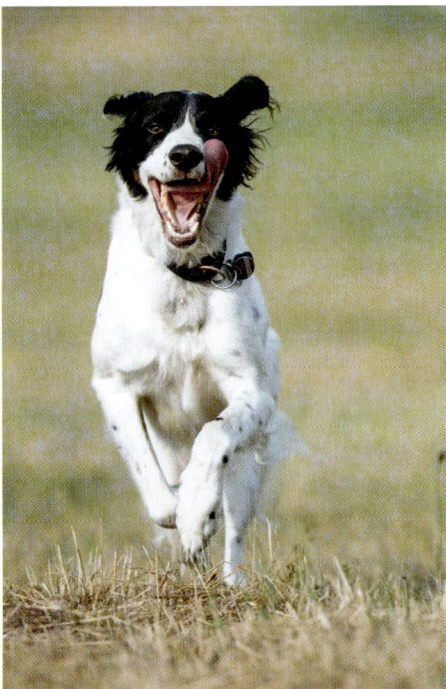

Fig. 128: Tracking fast-moving subjects like this running dog is a job for the **phase detection autofocus** (PDAF).

TIP 77 | AF-S or AF-C?

Your X camera features two basic AF modes:

■ **AF-S (AF Single) is meant for stationary subjects**. Once you half-press the shutter button, the camera will focus on the object covered by the active AF frame and lock the distance (as long as you keep the shutter button half-depressed). You can either fully press the shutter button to take the shot, or you can take your finger off the shutter release and try again.

■ **AF-C (AF Continuous) is meant for moving subjects,** especially those that move toward or away from the camera. When you half-press the shutter button, the camera starts focusing on the object covered by the active AF frame and continuously adjusts the distance to the moving object while you keep the shutter button half-depressed. In the live view of older or less advanced entry-level models, this may look like the camera is continuously hunting, while the green AF confirmation dot in the bottom-left corner of the screen keeps going on and off. Just make sure that the active AF frame or AF zone always covers the part of the image that is supposed to be in focus.

Every camera experiences a small delay between pressing the shutter and recording the image. This shutter lag can be considered by the predictive PDAF: the camera isn't focusing on the object's current position, but on the position the object is *predicted* to be when the image is captured. Predictive autofocus is also possible with CDAF, though to a lesser degree of performance.

While AF-C focuses using the set working aperture, AF-S can open the aperture beyond working aperture to improve the AF performance in poor light. This also improves the focusing accuracy due to the reduced depth of field caused by the wide-open aperture.

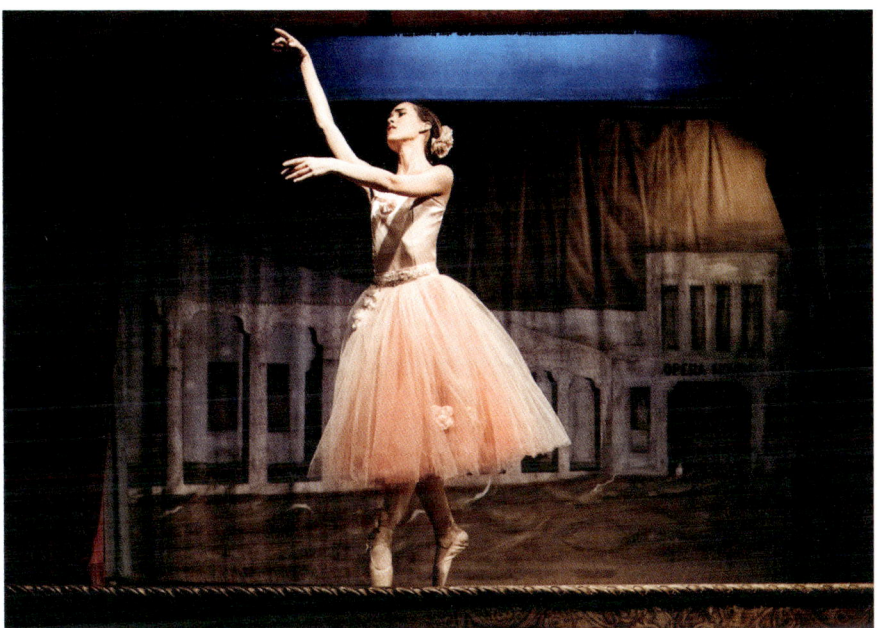

Fig. 129: When shooting with **AF-C in poor light**, it helps to keep the aperture wide open.

Single Point AF vs. Zone AF vs. Wide/Tracking AF	TIP 78

SHOOTING MENU > AF/MF SETTING > AF MODE lets you choose between SINGLE POINT, ZONE, or WIDE/TRACKING autofocus. Several recent X camera models also offer an ALL option, which lets you seamlessly select one of the three AF modes simply by changing the size of the focus frame or zone.

If your X camera doesn't offer Zone AF or Wide/Tracking AF modes, chances are it's an older model. Don't worry! You can still benefit from most tips in this chapter as long as they apply to Single Point AF.

■ **Single Point AF** mode is my recommended AF setting for most applications. In this mode, you can manually select one of many available focus frames (up to 425 in the X-T3 and GFX). Try to avoid old habits like using only the central frame in concert with the focus and recompose [65] technique. It's better to compose the shot and *then* select a suitable AF frame that covers the part of the image that you want to be in perfect focus. This helps you avoid focus errors that invariably occur when you pan the focus plane. Such focus errors may be irrelevant with long focal lengths and small aperture openings (larger depth of field), but they can be quite unpleasant with wide-angle lenses, a wide aperture opening (small DOF), and in situations with a short distance between the camera and the subject. Single Point AF can be used in concert with both AF-S and AF-C.

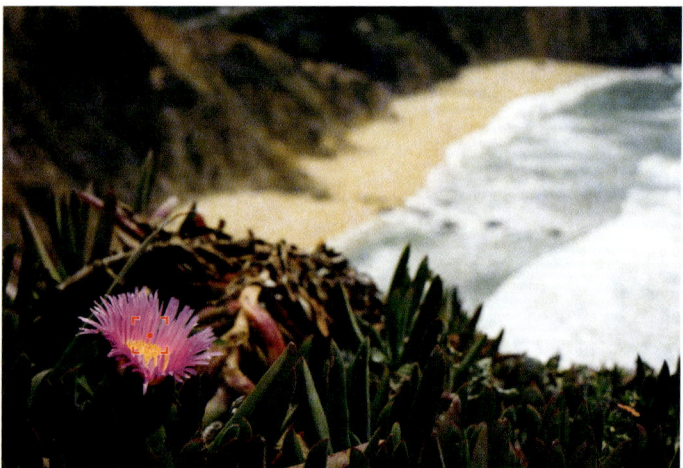

Fig. 130: Shooting with **minimal depth of field,** you can't afford to use a focus and recompose habit because it would quickly lead to soft results that appear out of focus. Instead, compose the shot, and then focus using a single focus frame that covers the part of the image that is supposed to be in focus.

■ You can think of **Zone AF** as an extension of Single Point AF. Basically, an AF zone is a particularly large AF frame that consists of a matrix of smaller AF points. In many recent X camera models, zones are available in sizes that cover 3×3, 5×5, or 7×7 out of a total of 91 AF points. Like

Single Point AF frames, AF zones can be moved around within the image area. Since they are larger than focus frames, AF zones make it easier to focus on moving subjects. In Zone AF mode, the camera will usually start looking for something to focus on in the center (crosshairs) of the selected zone and then expand its search toward the edges of the zone until it finds a target. Like Single Point AF, Zone AF works in concert with either AF-S or AF-C.

- When you combine **Wide/Tracking AF** mode with **AF-S,** the camera scans the entire image frame and automatically selects several focus frames. It's a bit like rolling dice, since the camera is simply looking for areas it can easily focus on. It doesn't know what's important in a scene. This changes when Wide/Tracking is used in concert with **AF-C:** This combination offers real 3D tracking of moving objects; that is, objects that not only move toward or away from the camera, but also left, right, up, or down within the image frame. To track such an object, select Wide/Tracking and AF-C and pick one of the available AF points. To start the tracking process, make sure the selected point covers the moving object you want to track. Half-press the shutter button to start the tracking process. While you keep the shutter button half-pressed, the camera will automatically follow the selected subject with a cloud of small AF frames as it moves across the image area.

Please note that Fujifilm has released an *AF Special Site* [66] detailing the autofocus modes and mode combinations that come with popular X series cameras.

Selecting an AF frame or AF zone	TIP 79

X cameras offer indirect and direct methods for selecting one of their many available focus frames in Single Point AF and for moving an AF zone around in Zone AF:

■ The *indirect* method requires you to *first* press the AF button and *then* use the selector buttons to pick an AF frame or move an AF zone. Some models feature a hard-wired AF button, others require you to assign the AF button function to an Fn button. After you have done so, press it to open the FOCUS AREA screen, where you can change the size and position of focus frames and AF zones. Please note that the X-E3 and GFX 50R don't offer selector buttons, so please use the direct focus stick or touchscreen method these models provide.

■ The *direct* method involves either using the touchscreen or the focus stick. This option is available in most newer X camera models. Make sure that the touchscreen-AF interface is set to AREA mode, then tap anywhere on the screen to select an AF area or zone. If your camera has a focus stick, you can use it like a joystick to move around the focus frame or AF zone. Press the focus stick to open the FOCUS AREA screen, where you can change the size and position of focus frames and AF zones.

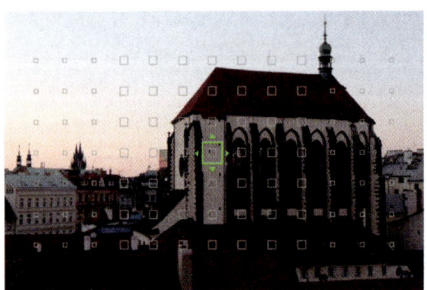 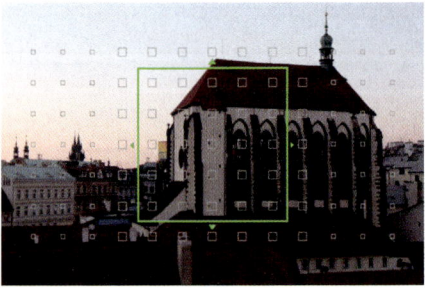

Fig. 131: Pressing the designated AF button or the focus stick opens the **FOCUS AREA screen,** where you can select a focus frame or AF Zone and change their size. With the new AF mode ALL, which is available in many recent models, changing the size automatically cycles through AF modes Single Point AF, Zone AF, and Wide/Tracking AF.

Choosing a suitable AF frame or AF zone size	TIP 80

Most current Fujifilm APS-C cameras offer a choice of 91 or 325 different AF frames in Single Point AF, and each frame comes in several sizes. You can change the size of an AF frame by pressing the focus stick (or designated AF button) and turning one of the command dials left or right to decrease or increase the frame size.

AF frame size affects the efficiency of CDAF and PDAF. A basic rule to follow is: *Make your AF frame as large as possible and as small as necessary.*

This is why:

- With a large AF frame size, the camera has more to work with and a better chance to find contrast in a target, especially when the light conditions aren't optimal. There's also a better chance the camera will be able to use the faster PDAF method when one of the PDAF-enabled AF frames is active. When PDAF isn't available, the camera will fall back to the slower CDAF.

- With a smaller AF frame size, the autofocus becomes more accurate. A small AF frame gives you better control over what *exactly* the camera is focusing on. Avoid AF frame sizes that are larger than the part of your image that needs to be in focus. For example, if your AF frame is larger than the head of the person you are focusing on, there's a chance that the camera will instead focus on the background behind them, especially if that background contains a lot of contrast.

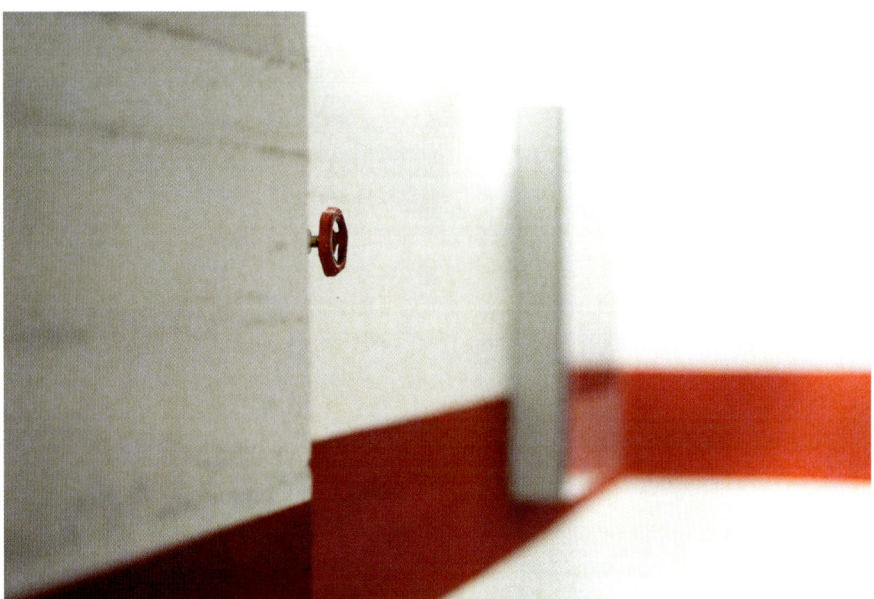

Fig. 132: To get tiny parts of an image in perfect focus, it's best to choose a **small AF frame size**.

In a similar fashion, you can change the size of AF zones by pressing the focus stick or designated AF button and turning the command dial left or right. You have a choice of three AF zone sizes: in most X cameras it's 3×3 (default), 5×5, or 7×7 out of 91 frames.

Since we can regard AF zones as very large AF frames, the same rules apply: larger zones are more convenient, and they potentially offer a faster AF response; but they are also potentially less accurate than smaller zones.

Keep in mind that the faster PDAF method is only available if the zone doesn't extend beyond the PDAF-enabled point matrix (only the X-T3 and future cameras with an X-Trans CMOS 4 sensor offer PDAF over the entire image area). As soon as an AF zone is configured to include at least one CDAF-only AF point, the focus system will switch to CDAF. You can easily tell the difference between AF points that are PDAF enabled and those that are CDAF only: the

PDAF-enabled points are displayed as larger squares than the surrounding CDAF-only points.

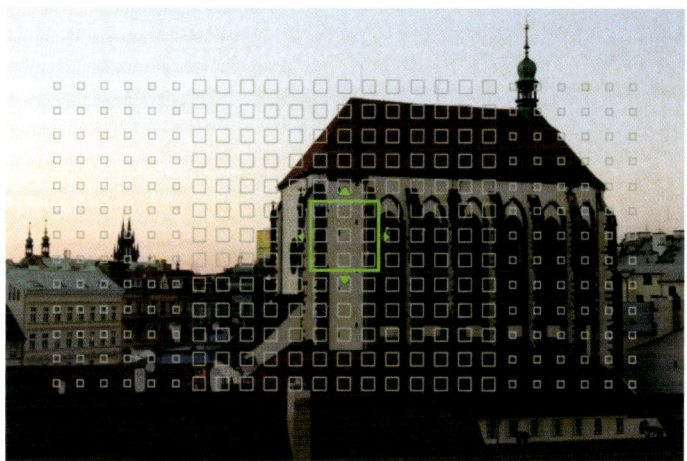

Fig. 133: In many X camera models (this example shows the X-T2), the **PDAF-enabled sensor area** is indicated by larger squares.

Manual focus and DOF zone focusing	TIP 81

In most X camera models, manual focus (MF) mode offers several focus aids:

■ A magnification tool with different magnification levels.

■ Focus peaking (Focus Peak Highlight) with two strength levels and optional colors.

■ Digital split image (only in cameras with PDAF).

■ Digital microprism (X-T3/X-Trans CMOS 4 only).

■ An electronic distance scale with depth-of-field indicators.

■ Instant AF: autofocus in MF mode, typically triggered by pressing the AF-L button in manual focus mode.

The digital distance scale can help you define a focus zone with pre-determined depth of field (DOF). Cameras with X-Processor Pro and X-Processor 4 offer two different DOF scales: a *pixel based* scale (recommended) and a *film format based* scale (not recommended). If you opt for PIXEL BASE in SHOOTING MENU > AF/MF SETTING > DEPTH-OF-FIELD SCALE, everything inside the DOF zone will look pixel-sharp even when the image is magnified to a 100% view. Please don't confuse manual zone focusing with Zone AF—they are completely different things.

Here's a zone-focusing example: using an 18mm lens on a 24 MP APS-C camera, manually set a distance of 15 feet and stop down to f/6.4. The DOF bars will show a depth-of-field zone that begins at around 12 feet and ends at around 30 feet. This means that everything located in this zone (between 12 and 30 feet) will appear equally in-focus in the final image. All you have to do is make sure that your subject is within that zone when you press the shutter button.

A special case of manual zone focusing is setting the hyperfocal distance [67]. This is the distance setting with the maximum DOF (all the way to infinity). Again, the electronic DOF scale can be very helpful: all you have to do is manually set the distance where the blue DOF bar on the right touches the infinity mark. For example, using an 18mm lens at f/16 on an APS-C camera with 24 MP, the hyperfocal distance is located at approximately 16 feet, with the pixel-sharp DOF zone extending from 9 feet to infinity.

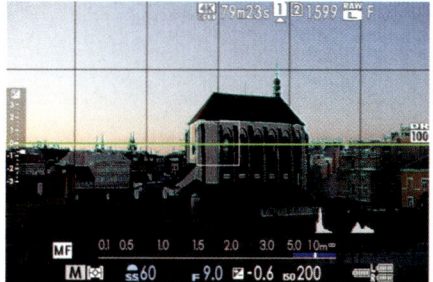 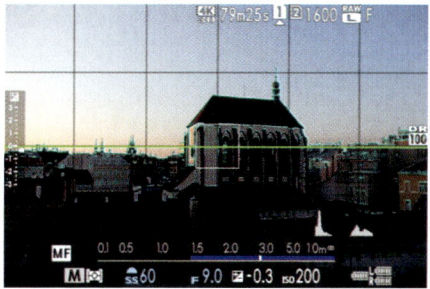

Fig. 134: Setting the **hyperfocal distance** with the electronic distance and DOF scale: instead of focusing on a predetermined distance, manually change the focus distance until the DOF bar touches the ∞ mark on the right end of the scale. This gives you the hyperfocal distance for a given aperture and focal length. This illustration shows the hyperfocal distance of a wide-angle lens at f/9 for both the PIXEL BASIS format (left) and FILM FORMAT BASIS format (right) on an X-T2.

Please note that depth of field is very much dependent on the circle of confusion (CoC) [68]. Fujifilm uses a very conservative CoC that guarantees pixel-sharp results even when the DOF zone is viewed at 100% magnification on a computer screen. Fuji is literally using the sensor's physical resolution as a benchmark. In PIXEL BASIS mode, everything that's located inside the electronic DOF zone will be rendered as sharp as the sensor can resolve it. In the age of pixel peeping, this is as good as it can get.

It's important to know that the engraved analog distance and DOF scales on the XF14mmF2.8, XF16mmF1.4, and XF23mmF1.4 lenses follow a different rule: the FILM FORMAT BASIS option. They are based on a much less conservative circle of confusion that is several aperture stops more generous than the electronic PIXEL BASIS scale. You can change the electronic scale to FILM FORMAT BASIS (and hence use a less conservative scale with all your lenses) in SHOOTING MENU > AF/MF SETTING > DEPTH-OF-FIELD SCALE. However, I want to reiterate that I do not recommend this setting. Instead, I recommend using the PIXEL BASIS scale.

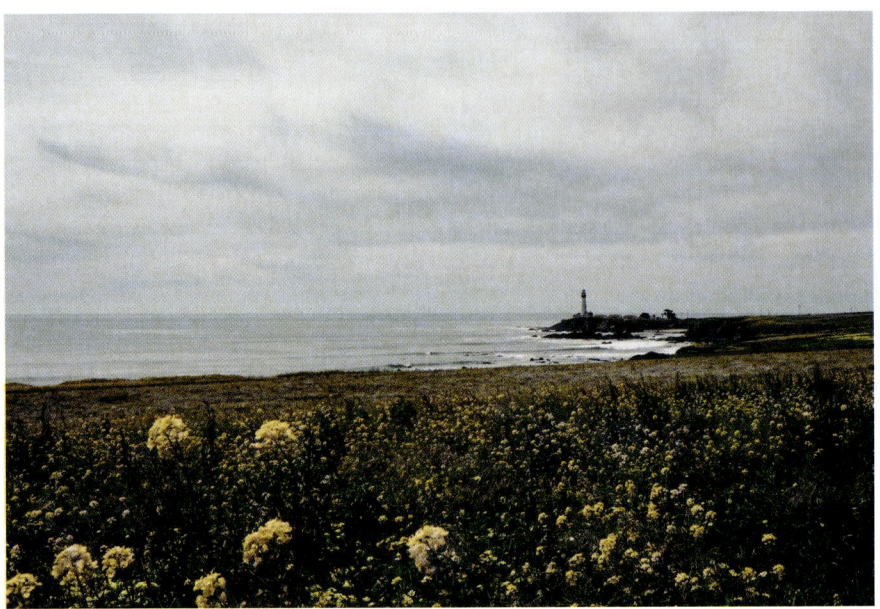

Fig. 135: This shot was manually focused by setting the **hyper-focal distance** for f/14 on the camera's electronic focus distance scale (XF27mmF2.8 Pancake).

If you are using an older X model that doesn't offer you a choice between a pixel and a film-format based DOF scale, do not worry: in these cameras, the DOF scale is always pixel based.

TIP 82	Manual focus assistants

Most X series cameras feature several MF assistants:

- **Focus Peaking** (or Focus Peak Highlight) emphasizes the edges of objects when they are in focus. This method is especially useful in concert with longer focal lengths and bright lenses with a tiny DOF.

- **Digital Split Image** tries to simulate the split image in-dicator of manual focus SLRs. It works best with vertical lines (or horizontal lines when the camera is held in portrait orientation). It uses the sensor's PDAF-enabled area, which is why the digital split image is just as large as the area covered by the central PDAF frames.

■ **Digital Microprism** is so far only available in the X-T3 and simulates a microprism that used to be popular in the manual-focus SLR days.

To quickly switch between the available MF assistants, you can press and hold the rear command dial for about a second while you are in MF mode.

You can watch a short video [69] demonstrating different manual focus assistants. There's also a video demonstrating the "real thing": actual analog split image and microprism focusing in an old Minolta SLR [70].

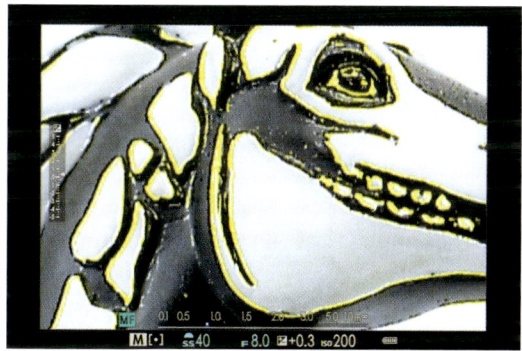

Fig. 136: **Focus peaking** is my favorite among the available manual focus aids. To make things even easier, it can be combined with the magnifier tool. In this X-H1 example, I opted for yellow outlines to indicate the areas of the scene that are in focus.

Using the Focus Check magnifier tool	TIP 83

The magnifier tool is available in most X camera models. It's helpful for checking if the current focus is spot-on. Press the rear command dial (either in AF-S/Single Point AF or in MF mode) to magnify the area that is targeted by the selected focus frame. Of course, this assumes that the rear command dial is operating with its default FOCUS CHECK Fn button assignment.

You can change the magnification level by turning the rear command dial. You can also combine focus check with any available MF assistants (focus peaking, digital split image, digital microprism). Please note that in digital split image and digital microprism mode, there's only *one* magnification level available.

By selecting SHOOTING MENU > AF/MF SETTING > FOCUS CHECK > ON, the magnifier tool is *automatically* activated when you turn the manual focus ring of a lens in MF mode. You can immediately cancel any automatic focus check by half-pressing the shutter button.

Analog to the AF-S and AF-C modes, there are many different focus frames available in manual focus mode (up to 425 in the X-T3 and GFX). These frames indicate which part of the image will be magnified when focus check is activated. As usual, you can change the active frame by pressing the focus stick or designated AF button and then moving the focus frame around with the selector keys or focus stick.

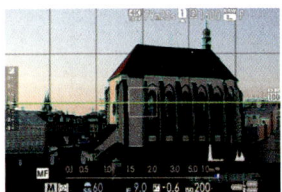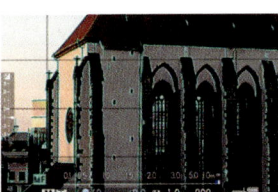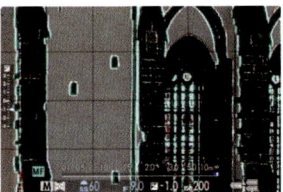

Fig. 137: Most X cameras offer two different **magnification levels**. This illustration shows the full image frame (left) as well as the lower (center) and higher (right) magnification levels of the Focus Check magnifier tool of the X-T2. To make things easier, the magnification was combined with focus peaking. Recent X models also allow you to move the magnified area with the focus stick or touchscreen while Focus Check is zoomed into the frame.

Please note that Focus Check is not available in AF-C mode.

Using Instant AF-S and Instant AF-C   TIP 84

Instant AF (or One-Touch-AF) allows you to autofocus the camera in manual focus mode. Usually, this works by pressing the AF-L or combined AE-L/AF-L button. A few cameras (like the X-T100) require you to assign Instant AF to an Fn button.

Instant AF always works with a wide-open aperture. Like the regular autofocus, its efficiency depends on the size of the selected focus frame.

Instant AF is the most precise AF method available, which also makes it a bit slower than the camera's normal autofocus. It can be combined with conventional manual focusing: you can use Instant AF to quickly autofocus on an object, then manually fine-tune the focus by turning the focus ring and using MF assistants like the magnifier and focus peaking.

Sadly, this convenient method of fine-tuning Instant AF with manual focus is *not* available when you are using lenses with manual focus clutches (XF14mmF2.8, XF16mmF1.4, and XF23mmF1.4).

Instant AF normally functions like AF-S, but in many recent X cameras, you can also set it to continuous focus with SHOOTING MENU > AF/MF SETTING > INSTANT AF SETTING > AF-C. In this mode, Instant AF will track the subject distance with AF-C as long as you keep the AF-L button (or designated Instant AF button) depressed in manual focus mode.

Unlike normal AF-C (that focuses with the working aperture), Instant AF-C can focus with a wide-open aperture, making it an option for stage and concert photography with moving subjects in poor light, where you want to shoot with AF-C and a stopped-down lens. Just keep the AF-L button depressed for continuous instant autofocus as you press the shutter button in the right moment.

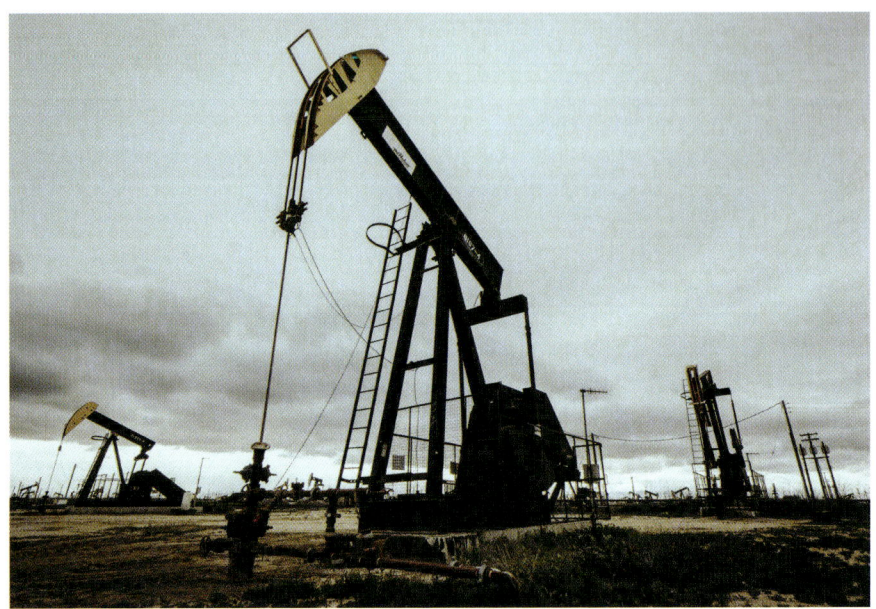

Fig. 138: **Instant AF** forces the lens to focus with a wide open aperture. This AF method is particularly accurate when you shoot with a stopped down wide-angle lens.

Please note that Instant-AF-C stops focusing as soon as you half-press the shutter button. To avoid unnecessary time lags between focusing and shutter release, it's best to first activate Instant AF-C by pressing and holding the AF-L button (or any other designated Instant AF button) to continually focus and then *immediately fully depress* the shutter button to take a shot.

TIP 85	Using AF+MF

AF+MF allows you to manually focus in AF mode by turn-ing the focus ring, all while holding the shutter button half-depressed. Select SHOOTING MENU > AF/MF SETTING > AF+MF > ON to enable this feature. To use AF+MF, your camera needs to be in AF-S autofocus mode.

Here's how it works:

- Autofocus on your subject as usual in AF-S mode by half-pressing the shutter button.

- Once the autofocus has been confirmed (green square[s]) or not confirmed (red AF warning), keep the shutter button half-depressed and rotate the focus ring of your lens to *manually* adjust the focus distance until you are satisfied. If focus peaking is enabled, it will automatically engage as soon as the focus ring is rotated and manual focus (MF) kicks in. You can also use the Focus Check function (AF/MF SETTING > FOCUS CHECK > ON) to automatically magnify the focus area as soon as you turn the focus ring. For this to work, make sure that AF-S and SINGLE POINT AF are set. You can also combine Focus Check magnification with focus peaking. Turn the rear command dial to change the magnification factor and press the rear command dial to manually enable/disable the live view magnification. Remember that all this has to be performed while you hold the shutter button half-depressed, so this might need some practice.

- When you are happy with your manual focus adjustments, fully depress the half-pressed shutter button to take the shot.

I see three main applications for AF+MF:

- **Manual focus in situations when autofocus fails:** Instead of losing time by changing the focus mode from AF to MF, you can immediately focus manually when the camera's AF fails to acquire the subject. Simply adjust the focus manually using the focus ring.

- **Correcting the camera's autofocus:** There are instances when you might want to fine-tune the autofocus of your camera by adjusting it manually. Again, focus peaking is available to make things easier, and you can enable

Focus Check to automatically show a magnified view of the focus area when you turn the focus ring.

- **Shifting the depth-of-field (DOF) zone or setting the hyperfocal distance:** After half-pressing the shutter button, AF+MF lets you quickly shift the DOF zone toward or away from the camera by turning the focus ring. The digital distance scale on the screen can be quite helpful here. For example, you can set the hyperfocal distance [71] by shifting the right tip of the DOF bar to touch the infinity mark of the digital distance scale.

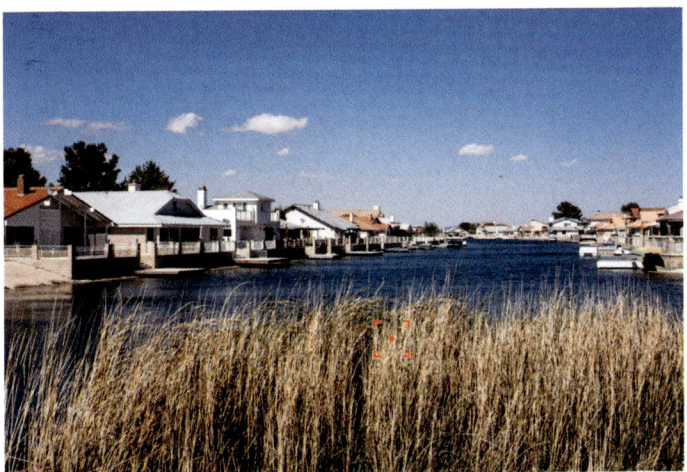

Fig. 139: In this example, I autofocused my X-T20 on the reeds by placing the AF frame right over them. I used a small aperture of f/9 for a decent amount of depth of field (DOF). Since the portion of the DOF zone that extends in front of the reeds toward the camera is useless in this case, I manually shifted the DOF zone away from the camera using **AF+MF**. The resulting DOF zone starts at the reeds and extends all the way back.

At first glance, the MF component of AF+MF may look like your regular manual focus, but it's not. While genuine MF is performed at a wide-open aperture, the MF part of AF+MF is performed at the selected working aperture. That's because the shutter button is half-pressed, so the camera has already been primed to take the shot with minimal shutter lag.

This also means that the EVF/LCD will display a live view image that shows the actual depth of field of the resulting image, and focus peaking will show an increasingly larger zone as being in focus when you stop down the lens. This can make it more difficult to nail your manual focus adjustment.

AF+MF also works with clutch-type lenses such as the XF14mm, XF16mm, or XF23mm. These lenses feature a clutch to mechanically switch between MF and AF mode. Since the focus ring of these lenses can only be turned when the clutch is in the MF position, you need the following configuration to get AF+MF to work:

- Enable AF+MF in the shooting menu.

- Select AF-S in the camera and MF on the lens (by pulling the clutch mechanism toward the camera).

- Use AF+MF as described above.

Here are a few tips regarding AF+MF and clutch lenses:

- Make sure that the manual focus ring of the lens has sufficient play to the left and right so you can make the necessary MF adjustments.

- The distance and DOF markings on your clutch lens have no meaning in the AF+MF configuration. Instead, use the digital distance/DOF scale that's displayed in the camera's viewfinder or on the LCD.

- To use clutch lenses in manual focus mode when AF+MF is on, both the lens *and* the camera must be set to MF.

Pre-AF: a relic of the past	TIP 86

Pre-AF brings the AF-C of older Fujifilm X cameras (like the X-Pro1) to more recent models: with Pre-AF set to ON, the camera will always focus on whatever is covered by the active AF frame, even when the shutter button is *not* half-depressed.

Pre-AF burns plenty of power because the autofocus in the lens is always working. On the other hand, using it can potentially result in a quicker AF response. When you are shooting action with telephoto lenses, Pre-AF may be helpful—but don't forget to pack a few extra batteries. Normally, I set this option (SHOOTING MENU > AF/MF SETTING > PRE-AF) to OFF.

| TIP 87 | Using face detection and eye detection |

Face detection is available in most X camera models. It's a combined autofocus and exposure metering mode that can even affect auto white balance. You can activate face detection with SHOOTING MENU > AF/MF SETTING > FACE/ EYE DETECTION SETTING and picking one of the four FACE ON options.

Here's what it does:

■ The camera scans the scene and detects human faces. It automatically focuses on one of the detected faces when the shutter button is half-pressed. When more than one face is detected, the camera tends to focus on the face that's closest to the center. That face will be highlighted with a green frame. The other detected faces will be highlighted with a white frame.

■ Face detection uses a custom version of weighted multi metering that puts an emphasis on the selected face. The goal is to deliver an exposure with correct skin tones. It may also influence the camera's auto white balance.

Face detection is both a blessing and a curse. It's a blessing when it works because it focuses directly on a face and makes sure that it's "correctly" exposed. It's a curse when the detection goes wrong, because it doesn't just mean that the focus might miss; it may also mess up your exposure metering.

The good news is that in many cases, face detection works, even with people who only show their profiles to the camera. The bad news is that face detection may not work well on folks wearing glasses.

Please note that the performance of face detection has been significantly improved in the X-T3 (and other upcoming cameras with X-Processor 4).

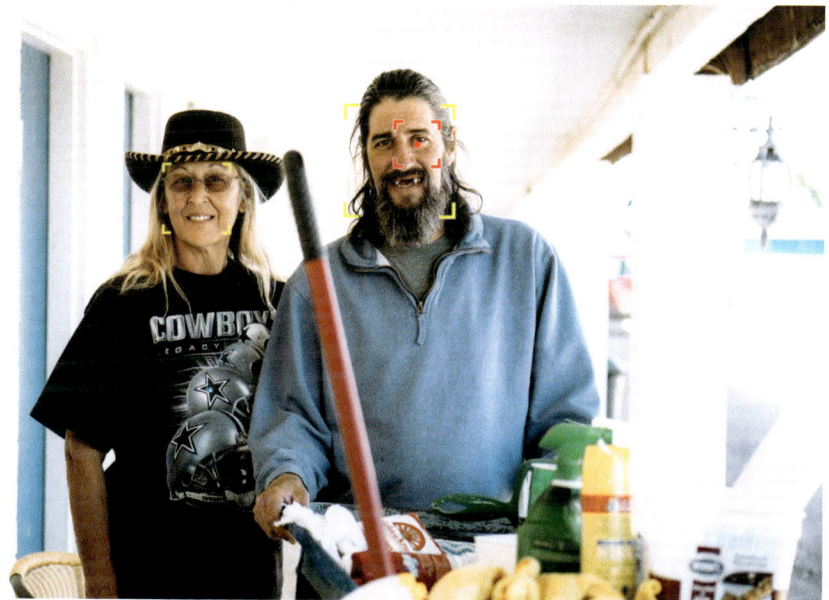

Fig. 140: **Face detection** is great for stationary scenes with one or more people looking at (or showing their profile to) the camera.

Here are a few helpful tips regarding face detection:

- It you want to take face detection exposure metering out of the equation (and I highly recommend that you do), you can set the camera to manual exposure mode **M**. While the *metering* will still be affected in this mode, the *exposure* itself will not. Alternatively, you can use the AE-L button to meter and lock the exposure and prohibit face detection from interfering with it while AE-L is active. You can still adjust your locked exposure with the exposure compensation dial.

- Face detection works with the full sensor area. This means that AF-C tracking performance of moving objects varies depending on which kind of AF method (PDAF or CDAF) can be used by the camera. In models prior to the generation of the X-T3, face detection isn't the best option when tracking an athlete or a child running toward the camera. With these older cameras, it may be better to use conventional AF-C mode with one of the central AF frames or an appropriate AF zone.

- Spot, center-weighted, and average metering aren't available when face detection is active. The camera is always using a derivate of multi metering.

- When face detection fails to detect a face in the scene, the camera will automatically fall back to the selected regular AF mode: Single Point, Zone, or Wide/Tracking. At the same time, exposure metering reverts to regular multi metering.

- AF-Lock is not available when face detection is active.

- In most cameras, face detection can be assigned to any function (Fn) button. Personally, I tend to assign it to the lower selector button.

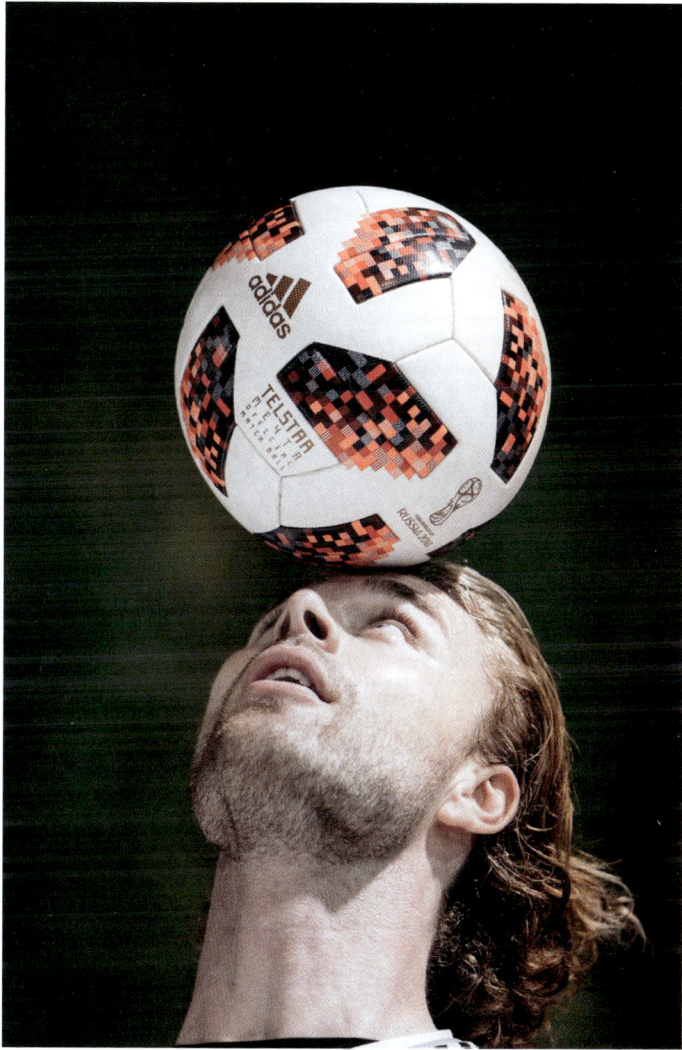

Fig. 141: For persons who are moving around, only the new X-T3 and upcoming models with X-Processor 4 are fast enough to confidently track their face with **AF-C and face/eye detection**.

Face detection accuracy can be improved with the optional eye detection feature. With the exception of the new X-T3 platform, eye detection is only available in AF-S mode. To activate it, select either FACE ON/LEFT EYE PRIORITY or FACE

ON/RIGHT EYE PRIORITY. You can also select FACE ON/EYE AUTO to make the camera focus on the eye that's closest to the camera, or select FACE ON/EYE OFF to deactivate eye detection during face detection.

In the viewfinder, the camera will highlight a detected eye with a small square and focus on it when you half-press the shutter button. In my experience, it doesn't hurt to leave this feature on all the time. I usually set it to EYE AUTO.

| TIP 88 | Using AF-Lock and AE-Lock |

Most X cameras offer either a dedicated AF-L or a combined AE-L/AF-L button that can be configured as "AF-L only." Some cameras also allow you to assign the AF-Lock function to an Fn button. In AF-S or AF-C mode, pressing the designated AF-Lock button locks the current distance setting. In SET UP > BUTTON/DIAL SETTING > AE/AF LOCK MODE, you can configure the button to function as an on/off switch (which is always my choice) or to work only while it is being pressed.

When AF-Lock is active, the camera won't refocus when the shutter button is half- or fully depressed. Instead, it will keep the focus at the previously locked distance. This is convenient when you want to take multiple shots of a non-moving subject in quick succession. With AF-Lock, you don't have to refocus every time to take another image. AF-Lock decouples autofocus and exposure metering: while AF-Lock is engaged, half-pressing the shutter button will only meter and lock the exposure, not the focus. Of course, this only applies if SHUTTER AF (in the SET UP > BUTTON/DIAL SETTING menu) is in its default ON position.

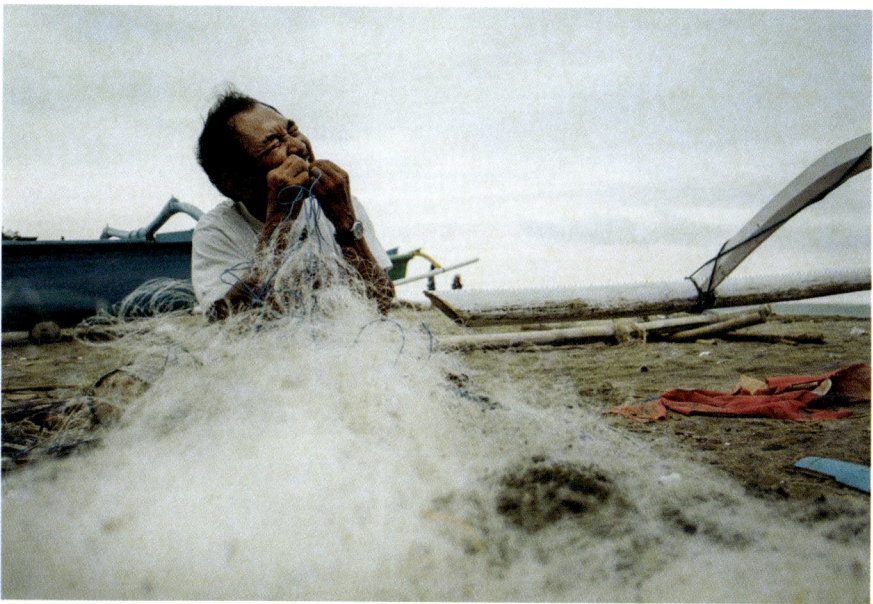

Fig. 142: With the slow CDAF of the original X-Pro1, using auto-focus and timing the decisive moment wasn't always easy. In this example, I wanted to capture a Bali fisherman in interesting split-second moments. To achieve this, I autofocused on the fisherman's head and then used **AF-Lock** to lock the focus distance. Now I was free to shoot the fisherman in various moments. All I had to do was press the shutter button. Thanks to the locked focus distance, there was almost no shutter lag, because the camera didn't have to refocus every time I took a shot.

In newer cameras with X-Processor Pro or X-Processor 4, you can also use an indirect form of AF-Lock that doesn't involve a dedicated AF-L button. Start as usual by taking one shot in AF-S mode. However, after taking the shot, do not *fully* release the shutter button, but only release it back to its *half-pressed* position. This will lock the focus of the previous shot (indicated by a tiny AF-L symbol in the live view), so when you now press the shutter button again (going from half press to full press), the camera won't refocus. Rinse and repeat as long as you want to take additional shots without refocusing.

In a similar fashion to AF-L, you can use the designated AE-L button to meter and lock exposure; in this case, half-pressing the shutter button will only change the focusing. You can even combine both AE-Lock and AF-Lock, so half-pressing the shutter will only set the working aperture and prime the camera.

| TIP 89 | Using AF-ON (back-button focusing) |

AF-ON brings genuine back-button focusing to most cameras with X-Processor Pro and X-Processor 4. However, it's not available in the X-Pro2 and X100F. Back-button focusing is a common practice with DSLR users. Simply put, AF-ON assigns the camera's autofocus to a function button. Press that button, and the camera starts focusing. Release it, and the focusing stops at the current focus position—until you press the AF-ON button again.

In other words: AF-ON performs the same autofocus function as half-pressing the shutter button (assuming that SHUTTER AF ON is set in the SET UP > BUTTON/DIAL SETTING menu). In AF-S mode, pressing AF-ON will perform a single focus search and lock the distance. In AF-C mode, AF-ON will continuously focus on a target as long as the button is pressed (just like half-pressing the shutter button).

As of December 2018, only the X-H1 offers a dedicated AF-ON button (instead of a dedicated AF-L button). In the X-T2, X-T3, X-T20, and X-E3, AF-ON must be assigned to an Fn button. To keep things simple and comfortable, it's best to replace the AF-L button with AF-ON. To do so, press and hold the DISP/BACK button until the Fn setting page appears. Scroll down to AF-L and select AF-ON from the list of available functions.

You can press and hold AF-ON while you simultaneously press the shutter. In AF-S, pressing and holding AF-ON will focus the camera and lock that focus while AF-ON is held, so simultaneously half-pressing or pressing the shutter button won't interfere with your locked focus. In AF-C, pressing

AF-ON means that the camera keeps tracking your target as long as AF-ON is pressed and held.

If you are a "religious" back-button-AF user (some DLSR converts are), you may find it more comfortable to entirely disable the shutter button's AF functionality by selecting SET UP > BUTTON/DIAL SETTING > SHUTTER AF > OFF, so AF-ON will be the only available method to autofocus in AF-S or AF-C mode.

In manual focus (MF) mode, AF-ON turns into Instant AF, just like the normal AF-L button.

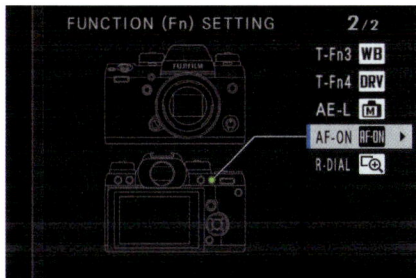

Fig. 143: **AF-ON** (a.k.a. "back-button focusing") is especially popular among (former) DSLR users. It allows you to activate the autofocus independently from the shutter button. Practically, you can focus with your thumb, so that half-pressing the shutter button with your index finger only locks the camera's exposure. This method can be used with both AF-S and AF-C.

AF-ON is simply an alternative user interface for accessing autofocus and AF-Lock, and it's sometimes combined with a SET UP > BUTTON/DIAL SETTING > SHUTTER AF > OFF setting (for both AF-S and AF-C) that completely relieves the shutter button of all focusing duties. Personally, I always assign AF-ON to the AF-L button.

Focusing in poor light	TIP 90

Low light can lead to poor contrast, making it more difficult for the camera to find and lock the correct autofocus distance. However, the amount of light that reaches the sensor depends not only on the brightness of a scene, but also on the brightness of the lens. The XF56mmF1.2 is 3.5 stops or EVs (exposure values) brighter than the XF18–55mmF2.8–4 kit zoom in its 55mm position. In other words, with the XF56mmF1.2 lens, the same scene can look 3.5 stops brighter to the camera's autofocus system. You can guess which lens will perform better when the lighting gets tough.

Don't be confused by appearances—it's true that the live view image in the viewfinder will look equally bright with both lenses, but that's only because the camera is electronically amplifying the live view display. Don't forget that autofocus needs *actual* light and contrast. When the light is poor, it's vital to target surfaces with contrast and, if possible, use a larger AF frame size.

One way of tackling a tough lighting situation is by using fast lenses, like the XF56mmF1.2, XF35mmF1.4, or XF23mmF1.4. You can also generate light—the camera's AF assist lamp can illuminate a subject to help the autofocus find better contrast. Be aware that the AF assist lamp can be easily blocked by an attached lens hood. Watch out for this and remove the lens hood if necessary. Since the AF assist lamp tends to concentrate on the center of the image, it works best in concert with one of the more central AF frames. To use the AF assist lamp, make sure to set SHOOT-ING MENU > AF/MF SETTING > AF ILLUMINATOR > ON.

An alternative to using the AF assist lamp is using a flashlight to temporarily illuminate a subject. If you are indoors, you can try turning on the lights in the room for a moment and using AF-Lock to lock the focus. Just make sure to meter the exposure *after* the lights are off again.

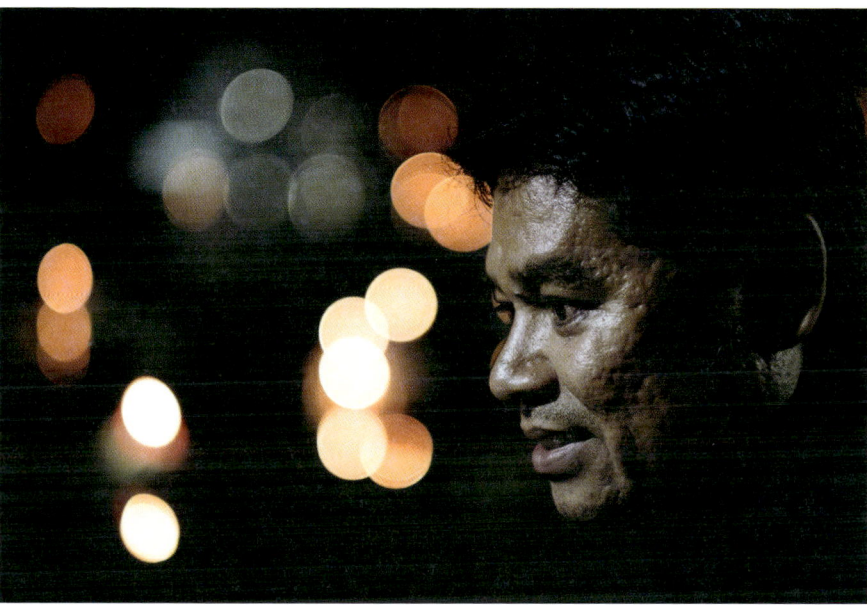

Fig. 144: In this **low-light shot,** the fast XF56mmF1.2 R lens made it easier on the autofocus system of my X-T2 to find its target in AF-S mode. In AF-S mode, low-light AF performance isn't related to the actually set working aperture, but to the maximum wide-open aperture that is available. In this particular example, it wouldn't have made a difference if I had set the aperture to 1.2 or 5.6 or 8, because in AF-S mode, the focusing system can temporarily open up to the widest lens aperture.

Important: If you intend to stop down the aperture of your lens in poor lighting, make sure to use either AF-S or manual focus with Instant AF-S or Instant AF-C as your focusing mode. Why? Because Instant AF always focuses wide-open. Try to avoid regular AF-C, because this mode will usually focus with your stopped-down working aperture, which will make things more difficult for your camera since less light will reach the sensor.

| TIP 91 | Macro: focusing at close distances |

The biggest challenge with shooting macro is the lack of depth of field. The slightest movement may cause the shot to be out of focus. That's why macro photography is usually performed using a tripod and manual focus, often with Instant AF, Focus Check (magnifier tool), and focus peaking. It's vital not to recompose after the focus has been set. To get a visual impression of the current DOF, you can half-press the shutter (make sure SHUTTER AE is ON) or assign PREVIEW DEPTH OF FIELD to one of your Fn buttons.

Macro shots usually require you to stop down the lens to increase the DOF. Since this can result in slower shutter speeds, it's important to make sure that the subject isn't moving too fast or out of the focus plane. Shooting a close-up of a flower in the wind may not yield excellent results.

If you don't want to use manual focus in macro mode, you can also focus automatically. Here's how:

- Set AF-S and Single Point AF, and select a small AF frame size.

- Reposition the small AF frame to exactly cover the part of the image that you want to be in focus. Quickly take the shot after you half-press the shutter—don't recompose.

- You can check your focus with the magnifier tool before taking a shot by pressing the rear command dial. After doing so, you can change the magnification factor by turning the command dial.

- Try not to shoot handheld; it's better to use a tripod.

- Stop down the lens and visually check the depth of field by half-pressing the shutter button or using the DOF pre-view function (remember that function can be assigned to any Fn button).

- Make sure there is sufficient light and try to shoot sub-jects that don't move in and out of the focus plane.

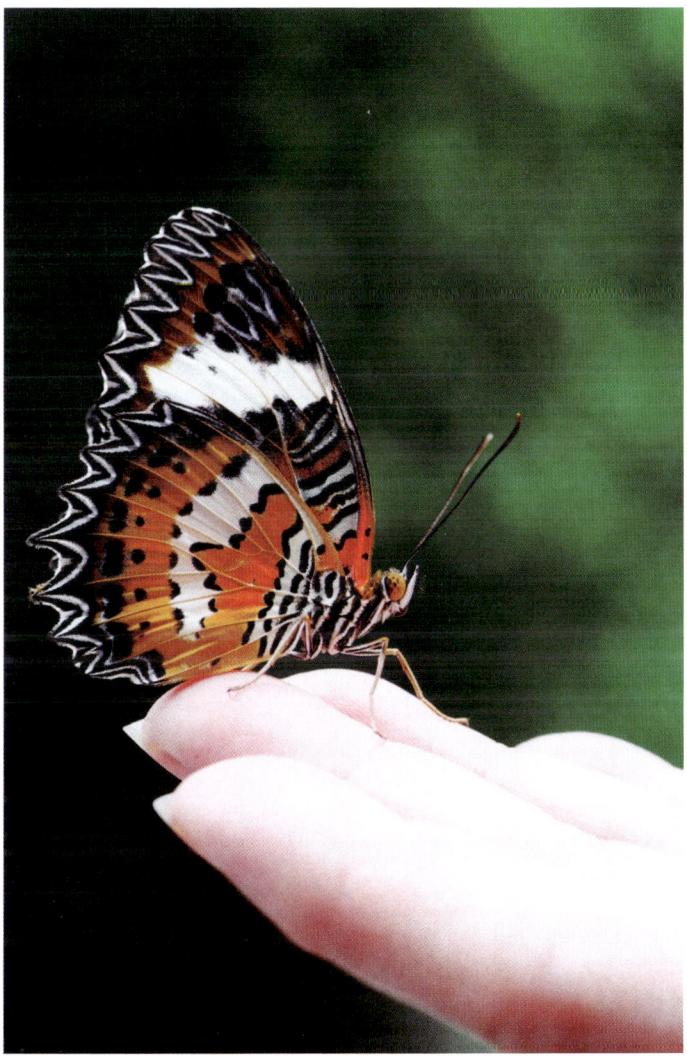

Fig. 145: **Macro shots** can be quite challenging due to their lack of DOF. That's why a tripod is highly recommended. With a little bit of luck, handheld shots are possible, as well. This handheld snapshot was taken in 2012 with the classic X-Pro1 and an XF60mmF2.4 R.

You can add macro capability to many of your existing XF and XC lenses by using Fujifilm's electronic macro extension tubes MCEX-11 and MCEX-16. You can download a PDF file [72] from Fujifilm's website that provides a chart that shows how these extension tubes enhance the magnification factor of compatible lenses. Please note that the camera's electronic DOF/distance scale doesn't reflect the use of macro extension tubes.

If you are a GFX user, you can get extension tubes, too: the MCEX-18G WR and MCEX-45G WR macro extension tubes can be combined with most GF lenses. According to Fujifilm, the 18mm version is the smallest possible size that meets the structural requirements, while the 45mm tube was designed to add 1:1 magnification to the GF120mmF4 R LM OIS WR Macro lens. Again, there is a PDF file [73] showing the magnification and distance specs for all available combinations of GF lenses and GF macro extension tubes.

| TIP 92 | Focus Bracketing |

The need for greater depth of field (DOF) [74] is a common issue for macro and landscape photographers. With increasing sensor resolution, diffraction blur [75] becomes a serious limitation. For example, to avoid visible diffraction with a 24 MP APS-C sensor, you should not stop down your lenses beyond f/11.

Even worse, many lenses have their "sweet spot" (the critical aperture delivering the best resolution and sharpness) [76] about two stops down from their maximum wide-open aperture. For example, my XF27mmF2.8 pancake delivers its maximum resolution around f/5.6.

For macro and landscape photographers, stopping down the lens to f/16 or f/22 isn't an option due to quality considerations. Not to mention that even at f/22, depth of field would still not be sufficient in many macro situations.

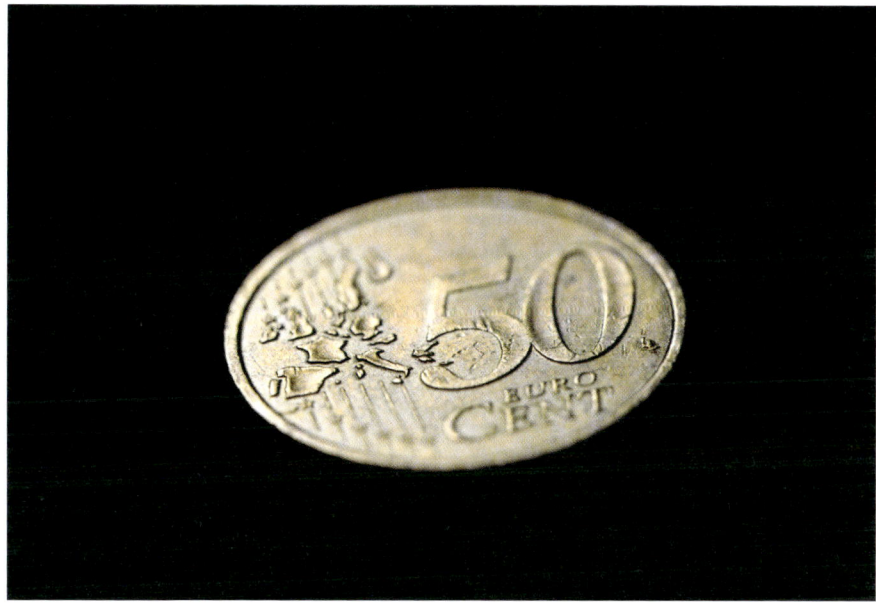

Fig. 146: A **regular macro shot** taken with a GFX 50S and a GF120mmF4 R LM OIS Macro lens with a MCEX-45G WR macro extension tube at f/8. Depth of field is limited to just a small portion of the subject.

What to do? A popular solution among ambitious photographers is *focus stacking* [77], which combines multiple images taken at different focus distances. Blending the individual source images in Photoshop or specialized software such as Helicon Focus [78] results in a single image with a greater depth of field.

Focus bracketing helps you automate the generation of the source material you need for focus stacking. As of December 2018, focus bracketing is available in the X-T2, X-H1, and X-T3, as well as the GFX 50S and GFX 50R. Additional legacy models might get it via firmware updates.

To configure focus bracketing in your X-T2, X-T3, or X-H1, select SHOOTING MENU > SHOOTING SETTING > DRIVE SETTING > BKT SETTING > FOCUS BKT. In the GFX 50S, you can select the focus bracketing configuration page directly in the SHOOTING SETTING menu.

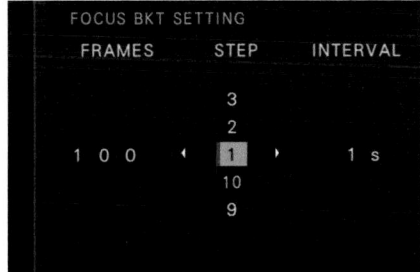

Fig. 147: The **focus bracketing** configuration screen allows you to set the number of frames that the camera should automatically take (FRAMES), the focus difference between individual shots (STEP), and the pause between individual shots (INTERVAL). The latter is useful to have the camera settle down after each shot to avoid shutter-induced vibration. If available, it's also recommended to activate the electronic first curtain shutter (EFCS).

To initiate a focus bracketing run, it's best to select MF and manually focus on the nearest point of your scene that you want to have in perfect focus. It's also recommended to stop down the lens to its "sweet spot." With macro lenses, that's typically two stops down their maximum aperture, while wide angle lenses often deliver peak performance three or four stops down.

Depending on your needs and time restraints, you can experiment with different step settings. To start the sequence, make sure that the camera is in BKT mode (DRIVE menu or dial) and that FOCUS BKT is selected as the BKT MODE, then press the shutter button. The camera will now take the set number of images or stop when it reaches infinity—whatever occurs first.

When the camera has finished recording the source images, you can merge them in Photoshop or specialized focus stacking software.

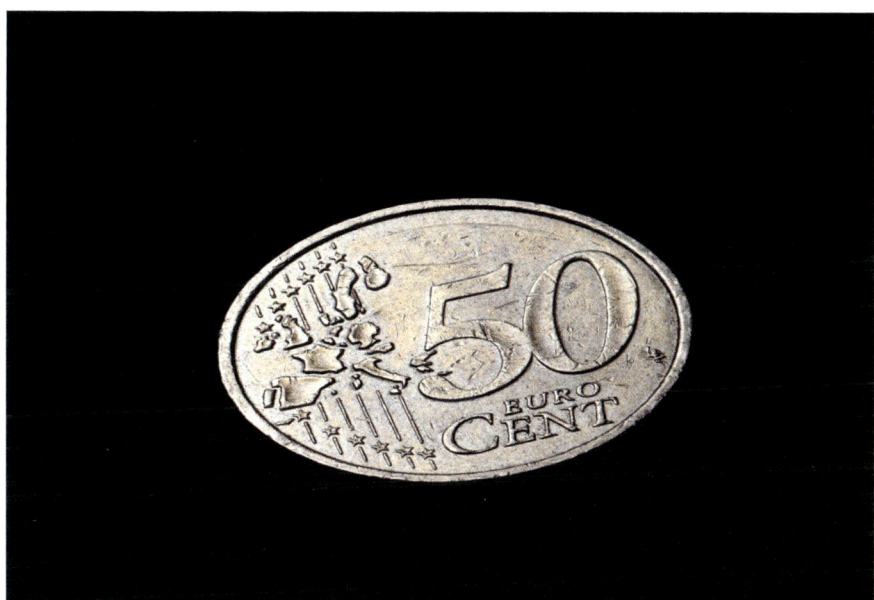

Fig. 148: This **focus stacking** example consists of 241 individual RAW files that were automatically recorded by my GFX 50S with a GF120mmF4 R LM OIS Macro lens and MCEX-45G WR macro extension tube at f/8. The RAW files were merged into a single DNG file using Helicon Focus. The DNG was then processed in Lightroom Classic CC.

Focusing on moving subjects (1): the "autofocus trick"	TIP 93

Rule of thumb: Use AF-S (Single) for stationary subjects; use AF-C (Continuous) for subjects that move toward or away from the camera. But, as usual, there's no rule without an exception: meet the so-called "autofocus trick" or "shutter mash" technique:

■ Set the camera to AF-S and single shot drive mode (S). Where available, make sure that High-Performance or Boot mode is on.

■ Use Single Point AF or Zone AF. Select an AF frame or zone position and size that cover the part of the moving subject you want to be in focus.

- Set a suitable exposure and make sure that the shutter speed is fast enough to avoid unwanted motion blur. Most action shots require shutter speeds of at least 1/1000s.

- Follow the moving subject in the viewfinder, making sure that the selected AF frame or AF zone always covers the part that needs to be in focus. Do *not* half-press the shutter button!

- *Fully* depress the shutter button in one swift motion when you want to take the shot. The camera will need some time to focus, so make sure the focus frame remains positioned on the moving subject while the camera is focusing. As soon as the camera can lock the focus, it will automatically take the shot. Depending on your X camera model, the time between fully depressing the shutter and the camera taking the shot can extend to a good fraction of a second.

The AF trick, also known as shutter mash, is based on the camera's autofocus priority logic. When you release the shutter, the camera *first* attempts to lock the focus, *then* take the shot. Since the delay between having locked the focus and releasing the shutter is very short, the moving subject ends up being in focus most of the time. This means that the AF trick works best with aperture settings that offer sufficient depth of field, and with subjects that don't move too fast toward the camera.

A negative aspect of this method is the delay between fully depressing the shutter button and the camera taking the shot. This makes it challenging to hit decisive moments and requires some amount of foresight from the photographer.

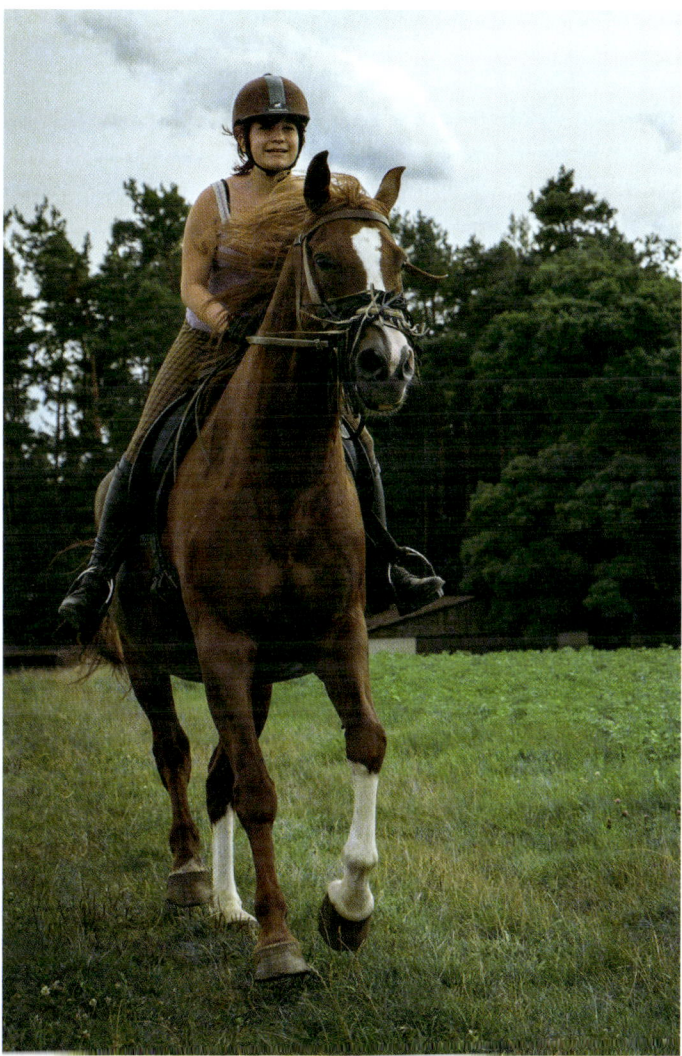

Fig. 149: A running horse captured using the **autofocus trick** or **shutter mash technique**. With older X camera models like the X100, X100S, X-Pro1, X-E1, X-M1, X-A1, or X-A2, this method is the only way to autofocus on subjects that are moving toward the camera. This sample image was taken with an X-E1.

TIP 94 Focusing on moving subjects (2): the focus trap

Setting up a focus trap is about pre-focusing on a location that a moving object will eventually pass through. This method can be useful with sports and other action that runs along a pre-determined course (track, street, trail, etc.).

This is how it works:

■ Set the camera to manual focus (MF).

■ Pre-focus on the location where you want to capture the moving subject. Select an aperture with sufficient depth of field (DOF) to make sure that all relevant parts of the object will be in focus.

■ Half-press the shutter button when the moving object is approaching the location you have in focus. The camera will lock the exposure and set the working aperture (assuming SHUTTER AE is ON).

■ Fully depress the shutter as soon as the object is about to cross the in-focus location.

There's only a very small shutter lag between half-pressing and fully depressing the shutter button. Depending on how fast the object is moving, it may be necessary to fully depress the shutter button a split second early.

Alternatively, you can set the camera to high-speed burst mode, increasing the chance that one or two frames will capture your fast-moving subject as it crosses your focus trap.

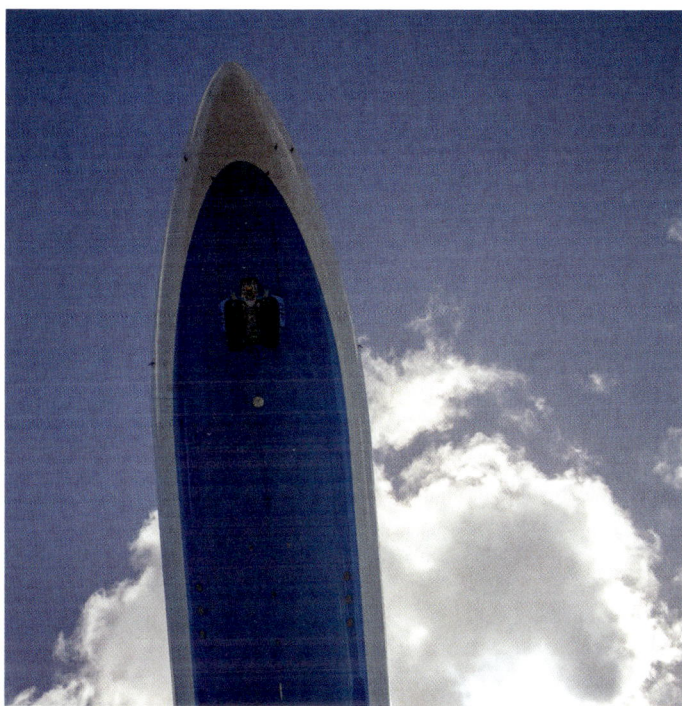

Fig. 150: **Focus trap:** To capture this landing Airbus A330 as it was flying over me at a distance of only a few meters, timing was essential. Instead of using autofocus, I pre-focused the 18mm lens on my X-Pro1 with sufficient depth of field and waited for the right moment with my camera primed and the shutter half-pressed.

You can also trap moving subjects in a set-up focus zone. Stop down your lens enough to create a sufficiently large DOF zone, and then wait until a subject enters the zone. This method is often used by street photographers with wide-angle lenses (typically 16–23mm) who can't afford to miss the decisive moment.

A variant of this method is panning [79] the camera with a slow shutter speed and a small aperture (plenty of DOF). The slow shutter speed makes sure that the background is blurred while the subject remains in focus.

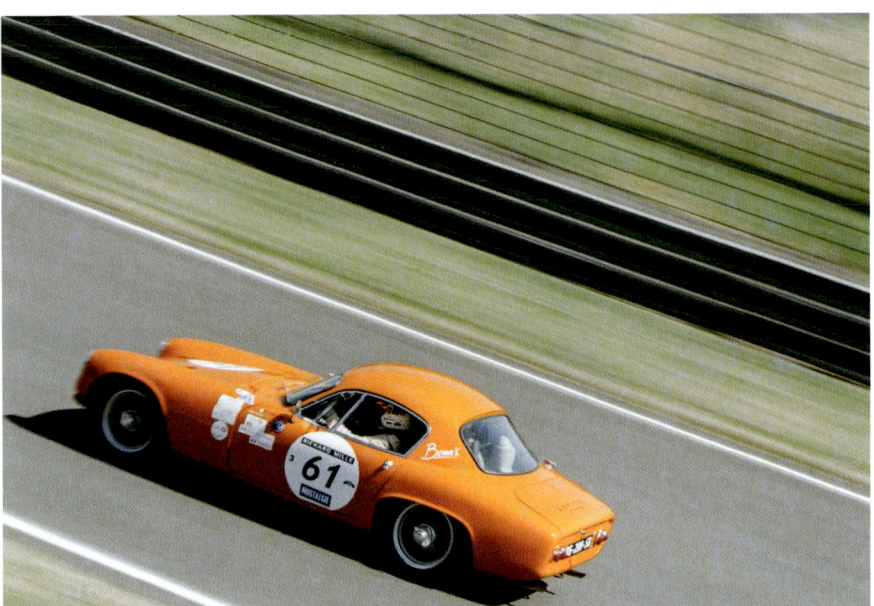

Fig. 151: **Panning** the camera in synch with a racecar at 1/60s: the slow shutter speed resulted in f/18 and more than sufficient DOF using a focal length of 50mm.

Focusing on moving subjects (3): autofocus tracking using Single Point AF, Zone AF, or Wide/Tracking AF

Predictive PDAF (phase detection autofocus) is available in most X cameras. It allows you to track moving subjects in three-dimensional space. Since the camera can calculate the movement of the object, it can automatically pre-focus on its predicted distance and compensate for any inherent shutter lag.

Please note that the X10, XF1, X-S1, X100, X-Pro1, X-E1, X-A1, X-A2, X-A3, GFX 50S, and GFX 50R don't offer PDAF at all. The X20 and X100S do feature on-sensor PDAF, but their AF systems aren't designed to track moving subjects and behave like the CDAF-only models with contrast detection autofocus.

Consequently, this tip is meant for users of the remaining X series models, such as the X-E2(S), X-T1, X-T10, X-Pro2, X-T2, X-T20, X-E3, X-H1, X-T3, XQ1, XQ2, X30, X70, X100T, and X100F. Xacti-made models like the X-A5, X-T100, and XF10 also offer PDAF with subject tracking, but its implementation is so slow and sluggish that many consider it hardly usable.

The X-T3 and future models with an X-Trans CMOS 4 sensor feature predictive PDAF that covers the entire sensor area. Users of these cameras don't have to care about restricting AF frames or zones to the camera's central PDAF area, because the entire sensor is the PDAF area.

Let's start with the **Single Point AF** and **Zone AF** modes:

- Set the focus to AF-C and make sure that High Performance or Boost mode is set.

- Set the camera to burst mode. I recommend a slow setting of 3 fps (cameras with an EXR II processor) or 5 fps (cameras with X-Processor Pro and X-Processor 4) that displays a real-time live view image between shots and supports all AF frames.

- If you are using Single Point AF, select one of the central PDAF-enabled autofocus frames. As of December 2018, only the X-T3 covers the entire sensor area with PDAF.

- If you are using Zone AF, select a zone that doesn't extend beyond the PDAF point matrix. If you use a zone that includes AF points outside this PDAF-enabled area, the camera can only use CDAF. Again, X-T3 users can happily ignore this restriction.

- Position the selected AF frame or AF zone to directly cover the subject or the part of the subject that you want in focus. Half-press the shutter button, and the camera will start tracking the subject covered by the AF frame or AF zone.

■ Keep the shutter button half-depressed as you follow the moving subject with the selected AF frame or AF zone.

■ Fully depress the shutter when you want to start taking a series of exposures. The actual burst speed (frame rate) depends on how well the camera can track the subject. As the camera is taking pictures, keep the selected AF frame or AF zone on the part of your image that is supposed to be in focus. This may be challenging at first, so practicing is important.

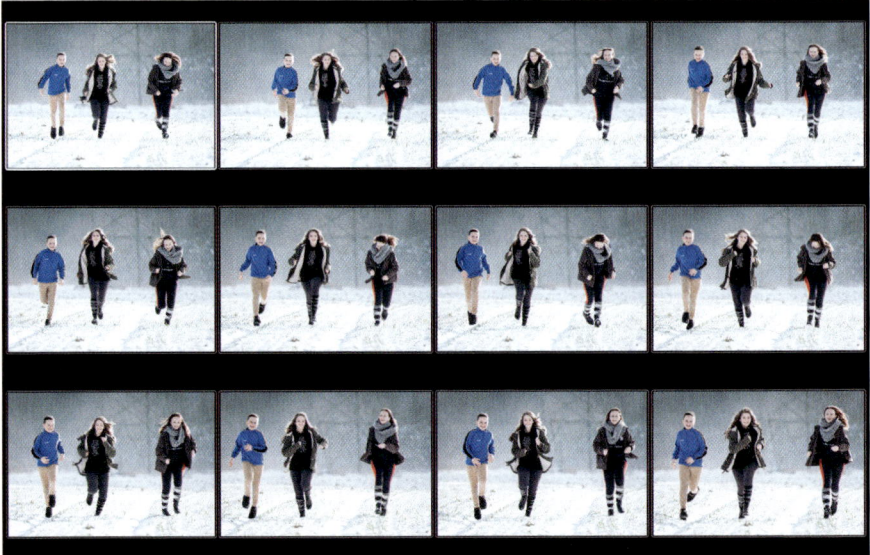

Fig. 152: **AF tracking** with AF-C and burst mode: The predictive autofocus was tracking one of the kids with the selected AF zone while they were running toward the camera. To make this kind of shot work, it's vital to follow the subject with the active AF frame or AF zone, making sure it's always covering the part of the subject that is supposed to be in focus.

In principle, AF-C tracking also works in single shot mode (DRIVE mode **S**, not to be confused with the AF mode **S**). In this case, the camera takes a single frame when the shutter button is fully depressed, then ends the tracking.

As an alternative to Single Point and Zone AF, you can also use **Wide/Tracking AF** mode in concert with AF-C to track a moving subject. This mode enables real 3D tracking, meaning the camera isn't merely tracking a subject's changing distance to the camera (z-axis), but also its left/right (x-axis) und up/down (y-axis) movements inside the image frame.

Here's how it works:

- Set the focus mode to AF-C and make sure that High Performance or Boost mode is active.

- Set the camera to **Wide/Tracking AF** and select a slow burst mode.

- Select one of the available tracking AF points. The point you select will serve as a starting point for your tracking action, so position it in a way that suits your composition.

- To identify your target, make sure that the selected AF point covers the object you want to track and half-press the shutter button. While you keep the shutter button half-pressed, the camera will use pattern recognition to automatically follow the object as it moves around the frame (or as you move the camera around) with a "cloud" of small green AF frames.

- Fully depress the shutter button and keep it pressed to take pictures at the selected burst rate.

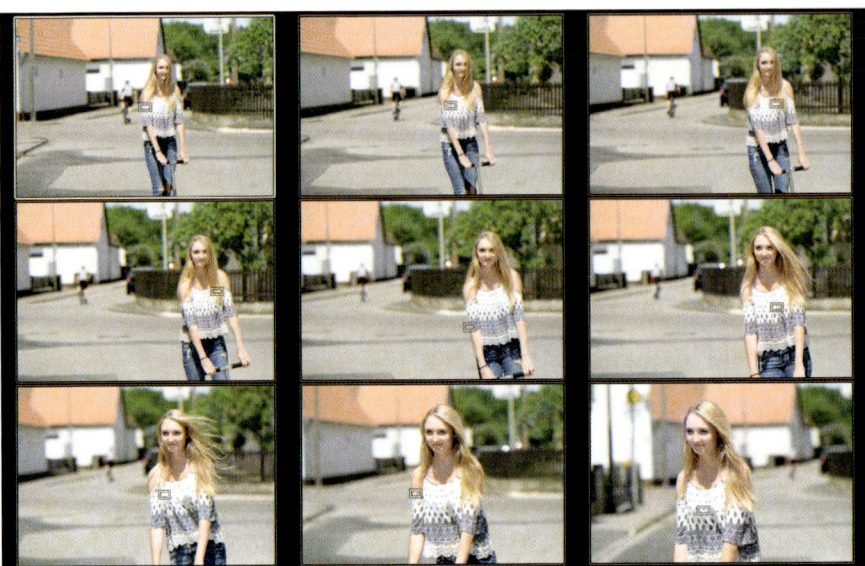

Fig. 153: AF-C in concert with **WIDE/TRACKING** and burst mode can track a subject in 3-dimensional space. To accomplish this, the camera is using pattern recognition to follow the designated subject as it moves.

Performance-wise, AF-C Tracking mode has long been a weakness with many X cameras. This changed for the better with the X-E3 and X-H1, as well as firmware upgrades for the X-Pro2, X-T2, and X-T20 that brought these models up to par. While the X-T3 offers the best 3D tracking among all X cameras, the X100F and older models with EXR II processors still suffer from lackluster tracking performance.

The same is true for AF-C tracking with face detection. As of December 2018, only the X-T3 offers great AF-C subject tracking in concert with face and eye detection. Previous X models are still using a weaker face detection algorithm that works with persons who are standing still, but falls apart with fast-moving subjects.

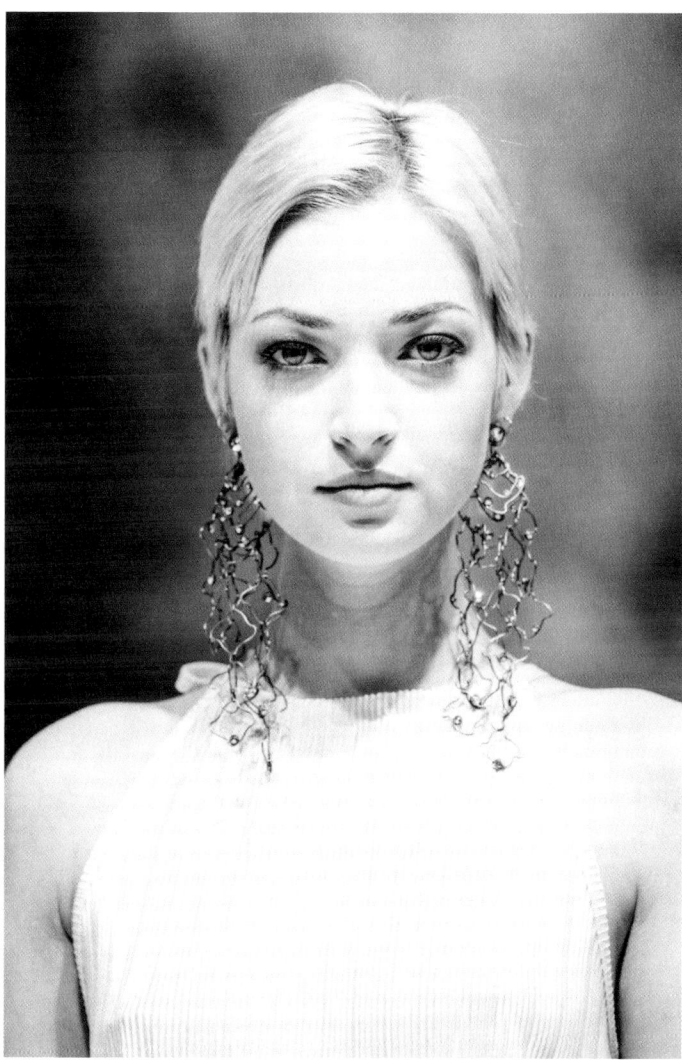

Fig. 154: **AF-C in concert with face detection** has traditionally been a weakness of X series cameras. This changes with the X-T3, which offers fast face- and eye-detection tracking. This example was shot wide open with the XF200mmF2 R LM OIS WR telephoto lens.

| Using AF-C custom settings

The X-Pro2, X-T2, X-T20, X-E3, X-H1, and X-T3 feature three parameters that allow you to customize the AF-C's behavior for a specific task or application:

■ **Tracking Sensitivity** (TS) specifies whether the camera should switch its focus to a different subject or retain its current focus to wait for the subject to reappear. This control is useful when the subject you are tracking disappears behind an obstacle or goes out of the frame, or when you aim at a new target with a different distance. Selecting 0 (zero) makes the camera switch its focus immediately, while choosing 1–4 progressively extends the time it will retain focus. Technically speaking, tracking sensitivity 0 will not predict an autofocus target's position when it's temporarily lost or obscured by something else. Tracking sensitivity settings of 1, 2, 3, and 4 will predict a lost or obscured target's position for another 0.4 seconds, 0.7 seconds, 1.0 second, and 1.3 seconds, respectively, before the AF-C locks on a new tracking target.

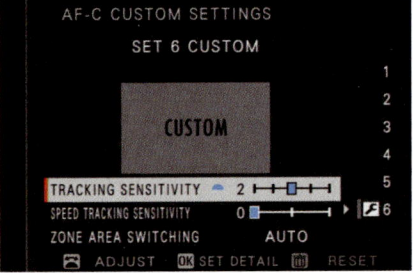

Fig. 155: By selecting a higher **TS** setting, the camera will wait a moment or two before it switches the continuous autofocus to a new target distance. The default setting is 2, which means the camera will give you about 0.7 seconds to re-aim the focus frame or zone back on your subject after you have lost sight of it. Higher TS settings are useful in situations where you want to track a specific subject with as little interference as possible.

- **Speed Tracking Sensitivity** (STS) controls the camera's tracking characteristics based on changes to the subject's speed. Selecting 0 (constant speed), the camera expects a steady movement when it predicts the subject's distance. Select 1 or 2, and the camera takes speed changes more and more into account when it's predicting subject movement, making it suitable for suddenly accelerating or decelerating targets like race cars

- **Zone Area Switching** (ZAS) is available only in the Zone AF mode and specifies which part of the focusing zone should be given focusing priority. CENTER maintains focus on the center of the zone. FRONT switches the focus to the closest subject (or part of a subject) anywhere inside the zone, which (in concert with a TS setting of 0) is great for immediately capturing new targets that suddenly move into a zone. AUTO tracks the subject you first focused on.

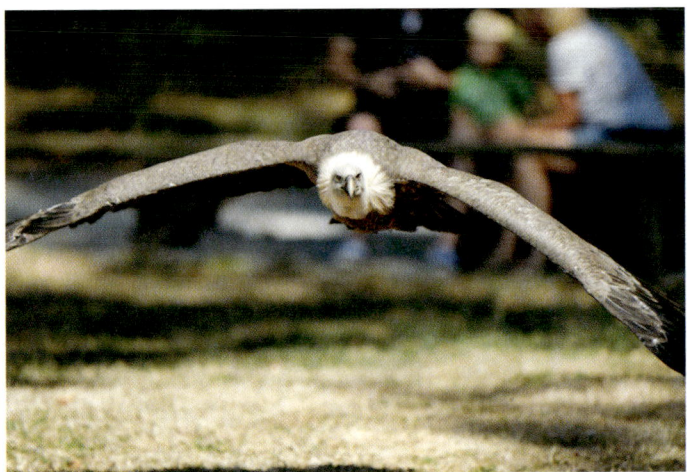

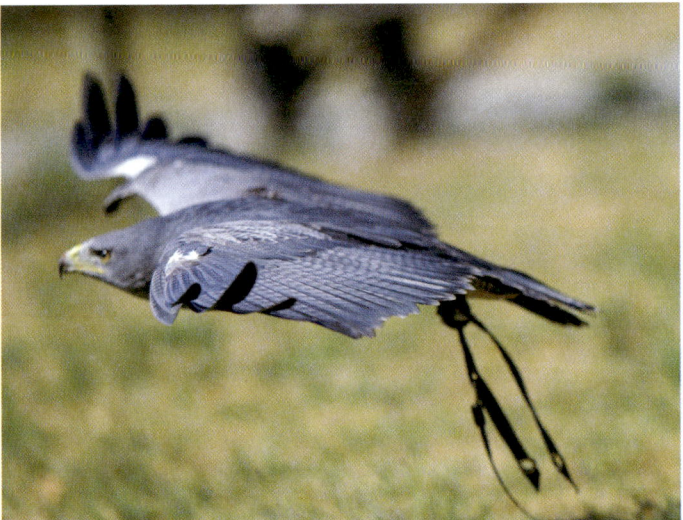

Fig. 156: By selecting FRONT as your **ZAS** setting, you can force the camera to focus on whatever part of the image inside your selected AF zone happens to be closest to the camera. In the case of the vulture that was flying toward the camera (above), a ZAS FRONT setting allowed me to focus on the bird's head and beak instead of the more prominent wings. However, using the same settings in a fly-by situation (below) only shifted the focus toward the left wing, which was closest to the camera within the 3×3 zone I had selected in my X-H1.

Unlike the X-T2, X-T3, and X-H1, the X-T20, X-E3, and X-Pro2 do *not* let you set these three parameters directly and independently. However, you can set them indirectly by choosing from several presets that cover typical AF-C shooting scenarios. Select SHOOTING MENU > AF/MF SETTING > AF-C CUSTOM SETTINGS, then pick one of the following available parameter sets:

- SET 1: STANDARD SETTING FOR MULTI-PURPOSE is the default setting and is our general AF-C setting. It's a great choice for situations where you don't have a clear understanding of how a specific custom setting could improve the AF-C performance. Its parameter settings are TS 2, STS 0, and ZAS AUTO.

- SET 2: IGNORE OBSTACLES & CONTINUE TO TRACK SUBJECT keeps the focus on a subject even when it's temporarily going out of the frame or is obscured by obstacles. This can be useful for following a specific target with the camera and ensuring that the target isn't lost when it's temporarily obscured by people, trees, or other obstacles that pass through the line of sight. Its parameter settings are TS 3, STS 0, and ZAS CENTER.

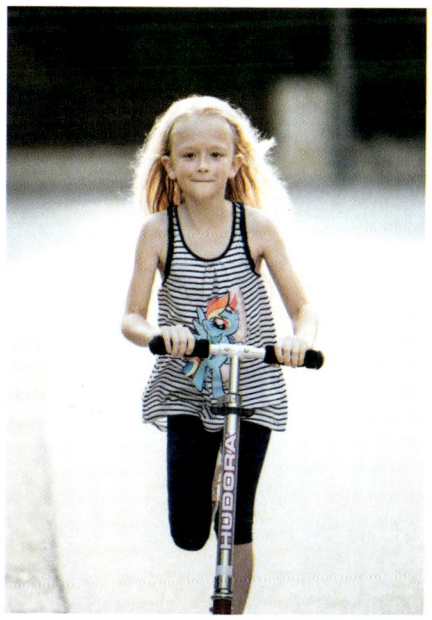

Fig. 157:
Set 2 is a good choice when you want to track a specific, steadily moving subject without interference, like this girl riding a scooter through the shot.

- SET 3: FOR ACCELERATING/DECELERATING SUBJECT is your typical racetrack mode. It takes changing relative speeds of subjects moving towards the camera into account. Whenever you have targets that rapidly accelerate or decelerate, this mode can be useful, especially in concert with XF lenses featuring high-speed linear autofocus motors. Its parameter settings are TS 2, STS 2, and ZAS AUTO.

- SET 4: FOR SUDDENLY APPEARING SUBJECT allows the camera to instantly focus on a subject that enters the focusing area, with priority given to any object (or any part of it) that is closest to the camera. It is ideal for subjects that suddenly appear in the focusing frame. Its parameter settings are TS 0, STS 1, and ZAS FRONT.

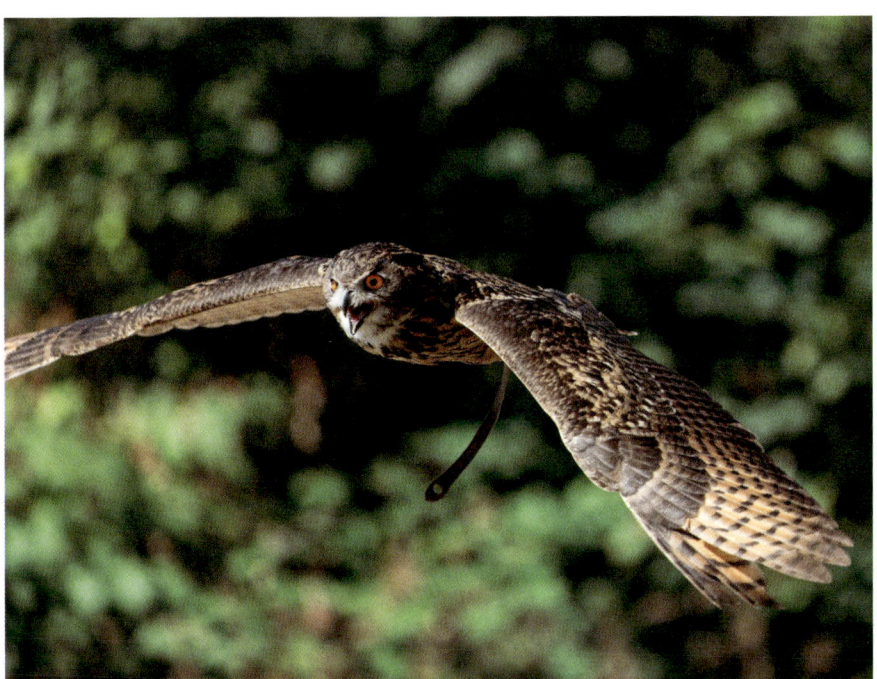

Fig. 158: **Set 4** makes sure that the AF-C immediately focuses on what's closest to the camera (as long as it's located anywhere inside the selected AF zone).

- SET 5: FOR ERRATICALY MOVING & ACCEL./DECEL. SUB-JECT is suitable for subjects that are moving at varying speeds in different directions, coming in and out of the focusing area. It is optimized for shooting field sports like soccer or tennis. Its parameter settings are TS 3, STS 2, and ZAS AUTO.

- SET 6: CUSTOM is currently (December 2018) only available in the X-T2, X-H1, and X-T3. It stores your individual setting for the three AF-C subject-tracking parameters TRACKING SENSITIVITY (TS), SPEED TRACKING SENSITIVITY (STS), and ZONE AREA SWITCHING (ZAS). Use this preset to manually create optimized settings for the specific movement characteristics of your subject.

Focus priority vs. release priority	TIP 97

The autofocus in your camera will *always* try to focus on a subject before it takes the shot. In this context, release priority vs. focus priority only refers to how the camera is behaving when the AF *fails* to lock on a target:

- Set SHOOTING MENU > AF/MF SETTING > RELEASE/FOCUS PRIORITY > AF-S PRIORITY SELECTION > FOCUS to stop the camera from taking a picture when the autofocus (AF-S) cannot lock onto a target (red AF warning).

- Set SHOOTING MENU > AF/MF SETTING > RELEASE/FOCUS PRIORITY > AF-C PRIORITY SELECTION > FOCUS to make sure that the camera only takes pictures in AF-C mode (particularly in concert with burst mode) when the autofocus can lock onto something.

Basically, selecting focus priority for AF-S and AF-C reduces the number of out-of-focus pictures on your memory card.

By default, the camera is set to release priority, following the motto, "better a misfocused shot than no image at all."

Since I am no friend of misfocused shots, my cameras are set to focus priority for both AF-S and AF-C.

Please note that when AF+MF is active in AF-S mode, the camera will always use AF-S Release Priority.

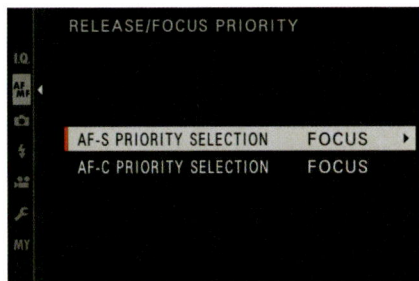

Fig. 159: Most X cameras allow you to select either **focus** or **release priority** for AF-S and AF-C. Personally, I opt for focus priority.

TIP 98 | Focusing in good light: What could possibly go wrong?

Many X series cameras find it difficult to determine a reliable and reproduceable focus distance when you are focusing on distant objects, such as a mountain, a building, or a wall. This is particularly common when you are in AF-S mode and one or more of the following conditions are met:

■ You are using a wide focal length.

■ You are using a slow lens with a small maximum aperture opening (such as f/3.5 or higher).

■ You are stopping down the lens in good lighting conditions (such as f/8 for a sunny landscape shot).

A typical example would be a bright and sunny day where you are focusing on a distant subject with nice contrast. You are using a focal length of 16mm, and you are stopping down the lens to f/8 in order to get sufficient depth of field.

What could possibly go wrong? As it turns out, quite a lot. You might notice that repeatedly focusing on the subject (by repeatedly half-pressing the shutter button) leads to a variety of different focus distances on the camera's distance scale. This is strange. After all, the distance between your camera and subject doesn't change, so you'd expect the autofocus to repeatedly and reliably deliver the same focusing result. However, in a situation like the one that I have described above (AF-S, sunny day, 16mm, f/8, distant subject), that's not necessarily the case.

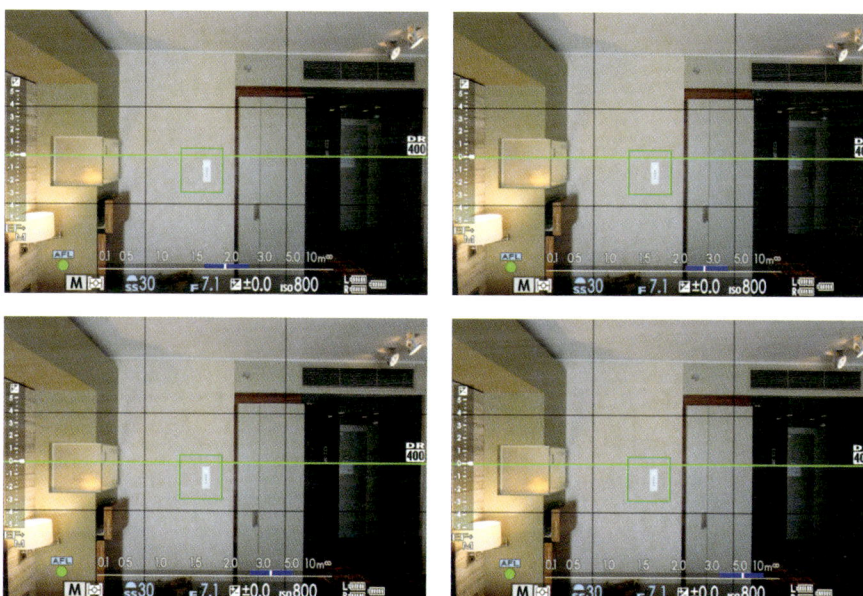

Fig. 160: Using AF-S with a stopped-down wide-angle lens in decent light can lead to unreliable autofocus results. You can test this unpleasant phenomenon by putting the camera on a tripod and repeatedly focusing on the same non-moving target (like a wall). In theory, the autofocus should always return the same focus distance, but as it turns out, it often doesn't. In this example, the wall was actually about 3 meters away from the camera, but repeated refocusing with a 16mm lens delivered random autofocus distances between 2 and 5 meters.

Why? I have a theory: By using a wide focal length in concert with a slower lens (or by stopping down a fast lens in bright light), the resulting focusing aperture delivers so much depth of field that the focus system has difficulty distinguishing between, say, a distance of 5 meters or 15 meters. For the AF system, it's all the same.

Let's be clear: When you are stopping down your lens in AF-S mode, the camera *might* focus with the maximum aperture opening of your lens, but it doesn't *have to*. In fact, the AF system will only open up the aperture when the light is poor. In bright light, however, AF-S will focus with an aperture closer to your set working aperture. This increases the DOF and, at the same time, decreases autofocus accuracy.

WHAT TO DO?

In situations like this, I recommend using Instant AF-S instead of regular AF-S. Instant AF forces the camera to *always* focus with the wide-open maximum aperture of your lens. This also means that a faster lens will work better and deliver more precise and reliable focusing results than a slower lens.

For example, if you stop down both lenses to f/8 for a landscape shot on a bright day, a XF16mmF1.4 will allow the camera to focus more precisely and with greater reliability than a XF16mmF2.8 lens, assuming that you are using Instant AF-S as your focusing method.

To use Instant AF, you have to set the camera to manual focus mode. You can then autofocus with the AF-L or AF-ON button (or whichever Fn button Instant AF has been assigned to). If you want to be sure, I recommend manually fine-tuning the focus with focus peaking and the magnifier tool. For scenes with a large depth-of-field, the DOF indicator can be of great help, too. Instead of accepting random autofocusing results, take control and set the DOF as *you* like it.

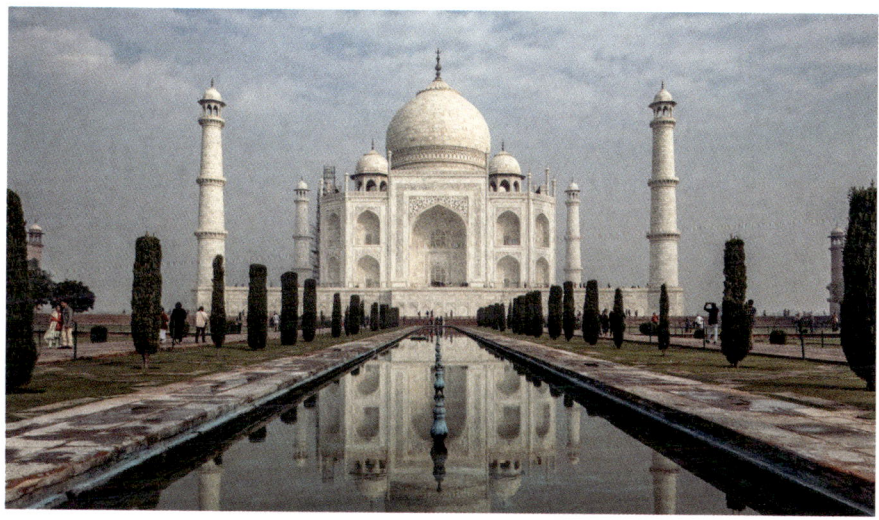

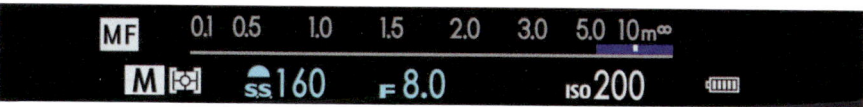

Fig. 161: When I'm taking pictures of landscapes, buildings or other subjects that don't move, I set the camera to **manual focus**. I can still use Instant AF-S to quickly autofocus on any part of the scene and then manually adjust the focus distance and DOF zone as needed. In this example of the Taj Mahal, I set the XF18–55mm kit zoom on my X-T2 to 18mm and f/8, then manually set a distance where the far end of the DOF bars touched the infinity mark of the electronic distance scale.

2.5 WHITE BALANCE, JPEG PARAMETERS, AND RAW CONVERSION

A great feature of all X series cameras is their ability to set white balance [80] and JPEG parameters before *and* after you take a shot, thanks to the built-in RAW converter. This gives you full control over the JPEGs that are generated in your camera.

It's not necessary to anticipate and set the perfect settings for each shot in advance because you can always generate different JPEG versions of a shot with the internal RAW converter. For example, you could create a version with bold Velvia colors, or a black-and-white version with strong contrast and minimal noise reduction. As long as you have access to the RAW file, you can change all JPEG parameters after the fact and use it to create as many different-looking JPEGs as you want.

Using the built-in RAW converter in the playback menu is quite easy because it offers the same functions that are available in shooting mode.

IMAGE QUALITY SETTING menu	RAW CONVERSION menu
(Exposure Comp. Dial)	PUSH/PULL PROCESSING
DYNAMIC RANGE	DYNAMIC RANGE
FILM SIMULATION	FILM SIMULATION
WHITE BALANCE	WHITE BALANCE
(incl. WB SHIFT)	WB SHIFT
COLOR	COLOR
SHARPNESS	SHARPNESS
HIGHLIGHT TONE	HIGHLIGHT TONE
SHADOW TONE	SHADOW TONE
NOISE REDUCTION	NOISE REDUCTION
GRAIN EFFECT	GRAIN EFFECT
COLOR CHROME EFFECT	COLOR CHROME EFFECT
D RANGE PRIORITY	D RANGE PRIORITY
B&W ADJUSTMENT	B&W ADJUSTMENT
LENS MODULATION OPTIMIZER	LENS MODULATION OPTIMIZER
COLOR SPACE	COLOR SPACE

Please be advised that GRAIN EFFECT, COLOR CHROME EF-FECT, D RANGE PRIORITY, B&W ADJUSTMENT, LENS MOD-ULATION OPTIMIZER, and COLOR SPACE settings aren't available in every X camera model.

Notable differences between shooting mode and after-the-fact RAW conversion in playback mode affect the first two items in this list:

- **Exposure corrections** made *before* you take a picture can affect aperture, shutter speed, and ISO. **Push/pull process-ing** applied *after* you have taken a picture only affects the ISO amplification. Effectively changing the ISO via push/pull processing also doesn't change the nominal ISO value in the EXIF data [81] of the JPEGs. Instead, Push/Pull processing in the internal RAW converter has the same effect as moving the exposure slider in external RAW conversion software, such as Adobe Lightroom, Silkypix, or Capture One.

- *Before* you take an image, you can select four different **dynamic range** options: AUTO, DR100%, DR200%, or DR400%. DR200% exposes the RAW file one ISO stop darker than indicated; DR400% exposes it two ISO stops darker. DR-Auto automatically selects either DR100% or DR200% (or DR400% in first-generation X cameras). *After* you have taken an image, you can still select different DR settings in the internal RAW converter. However, you can only *reduce* the DR after the fact, not increase it. If you are working on a RAW file that was recorded with DR400%, you can reprocess it to create JPEGs with DR400%, DR200%, or DR100%. A DR200% RAW file can be reprocessed with DR200% or DR100%, but not DR400%. And a DR100% RAW file can only be reprocessed with DR100%. The same restrictions apply to the D RANGE PRIOITY settings STRONG, WEAK, and OFF.

The correct **white balance** ensures that neutral (white or gray) areas of an image appear without color tints, regardless of the light conditions. At the same time, the results are usually not supposed to look clinically neutral. Your X camera masters this task quite well, so you can rely on the Auto white balance setting to get it right most of the time.

However, "most of the time" is not "all the time." There are instances when the white balance is off, or when you *want* it to be off. For example, you may want to emphasize a sunset with a warmer white balance. In such cases, it makes perfect sense to manually set the white balance in advance or after the fact.

X series cameras offer a variety of options to manually set the white balance:

- Several white balance presets for typical situations, such as sunny weather (Fine), cloudy skies (Shade), and tungsten light (Incandescent).

- A Kelvin option to manually set the color temperature.

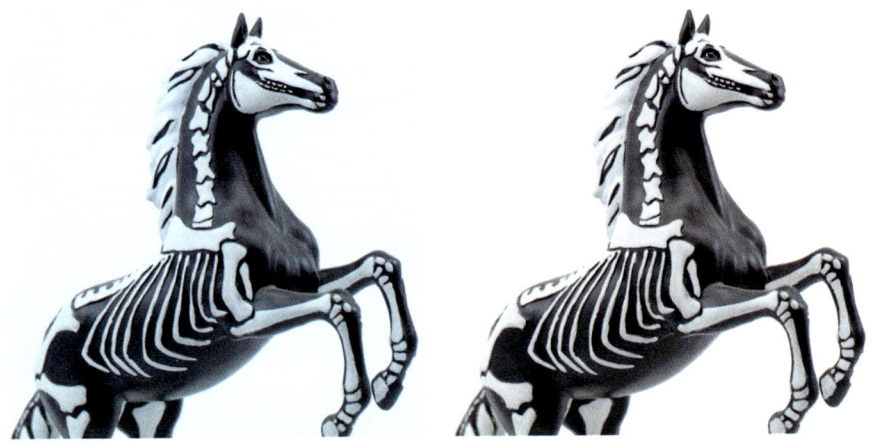

Fig. 162: AUTO white balance isn't always right. However, you can always adjust white balance later with the built-in or an external RAW converter. In this case, a simple **white balance preset** change from AUTO (left) to FLUORESCENT LIGHT-1 (right) did the job.

- Custom white balance that meters a white or neutral surface (like a white wall) under the current light conditions. This way, the camera can adjust the white balance to make the surface appear neutral.

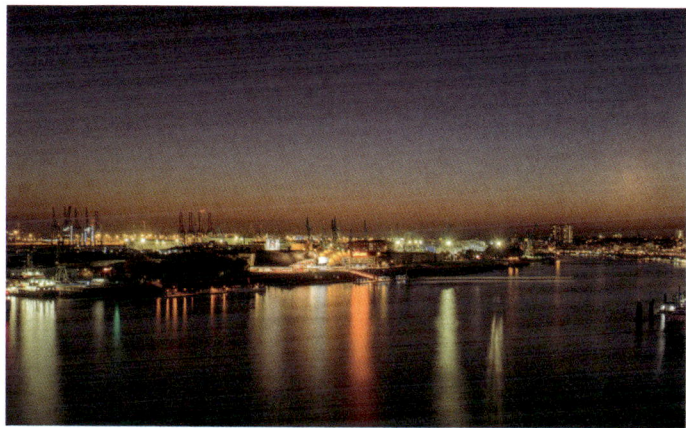

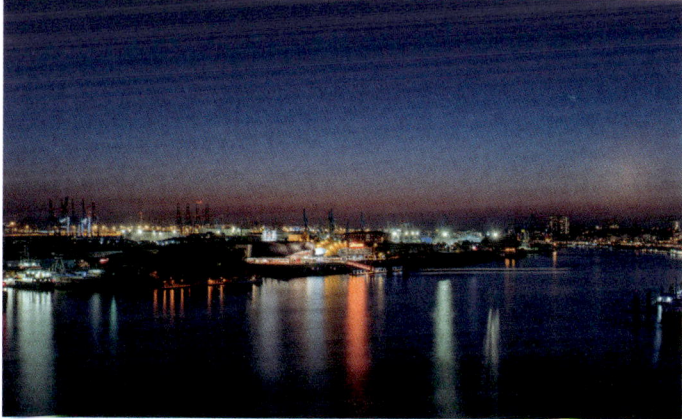

Fig. 163: Two versions of the same shot processed with **different white balance settings**. The image above shows the WB Auto setting without further corrections; the image below shows the same shot after a manual white balance adjustment in Adobe Lightroom. While white balance can also be adjusted with the camera's built-in RAW converter, extensive changes like this one are easier to accomplish with external RAW conversion software.

| TIP 99 | Custom white balance: a little effort can go a long way. |

This useful function is only available *before* you take a shot, because you are metering the white balance of the actual scene. Custom white balance allows you to calibrate the camera's white balance toward a part of your scene that you want to appear neutral in the final image.

Here we go:

■ Select SHOOTING MENU > (IMAGE QUALITY SETTING >) WHITE BALANCE > CUSTOM.

■ Point the camera toward a surface that you want to use as a neutral reference—for example a white wall or a gray card [82]. Make sure that the surface is large enough to be fully covered by the white balance metering frame in the viewfinder. Come closer to your subject or zoom in if you need to.

■ Fully press the shutter button to meter and set the new custom white balance. The live view will change accordingly and simulate the adjusted color temperature. If you are happy with the result, confirm it by pressing the OK button.

You can use the same procedure with a firing flash unit. In this case, the custom white balance will meter the mix of flash-light and surrounding light that hits your neutral reference surface.

Don't worry! You are under no obligation to use the custom white balance later during RAW conversion. It's simply one of many options, and you can always adjust it later as you please. For example, you can use the built-in RAW converter with a manual KELVIN setting or select one of the white balance presets (usually FINE, SHADE, FLUORESCENT LIGHT 1–3, INCANDESCENT, and UNDERWATER). You can even apply AUTO white balance anytime later because the camera will always save its automatic white balance reading for later use by the internal RAW converter.

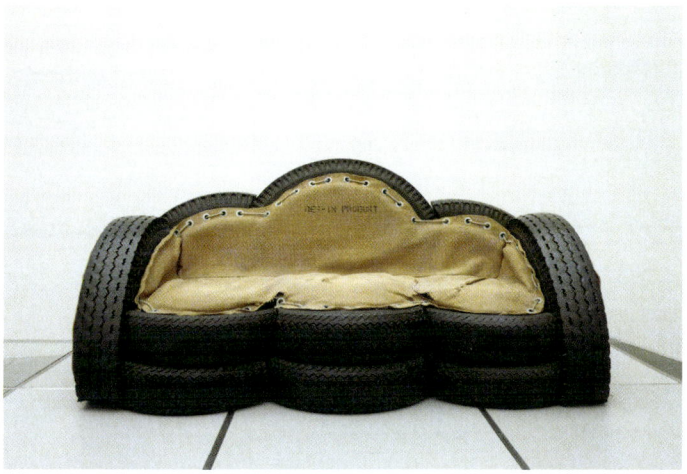

Fig. 164: A **custom white balance** setting was used to take this shot. The wall behind the sofa served as a neutral reference.

| Infrared photography | TIP 100 |

Since X series cameras are known for their weak IR-blocking filters in front of their sensors, they are deemed quite suitable for infrared photography. You'll need an infrared filter in front of your lens, typically of the R72 kind, which is available from most filter vendors. This filter blocks all light wavelengths except infrared, making sure only infrared light reaches the sensor.

To minimize the resulting red tint in the live view (and JPEGs), set the color temperature to the minimum of 2500 Kelvin. You can also select one of the various black-and-white film simulation modes to eliminate colors in the viewfinder (and JPEGs).

Since the R72 filter blocks a large percentage of light, it's useful to shoot with a tripod.

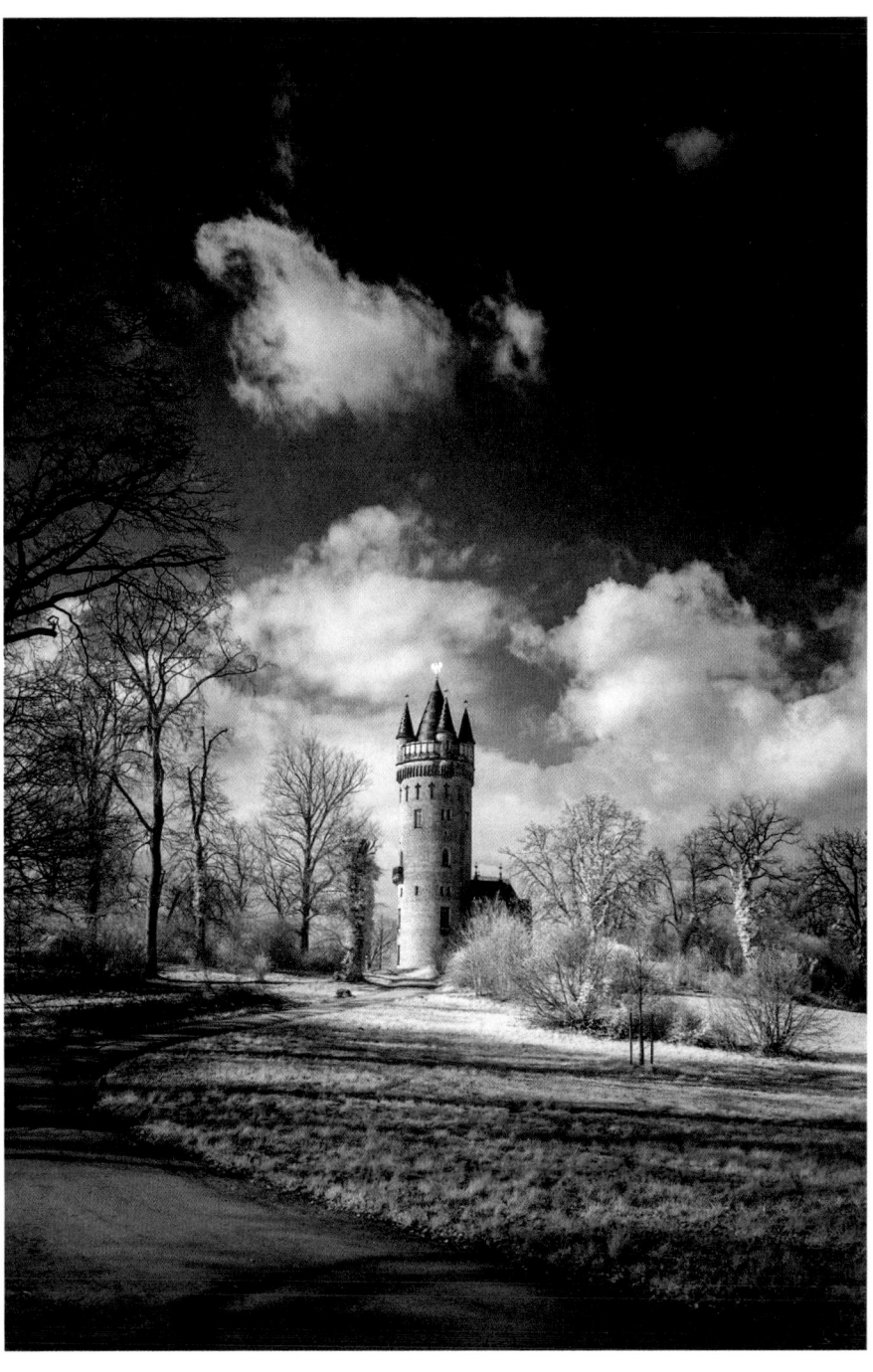

Changing color tints with WB SHIFT	TIP 101

WB SHIFT offers the opportunity to correct (or introduce) a color tint in any shot. You can adjust the color tint as an addition to any white balance setting—either before you take a shot or in the built-in RAW converter.

You can individually set a *different* white balance shift for each of the camera's white balance options (Auto, Kelvin, WB presets, and Custom white balance settings). You can do this by changing the tint between green and red on the X-axis and between yellow and blue on the Y-axis of the display that automatically appears when you select one of the white balance options.

I recommend a neutral setting here to avoid confusion. As mentioned before, there's a different white balance shift setting for each of the white balance options, meaning the camera can store up to a dozen different white balance shift settings at once. This makes it easy to forget a previously set correction, which is why I recommend introducing white balance shift only during RAW conversion. You can see, for example, that the skin tones in a portrait may require an adjustment.

Fig. 165: This **infrared image** (left) by X Photographer Mehrdad Abedi was processed in Adobe Lightroom and shot with a R72 filter (Credit: www.qimago.de).

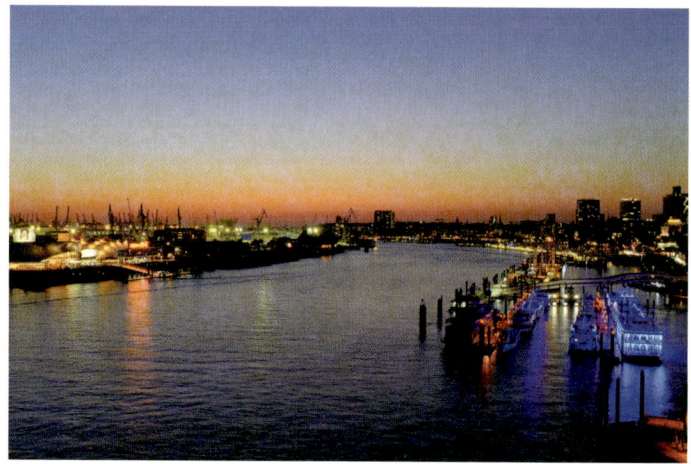

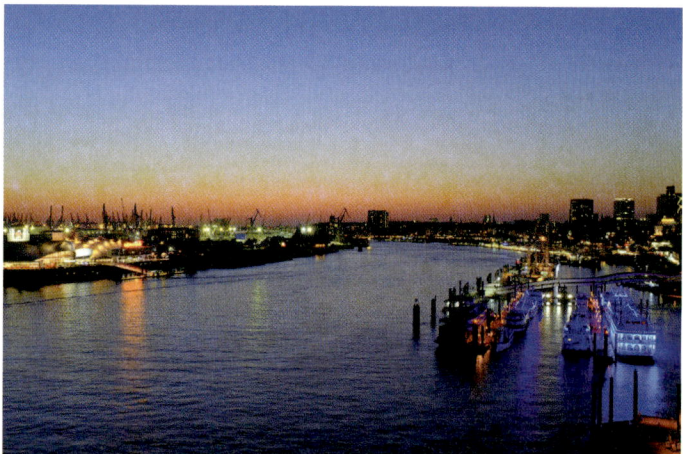

Fig. 166: WB SHIFT in action: The example above shows a straight-out-of-camera image (SOOC JPEG) with the AUTO white balance settings. Below, you can see the same image, again straight out of camera and with AUTO white balance, but with an additional WB SHIFT of BLUE +3 and RED −3 to make it look cooler than the original.

Important: WB Shift is only available for in-camera JPEGs from the built-in RAW converter. When you process a RAW file externally with Adobe Lightroom or similar software, any WB Shift settings that were active when you took the image will be disregarded.

| White balance and monochrome images | TIP 102 |

You may think that white balance adjustments don't affect black-and-white images, because monochrome shots only consist of neutral shades of gray. In reality, your white balance settings still affect the *underlying* color information that your monochrome conversion is based on.

Black-and-white photography is color photography with an additional dimension of difficulty. This added dimension is determining how different grayscale levels are assigned to different colors. Since your white balance settings affect the colors of the underlying shot, they also affect the grayscales of the color-to-monochrome conversion.

Black-and-white images can be created either in-camera (with the MONOCHROME and ACROS film simulations) or externally with RAW conversion software such as Adobe Lightroom, Capture One, or Silkypix. When you set your X series camera to ACROS or MONOCHROME, it is still re-coding RAW *color* images, which are then converted into black-and-white JPEGs.

Knowing this, you can manipulate the look of your black-and-white conversions by changing the white balance during RAW conversion—either in-camera or externally in software like Lightroom. In-camera with the built-in RAW converter, you can use one of the white balance presets, or select a manual Kelvin setting between 2500K and 10000K.

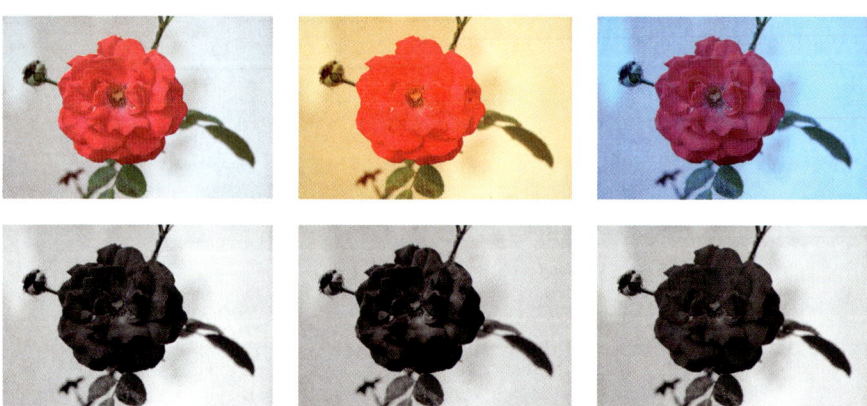

Fig. 167: **White balance and monochrome:** In the upper row, this illustration shows the same color image with Auto white balance (left), a 2500K setting (center) and a 10000K setting (right). The lower row exhibits monochrome conversions of the above images, all three made with a MONOCHROME+G FILTER film simulation and a SHADOW TONE +4 setting. The different underlying white balance settings have a visible impact on the appearance of the monochrome conversions.

TIP 103	Using film simulations

The importance of film simulations for the overall look of a JPEG is often underestimated. Film simulations influence color grading, color saturation, dynamic range, and contrast in the resulting JPEGs. Picking a film simulation should always be the first step when adjusting JPEG parameters. As with all JPEG settings, film simulations have no effect on the actual RAW file (the digital negative). They only affect the JPEGs that are generated in the camera (the digital prints). Most current X camera models offer six or seven different color film simulations, eight black-and-white modes, and one sepia option:

■ PROVIA is the standard, all-purpose setting. The name reminds us of Fuji's popular Provia slide film.

- ASTIA is another color slide film derivate with softer highlights and pleasing skin tones. It's often used for portraits but can also work with landscape shots that feature vegetation and blue sky.

- VELVIA is a very contrast-heavy, color-saturated derivate of the legendary Fuji Velvia slide film. It's mostly used for landscape and nature shots and is rather unsuitable for portrait work.

- CLASSIC CHROME reminds us of the golden era of *LIFE* magazine color photography. The distinctive look of Classic Chrome is equally suitable for landscapes and portraits.

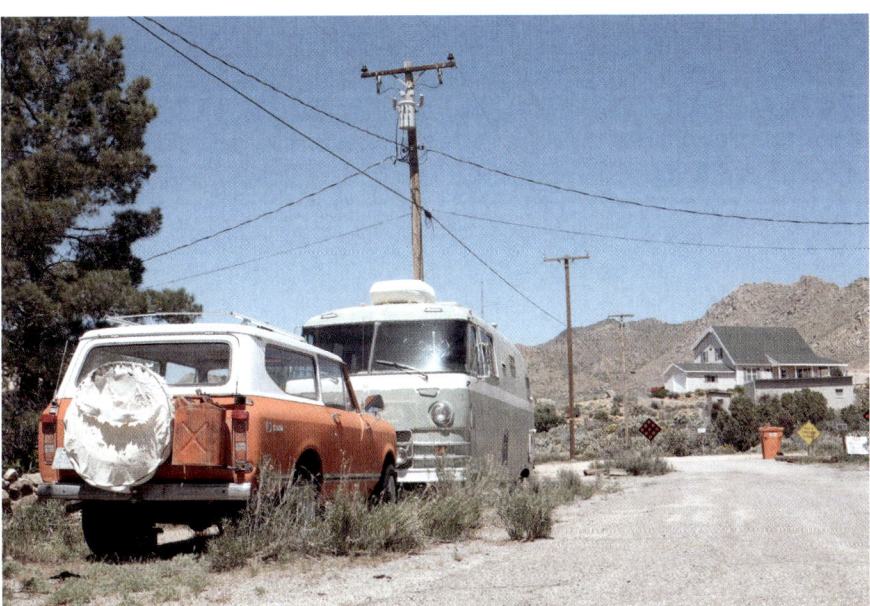

Fig. 168: The distinctive look of **CLASSIC CHROME** has earned it much popularity in a very short time.

- PRO NEG. HI is derived from a professional color negative film that was specifically made for portraits. It delivers accurate and pleasing skin tones with nice contrast, adding some punch to the image without adding too much color to faces.

- PRO NEG. STD is a rather neutral film simulation. Featuring flat contrast, subdued colors, and high dynamic range, it can look dull at first, but the JPEGs are usable for further post-processing. Fuji recommends this film simulation for studio portraits in a flash setup.

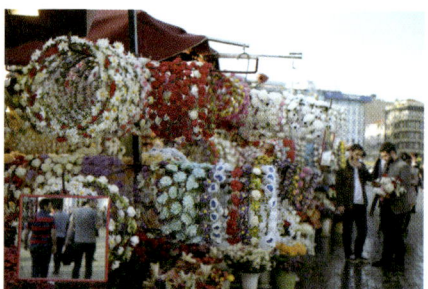 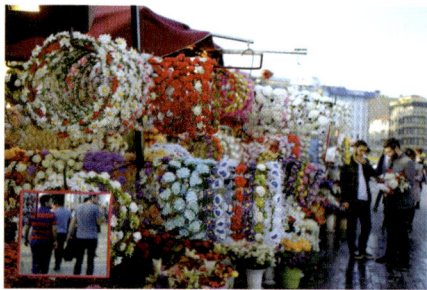

Fig. 169: **Antagonists:** PRO NEG. STD and VELVIA illustrate the spectrum of Fuji's different film simulation modes. On the left you can see the PRO NEG. STD version of a shot, and on the right its VELVIA cousin.

- ETERNA is the most neutral film simulation in the X series. As of December 2018, it was only available in the X-H1 and X-T3. Though Eterna was designed as a flat and desaturated film simulation for video production, it's also our preferred low-contrast, high dynamic range profile for RAW photography.

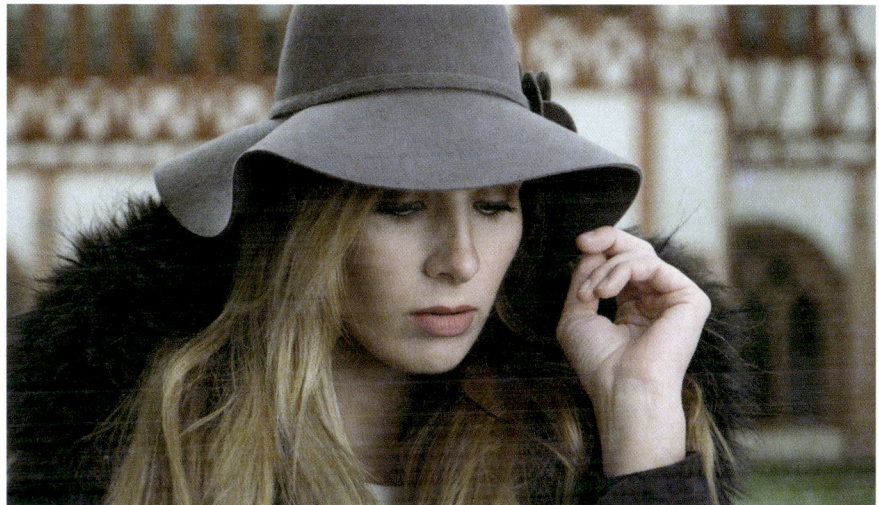

Fig. 170: ETERNA is a flat film simulation profile with a cinematic look. It is named after Fujifilm's discontinued Eterna motion picture film. With low contrast, high dynamic range and desaturated colors, it's ideal for video production work. That said, it can also be used as a flat RAW shooter profile (along with Highlight Tone −2 and Shadow Tone −2 settings) or for neutral, cinematic JPEGs like this sample image.

- MONOCHROME is Fuji's standard black-and-white conversion. Black-and-white photography is based on assigning different gray levels to different colors of a scene. To increase the contrast, many photographers combine MONOCHROME with increased SHADOW TONE and HIGHLIGHT TONE settings. Additionally, noise reduction is often decreased to reveal more detail and display more noise, which gives the appearance of film grain.

- MONOCHROME+Ye FILTER adds a digital yellow filter to the black-and-white conversion. This typically results in a slight increase of contrast because yellow parts of the scene will be represented by brighter gray tones.

- MONOCHROME+R FILTER adds a red filter to the black-and-white conversion. This means that skin tones will become brighter, which will camouflage reddish skin impurities. Conversely, blue skies will be darkened, adding contrast between clouds and the sky.

■ MONOCHROME+G FILTER adds a green filter to the black-and-white conversion. This filter will add texture to skin tones and can potentially emphasize impurities.

■ SEPIA results in a sepia-toned monochrome JPEG for an antique touch.

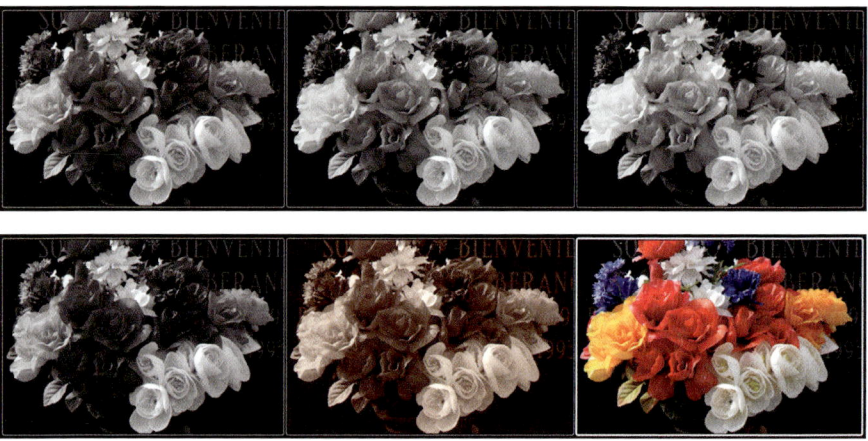

Fig. 171: **Comparing B&W options:** From left to right, top row: unfiltered B&W, yellow filter, and red filter. Bottom row: green filter, sepia, and the original shot in color.

■ ACROS is a more sophisticated alternative to the regular MONOCHROME settings. It's also available in four versions: no filter, or with either a yellow, red, or green filter. It reminds us of Fujifilm's analog Acros film and offers a quite cinematic look. This is partly because ACROS includes a noise-dependent analog film grain simulation that transforms regular image noise into analog-looking grain. In cameras with X-Processor Pro, the grain even fills areas with blown highlights and blocked shadows, creating a smooth transition between textured and blocked/blown image areas. Sadly, X-Processor 4 in the X-T3 doesn't offer this particular "soft clipping" quality and can consequently be considered a step backward in the image-quality department.

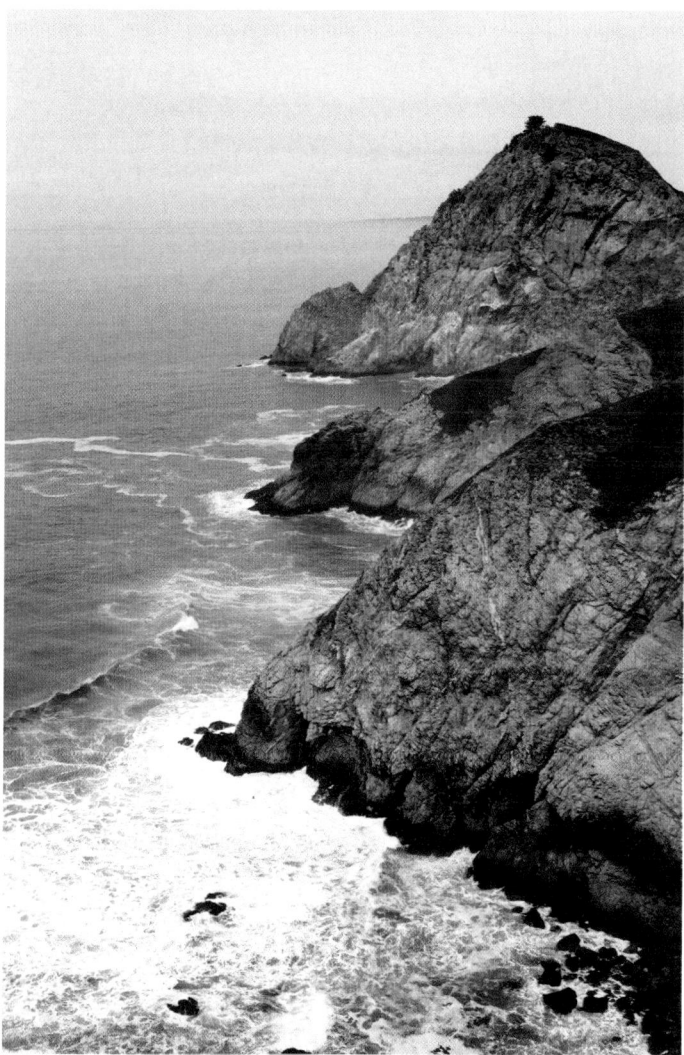

Fig. 172: ACROS has quickly become a favorite among X series users. Due to its high processing requirements, this sophisticated monochrome film simulation is currently only available in cameras that are equipped with X-Processor Pro or X-Processor 4.

The noise-dependent analog film grain simulation of ACROS is based on innovative noise shaping. To make it visible, your image must contain some noise, so it's best to set in-camera noise reduction to a minimum. Even at base ISO, there's already a subtle difference between ACROS and the regular MONOCHROME film simulation—as long as you set noise reduction to −4 in order to give the noise-shaping algorithm something to work with.

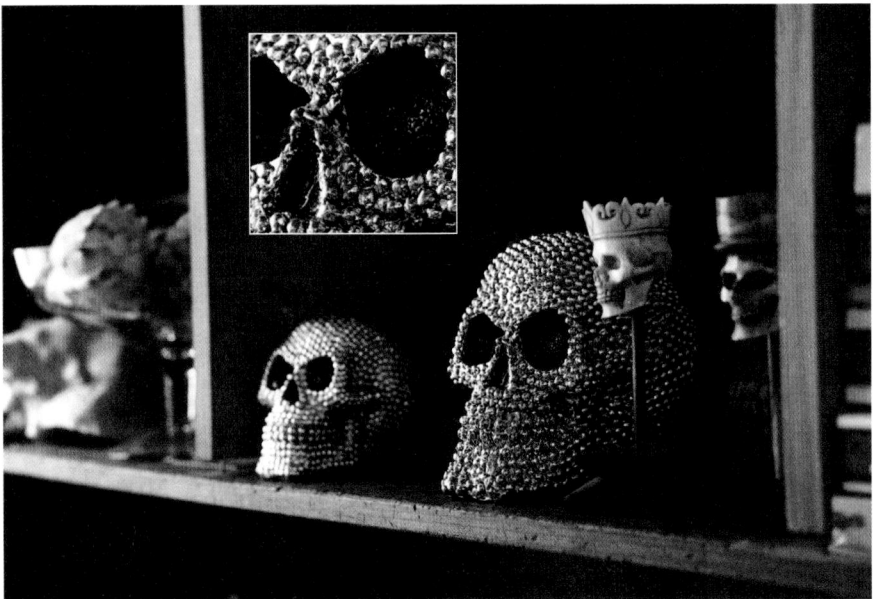

Fig. 173: Even at ISO 25600, the noise shaping of the **ACROS film simulation** delivers a natural-looking result with high resolution and fine details.

The best way to learn about film simulations is to try and compare the different options for yourself. The easiest way to do so is with the camera's internal RAW converter. Take one RAW file and process it with all available film simulations, then import the JPEGs into your computer and compare them on your monitor.

In cameras with X-Processor Pro and X-Processor 4, you can also use X RAW STUDIO [83] to conveniently remote control your camera's built-in RAW converter from your Mac or your Windows PC.

Using the GRAIN EFFECT   TIP 104

Fujifilm is all about great film simulations with an organic look. For example, adding "analog film grain" to a digital image can be useful to achieve a more natural look with enhanced micro contrast.

GRAIN EFFECT is available in cameras with X-Processor Pro and X-Processor 4 and offers three settings: OFF, WEAK, and STRONG. GRAIN EFFECT adds a layer of randomized, simulated film grain to the image. It can be used with all film simulations. Like ACROS, it fills blown highlights and blocked shadows with smoothly transitioning grain—as long as you use a camera with X-Processor Pro. Sadly, in the X-T3 with X-Processor 4, this benefit is lost.

Please note that I do *not* recommend using GRAIN EFFECT in concert with the ACROS film simulation—it would mix two different grain effects. After all, ACROS already brings its own noise-dependent grain to the table.

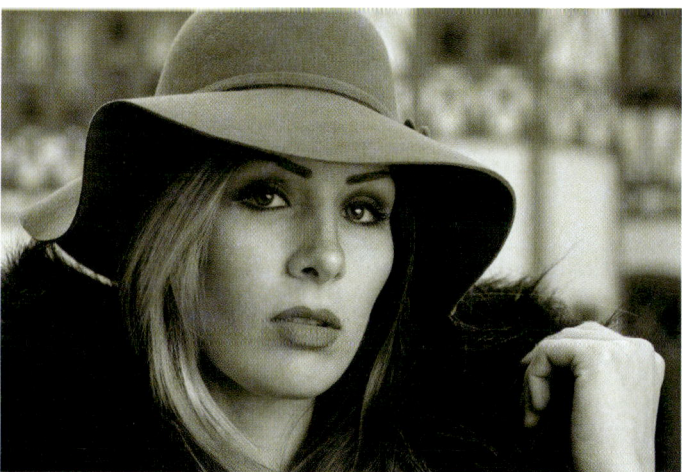

Fig. 174: Even at base ISO, using the ACROS film simulation in concert with minimal noise reduction (–4) already results in a subtle grain effect that adds organic texture to the image. This sample was shot with an X-H1 at ISO 200.

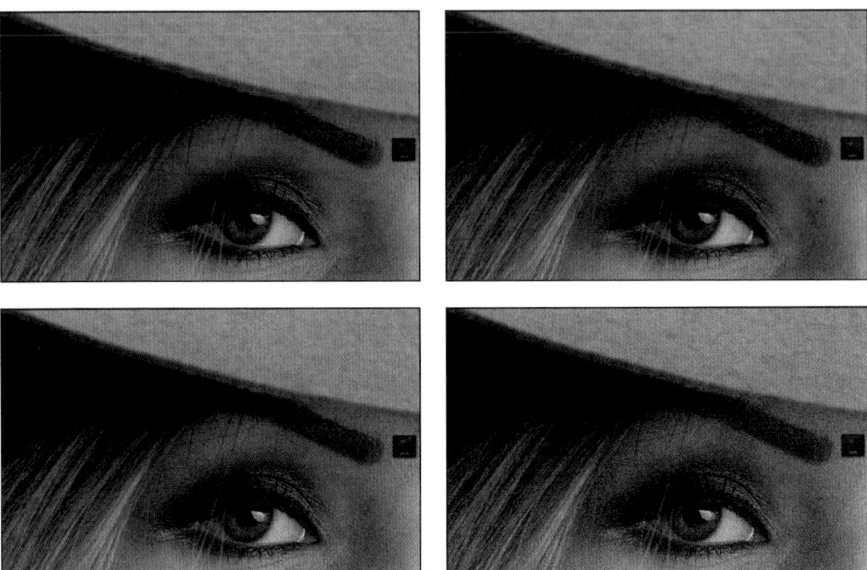

Fig. 175: GRAIN EFFECT adds natural-looking analog grain to all film simulations, providing extra texture and micro contrast for an organic look. These zoomed-in samples show the same image as before in four variations, all processed in-camera with minimal noise reduction: MONOCHROME with GRAIN EFFECT OFF (top left), ACROS with GRAIN EFFECT OFF (top right), MONOCHROME with GRAIN EFFECT WEAK (bottom left), and MONOCHROME with GRAIN EFFECT set to STRONG (bottom right). As you can see, the built-in noise shaping of ACROS holds its own without adding another layer of artificial grain via the GRAIN EFFECT setting.

Adding artificial grain may not be necessary for shots that were taken with ISO settings of 800 or higher. Instead, you can reduce the NOISE REDUCTION setting to −4 to preserve as much noise (and detail) as possible and allow the camera to do its magic.

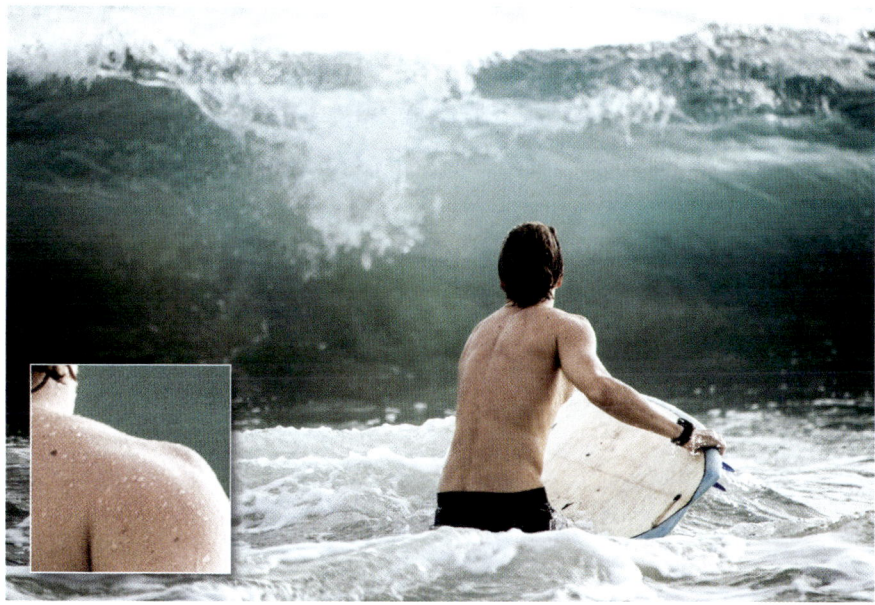

Fig. 176: **Grain effects** are also available in some external RAW converters and post-processing software. This sample shows a Lightroom-processed image with a subtle grain effect. Artificial grain is primarily about adding texture and micro contrast to an image. In most cases, the grain itself will be invisible at normal viewing distances. Subtle extra grain can also be used to trick hosting services and websites into applying less JPEG compression to out-of-focus areas when you upload images to share online. Less compression means larger files and smoother tonal transitions with less artifacts.

Contrast settings: adjusting highlights and shadows	TIP 105

A useful feature of the X series is its ability to independently set the contrast [84] for dark and bright parts of a JPEG image using the HIGHLIGHT TONE and SHADOW TONE settings. These settings can also be used to extend or reduce a JPEG's dynamic range by lifting dark shadows or lowering bright highlights. To increase the overall contrast of a shot, you can increase both parameters in tandem by choosing a setting on the plus side. To reduce the overall contrast, pick a negative setting for both parameters.

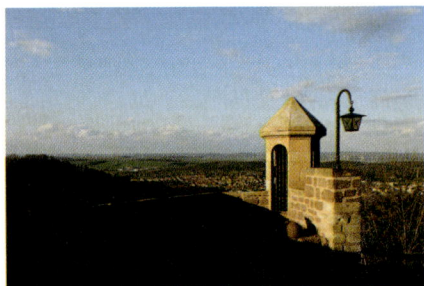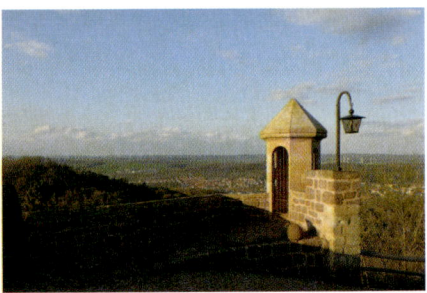

Fig. 177: Comparing **Shadow Tone** settings: The image on the left shows a SHADOW TONE +2 version; the image on the right shows the same RAW file processed with SHADOW TONE −2. Shadows and dark midtones are lifted by the reduction of the JPEG's shadow contrast, while the highlights remain untouched.

It's worth mentioning that increased contrast also enhances the impression of image sharpness and color saturation. This demonstrates that JPEG parameters always work in concert with each other.

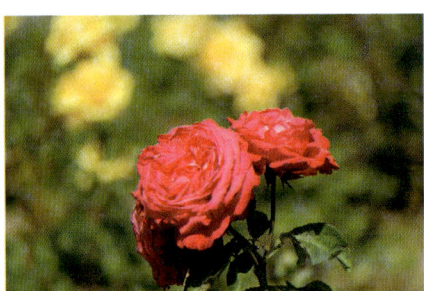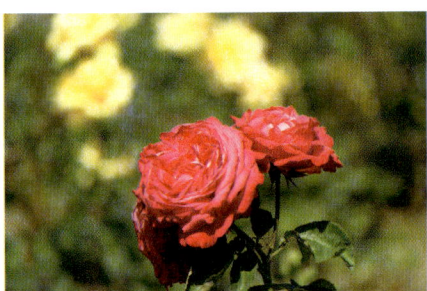

Fig. 178: Comparing **Highlight Tone** settings: The image on the left shows the HIGHLIGHT TONE −2 version of a shot; the image on the right shows the same RAW file processed with HIGHLIGHT TONE +2. Increasing the highlight contrast leaves the shadows and darker midtones untouched.

Skin tones and noise reduction: smooth or with texture?   **TIP 106**

The smoothness of surfaces (such as skin tones) at higher ISO settings is best controlled by reducing the NOISE RE-DUCTION setting. To reveal more detail and achieve less skin smoothening with in-camera JPEGs, you can decrease the noise reduction to −2 or lower.

If this still doesn't meet your demands, you can switch to an external RAW converter to turn RAW files into JPEGs or TIFFs. Current versions of RAW File Converter EX, Silky-pix, Adobe Lightroom and Capture One offer copies of the camera's internal film simulation modes. This means you can replicate the famous Fuji Colors and enjoy more control over many processing parameters.

Please note that RAW files recorded with extended DR settings (DR200%, DR400%) may require additional manual processing in external RAW converters if you want them to match the look of your camera's built-in film simulations. You'll have to tone-map the image and manually recover blown highlights. In Lightroom and Adobe Camera Raw, you can combine the sliders for exposure, highlights, shadows, whites, and blacks to get the job done.

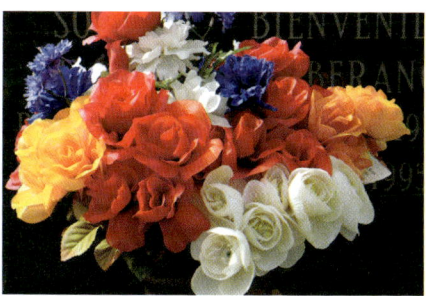 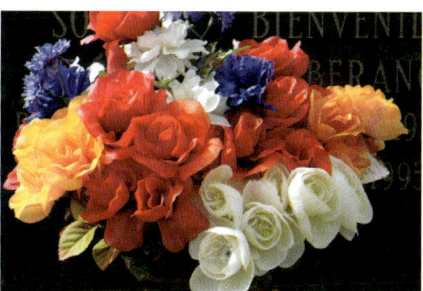

Fig. 179: In models with X-Processor Pro and X-Processor 4, the built-in film simulations and their copies in Adobe Lightroom look almost identical. This example shows a Provia JPEG from an X-Pro2 (left) and its Lightroom counterpart (right).

TIP 107 Color saturation

After picking a suitable film simulation mode, you still might want to change the color saturation [85] of an image. You can do so with the COLOR setting.

Too much color saturation can obscure texture and details. For example, VELVIA is a very saturated film mode that may sometimes require a reduction in color saturation.

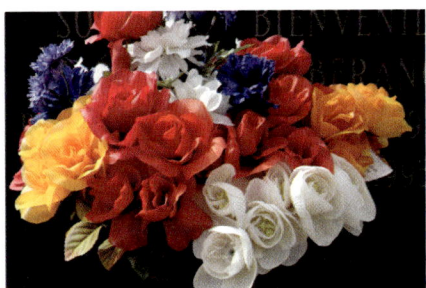 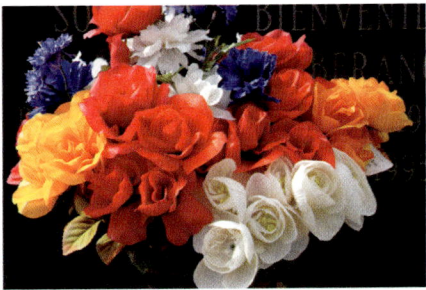

Fig. 180: **Color saturation:** The left image shows a PROVIA version with COLOR −4; the right image shows the same RAW file processed with COLOR +4.

TIP 108 The COLOR CHROME EFFECT

As of December 2018, the Color Chrome effect was only available in the GFX and X-T3. It is a calculation-heavy process that adds depth to saturated colors in an image. This is why I don't recommend using this setting in shooting mode. Instead, apply it as needed after the fact with your X camera's built-in RAW converter.

COLOR CHROME EFFECT offers three settings: OFF, WEAK and STRONG. It can be applied in concert with any film simulation, but it obviously has little or no effect when used with ACROS or MONOCHROME.

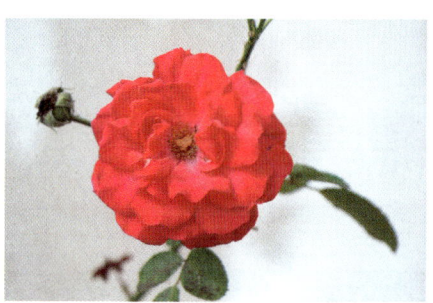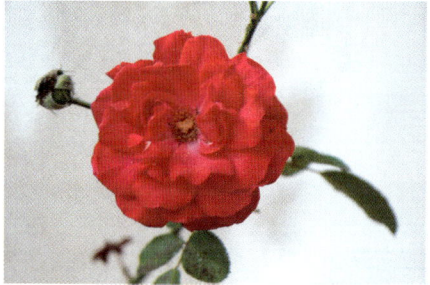

Fig. 181: This example illustrates how a regular Provia image (left) is changed by adding a COLOR CHROME EFFECT STRONG setting (right).

B&W ADJ.: adding color tints to monochrome images	TIP 109

In many cases, printed black-and-white photos aren't just black and white, but have a warm or cool color tint. Even in photographic books, it's common practice to add at least one color to monochrome pictures in order to increase the number of tones that can be realized during the printing process.

The X-T3 is Fujifilm's first X camera that allows adding a warm or cold color tint to ACROS and MONOCHROME images. With the B&W ADJ. setting, you can change the neutral look of black-and-white images with a Warm/Cool adjustment in ±9 steps.

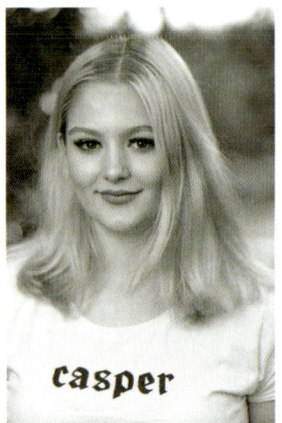 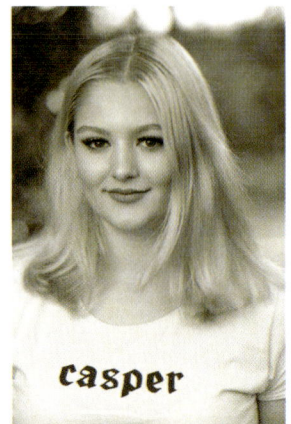 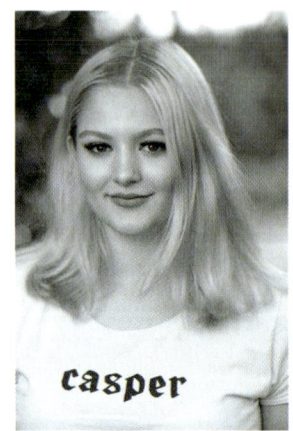

Fig. 182: This example illustrates the effect of the B&W ADJ. setting on monochromatic JPEGs: The left sample shows an ACROS image with a neutral Warm/Cool setting of 0. The center sample is the same shot, but with Warm/Cool set to +4. On the right, we have the image with a Warm/Cool −4 setting.

| TIP 110 | Color space: sRGB or Adobe RGB? |

A color space [86] is a way of organizing available colors. Most X series cameras offer two options: sRGB [87] and Adobe RGB [88]. Both color spaces contain the same *number* of colors, but not the *same* colors—their gamuts [89] are different.

Adobe RGB covers a larger gamut than sRGB because its colors are optimized for CMYK printing. On the other hand, sRGB is optimized for computer monitors and all kinds of high-resolution displays, such as HD and UHD TVs, smartphones, and tablets. Since Adobe RGB encompasses a wider gamut than sRGB, the gaps between neighboring colors and tones are wider because both color spaces contain the same number of colors. Adobe RGB must spread this number over its larger gamut. This larger gamut (compared to standard sRGB) is why Adobe RGB is also known as an extended color space.

Users often misunderstand and assume that "extended" means "better." It does not. The additional colors in Adobe RGB are only useful if you intend to print your JPEGs or TIFF files with a commercial CMYK printer. This requires a calibrated workflow and a wide-gamut monitor that can display the Adobe RGB gamut. However, most computer monitors are only capable of displaying the sRGB gamut. Using Adobe RGB on such a monitor would be like working with closed eyes because you wouldn't be able to see many of the colors you are using.

For most users (including me), sRGB is the best choice of color space. Images rendered in this color space can be viewed, processed, and printed on a wide variety of devices without unpleasant surprises. In any case, you should cal-ibrate your computer monitor with hardware like Spyder. Uncalibrated screens will not give you an accurate repre-sentation of the colors in your images.

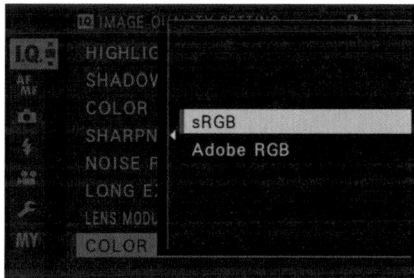

Fig. 183: Always set your camera's internal color space to **sRGB**. The color space setting in this menu only applies to JPEGs from your camera, including the live view image on the LCD and EVF (the camera displays only support sRGB). Since RAW files don't have an assigned color space, you can always create new JPEGs with a different color space either with your camera's built-in RAW converter or with external RAW conversion software.

Using custom settings (usage profiles)

Most X series cameras offer up to seven custom settings (C1 to C7) that can hold sets of camera settings for quick access. The available settings are:

- ISO (including Auto-ISO)
- Dynamic range
- D-Range priority
- Film simulation
- B&W adjustment
- Grain effect
- White balance
- Highlight tone
- Shadow tone
- Color
- Color chrome effect
- Sharpness
- Noise reduction

Please note that not all of these parameters are available in all X camera models.

Basically, custom settings comprise your camera's JPEG parameters with the addition of ISO (for cameras without a dedicated ISO dial) and dynamic range settings.

Custom settings or usage profiles aren't camera modes. They are storage spaces for sets of settings than can be quickly retrieved (usually via the Quick menu) to replace the currently active camera settings with new ones. Custom settings are mere shortcuts—time-savers that allow you to quickly change several of your camera's current settings at once instead of changing parameters one by one.

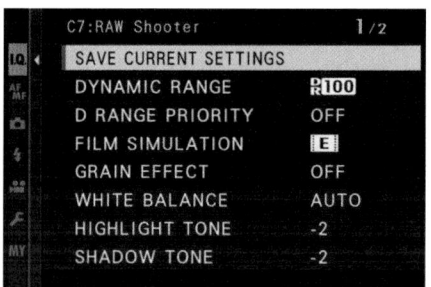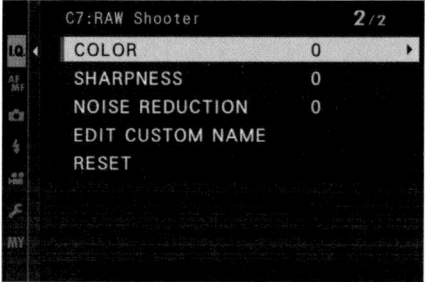

Fig. 184: Most X cameras offer three or seven **custom settings**. These usage profiles are shortcuts that allow you to quickly change or replace some of your current camera settings. Sadly, custom settings are limited to JPEG parameters, DR settings, and ISO.

The best way to select a custom setting is via the Quick menu:

■ Pull up the Quick menu by pressing the Q button and select one of the available custom settings (C1 to C7).

■ At this point, you can make changes to individual items of the retrieved parameter set using the Quick menu. Once you change a parameter, it is marked with a red dot.

■ When you are happy with your settings and changes, you can make them your new current settings by pressing the OK button or by half-pressing the shutter button. In the upper-left section of the Quick menu, the currently active settings are always marked with the word BASE. It also displays the custom setting that was last retrieved; for example, C1.

What kind of custom settings may be useful? Here are a few suggestions:

■ Make sure to save your favorite all-purpose default settings in one of the user profiles (such as C1). This enables you to quickly revert to your default settings.

■ RAW shooters can use a RAW shooter profile with dynamic range set to DR100%, HIGHLIGHT TONE −2,

SHADOW TONE −2, and ETERNA or PRO NEG. STD film simulation.

■ You could create profiles for black-and-white or infrared shooting. For example, a black-and-white profile could contain one of the eight B&W film simulations, minimal noise reduction, and additional highlight and shadow contrast.

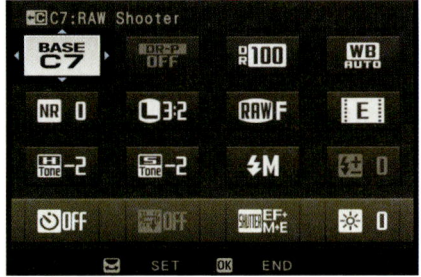

Fig. 185: Selecting C7 in the Quick menu of my X-H1. The C7 **custom setting** is traditionally the spot where I keep my "RAW Shooter" settings. To help you remember what each of the (up to) seven custom settings does, you can assign them memorable labels such as "RAW Shooter."

| TIP 112 | Working with the built-in RAW converter |

The RAW converter in your X series camera serves two main purposes:

■ You can create different versions of a shot; for example, a colorful Velvia version and a gritty black-and-white version of the same image. Not sure what's best or what you want? Quickly create multiple versions with different film simulations and varying JPEG parameters, then sort them out later at home on your calibrated computer screen.

■ You can improve your JPEGs after the fact. Since it's hard (if not impossible) to guess and set the perfect JPEG settings for each shot in advance, it's more convenient to adjust these parameters later when you have time to look at your results. You can easily change parameters like white balance, color saturation, contrast settings, sharpness, or noise reduction. You can also adjust the exposure and try different film simulations.

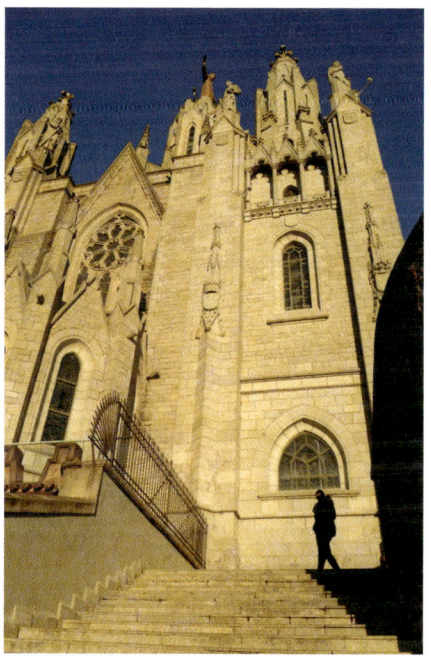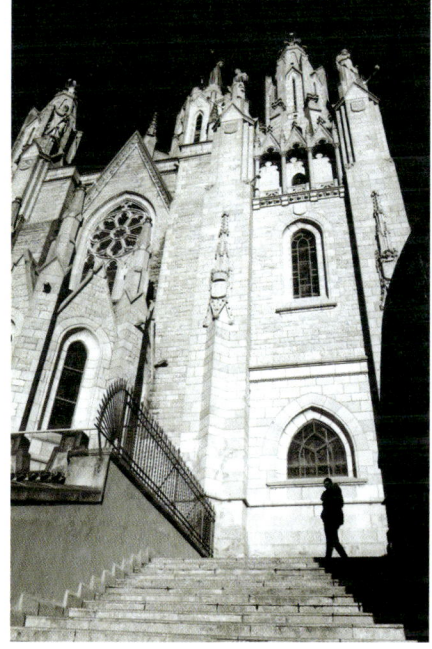

Fig. 186: Using the **built-in RAW converter** to change the look of a shot: The left image shows the scene as it was recorded with the camera's default settings. On the right, you can see the same shot processed with ACROS+Red Filter and maximum contrast (SHADOW TONE +4 and HIGHLIGHT TONE +4).

Here are a few things you can accomplish with the built-in RAW converter:

- Use PUSH/PULL processing to brighten (push) underexposed shots or darken (pull) overexposed images.

- Use the contrast settings (SHADOW TONE and HIGH-LIGHT TONE) to selectively adjust the contrast of dark or bright parts of your image. It's perfectly adequate to combine these functions with PUSH/PULL processing. To generate JPEGs with maximum dynamic range for further post-processing on your computer, it may be useful to set both contrast parameters (shadows and highlights) to −2 and use a neutral film simulation like PRO NEG. STD or ETERNA.

■ Adjust the color saturation of your JPEGs with the COLOR parameter. Reducing the color saturation can recover texture when one or more of the color channels appear oversaturated.

■ Use SHARPNESS and NOISE REDUCTION in opposition with each other: increase sharpness while diminishing noise reduction to obtain more texture in high-ISO shots.

■ Adjust the white balance using one of the presets or a Kelvin value to make your shot look warmer or cooler. Use WB SHIFT to correct or introduce a color tint.

■ Want to know what the Lens Modulation Optimizer (LMO) is doing? Take a RAW sample and process JPEGs with and without LMO in the internal RAW converter. Then, compare the results on a computer screen. Happy pixel peeping!

■ Picked the wrong color space? No problem! Just reprocess the shot with the correct color space.

To process RAW files that have already been transferred to a computer, you can use the free X RAW STUDIO application as a remote control interface for your camera's built-in RAW converter.

By the way: Your specific X camera cannot process RAW files from X series models other than your own. For example, the built-in RAW converter of an X-T2 cannot process RAW files that were taken with an X-T20. However, you can process RAW files that were shot with a different copy of the same model.

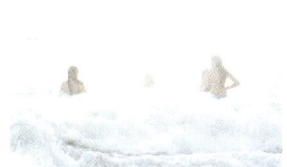 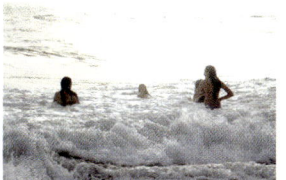 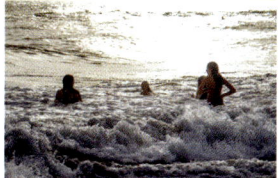

Fig. 187: You can also use the **built-in RAW converter** to correct a shot: The left image shows an overexposed sample shot that was recorded with my X-Pro2's default settings and DR400%. In the middle, you can see the same shot processed in-camera with a PULL of –2 EV, maximized shadow contrast (SHADOW TONE +4), and the VELVIA film simulation. To complete the comparison, the version on the right was created with Adobe Lightroom.

Working with X RAW STUDIO	TIP 113

The built-in RAW converter of X series cameras is a practical tool for on-the-fly RAW conversions in the field. You can use your camera's LCD or EVF display (I recommend the latter) to create new and improved JPEGs from RAW files that are saved on the SD card in your camera.

But what if your RAW files have already been transferred from the SD card to a computer? Instead of copying them back to a card and processing them in-camera, there's a better and more comfortable way: FUJIFILM X RAW STUDIO.

X RAW STUDIO is a free download for Windows and macOS [90]. Don't confuse it with a stand-alone RAW converter, though. Basically, X RAW STUDIO is a PC/Mac-based remote control and user interface for the built-in RAW converter of your X series camera. This means that X RAW STUDIO doesn't work without your camera, which has to be tethered to your Mac or PC via USB.

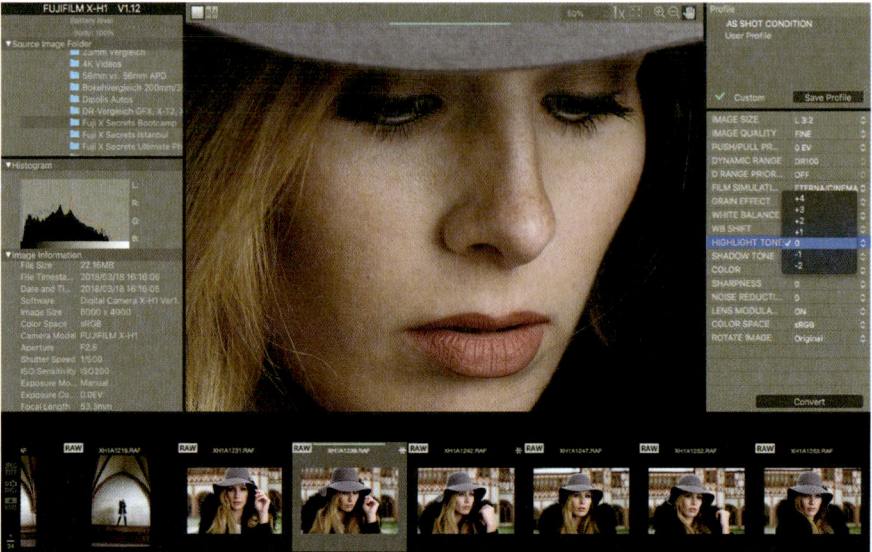

Fig. 188: **FUJIFILM X RAW STUDIO** is a simple way to remotely control the built-in RAW converter of your camera and use it to process RAW files that are stored on your Windows PC or Mac. The free app sends RAW files from your computer to the camera via an USB connection, where they are remotely processed to "in-camera JPEGs" that are immediately returned to your PC. You get the best of both worlds: The ease of use of a computer interface (with a large display and convenient storage for all your images) is combined with the processing power and image quality of your camera's internal RAW converter.

X RAW STUDIO works with X-Processor Pro and X-Processor 4. As of December 2018, compatible cameras included the X100F, X-Pro2, X-T2, X-T20, X-E3, X-H1, X-T3, GFX 50S, and GFX 50R. The X100F, X-Pro2, X-T20, and X-E3 connect with a USB 2.0 Micro cable, while the X-T2, X-H1, and GFX 50S can be tethered with either a USB 2.0 Micro or a faster USB 3.0 Micro connection. The X-T3 and GFX 50R work with a modern USB-C connection.

Set-up your camera to work with X RAW STUDIO by selecting SET UP > CONNECTION SETTING > PC CONNECTION MODE > USB RAW CONV./BACKUP RESTORE, then connect it to your Mac or PC via USB while X RAW STUDIO is running.

Operating the software is mostly self-explanatory, but feel free to consult Fuji's online manual [91].

Since it runs on a computer, X RAW STUDIO offers a more comprehensive user interface than the stand-alone converter in your camera. You can copy and paste development settings from one image to others, and you can set-up and save development presets for later use. Batch-processing of multiple RAW images is also no problem.

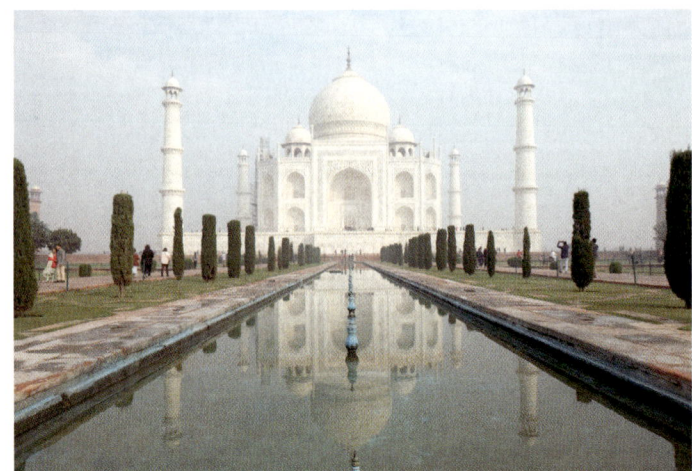

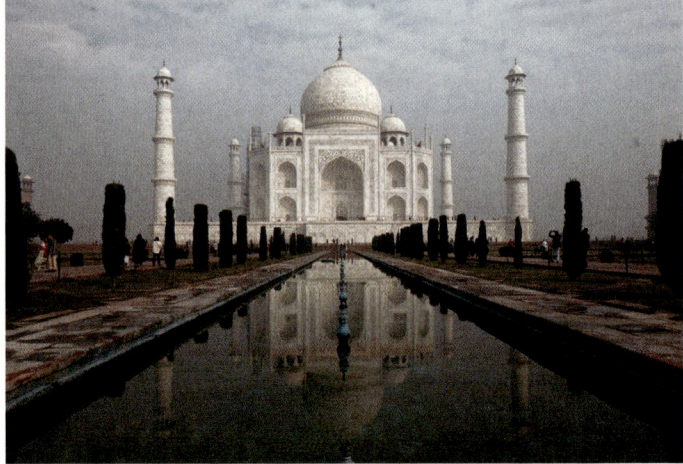

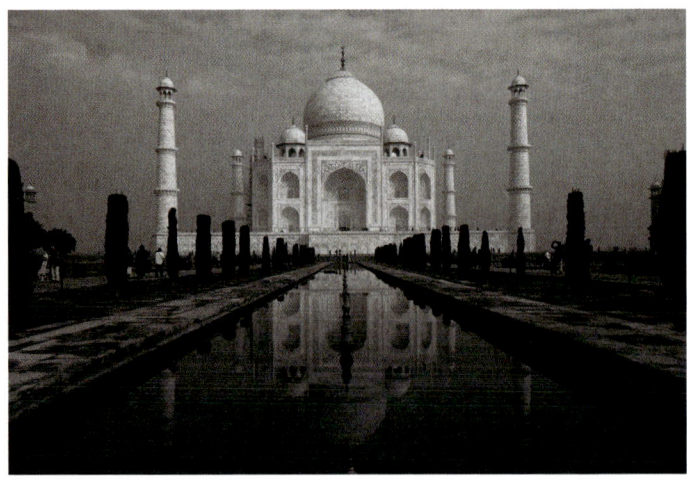

Fig. 189: **X RAW STUDIO** offers a straight-forward workflow. You begin with selecting a RAW image from your computer's hard drive. In this case, I chose a shot of the Taj Mahal that I took with my X-T2 and an XF18–55mm kit zoom. The image is automatically processed and displayed with the camera settings that were active when I took the shot (top image). In this case, I used the camera's factory defaults with PROVIA.

The center image is the same RAW file after processing it with different settings. After changing the film simulation to CLASSIC CHROME, I lowered the exposure by applying a PULL of −1.33 EV, raised HIGHLIGHT TONE to +4 for brighter highlights, reduced NOISE REDUCTION to −4 to reveal maximum detail, and applied SHARPENING +3, because I was unlucky enough to bring a soft XF18–55mm lens copy with me to India. After clicking on the Convert button, the app saved the new and improved JPEG on my Mac, using the same directory as the underlying RAW file.

The image below is a second processing variant of the same shot, this time using MONOCHROME+R FILTER, PULL −1.33 EV, HIGHLIGHT TONE +4, SHADOW TONE +1, NOISE REDUCTION −4, and SHARPENING +3. I also changed the white balance to 4500K and applied a WB shift of R: −5 and B: +7 for a little bit more drama.

Comparing external RAW converters	TIP 114

So far, we have talked a lot about the built-in RAW converter. It's a great tool to create JPEGs. It's also easy to use, because it utilizes the same functions and parameters that are available in the shooting menu. But what about diehard RAW shooters who don't care much about in-camera JPEGs, Fuji colors, or the built-in RAW converter? Those guys (I tend to be one of them from time to time) require an external RAW converter to process their RAW files.

In this tip, I'll compare how popular external RAW processors handle specific features of your X series camera:

- **RAW File Converter EX** comes free with your camera. This software is currently based on version 8 of the Japanese **Silkypix** [92] RAW processor that is also commercially available in version 9. If you want to use all the features of this software, you might want to upgrade to the latest "real" version of Silkypix. As a Fujifilm camera user, you are eligible for an upgrade discount in many territories. Please note that the current RAW File Converter EX version 3 also supports Fujifilm's film simulation modes. This software is available as a free download [93].

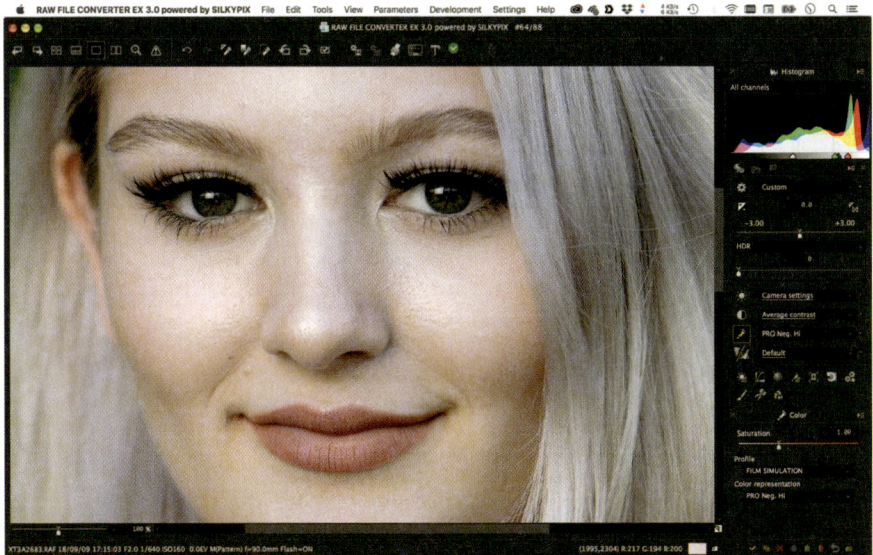

Fig. 190: **RAW File Converter EX** is a free download on the Fujifilm website. It's available in versions for Windows and macOS, and it only works with RAWs from Fujifilm cameras. The current RAW File Converter EX version 3 is based on the Japanese Silkypix 8 converter and therefore lacks the new shadow and highlight recovery functions of Silkypix 9.

■ The most popular RAW converter is **Adobe Lightroom** [94]. Its processing module is also available in Photoshop as **Adobe Camera Raw (ACR)**. There are now actually two versions of Lightroom: Lightroom CC and Lightroom Classic CC. Whenever I mention "Lightroom" or "Lightroom CC" in this book, I actually refer to "Adobe Lightroom Classic CC," which is Adobe's new name for the PC/Mac-based desktop version of the app.

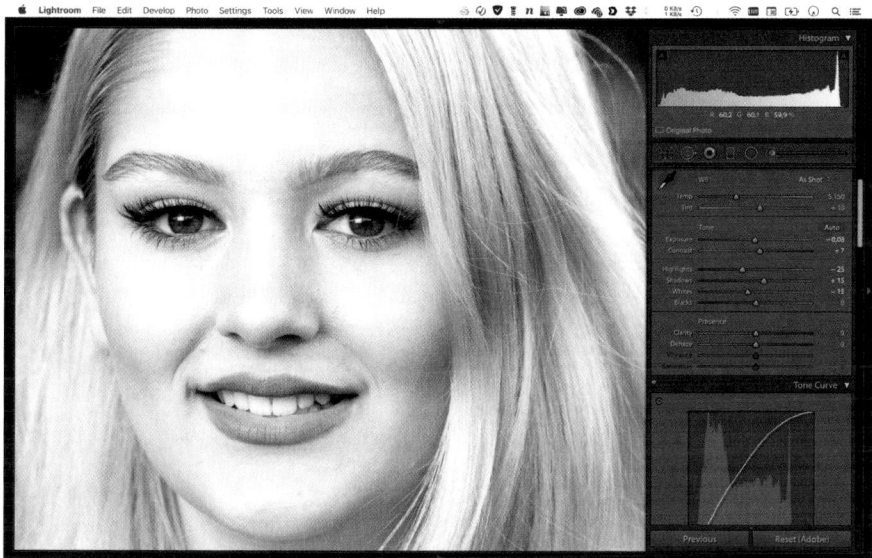

Fig. 191: **Adobe Lightroom Classic CC,** Lightroom CC, and Adobe Camera RAW are just different names for the world's most popular RAW conversion engine. The software is considered an industry standard. Subscribers use it on Windows and macOS as well as on Android and iOS devices, where it offers cloud-based workflow synchronization across all platforms. Current versions of Lightroom are only available via a subscription-based payment model, mostly in a bundle with Adobe Photoshop.

- **Capture One Pro** is similar to Lightroom and deeply rooted in the professional community. It's made by PhaseOne [95], the same folks who are building medium-format cameras and digital camera backs. At Photokina 2018, Fujifilm and PhaseOne entered into a 5-year agreement that ensures that Capture One fully supports existing and upcoming X series models, including the GFX. There is now also a special version of Capture One Pro for Fujifilm [96] as well as a free Capture One Express software for the Fujifilm X series. Please note that all Capture One versions are the same download file, with different feature sets being activated depending on what license you pick on the activation screen.

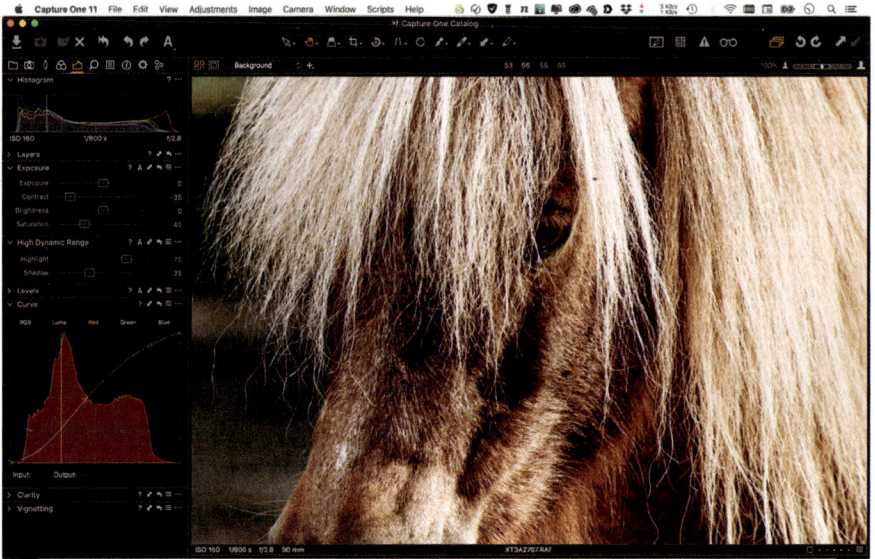

Fig. 192: **Capture One Pro** is a comprehensive RAW converter particularly popular among professionals and PhaseOne medium-format photographers. You can activate the software as a free Capture One Express for Fujifilm version, as Capture One Pro for Fujifilm, or as the regular Capture One Pro version that works with RAW files from 500+ cameras, including Fujifilm. You can also choose between subscriptions and perpetual licenses [97].

- A great RAW processor for macOS users is **Iridient Developer** from Iridient Digital [98]. Even more popular among Fujifilm users is **Iridient X-Transformer** for macOS and Windows, which can be launched from a plug-in in Adobe Lightroom. It converts Fujifilm RAF files into pre-demosaiced DNG files that can be perfectly processed in Lightroom, thus combining the strengths and benefits of Iridient Developer and Lightroom.

- **Photo Ninja** from PictureCode [99] is another interesting option. Like Iridient Developer, it can extract a great amount of sharpness and detail from Fuji's X-Trans RAWs. It also contains a module for adaptive tone-mapping, offers competent noise reduction, and features a special algorithm to restore blown highlights.

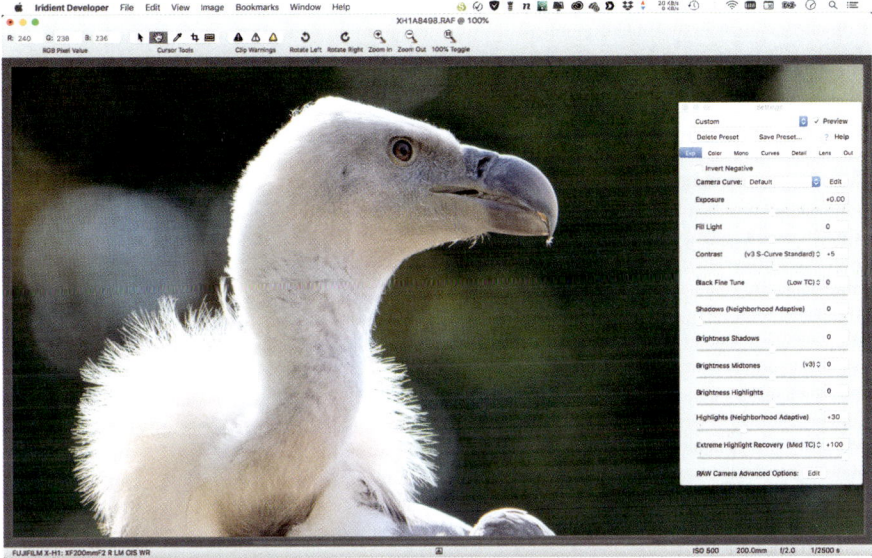

Fig. 193: **Iridient Developer** is a macOS-based RAW converter that is known for delivering great results with X-Trans RAWs. This led to a spin-off converter named Iridient X-Transformer for Windows and macOS, which works particularly well as a companion software to Adobe Lightroom.

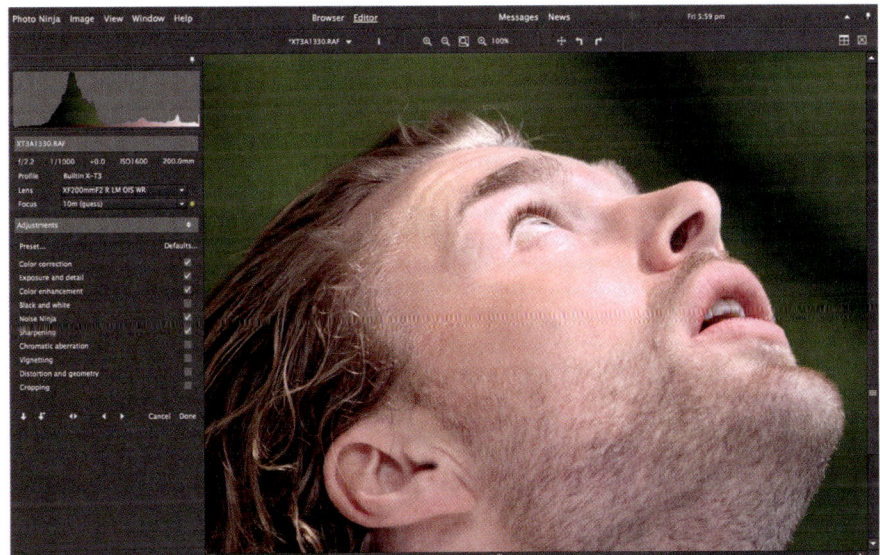

Fig. 194: **Photo Ninja** is a no-nonsense RAW converter for macOS and Windows that works well with X-Trans files. While its graphical user interface is hopelessly outdated, the modules for tone-mapping, highlight recovery, and noise reduction (Noise Ninja) are very powerful.

Which RAW converter is right for you? That's up to you! Luckily, you can download free trial versions of all mentioned programs to find out for yourself. That said, it can be helpful to make a quick comparison that tells you how well some important Fuji-specific features are supported by each alternative.

Those features are:

- Original Fujifilm film simulations
- Shots taken with extended DR settings (DR200%, DR400%)
- Digital lens corrections (distortion, vignetting, etc.)

Let's have a look...

FUJIFILM FILM SIMULATIONS

Provia, Astia, Velvia, Classic Chrome, Eterna, Pro Neg. Hi, and Pro Neg. Std make up the color backbone of the X series. Together, they constitute the Fuji Colors. However, the makers of external third-party RAW converters often have their own ideas about the look of processed Fuji RAWs.

- The **built-in RAW converter** is the benchmark reference for external RAW converters when it comes to emulating Fuji Colors.

- In their current iterations, **RAW File Converter EX** and **Silkypix** fully support Fuji's own film simulation modes.

- **Adobe Lightroom** and **Adobe Camera Raw** also feature camera profiles that closely emulate Fuji's film simulation modes—as long as you are shooting in DR100% mode.

- **Capture One Pro** now officially supports Fuji's film modes for X cameras with X-Processor Pro and X-Processor 4, thanks to their new collaboration with Fujifilm.

- **Iridient Developer** offers support for Fuji's film simulation modes but hasn't provided updated profiles that are optimized for the GFX and cameras with X-Processor Pro and X-Processor 4. The reason is simple: If you use the popular **Iridient X-Transformer** as a Lightroom plug-in, you have full access to Lightroom's own Fujifilm profiles, which closely match the film simulations in cameras with X-Processor Pro and X-Processor 4.

- **Photo Ninja** doesn't support Fuji's film simulations.

EXTENDED DYNAMIC RANGE (DR200%, DR400%)

Using the DR function results in RAW files that are exposed with an ISO setting that is 1 EV (DR200%) or 2 EV (DR400%) lower than indicated in order to protect critical highlights. The darker ISO exposure of the RAW data is compensated during RAW conversion by a digital ISO push of the same amount that only affects shadows and midtones.

- The **built-in RAW converter** is the benchmark here, since it fully automates the tone-mapping process of partially pushing the shadows and midtones back to where they belong.

- **Silkypix** and **RAW File Converter EX** are smart citizens, too: they recognize RAW files with DR200% and DR400%, and they push them up by 1 or 2 EV, then automatically recover the blown highlights by adjusting the highlight recovery slider accordingly. That said, the results don't necessarily look exactly like the JPEGs from the camera.

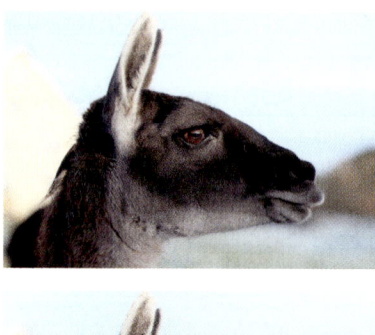
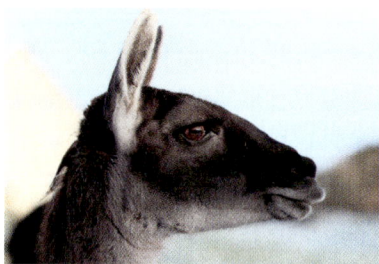
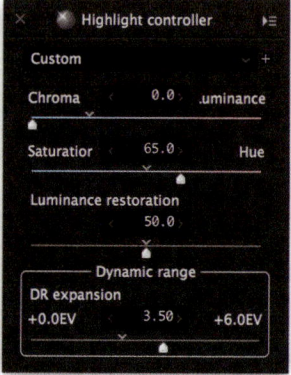

Fig. 195: The unique pastel highlights' look of a straight-out-of-camera DR400% JPEG (top) isn't easy to replicate with external RAW converters. With RAW File Converter EX and Silkypix, you can get close (bottom) by tweaking the highlight control's default settings (right).

- **Lightroom** and **Adobe Camera Raw** are also smart enough to recognize RAWs with extended DR settings, and they automatically push the exposure up 1 or 2 EVs when the RAWs are opened in the software. However, recovering the highlights isn't an automated process; it's the user's job. This can become challenging because Lightroom's exposure-related sliders work in a different way than Fuji's internal tone-mapping.

- **Capture One Pro** works like Lightroom and applies a push of 1 or 2 EV to RAWs that were recorded with a DR200% or DR400% setting. There's also a slider to recover highlights that may have disappeared during this push, but the results look different from Fuji's own DR tone-mapping. However, DR200% and DR400% settings in RAW files from cameras with X-Processor Pro or X-Processor 4 are fully emulated if you are using one of the official Fujifilm film simulation profiles in Capture One. The results look similar to the original DR200% and DR400% JPEGs from the camera.

- **Iridient Developer** operates like Lightroom and Capture One, automatically pushing RAW files that were recorded with a DR200% or DR400% setting. There's also a Highlight Recovery slider to restore highlights that may have vanished, and here's the good news: the results very much resemble the look from the camera's internal RAW converter. Well done! **Iridient X-Transformer** doesn't create JPEGs and relies on Lightroom to recover highlights. Lightroom treats DR200% and DR400% X-Transformer DNGs just like DR200% and DR400% RAF files.

- **Photo Ninja** uses its own powerful adaptive tone-mapping module, and hence doesn't really bother emulating Fuji's simple tone-mapping. There are several sliders to adjust a RAW file's exposure during processing.

DIGITAL LENS CORRECTIONS

Digital lens corrections affect three areas: devignetting, distortion correction, and the removal of chromatic aberrations (CAs). The information to perform such corrections is stored in the metadata of each RAW file. Every RAW converter can potentially read and use this metadata to apply appropriate image corrections. However, not all converters are able to do so.

- The **built-in RAW converter** supports all types of lens correction, including the camera's Lens Modulation Optimizer (LMO), which isn't available in external RAW converters.

- **Silkypix** and **RAW File Converter EX** can read and process the RAW metadata for distortion correction, devignetting, and CAs. All corrections are automatically applied and can't be controlled by the user.

- **Lightroom** and **Adobe Camera Raw** can also process lens-correction metadata and automatically apply the respective corrections in the background. It's currently not possible to control or stop the application of these lens corrections. That said, Lightroom offers *additional* correction profiles for the lenses of X100 series cameras *on top* of the metadata-based digital lens corrections. With these additional profiles, distortion and vignetting can be further corrected or even over-corrected.

- **Capture One Pro** can also process lens-correction metadata. Unlike Lightroom and Silkypix, it allows users to control the intensity of the corrections or switch them off altogether. There's also an option to reduce diffraction blur.

- **Iridient Developer** can use lens-correction metadata, too. Like Capture One, it also provides control over the extent of the corrections. In a similar fashion, **Iridient X-Transformer** offers checkboxes to switch off any of the three metadata-based lens-correction parameters. This means that X-Transformer, when used as a Lightroom plug-in, can serve as a way around Lightroom's current inability to disregard RAW metadata-based lens corrections.

- **Photo Ninja** ignores all lens-correction metadata. Instead, the software asks the user to provide suitable profiles or to manually correct distortion, vignetting, and CAs.

Automatic lens metadata corrections can look a bit different depending on the RAW converter because each converter tends to interpret the data differently.

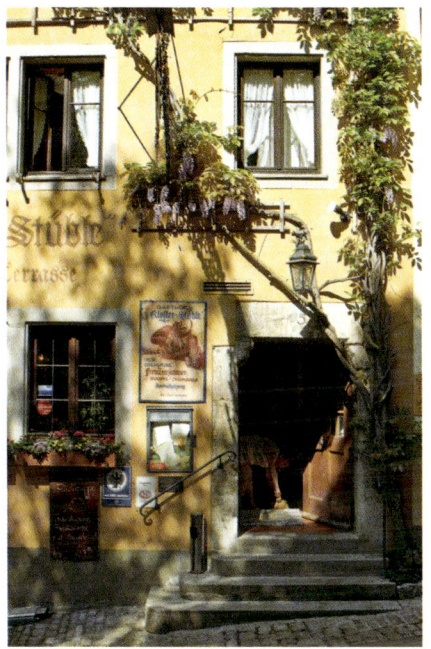 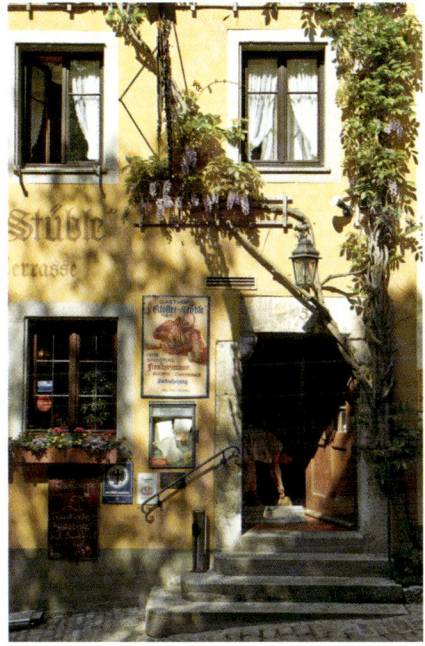

Fig. 196: **Digital lens correction:** This shot was taken with a Zeiss Touit 1.8/32 lens. The left image shows the shot without digital distortion correction. On the right, you can see how Capture One Pro applied the digital distortion correction to straighten the lines.

Sharpening RAWs with Adobe Lightroom	TIP 115

Sharpening X-Trans RAW files in Adobe Lightroom is a controversial topic on the internet, especially when it comes to landscape shots with grass and foliage.

As a general rule, you should always sharpen an image near the end of your editing process. Clarity, contrast, and color settings all impact how crisp or soft an image looks, so make sure that those parameters are set before you finalize the sharpening.

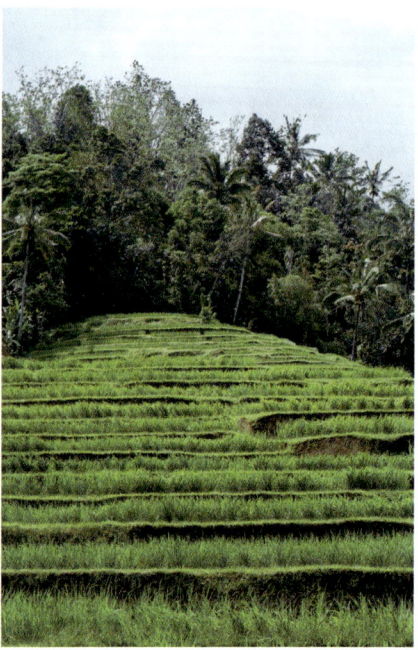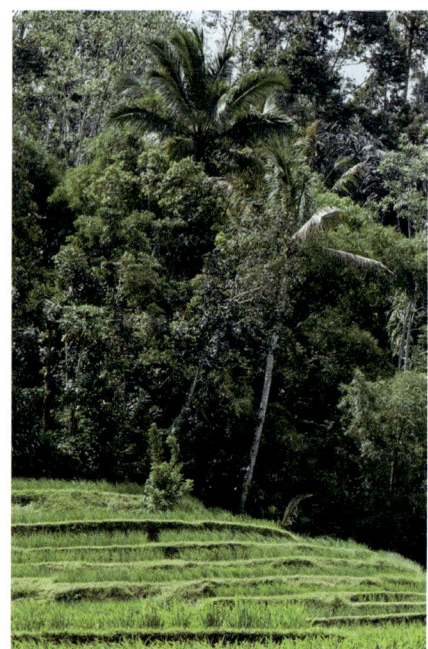

Fig. 197: X-Trans sensor shots of vegetation and foliage are considered difficult to **sharpen with Adobe Lightroom** and Adobe Camera RAW (ACR). This 16 MP example from Bali was taken with an X-Pro1 and XF60mmF2.4 R Macro lens at f/8 and 1/250s. The full image is printed on the left. On the right, you can see a zoomed-in crop of the shot.

Lightroom's *Sharpening* panel consists of four sliders:

■ Amount
■ Radius
■ Detail
■ Masking

I recommend beginning with the Masking slider. This parameter defines what parts of your image are affected by the sharpening settings. This is essential: If you apply sharpening to areas that don't require sharpening (like out-of-focus areas, the sky, or subjects with smooth surfaces), all you get are unpleasant artifacts and false detail. This applies equally to images from Bayer and X-Trans sensors, the only difference being that Bayer artifacts tend to look "nicer" and are often confused with actual detail, not the false detail that they really are.

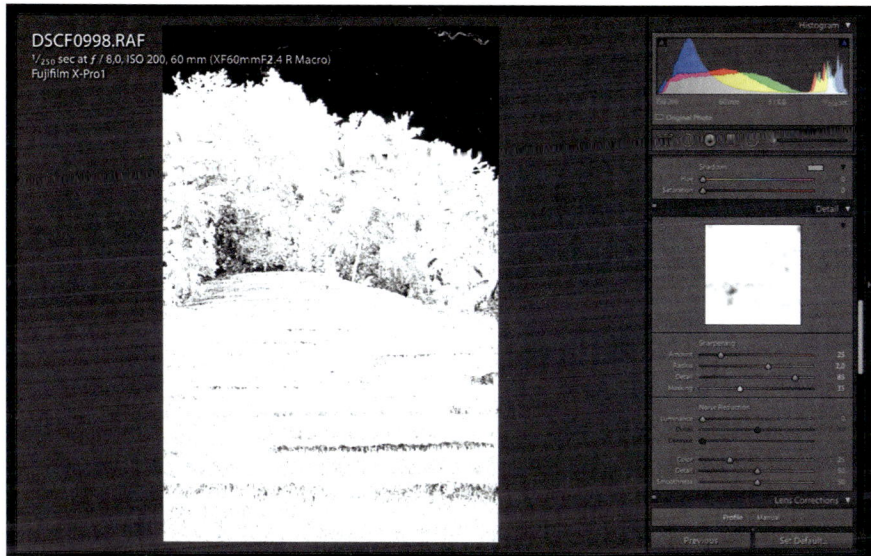

Fig. 198: **Masking the image** is usually the first step of any Lightroom sharpening protocol. To select a fitting mask, hold down the Option (Alt) key while you move the Masking slider. The black-and-white mask tells you what areas of the images will be affected by your sharpening settings: bright areas will be sharpened; dark areas won't. In this case, I opted for a Masking setting of 35 to make sure that I sharpened the entire landscape, but not the sky.

Over-sharpening an image in Lightroom/ACR leads to worm-like artifacts that are particularly unpleasant to look at when they occur in areas that don't require sharpening in the first place.

The Amount, Radius, and Detail sliders are responsible for sharpening the areas that haven't been masked out via the Masking slider. To avoid sharpening artifacts, you can move *either* the Amount *or* the Detail slider further (or even far) to the right—but you shouldn't move them very far in tandem. You can select high settings for Amount as long as you keep Detail in the single-digits. In the same fashion, you can move Detail up even to its maximum settings of 100 as long as you keep the Amount slider well below 30.

The Radius slider defines the thickness of the sharpening outlines. A higher Radius value (typically 1.5–2.0) results in a bolder or thicker sharpening at the cost of obscured detail. As a basic rule, you should use lower Radius settings if your image contains plenty of actual fine detail. Use higher Radius settings with images that are less detailed—for example due to camera shake, motion blur, subpar focusing, or a soft lens. A higher Radius setting can also be useful with difficult subjects such as foliage and vegetation, because it helps obscure false detail that can occur as part of the demosaicing process.

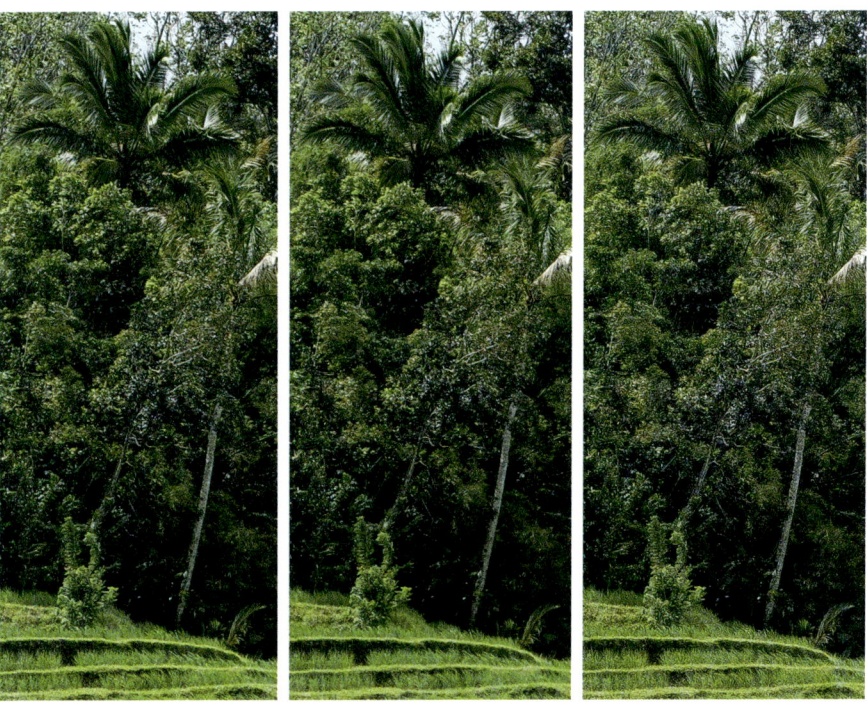

Fig. 199: **High settings for Amount or Detail** are only tolerable when you don't overly increase both parameters together. The zoomed-in example on the left was processed with an Amount/

Radius/Detail/Masking setting of 100/2/10/35; the one in the middle was processed with 30/2/100/35; the example on the right was sharpened with 75/2/75/35 and is clearly overdone with artifacts.

In many cases, soft RAW images can already be sharpened just by increasing the Radius setting.

Using Iridient X-Transformer	TIP 116

X-Transformer [100] is the perfect companion tool for the Adobe Lightroom users among us. It's a neatly integrated app that offers enhancements in three important categories:

- Better dynamic range
- Improved demosaicing
- Finer sharpening

Since X-Transformer works as a plug-in app for Lightroom, you get these improvements without sacrificing any Lightroom functionality. X-Transformer transforms Fujifilm RAF files into pre-demosaiced RGB DNG files that can be processed in Lightroom just like any other RAW file. You can still apply all film simulations, profiles, settings and presets, and adjust the white balance as needed.

To install the Lightroom plug-in, open the X-Transformer app and select HELP > INSTALL LIGHTROOM PLUG-IN. To transform a Fujifilm X series RAW film into a pre-demosaiced X-Transformer DNG, all you have to do is highlight the RAW files(s) in Lightroom's Library or Development module and select FILE > PLUG-IN EXTRAS > PROCESS SELECTED RAF(S) TO DNG. It's a fully automated process.

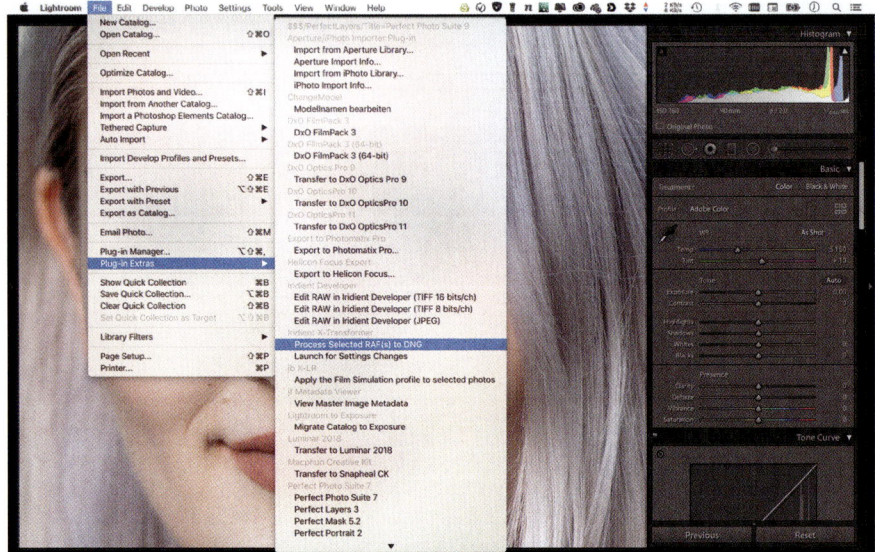

Fig. 200: **Transforming RAFs to X-Transformer DNGs** is easy, thanks to the plug-in structure of the app. After selecting the RAF files that you want to transform, all you have to do is execute PROCESS SELECTED RAF(S) TO DNG. Lightroom will then pass the selected RAF(s) to X-Transformer, which turns them into pre-demosaiced DNGs and hands the results back to Lightroom where they are automatically linked to the original RAF files.

Using X-Transformer as a pre-processing stage can be helpful in situations where you want to maximize your camera's dynamic range by pulling up shadows and midtones by several(!) stops. X-Transformer's benefits in this regard are most visible with RAWs from older 12-bit cameras like the X-E1 and X-Pro1, and with shots that were taken with the electronic shutter (ES).

To maximize dynamic range, your camera's sensor needs to be ISOless. But that's just half of the story. It's also important to use a RAW converter that correctly handles pushing up RAW files by several stops. As we now know, Lightroom delivers better results when it is pushing X-Transformer DNGs than original RAFs.

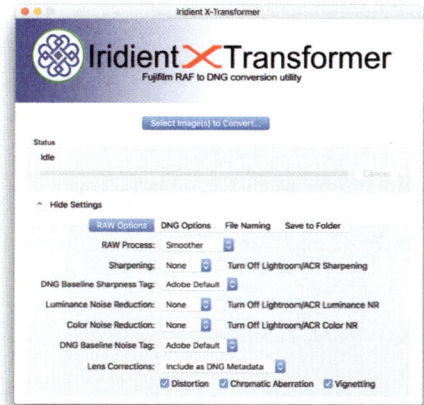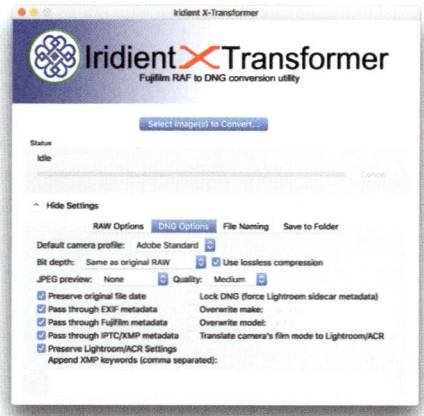

Fig. 201: To make sure that X-Transformer DNGs can be processed in Lightroom with the same settings of their original RAF versions, it's essential to **configure X-Transformer** appropriately. The screen-shot on the left shows my suggested *RAW Options* settings. On the right, you can see my preferred *DNG Options*. With these settings, all adjustments that you have already applied to the original RAF in Lightroom will be copied and applied to the X-Transformer DNG.

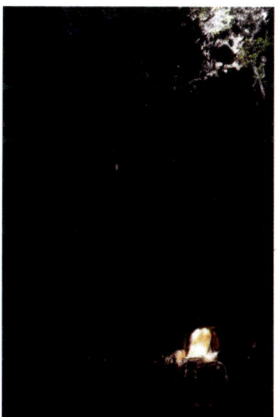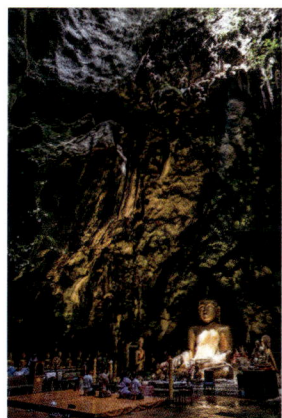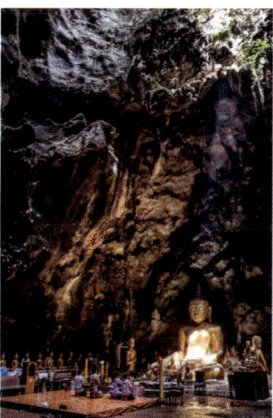

Fig. 202: This X-E1 example illustrates how X-Transformer helps **improve Lightroom's dynamic range** capability. On the left is the original exposure to the highlights at base ISO 200. In the middle, you can see the Lightroom-processed RAF with a strong push of the shadows and midtones. The image on the right shows the same Lightroom processing, but now of the DNG from X-Transformer. The green tint and blocked shadows of the RAF version have dis-appeared.

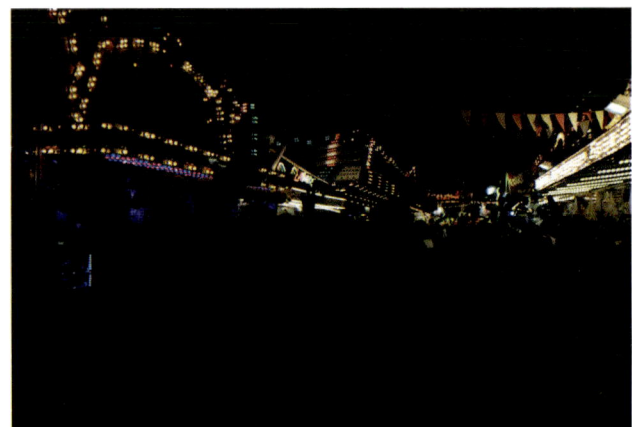

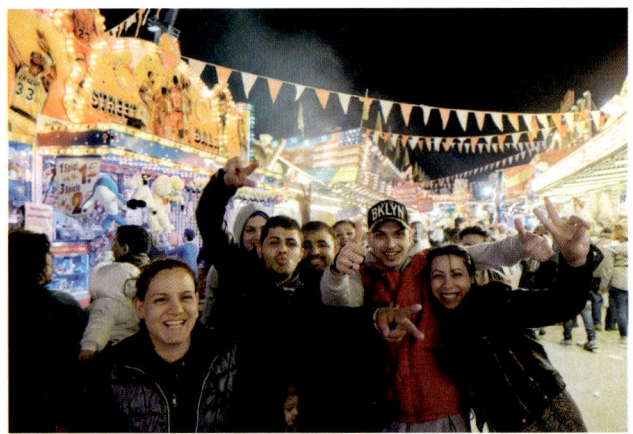

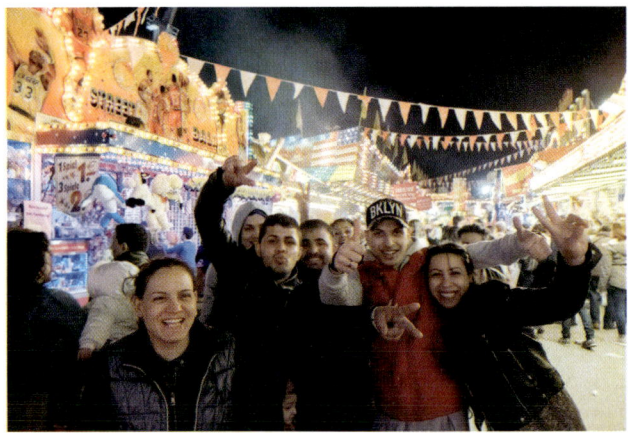

Fig. 203: (Left) Here's another pretty **extreme dynamic range** example, this time from an X-T1 (14-bit sensor) and with a push of approximately +5 EV. The top image shows the original exposure at base ISO 200. The image in the middle is the Lightroom-processed version of the RAF, and at the bottom you can see the X-Transformer DNG with the same Lightroom development settings. Again, the DNG from X-Transformer delivers better tonality in the dark areas.

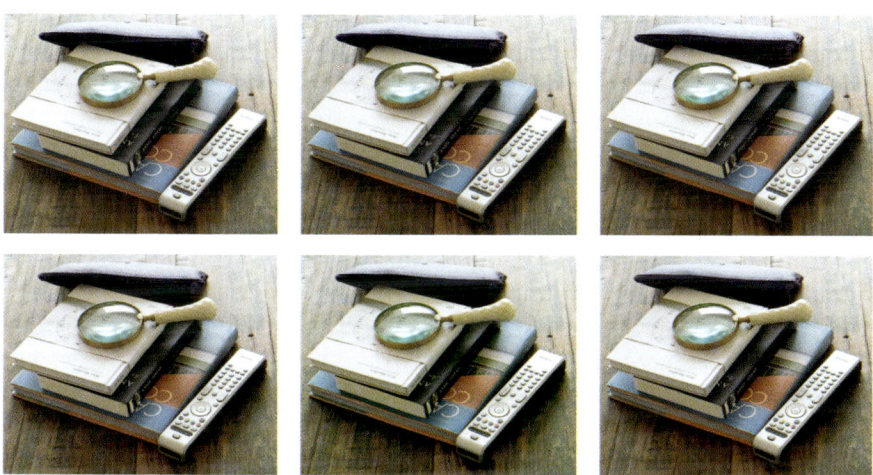

Fig. 204: X-Transformer DNGs are also beneficial for **pushing RAW files that were taken with the electronic shutter**. This example was shot with an X-T10, and the RAWs were processed in Lightroom.

Top left: mechanical shutter ISO 6400 RAF file; top center: mechanical shutter ISO 200 RAF file pushed 5 EV; top right: mechanical shutter ISO 200 X-Transformer DNG file pushed 5 EV.

Bottom left: electronic shutter ISO 6400 RAF file; bottom center: electronic shutter ISO 200 RAF file pushed 5 EV; bottom right: electronic shutter ISO 200 X-Transformer DNG file pushed 5 EV.

The pushed RAF that was taken with the electronic shutter (bottom center) clearly can't match its pushed X-Transformer DNG cousin (bottom right). It's also inferior to Lightroom's version of the pushed mechanical shutter RAF (top center). So, let's not blame the camera or the electronic shutter; It's the RAW converter! In this case, it's Lightroom's inability to competently push the original RAF up 5 EV. Take the detour via X-Transformer and your results will very much improve.

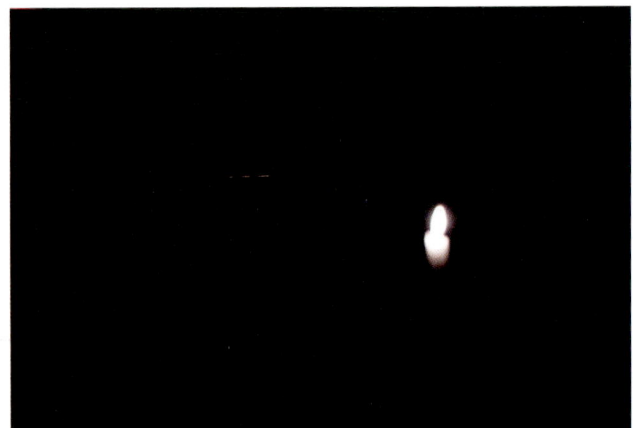

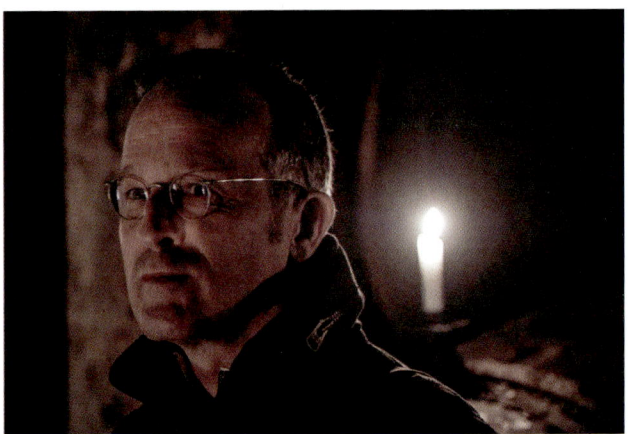

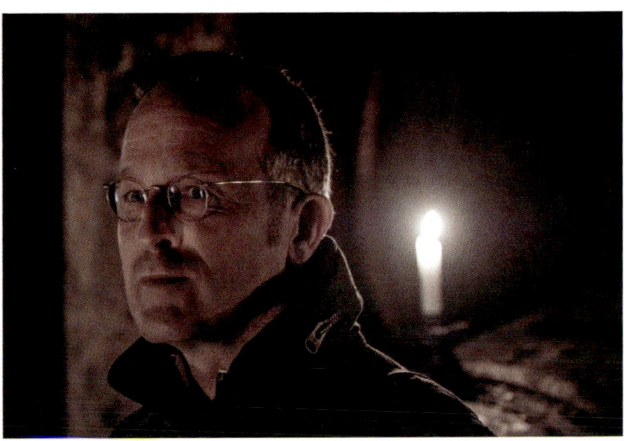

Fig. 205: In this final example we examine a mechanical shutter shot taken with an X-H1—another 14-bit camera, but with a more current X-Trans CMOS III sensor. As usual, the top image shows the original exposure, this time at ISO 800, which is the camera's dual conversion gain level. In the middle, we see the ISO 800 RAF file after being pushed approximately +4 EV in Lightroom. The image below is the same shot with our usual X-Transformer detour, pushing the X-Transformer DNG file with exactly the same Lightroom settings as the original RAF file. Once again, we can see a slight improvement in coloration and shadow rendering.

Please note that the detour via X-Transformer isn't recommended as a general rule for *all* your images. Instead, it's meant as a better alternative for those rare occasions when you literally have to push your X series camera to its dynamic range limits—especially with shots that were taken with the electronic shutter or with older 12-bit cameras.

Another aspect of using X-Transformer is its demosaicing algorithm, which is considered superior to Lightroom's own processing. By feeding Lightroom with a pre-processed DNG from X-Transformer, you can combine Lightroom's feature set with X-Transformer's demosaicing and get the best of both worlds. I'm always using X-Transformer's *Smoother* demosaicing option to avoid artifacts.

Iridient X-Transformer also offers its own sharpening algorithm that is supposed to deliver more details results with less artifacts. Here's the catch: You can't apply Masking to X-Transformer's sharpening, so the process will always apply to the entire image, including areas that don't require any sharpening. To replace Lightroom's sharpening with X-Transformer's alternative, you have to use a different set-up:

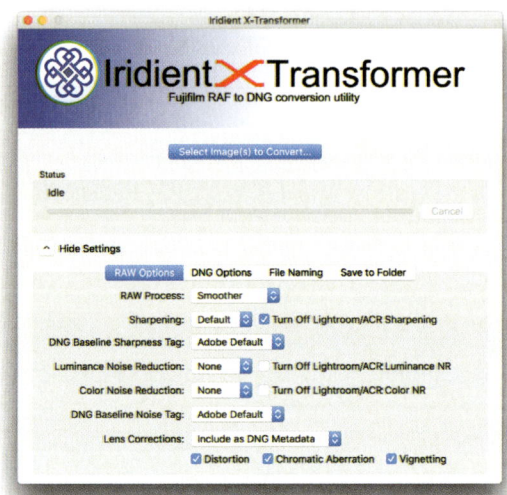

Fig. 206: To use X-Transformer's own sharpening, set the Sharpening pop-up menu to Default (or any other value except None) and check the "Turn off Lightroom/ACR sharpening" box. This will apply X-Transformer's own sharpening algorithm to the image during its DNG transformation. At the same time, Lightroom's sharpening will be set to zero.

Is it worth it? Yes and no. Indeed, X-Transformer's own sharpening can deliver finer details. But at the same time, the lack of masking means that smooth areas like the sky get unnecessary artifacts. *(Fig. 207)*

Important: Don't confuse X-Transformer's DNG files with regular DNG files (like those from Adobe's own DNG converter). X-Transformer DNGs are pre-demosaiced DNGs that you should only use as add-ons to your original Fuji RAF files. Never delete your RAFs, because you will need them again for reprocessing when new versions of X-Transformer become available, for different RAW converters, or for future versions of Lightroom with improved process engines. The same applies to Adobe's own DNG converter: If you use it to convert RAFs to DNGs, always keep the RAFs after the conversion! Adobe's DNGs contain less metadata information than the original RAFs, and they basically marry you to Adobe products, be-

cause opening DNGs in RAW converters other than Adobe's may be impossible or lead to inferior results. Only keeping the RAFs ensures that you your RAW processing is future-proof.

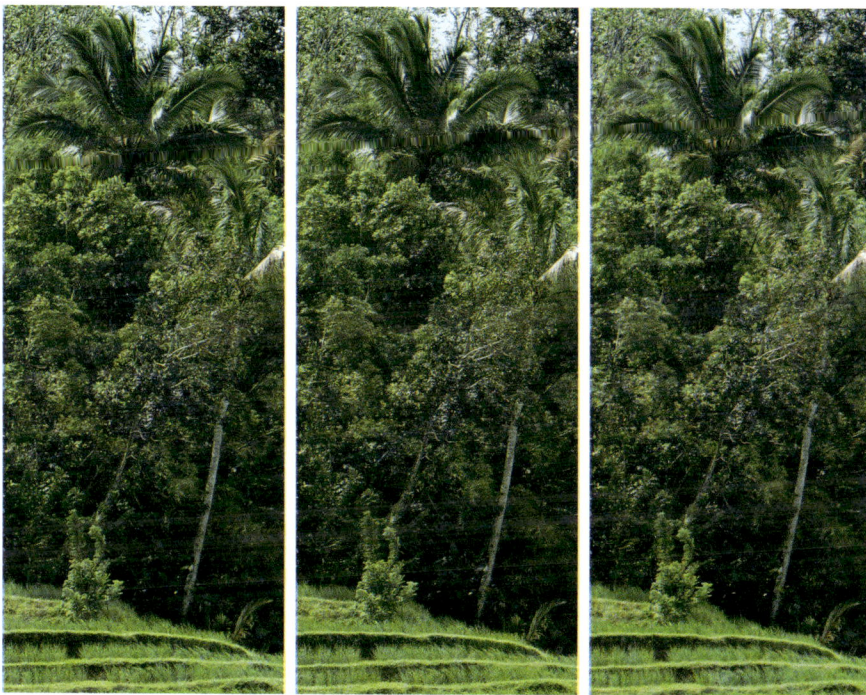

Fig. 207: In this illustration, we compare all three demosaicing/ sharpening options that are available when you are using Lightroom and X-Transformer: The image on the left is a crop of the Lightroom-processed RAF file with a 25/2/85/35 sharpening setting and no X-Transformer involvement. In the middle, we have the X-Transformer DNG processed with Lightroom sharpening 25/1.4/85/35 and no X-Transformer sharpening. The image on the right shows the X-Transformer DNG with X-Transformer's default sharpening and no Lightroom sharpening at all. Again, you can decide whether any differences are worth the detour via X-Transformer.

TIP 117	Displaying EXIF metadata

Digital cameras save information about every recorded image in the EXIF [101] data of each RAW or JPEG file. This data can be useful to RAW converters and cataloging software, but it can also be useful to you to help you understand how an image was exposed.

EXIF data consists of information about exposure parameters, camera settings, date and time, focal length, AF settings, white balance, JPEG parameters, DR mode, digital lens-correction data, serial numbers of cameras and lenses, etc. Many of these data points are saved in an area called "maker notes," which contains information on camera features that are specific to a certain brand (like Fujifilm).

ExifTool can read the EXIF data and is also able to make sense of maker notes. ExifTool is rarely stand-alone. Instead, you can get it as part of other image utilities, such as ExifTool GUI for Windows or GraphicConverter for macOS users.

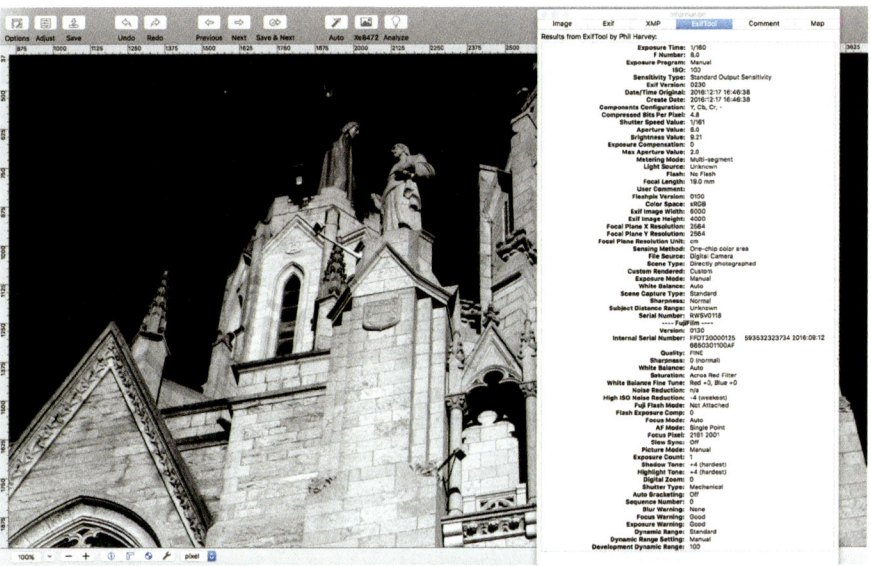

Fig. 208: **EXIF data** of an X100F shot in GraphicConverter: There's a vast amount of information about every image, including brand-specific Fujifilm maker notes.

2.6 FLASH PHOTOGRAPHY

This book covers Fujifilm's current flash system, which is available in the X-T1 and all X series cameras with X-Processor Pro or X-Processor 4, such as the X-Pro2, X-T2, X-T20, X-E3, X-H1, X-T3, X100F, and GFX lineup. If you are using an older or Xucli-built model, most of the information in this chapter still applies, but be advised that high-speed sync (HSS/FP) isn't officially available in cameras with focal plane shutters and that the user interface is different. In addition to that, manual flash control is limited, and there's no built-in wireless master/slave remote flash system.

Also note that the built-in camera flash and the tiny EF-X8 add-on flash for the X-T1, X-T2, X-T3, X-H1, X-Pro2, and X-E3 behave the same. The EF-X8 is Fuji's add-on flash for X series models that don't offer a built-in flash. It doesn't need a battery since it obtains its power from the camera it's mounted on. However, the GFX series doesn't work with the EF-X8, so you have to use a "real" external or hot shoe mounted flash with one of these cameras.

Flash photography means taking a double exposure. The lighting in a flash shot always consists of two components: **surrounding light** and **flash light**.

■ The **surrounding-light** component is metered like a regular exposure. Your camera is metering the scene with multi, average, center-weighted (if available), or spot metering, while the auto exposure mode (**S**, **A**, or **S**) automatically selects suitable exposure parameters based on your adjustment of the exposure compensation dial. As usual, the live view and live histogram are your friends. You can also set the exposure of the surrounding-light component manually in mode **M**, which is my preferred method in almost all situations. Basically, exposing for the surrounding-light component works exactly like exposing a scene without flash.

■ The **flash-light** component can be automatically metered and adjusted by the camera to match the overall exposure. To accomplish this, the camera employs a so-called TTL metering system [102]. TTL stands for Through The Lens. It means that the flash light is entering the camera through the lens before it's metered with the image sensor. This happens with the help of a weaker pre-flash that is emitted solely for metering purposes. You can bias the strength of the automatic flash-light component either on the FLASH FUNCTION SETTING page, or directly on external Fujifilm TTL flash units like the EF-X20 or EF-X500. Please note that while the live view and live histogram provide a preview of the surrounding-light component, they completely ignore the flash-light component that will be added to the final image.

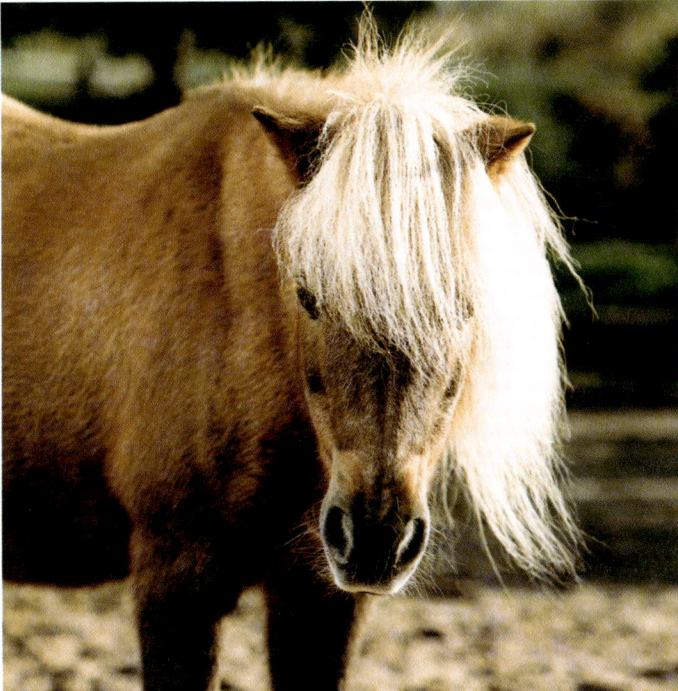

Fig. 209: In many cases, **flash photography** is about balancing the natural surrounding light and the artificially added flash light.

Besides Fujifilm-branded or Fujifilm-compatible TTL flash units, you can also use generic third-party flash units. Pretty much everything that fits onto the hot shoe works. Using generic third-party flash units means that TTL flash metering is no longer available, so you must manually set the flash energy output. You can also use automatic flash units that use their own built-in light sensor to automatically measure and adjust the flash output independently from the camera.

The TTL flash logic in your X camera supports several flash modes that can be selected in the Quick menu or on the SHOOTING MENU > FLASH SETTING > FLASH FUNCTION SETTING page:

- TTL FLASH AUTO is only available in auto exposure mode **P** and automatically fires an available flash unit if the camera decides it's necessary. It's a silly mode, since you probably know better than your camera whether or not you want to use a flash. When the flash is firing, it works just like regular TTL, which is our next mode.

- TTL STANDARD (formerly known as FORCED FLASH) always fires an active flash unit. This setting is available in all four exposure modes (**P**, **A**, **S**, and **M**).

- TTL SLOW SYNC works like standard TTL but allows shutter speeds as slow as 1/8s to better capture the surrounding-light component. This can be helpful when the light is poor, and you still want to capture more of the background. This setting is only available in exposure modes **P** and **A**.

- MANUAL FLASH works like TTL SLOW SYNC but allows you to manually specify the light emission power. This setting is available in all four exposure modes (**P**, **A**, **S**, and **M**).

- COMMANDER is a trigger flash that optically releases external flash units (or slaves) that feature an optical trigger sensor (like Fuji's EF-X20 and several third-party flash units). Please note that you must *manually* adjust the power output of the triggered slave flash. Don't forget that the commander flash is also emitting flash light that can affect the overall exposure of your scene, especially when you are shooting with high ISO settings. COMMANDER is available in all four exposure modes (**P**, **A**, **S**, and **M**).

- OFF makes sure that no flash is fired, even when the flash is switched on and connected to the camera.

- In the FLASH FUNCTION SETTING page, there is an option to specify whether the flash is supposed to fire on the FRONT (1st) or REAR (2nd) curtain. This option is available in all flash modes, and it is relevant for shooting moving subjects at slow shutter speeds. Since flash photography is a double exposure, it makes a difference whether the flash is fired at the beginning or at the end of a longer exposure. With the higher-end EF-X500 flashgun, there's also an option called FP, which stands for Focal Plane. This is Fuji's version of HSS, a.k.a. High-Speed Synchro-nization, which allows firing the flash at all mechanical shutter speeds up to 1/4000s or 1/8000s. Please note that the HSS function is not available (and also not required) in leaf-shutter models like the X100/S/T/F, X30, X70, or XF10, because their leaf shutters inherently allow official flash sync speeds of up to 1/2000s.

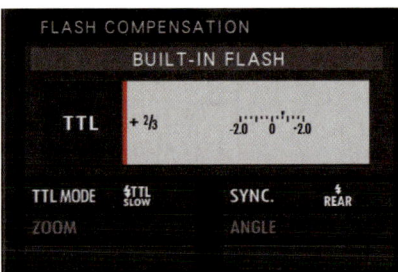

Fig. 210:
The FLASH FUNC-TION SETTING page lets you control flash parameters such as flash mode, sync. mode, and flash expo-sure compensation.

Flash photography in modes **P** and **A**:
slow shutter speed limits   TIP 118

In exposure modes **P** and **A**, the camera automatically selects suitable shutter speeds to capture the surrounding-light component of the scene.

- In flash modes TTL AUTO, TTL STANDARD, and COMMANDER, the slowest available shutter speed is approximately half the reciprocal of the focal length. For example, shooting with a 55mm focal length, the slowest available shutter speed will be 1/110s. This is a hard limit. Another hard limit in these modes is 1/30s. No matter what focal length is in use, the camera will not use a slower shutter speed than that. These hard limits mark the point where the surrounding-light component (usually the scene's background) can end up underexposed. There are exceptions, though. *Exception number 1:* Lenses with built-in and active OIS ignore the reciprocal rule and only follow the hard minimal shutter speed limit of 1/30s. *Exception number 2:* Auto-ISO can overrule both shutter speed limits for flash photography (the reciprocal limit and the 1/30s minimum) if you set a slower minimum shutter speed in Auto-ISO, such as 1/15, 1/8, or 1/4s. To achieve even slower shutter speeds in concert with flash photography, you should use mode **S** or **M**.

- TTL SLOW SYNC and MANUAL FLASH allow the camera to use slower minimum shutter speeds with flash photography. There's only one hard limit of 1/8s, which is independent from the focal length or an active OIS. To achieve even slower shutter speeds, you should use mode **S** or **M**.

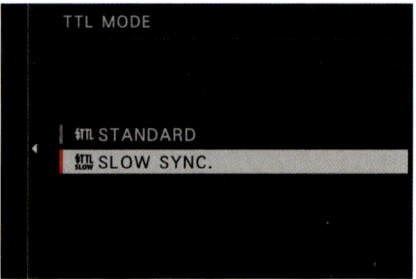

Fig. 211: If you insist on using the AE modes **P** or **A** to automatically expose the surrounding-light component of your flash image, selecting TTL SLOW SYNC will reduce the minimum shutter speed that the camera can use to sync with the flash to 1/8s. Please note that this may still be too fast to properly expose the background in low-light situations. That's another reason why I highly recommend exposing the surrounding-light component in mode **M**. Of course, the main reason is maintaining full control over the look of the picture and the balance between surrounding light and flash light.

Note: As of December 2018, the X-T3 with firmware 1.02 didn't follow these rules for regular and slow flash sync in exposure modes **A** *and* **P***, especially in concert with Auto-ISO. Hopefully, this will be fixed in a future firmware release. Until then, X-T3 users should not use flash in exposure modes* **A** *and* **P***.*

TIP 119	Controlling the surrounding-light component

When you are metering a scene with your X camera, you will quickly realize that it doesn't make any difference whether the flash function is turned on or off while doing so. The metering result will always be the same. In other words, the camera is metering the surrounding-light component always in the same way, with or without flash. In case you choose to use a flash, the flash-light component will simply be *added* to the surrounding-light component.

This is important because it tells us that we don't have to fear some camera voodoo that may or may not influence the metering of the surrounding light as soon as we switch on a flash. Instead, we can be certain that the camera's metering will always deliver consistent results. This also means that it's *our* job to balance both light components; for example, we can reduce the surrounding-light component to make room for more flash light in the composite exposure.

If you want to use the TTL flash as a fill light to brighten a dark foreground (such as a backlit person), the flash-light component will brighten the foreground by filling in the light that's missing. However, if you use the flash on a scene that's already fully exposed by natural light, the camera's TTL flash metering will probably conclude that no additional light is needed. A forced flash would still fire, but with minimal output; it would probably be almost invisible in the resulting shot. To emphasize the flash-light component, you must reduce the exposure of the surrounding-light component.

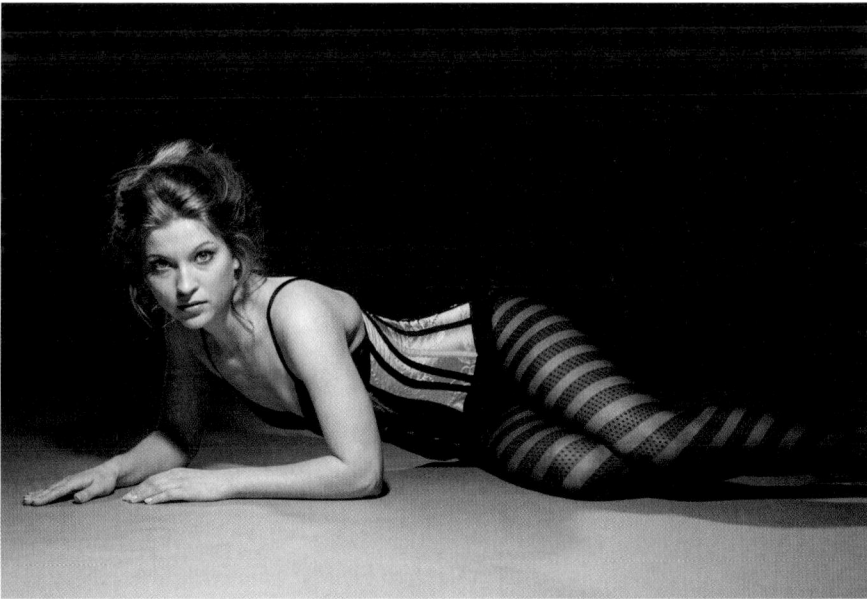

Fig. 212: **Reducing the surrounding-light component** to darken the background leaves more room for the flash-light component. This is particularly easy in a studio, where you have full control over the intensity of both light components.

Here's how it works:

■ You can control the exposure of the surrounding-light component either with the exposure compensation dial or by setting an appropriate manual exposure (ISO, aperture, shutter speed). Less surrounding light will prompt the TTL flash metering to add a stronger flash-light component, since the TTL flash system will always try to deliver balanced results. Changing the exposure compensation dial has no effect on the flash component of the shot; it only affects the exposure of the surrounding-light component.

■ To control the surrounding-light component in manual mode **M** using the live view and the live histogram, make sure that the exposure preview in manual mode is enabled by selecting SET UP > SCREEN SET-UP > PREVIEW EXP./WB IN MANUAL MODE > PREVIEW EXP./WB.

■ In a studio setting, you often want to minimize the surrounding-light component and illuminate your subject entirely with flash light. In such cases, I recommend smaller aperture settings (larger aperture numbers), base ISO 200, and a fast shutter speed. The fastest official flash synchronization speed of X series cameras with focal plane shutters is either 1/125s, 1/180s, or 1/250s, depending on your model. To compose a studio scene with very little surrounding light in mode **M**, make sure that the exposure preview in manual mode is disabled by selecting SET UP > SCREEN SET-UP > PREVIEW EXP./WB IN MANUAL MODE > OFF. Otherwise, it will be hard for you to see anything in the viewfinder other than darkness.

■ Sometimes the fastest available flash sync speed will still overexpose the surrounding-light component, even at base ISO. Yes, you could stop down the aperture, but this might negate the purpose of achieving a nice subject-to-background separation with little depth of field.

In such a case, it's useful to attach a neutral density filter [103] to the lens to reduce the amount of light that hits the sensor by 3 to 6 stops. Alternatively, you can use a Fuji-compatible flash that supports high-speed sync (HSS).

■ Like the DR function, flash light is often used to reduce the contrast between a darker foreground subject and a brighter background. You can combine both features (flash and the DR function), which may be useful if the background—when viewed isolated from the fore-ground—still contains so much contrast that DR expansion is required. Think of a night scene with city lights, street lamps, and bright billboards in the background. In such a scenario, a flashgun could illuminate a person standing in the foreground, while the DR function (DR400%) would help capture the bright colors and textures of the city lights. DR400% is also useful when you are illuminating scenes with subjects that expand deep into space and don't have an equal distance to the camera. In such cases, DR400% will give subjects that are closer to the flash light an additional overexposure protection of 2 EV, which can be retrieved during external RAW conversion of your shot.

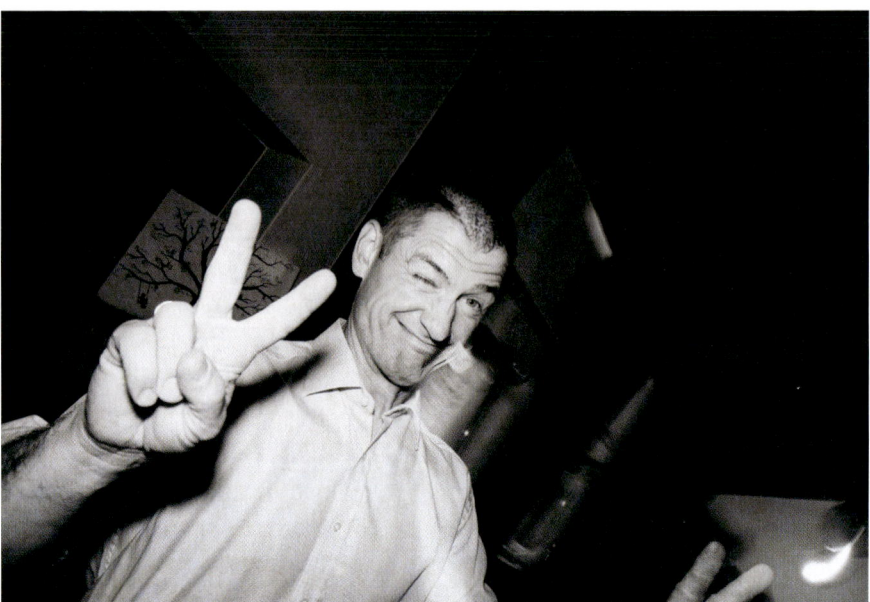

Fig. 213: Shooting close-ups with **a hot shoe flash and a wide-angle lens** can make things tricky. For this snapshot, I used an X-T10 with a Nissin i40 TTL flash and an XF16mmF1.4 lens at f/6.4, 1/6s, and ISO 800/DR400% in exposure mode M. The hand of the party guest happens to be much closer to the camera (and hence the TTL flash) than his face, so with every "normal" camera, the hand would either be overexposed, or the face would be underexposed by the flash light. Not with Fujifilm, though. The DR function comes to the rescue: By manually setting DR400%, the guest's hand can be overexposed up to 2 EV by the TTL flash—we can still fully recover it in during external RAW conversion. In this case, I used Lightroom.

- The previously discussed hard limits for minimum shutter speed in modes P and A can lead to an underexposed surrounding-light component. However, these limits can be somewhat useful because they prevent shaky or blurred backgrounds in hand-held shots. This isn't an issue when using a tripod, so you could circumvent the limits by selecting TTL SLOW or by manually setting a slow shutter speed in S or M mode. I personally recommend using mode M.

- Surrounding light and flash light frequently exhibit different color temperatures, which makes it difficult to find a white balance setting that suits all parts of the image. Luckily, some RAW converters (like Lightroom) allow selective white balance editing in an image. Another method is to use a gel filter in front of the flash unit to warm or cool the flash light to better match the surrounding light.

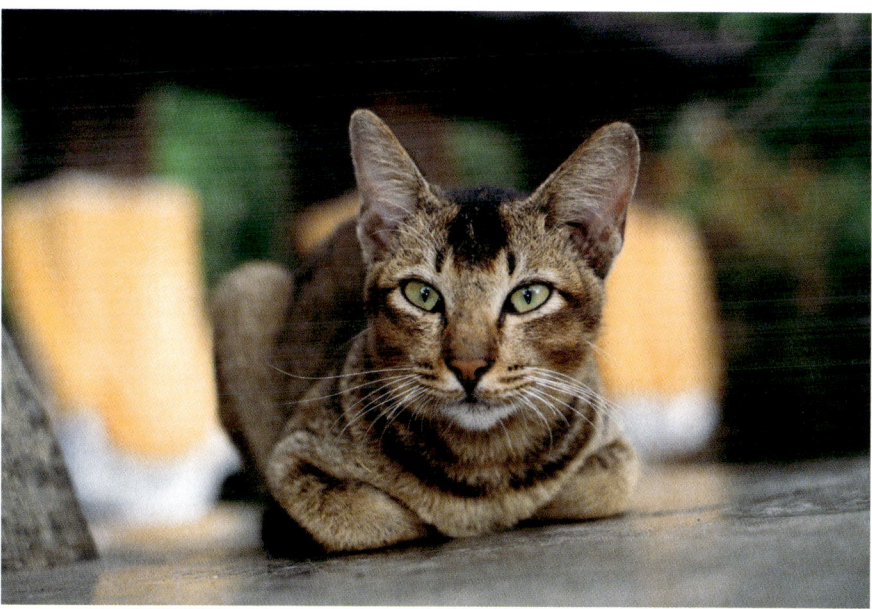

Fig. 214: With plenty of **surrounding light,** the flash-light component takes a backseat. In this example (taken with an X-Pro1 and an EF-20), it simply added a spark to the cat's eyes. The best flash shots are often those that are hard to identify as flash photography.

TIP 120 **Controlling the flash-light component**

If the flash-light component of your image turns out too bright or dark, you can bias the camera's TTL flash system:

■ To bias the flash-light component of your shot, you can adjust the flash exposure compensation in the camera on the SHOOTING MENU > FLASH SETTING > FLASH FUNC-TION SETTING page or on many external TTL flash units. Combining the in-camera flash compensation with an additional compensation setting on the flash unit itself will simply add up both corrections (the EF-X500 and Metz M400 are exceptions to this rule).

■ You will often get nicer-looking results by bouncing the flash off the ceiling, as this softens the flash light. Of course, bouncing the flash light requires more power, so you may need a stronger flash. It's also worth noting that bouncing the flash from a colored surface will tint the light accordingly.

■ To add a tint or change the color temperature of your flash light, you can attach colored gel filters in front of your reflector. The color temperature of unfiltered flash light usually corresponds to regular daylight.

■ The range of your flash unit depends on the set aperture, the ISO setting, and (of course) the power setting. In TTL mode, the camera is automatically adjusting the light output of your flash, but many flash units can also be set to manual. This way, you are the one setting the power output of the flash. In manual mode **M**, changing the shutter speed doesn't affect the brightness of the flash-light component of your shot, as long as you remain at or below the official maximum sync speed. Hence, changing the shutter speed is a quick way to adjust the exposure of the surrounding-light component without messing with your carefully balanced manual flash-light setup.

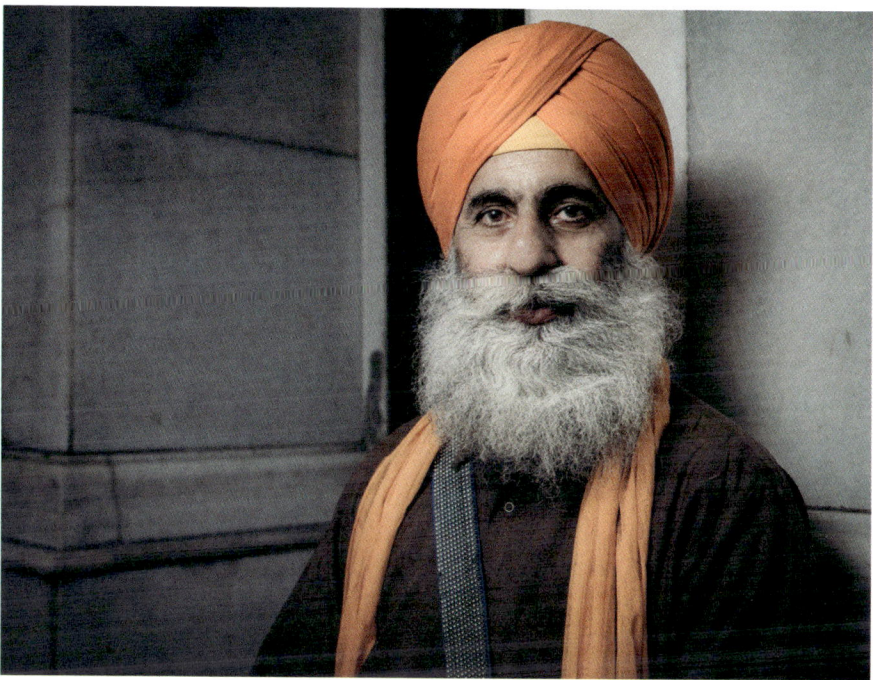

Fig. 215: Having **full manual control over both light components** is my preferred and recommended way of merging flash light and surrounding light—as long as there's enough time to make the necessary adjustments. For this quick street portrait in Delhi, a friend was holding a Godox AD200 radio flash [104] with an attached umbrella from my left as I took the shot with manual exposure settings (f/8, 1/125s, ISO 400) on my GFX 50S with a GF32–46mm lens set to 64mm. Manual control over the flash-light output was established with a Godox X1T-F [105] radio transmitter.

■ Don't forget that when using an on-camera hot shoe flash, large lenses and lens hoods can block parts of the flash light, resulting in unpleasant shadows. It's better to remove the lens hood or to use an off-camera flash.

■ Some wide-angle lenses cover a larger angle of view than the reflector of your flash can handle. This results in unpleasant vignetting. In such cases, bouncing the flash light off the ceiling can be helpful. Alternatively, you can attach a diffusor to the flash reflector. Many flash units feature built-in diffusors—just don't forget to flip it on.

| TIP 121 | Front- versus rear-curtain flash synchronization |

Flash photographs are double exposures consisting of surrounding light and flash light. When you shoot the surrounding light with a slow shutter speed, there is the question of when the flash (with its much faster speed) should fire. Normally, the flash is fired along with the shutter opening its FRONT (or 1st) curtain at the *beginning* of an exposure. However, selecting the REAR (or 2nd) curtain makes the flash fire at the *end* of the exposure when the rear shutter curtain closes.

Naturally, moving objects change their position during the exposure of a shot. Synchronizing the flash with the rear curtain ensures that moving objects are frozen where they are located at the end of the exposure as opposed to at the beginning. This often results in the moving object appearing more natural in the image.

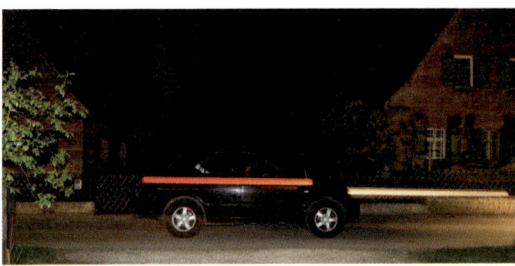

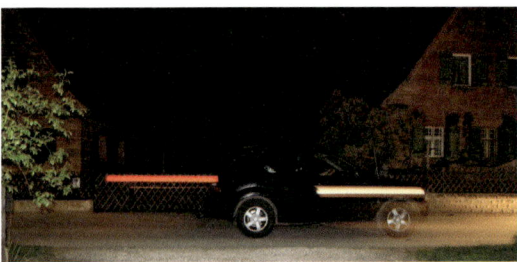

Fig. 216:
Front- versus rear-curtain sync: This example shows the same scene photographed with front-curtain sync (above) and rear-curtain sync (below). The shot above shows how the flash freezes the moving vehicle at the beginning of the exposure, while the shot below shows it being frozen at the end of the exposure. The rear-curtain version looks more natural and avoids the false impression of the car moving backward. This is also a good example to examine the nature of flash photographs as double exposures. You can see how the slow shutter speed captures the moving vehicle as a blurry trail of light, while the fast flash instantly freezes parts of it.

Flash synchronization: where's the limit?	TIP 122

The maximum flash sync [106] speed of most X series cameras with interchangeable lenses (and hence focal plane shutters) is 1/180s. The X-Pro2, X-T2, X-T3, and X-H1 offer 1/250s, and the large shutter of the GFX syncs at 1/125s or slower. Thanks to their leaf shutters, fixed-lens cameras like the X100 series can officially sync flash as fast as 1/2000s.

- In exposure modes **P** and **A**, the camera will never offer a shutter speed faster than the official maximum sync speed. If this is too slow for the current light conditions, the surrounding-light component will be overexposed. In this case, the shutter speed will be displayed in red. To avoid overexposure, stop down the lens, reduce ISO (but never below base ISO), or use a neutral density (ND) filter [107] in front of the lens.

- In exposure modes **S** and **M**, you can select shutter speeds faster than the maximum sync speed. Your camera will honor these settings in flash mode, but there is a price to pay: the resulting images will display some partial shadowing of the flash. It's often possible to use shutter speeds that are a little bit faster than the official maximum sync speed without visible negative effects—it depends on the type of flash you are using. Its power setting plays a role, as well. Proceed at your own risk!

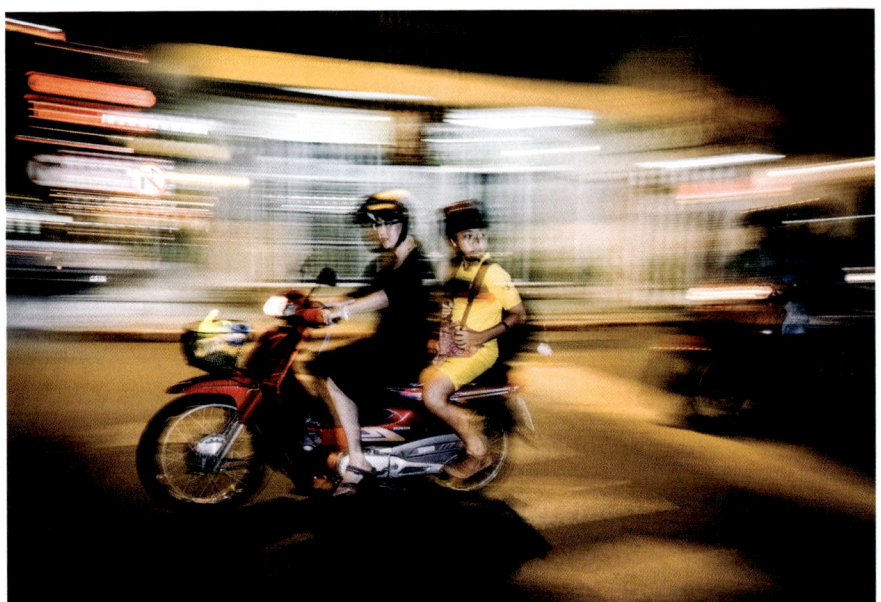

Fig. 217: Many photographers wish to use a **flash sync speed** faster than the maximum sync speed of their camera. That said, it's also possible to deliberately use very slow synch speeds to create a blurry background behind a more contoured flash-lit foreground. This was taken with an X-T2 and an EF-X500.

- High-speed synchronization (HSS, also known as FP mode) up to 1/4000s or 1/8000s is officially supported by the X-T1 and cameras with X-Processor Pro and X-Processor 4, but not available with many Fuji-TTL-compatible flashguns. As of December 2018, the only HSS-compatible flash from Fujifilm was the EF-X500. Luckily, several Fuji-TTL-compatible third-party flashguns and systems (Godox, Metz M400, etc.) support HSS, as well.

- HSS/FP consumes more flash power, so you may need a more powerful flashlight to compensate HSS-related losses. Depending on the brand and type of your flash, the effective power reduction that occurs at the transition point between normal sync and high-speed sync can vary between 2/3 EV (Godox AD200 or AD600) and almost 2 EV (some speedlights).

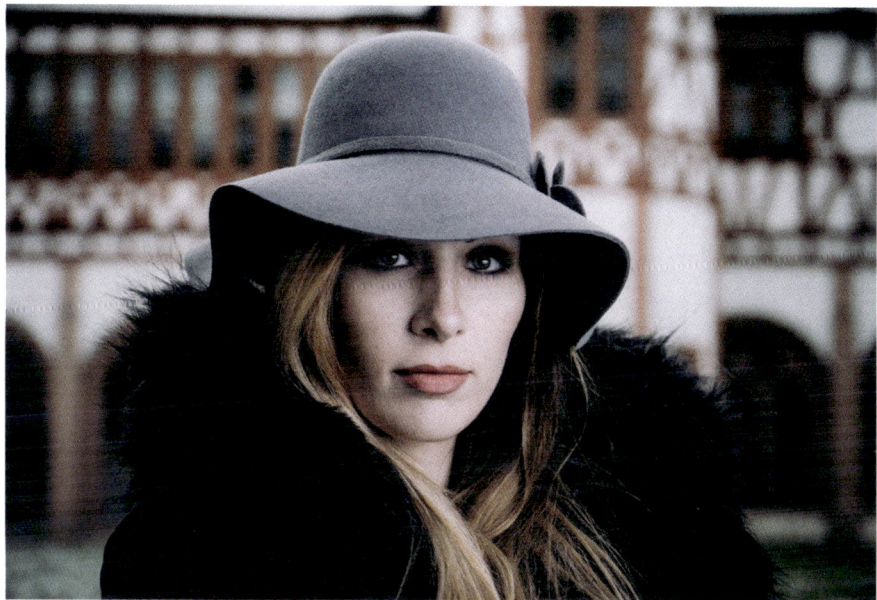

Fig. 218: This manually controlled **HSS** shot was taken with an X-H1 at a shutter speed of 1/500s, using a Godox AD600B [108] with a gridded 120cm Phot-R Octabox [109] and a Godox Xpro-F [110] radio controller.

X cameras with a **leaf shutter** (like the X70 or X100 series) don't offer HSS due to their inherently faster flash sync speeds. For example, the official flash sync speed of the X100 series is 1/2000s, but you can go faster as long as your flash can keep up with the increasingly small firing window.

Using wireless flash (TTL and manual) with leaf-shutter cameras at fast shutter speeds doesn't result in an HSS-related power reduction, but it can impose other sync restrictions, because the transmitter on the camera needs time to communicate with the off-camera flash. This latency can reduce the maximum effective sync speed of your setup. In my experience, light-based communication (such as the Fujifilm EF-X500 or Metz M400) results in less latency than radio-based communication (like the Godox 2.4 GHz system).

With leaf-shutter cameras, I recommend 1/500s as a safe maximum sync speed for off-camera radio flash units operating at or near full power. With less output power, faster shutter speeds of up to 1/1000s are also possible.

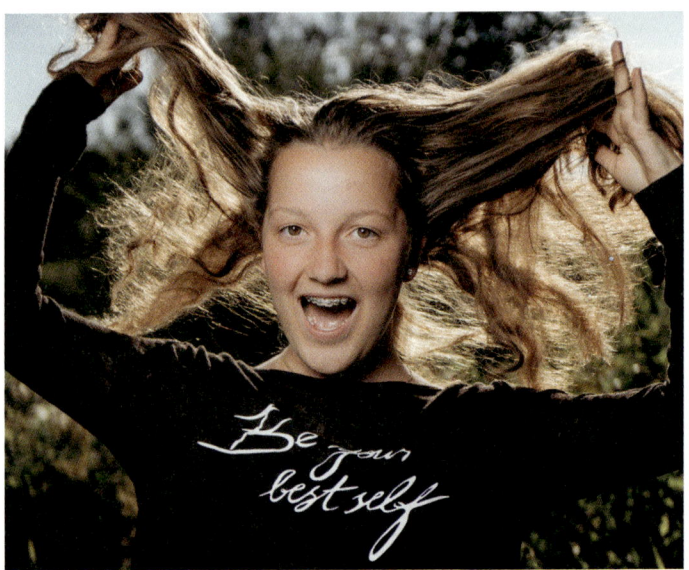

Fig. 219: This **wireless flash shot** was taken with an X100F at a shutter speed of 1/800s using a Godox X1T-F radio transmitter and a Godox TT600 [111] flash mounted in a square softbox.

TIP 123	Red-eye removal: a two-step affair

If the flash and your subject share almost the same optical axis (a frequent occurrence with the built-in flash or a clip-on flash), this can lead to the red-eye effect [112]: an unpleasant red reflection in the eyes of humans or animals.

■ If you pull up SHOOTING MENU > FLASH SETTING > RED EYE REMOVAL and then select either FLASH or FLASH+REMOVAL, the camera will emit a pre-flash prior to each shot that forces your subject's pupils to contract, thus reducing or eliminating the red-eye effect.

■ In addition to the pre-flash, there's *another* red-eye removal tool available: selecting REMOVAL (or FLASH+RE-
MOVAL) in the FLASH SETTING > RED EYE REMOVAL
menu will detect and remove unpleasant red-eye effects
in a JPEG after the fact. This function is also available
in PLAYBACK MENU > RED EYE REMOVAL in case you
decide to use it later. If you want to keep a copy of the
unretouched JPEG, select SET UP > SAVE DATA SET-UP >
SAVE ORG IMAGE > ON. The RAW file isn't affected by
this variant of red-eye removal.

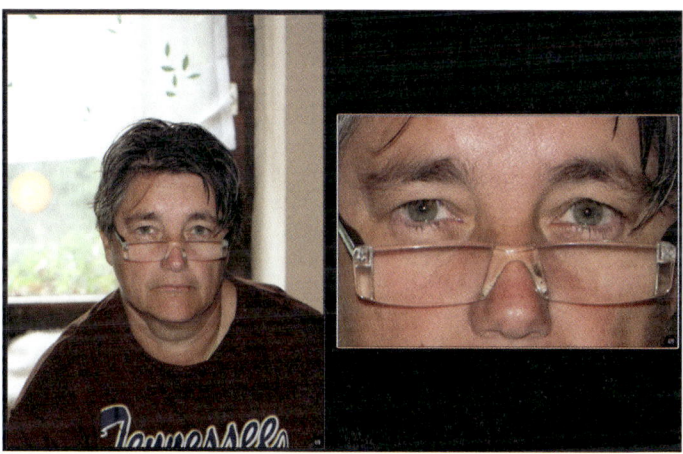

Fig. 220: The **red-eye removal** function emits a pre-flash that is
bright enough to prompt your subject's pupils to contract.

Using TTL-Lock	TIP 124

TTL-Lock works like AE-Lock: Where AE-Lock locks the exposure of the surrounding-light component, TTL-Lock locks
the exposure of the flash-light component. To use TTL-Lock,
you have to first assign it to one of your camera's Fn buttons.

TTL-Lock can work in one of two ways:

■ Keep and lock the exposure of the most recent flash
exposure when you press the TTL-Lock button (FLASH
SETTING > TTL-LOCK MODE > LOCK WITH LAST FLASH).

■ Meter the flash exposure with a metering flash when you press the TTL-Lock button and immediately lock the metered result (FLASH SETTING > TTL-LOCK MODE > LOCK WITH METERING FLASH).

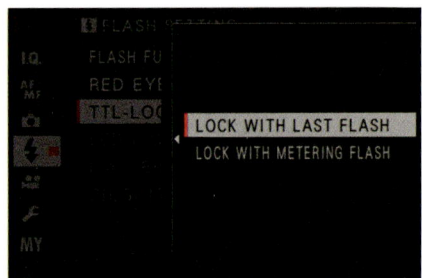

Fig. 221: Pressing the designated **TTL-Lock** button can work in two ways: either lock the flash exposure of the previous shot or fire a TTL metering flash and immediately lock the metered exposure. You can configure these options in the TTL-LOCK MODE menu.

TTL-Lock is practical in situations where you want to take more than one picture of the same scene and maintain a consistent flash output for the entire series. A typical method involves setting the LOCK WITH LAST FLASH option, then taking a few test shots of the scene and applying flash exposure compensation until the result looks great. Now press TTL-Lock to lock and maintain this "perfect" flash exposure while you take additional pictures of the scene.

| TIP 125 | Tiny slave: the Fujifilm EF-X20 |

Fuji's TTL system flash EF-X20 was specifically designed for retro-style cameras like the X-Pro1, but it also works nicely with other models. Besides using it as a TTL flash, you can also set its output power manually. You can even trigger it wirelessly with another flash, such as the camera's commander flash.

■ Set the flash mode in your camera to COMMANDER.

■ Move the mode switch on your EF-X20 to the N position.

- Manually set the desired flash output on your EF-X20. There are seven levels, from 1/1 (full power) to 1/64.

With this setup, the built-in flash of your camera (or an attached EF-X8, or another clip-on flash) will wirelessly trigger the EF-X20. Please consider that the light emitted by the commander flash can still affect your image.

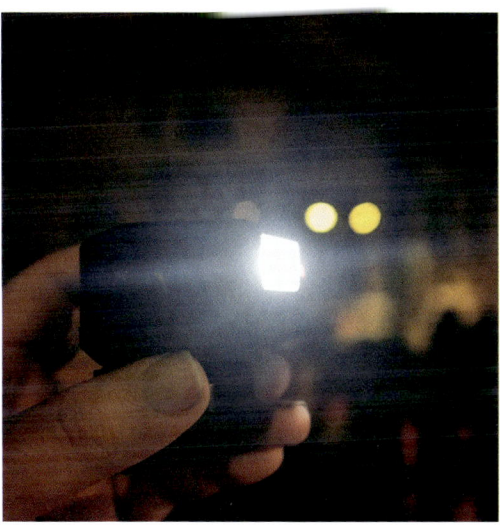

Fig. 222: An optically triggered **EF-X20** slave flash.

Grand master: the Fujifilm EF-X500   TIP 126

The EF-X500 is Fuji's version of a professional flashgun, with wireless TTL control of several flash units (organized in up to three independent groups) and stroboscope flash. There's a secondary LED reflector that can be used as a catch light [113], a more powerful AF assist lamp, or a video lamp. It also features FP high-speed sync to support shutter speeds of up to 1/8000s.

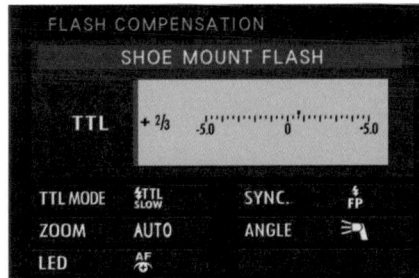

Fig. 223: With the fully featured **EF-X500** attached, the FLASH FUNCTION SETTING page adds several new items, including high-speed sync (FP), zoom settings, a reflector angle control, and control of the secondary LED, which can be used as an AF assist lamp and/or a catch light.

You can use the EF-X500 as a single clip-on flashgun or as a master/slave in setups with multiple wireless flash units. Communication between master and slave units is light based.

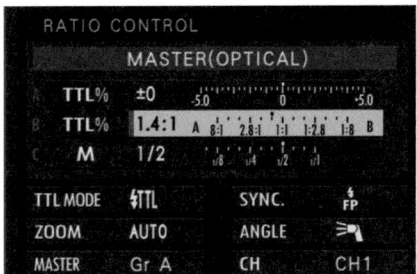

Fig. 224: In **TTL master mode,** one EF-X500 can control several compatible flashguns in three independent groups (A, B, C) via a light communication protocol. Each group can be controlled via direct TTL, a ratio of another TTL group, or fully manually.

While the EF-X500 is fully featured and delivers good quality, there are also a few negative aspects to it:

■ The flash is quite large, heavy, and expensive.

■ Wireless TTL control is realized with outdated light signals instead of state-of-the-art radio transmission.

■ Users must buy and attach either a heavy and expensive EF-X500 or a Metz M400 as a wireless master controller. The built-in camera flash or an EF-X8 cannot be used as master control flashes.

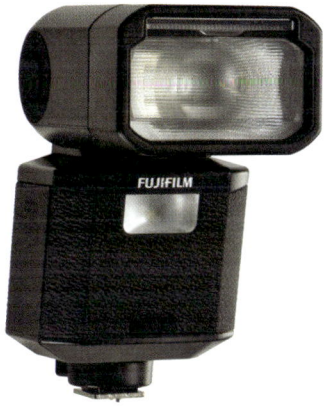

Fig. 225: The **EF-X500** is Fujifilm's pro speedlight. It leans a bit to the large, heavy, and expensive side. At this level, one would ex-pect wireless TTL based on radio transmission instead of outdated light signals.

Luckily, a growing number of independent manufacturers are offering Fuji-compatible flash solutions with wireless radio TTL, multi-group support, and HSS/FP high-speed-sync. I can particularly recommend options from Godox and the Metz M400.

Good alternative: the Metz M400	TIP 127

Metz was one of the first flash manufacturers to support Fujifilm's new flash system, including HSS/FP high speed sync, the AF assist lamp, and convenient control via the camera's flash configuration page. This makes the Metz M400 [114] an interesting alternative to the larger and more expensive EF-X500.

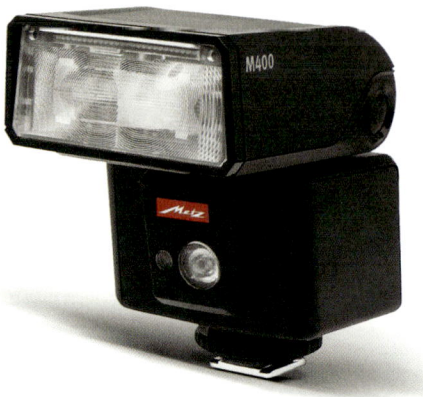

Fig. 226: If you are looking for a fully compatible shoe-mount flash that is more affordable and less bulky than the Fujifilm EF-X500, the Fujifilm edition of the **Metz M400** might be just right for you.

The M400 is based on a "fly-by-wire" user interface that doesn't feature dials with fixed markings. Instead, there are four generic control buttons and an LCD display that can be read day and night. Thanks to this flexible user interface, the M400's firmware can be fully compatible with any camera. Also, there are never any discrepancies between flash settings made in the camera and those made directly on the flash unit. Most flash functions can be conveniently accessed and changed on the flash configuration page and in the menus of your camera.

In addition to this, Metz keeps improving its flash firm-ware and provides free updates that can be applied by the user via the flash unit's built-in USB interface. This ensures compatibility with upcoming Fujifilm cameras and future feature changes.

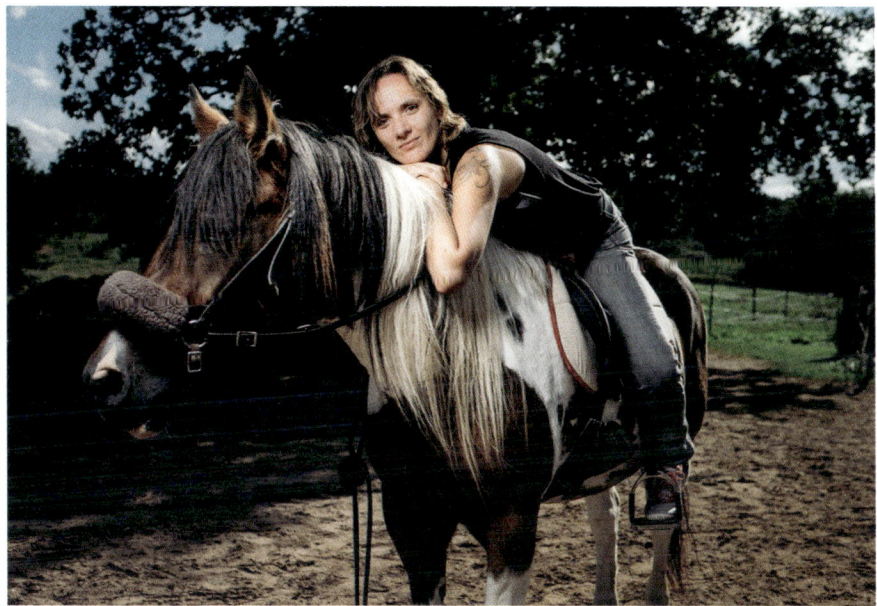

Fig. 227: Despite its compact size, the **Metz M400** packs enough punch to be used with small light modifiers. In this example, I put it in a 40×40cm softbox and triggered it remotely with an EF-X500 on my X100F. Thanks to this camera's leaf shutter, I could sync the Metz flash wirelessly at 1/500s without HSS (and hence without any HSS-related power loss).

Serious bargain: the Godox X system	TIP 128

If you are looking for an affordable radio flash solution that meets professional standards and is not only compatible with the Fujifilm X series, but also with cameras from Canon, Nikon, Sony, Olympus, Panasonic, and Pentax, it's hard to ignore the Godox company from Shenzhen, China. You may already know some Godox products under one of several rebrands, such as Adorama's Flashpoint, Neewer, MoLight, Pixapro, StrobePro, or Quadralite.

Apart from its affordability and compatibility across all major camera brands and their corresponding flash standards, the main appeal of the Godox X system is its scalability. For example, you can start out with a Fuji-compatible

X1T-F radio transmitter [115] along with 3 wireless TT600 speedlights [116], 3 compact light stands with tilting speed-light brackets, and 3 gridded softboxes—all for less than US $450. That's about the price of a single, bare-bones Fujifilm EF-X500 speedlight without any accessories.

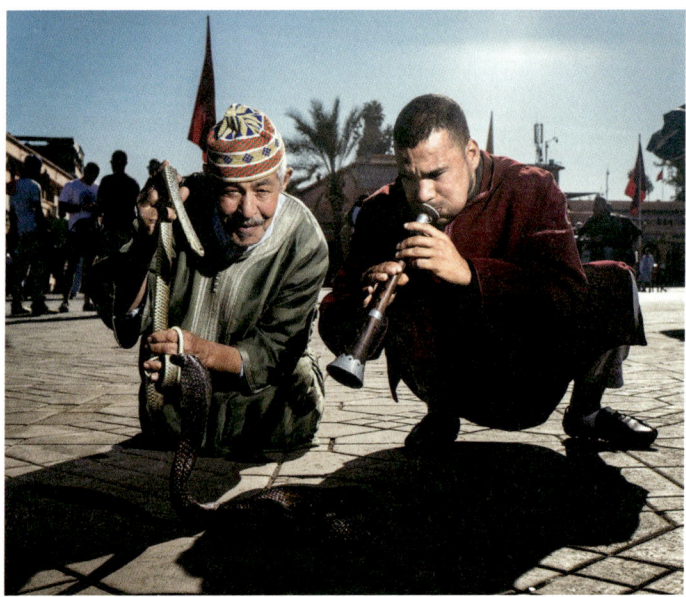

Fig. 228: This **wireless flash shot** was taken with an X100F at a shutter speed of 1/250s, using a Godox X1T-F radio transmitter and a bare-bones Godox TT600 speedlight (handheld by a friend without any modifiers).

If you crave for more power and flexibility, you can obtain one or more copies of the highly versatile, portable Godox AD200 pocket flash [117] with 200 Ws output power. It comes with two different flash heads (a Fresnel and a bulb head), and it can be further expanded with a round flash head [118] or an LED head [119]. There's also a decent choice of custom-fit accessories [120] that you can mount either directly or on a lightweight extension head [121]. Alternatively, you can put the AD200 in a Bowens-type speedlight bracket [122] or combine two AD200 units in an AD-S2 bracket [123] for a more powerful, yet portable, 400 Ws studio flash.

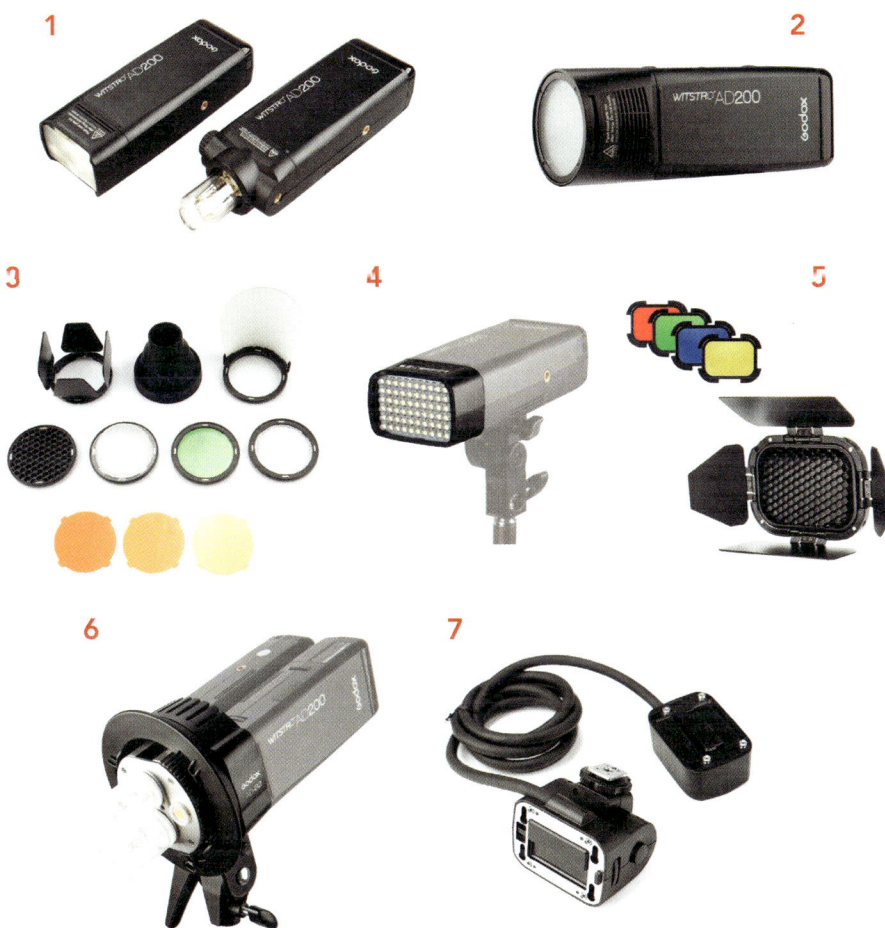

Fig. 229: The **Godox AD200** is one the most innovative flash units on the market today. For approximately US $300, you get a portable 200 Ws flash with a Li-Ion battery and Fresnel and bare-bulb heads (1) along with a battery charger and lampstand mount, all in a protective carrying case. You can expand the AD200 with a round flash head (2) and a set of fitting magnetic light modifiers (3). There's also an LED head option (4) and a barn-door kit with color gels (5) that fits on the Fresnel and LED heads. You can combine two AD200 units to a 400 Ws outfit with a Bowens and Speedring mount (6) or reduce lightstand weight with a flash-head extension cable (7). You can also directly mount a variety of portable Godox light modifiers on the bare-bulb head [124] or put the AD200 in an S-type bracket for compatibility with hundreds of Bowens and Speedring accessories.

The sheer number of Godox products and accessories can easily be overwhelming. Luckily, there's help on the internet. For example, Robert Hall has assembled a great Godox X system introductory guide [125] with videos, and Flashhavoc has an informative 3-part article [126] with a complete Godox overview.

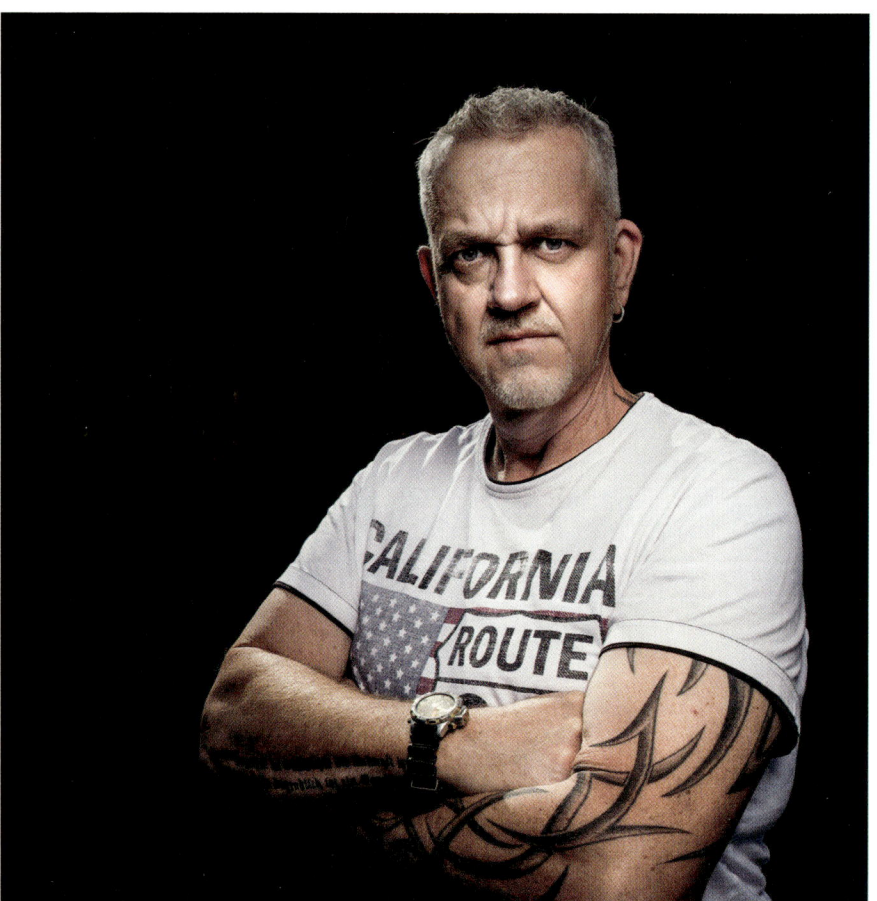

Fig. 230: I took this **simple but effective portrait** outdoors using a single Godox AD200 with an AD-S7 multi-softbox that was located right above the camera using a hand-held boom. I placed my model in front of an old wooden barn for a dark and textured background. The sun served as my backlight, so I didn't need a second flash. I used the GFX 50S with a GF32–64mmF4 lens at 32mm and f/14, 1/125s, ISO 100.

Generic third-party flash units	TIP 129

Basically, you can use any modern flashgun from any vendor with your X camera, as long as you are prepared to set its power manually. You can connect third-party flash units directly to the camera's hot shoe or use a cable or a wireless (radio) triggering device.

The camera's TTL modes aren't available when you are using generic third-party flashes because the camera isn't *metering* the flash light, it's only *triggering* the flash. There's also no HSS support.

This makes using generic flash equipment possible but inconvenient. Luckily, major flash brands like Broncolor, Profoto, and Elinchom are now supporting Fujifilm with dedicated transmitters for the Fujifilm X series. They also support HSS.

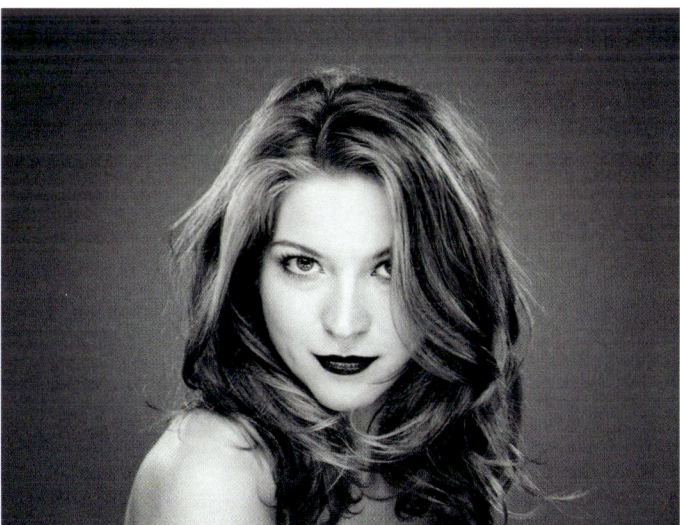

Fig. 231: Manually controlled **studio flash shot** using an X-Pro1 and an XF18–55mm zoom lens.

Important: Attaching Canon-compatible TTL flash equipment to the hot shoe could result in the camera overheating and performing an emergency shutdown. While Fujifilm and Canon share the same the physical hot shoe contacts, the protocols are not compatible. In this case, either tape off the TTL contacts of your device or use an adapter that only loops the sync signal from the camera to the flash.

TIP 130 Getting started with on- and off-camera flash photography

---

Traditionally, the Fujifilm X series has been targeting street and travel photographers. It was rarely the first choice of serious flash and studio photographers, and until 2017, the X series wasn't even fully supported by major flash system manufacturers.

For users of mirrorless cameras, there's also a fundamental difference between shooting with flash and with regular light. Using a mirrorless X camera, we can use the live view along with the live histogram to manually set the perfect exposure that protects the critical highlights of a scene. We can use "JPEG settings for RAW shooters" and the DR function to master demanding exposure situations with ease. Thanks to WYSIWYG, we already know exactly how the JPEG will look like before we press the shutter button. There are no surprises. Life is good.

Flash photography is different: There is no WYSIWYG experience for the flash-light component—we have to shoot first and check later. It's an informed trial-and-error approach, where we start out with flash setups and settings that we *think* are right, then take a few test shots and adjust the setup and settings accordingly. In hectic or volatile situations, we may even have to trust the automatic TTL flash exposure.

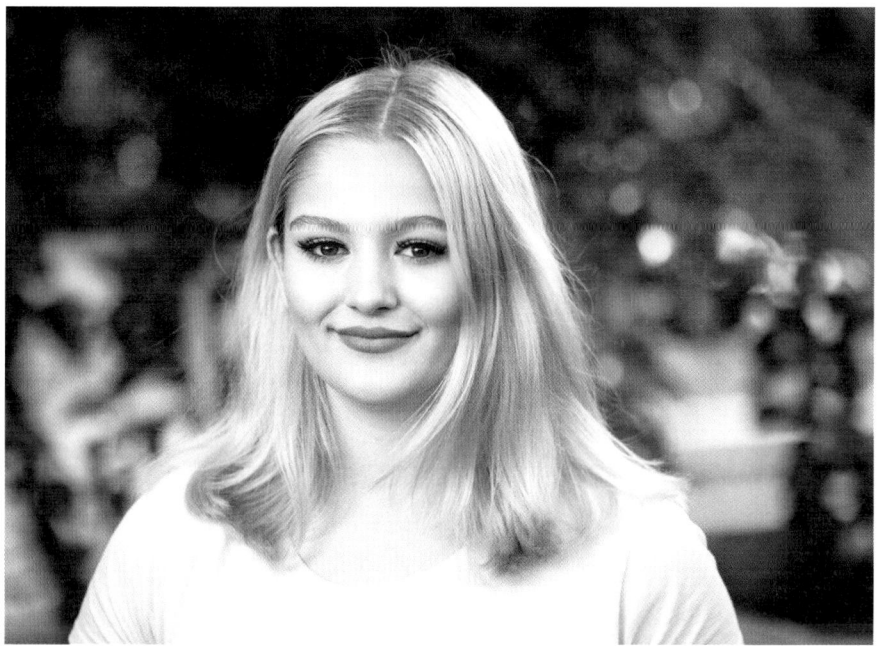

Fig. 232: Flash photography is less complicated than many people think. Starting out, you can play your part by opting for a simple
one-flash setup and lightweight equipment that can be moved
around easily. In this example, I used an X-T3 with an XF90mmF2
lens (ISO 160, f/2, 1/640s HSS) and an inexpensive Godox TT685F
speedlight [127] with a foldable 80×80cm softbox. A Godox Xpro-F
was used to control the flash output and trigger the flash via radio.

As a mirrorless photographer, getting started with flash
photography involves a little leap of faith. You have to
surrender WYSIWYG control and accept trial and error as a
workable method to determine the correct exposure of the
flash-light component.

At least gear limitations are now a thing of the past for
users of Fujifilm cameras: Most major flash brands support the X series, and with Godox, we have a scalable and
affordable system that meets even the most demanding
requirements and is very comfortable to work with.

To correctly expose a flash image, you can follow these basic guidelines:

■ Start out by manually exposing the surrounding-light component of your shot "to taste," just like you'd do for a regular shot without flash. Often, this involves under-exposing the surrounding-light component for dramatic effect, or to simply leave room for the flash-light component in backlit scenes. As always, make sure that critical highlights aren't blown by your exposure setting (use the live view and the live histogram), so be prepared to use DR200% or DR400% for highlight recovery. You should always have an eye on the shutter speed setting to make sure that it doesn't exceed the camera's maximum sync speed. If it does, you can either stop-down the lens, use an ND filter, or employ HSS/FP if your flash supports it.

■ After the surrounding-light component of your shot has been manually set, it's time to take care of the flash-light component. As usual, the best course of action is a manual setup with a few test shots that show you the best flash placement and output for your scene. Trial and error are your friends. If your shooting situation is more volatile (a.k.a. rapidly changing), you can also use TTL flash. In this case, I recommend setting DR200% or DR400% as a safeguard against flash overexposure. This is also recommended for clip-on flashes.

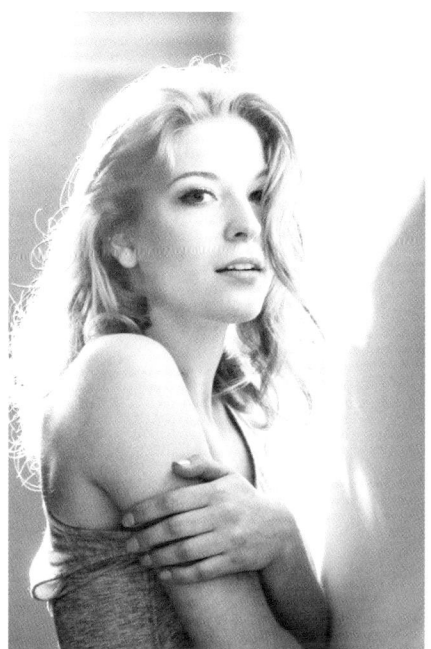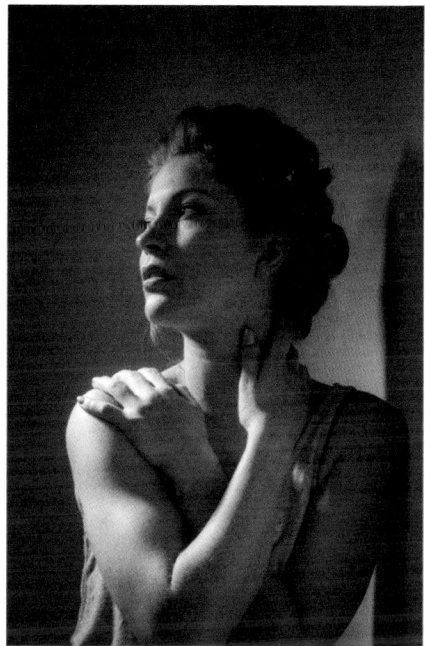

Fig. 233: Even **the most basic off-camera flash setup**—one studio strobe with a standard reflector, a model in front of a blank white wall, and no relevant surrounding light—offers many opportunities to experiment with different lighting styles. This example demonstrates a high-key (left) and a low-key setting (right), both shot with an X-Pro1 and an XF18–55mmF2.8–4 R LM OIS lens.

To learn more about flash photography, I can recommend these books:

- **One Flash!** [128]
  Great Photography with Just One Light
  by Tilo Gockel

- **The Flash Book** [129]
  How to fall hopelessly in love with your flash, and finally start taking the type of images you bought it for in the first place
  by Scott Kelby

■ **The Photographer's Guide To Posing** [130]
Techniques to Flatter Everyone
by Lindsay Adler

Additionally, you can have a look at David Hobby's STRO-BIST blog [131] and consider attending enlightening studio or on-location workshops with gifted X Photographers like Damien Lovegrove [132] or Piet Van den Eynde [133].

2.7 USING ADAPTED LENSES

Thanks to its short flange-back distance, the X-mount system can host almost every existing full-frame, medium format, cinema (Super 35 and larger), or APS-C lens. All you need is a fitting adapter. This means that in addition to about three dozen native lenses, you have access to hundreds of additional modern and legacy lenses.

It's a similar situation with the GFX and its G-mount: Using dumb or smart adapters, you can not only adapt many classic medium-format lenses, but also a large collection of classic and current full-frame (35mm format) DSLR lenses.

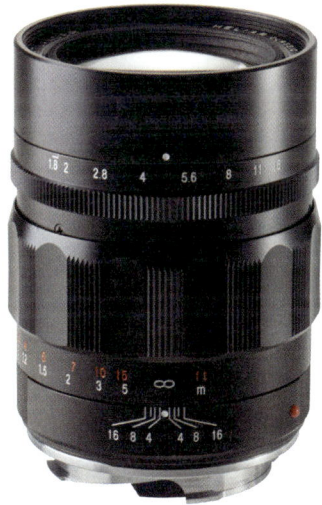

Fig. 234: Leica M-mount lenses like this affordable **Voigtländer Heliar 75mmF1.8** can be mechanically adapted to Fujifilm X- or G-mount cameras.

TIP 131	Finding the right lens adapter

X-mount and G-mount lens adapters are available for many old and current third-party mounts. Here are a few tips to help you find the right adapter for your legacy lens:

■ Adapters are available at many price and quality levels, and you get what you pay for. Don't buy too cheap or you may end up buying twice. The German manufacturer Novoflex is setting the benchmark here, but even their simple mechanical adapters can be more expensive than the lens you are adapting. Asian manufacturers like Kipon or Metabones enjoy a good reputation, and they all offer adapters for a wide variety of lens mounts.

■ With dumb (a.k.a. merely mechanical) adapters, third-party lenses can only be used as manual focus lenses with manual mechanical aperture control. Smart electronic adapters can translate between Fuji's AF protocol and the AF protocols of popular brands like Canon, and they can also control the aperture of the lens. Some even support the OIS of the third-party lens.

■ With dumb adapters, adapted lenses always operate with a manually set working aperture. This means that when you are stopping down the lens, the live view and live histogram of your camera must contend with the smaller aperture's reduced amount of light. It also means that mechanically adapted lenses can only be used in exposure modes **A** or **M**. With smart adapters, all exposure modes should be available.

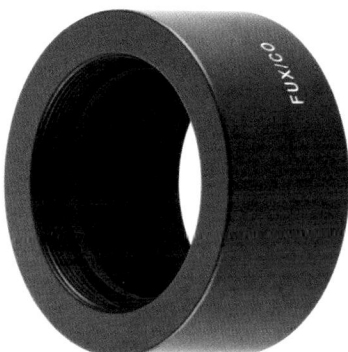

Fig. 235: Mechanical **M42 adapters** like this high-end model from Novoflex allow you to connect legacy M42 screw-mount lenses to X-mount cameras.

- Many modern third-party lenses that don't feature a manual aperture ring can still be mechanically adapted to your camera, but you can't change their aperture while they are connected via a dumb adapter. That's why some of these adapters feature a mechanical replacement aperture, but the results produced by these devices will differ from the results created by the original lens. If available, use a smart adapter for such lenses.

- Modern electronic features like optical image stabilization (OIS) aren't supported by dumb adapters since there is no communication or power transfer between the camera and the adapted lens. In fact, the camera believes that there's no lens attached at all. Some smart adapters do offer OIS support.

- *Speed Booster Ultra* from Metabones offers the fascinating possibility to attach full-frame legacy lenses from Contax/Zeiss, Canon FD, Nikon G, Minolta MD, and Leica R to X-mount cameras without changing their angle of view or cropping the image on your camera's smaller APS-C sensor. With Speed Booster, your APS-C camera sees what a full-frame (35mm format) camera would see. Speed Booster is a focal reducer—basically the opposite of a teleconverter [134]. It reduces the focal length of the adapted lens by a factor of 0.71. At the same time, the brightness (speed) of the lens is increased by about one stop. At 400 to 600 dollars apiece, Speed Booster adapters aren't cheap. However, they offer better quality than knock-off products like the Lens Turbo II by Zhongyi Mitakon.

■ Fujifilm offers its own X-mount adapter for Leica M-type full-frame lenses. This is a regular adapter (no Speed Booster), but it features electronic contacts, so your camera will recognize the adapter when it's mounted. It also features an Fn button that provides direct access to the camera's MOUNT ADAPTOR SETTING menu. With all other dumb adapters, you must set SHOOT WITHOUT LENS > ON to take a picture (usually found under SET UP > BUTTON/DIAL SETTING).

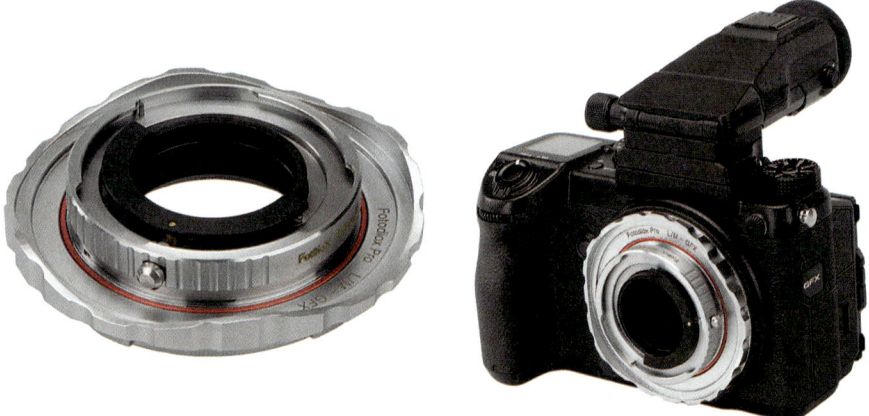

Fig. 236: There's no official Fujifilm M-mount adapter for the GFX, but you have a choice of third-party offerings. The **Fotodiox Pro Double Adapter** even combines two G-mount adapters in one design: you can connect Leica M-mount and Alpa 35mm SLR mount lenses to a GFX.

- Similar to the M adapter, Fujifilm also offers a dedicated H MOUNT ADAPTER G to use Fujifilm/Hasselblad H lenses on a GFX.

- Caution: don't use cheap macro lens adapters with electronic contacts. These knock-off adapters are designed to serve as macro spacer rings for native X mount or G-mount lenses. They promise full AF functionality thanks to their electronic contacts, but in reality, these adapter rings can be a bad fit and can damage your camera and lenses. Instead, I recommend using Fujifilm's own electronic macro extension tubes.

- If possible, don't combine more than one adapter. Stacking adapters leads to a measurable and visible loss in quality. Instead, get the right adapter for your lens.

Adapting third-party lenses	TIP 132

When you connect third-party lenses to your camera via a mechanical (dumb) adapter, the camera won't notice it due to the lack of electronic contacts. It will think there's no lens attached at all.

- To make the camera work with mechanically adapted lenses, select (SET UP > BUTTON/DIAL SETTING >) SHOOT WITHOUT LENS > ON.

- Enter the focal length of your adapted lens in the SHOOTING SETTING > MOUNT ADAPTOR SETTING > LENS REGISTRATION menu. You can either select the focal length from one of four presets or enter it manually in LENS 5 or LENS 6. Always enter the actual focal length of the adapted lens (the number that is printed on the lens), not its full-frame (for APS-C cameras) or medium-format equivalent (for GFX cameras). This ensures that the EXIF data will display the correct focal length, and it will also adjust the bright frame in the X-Pro1 and X-Pro2. The only exceptions are cases when you are using a special optical adapter that changes the focal length of the adapted lens, such as a Metabones Speed Booster for the X-mount (focal length reduction), or a Laowa Magic Format Converter for the G-mount (focal length increase). Entering the correct focal length is especially important if you use a camera with IBIS, like the X-H1.

Please note that the menu locations mentioned above refer to cameras with X-Processor Pro and X-Processor 4. Older/ other X camera models with interchangeable lenses still offer the same features for adapted lenses, but you may have to find them at different menu locations.

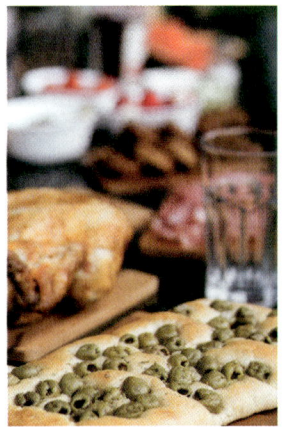 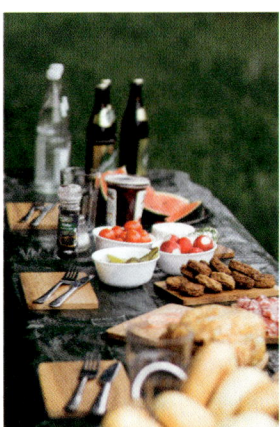 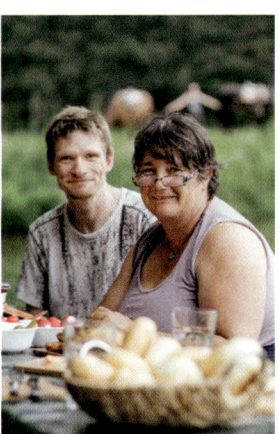

Fig. 237: **Third-party lenses with "character"** can help you achieve images with a distinctive look and bokeh. For this series, I attached a Voigtländer Heliar 75mmF1.8 M-mount lens to my X-E1.

TIP 133 | Exposing with mechanically adapted lenses

Mechanically adapted lenses (dumb adapters) can be used in exposure modes **A** (aperture priority) and **M** (manual mode). There are also a few notable differences between exposing with native lenses and adapted lenses:

- Native lenses close to working aperture when the shutter is half-pressed or when the shot is taken. Mechanically adapted lenses always operate with the aperture set by the user. As soon as you stop down an adapted lens, less light reaches the sensor and the camera's exposure metering. Stopping down adapted lenses increases the depth of field in the viewfinder.

- Since less light reaches the sensor when the lens is stopped down, the camera must increase the live view image amplification to display an accurate WYSIWYG simulation of the scene. This decreases the quality of the live view image and can also negatively affect the live view's frame rate.

- Since the camera thinks there's no lens attached at all, the aperture is always displayed as F0 in the viewfinder (and f/1 in the EXIF data). There's no way for the camera to know which aperture has been set on a mechanically adapted lens.

- Shooting in poor light with mechanically adapted lenses can be tricky when you stop down the aperture. It's possible to reach the live view's amplification limit. Once this limit is reached, the live view and live histogram cannot display the actual brightness of the scene, so it appears darker than the image that will be exposed. However, exposure metering will still work correctly, and the camera will display the correct shutter speed.

- Since the electronic live view cannot control the aperture of a mechanically adapted lens, it takes longer for the camera to adjust to abrupt brightness changes. You can test this yourself by quickly panning the camera from a bright scene to a dark scene and vice versa. With adapted lenses, the camera may need a few seconds for the live view to adapt to the changing brightness levels.

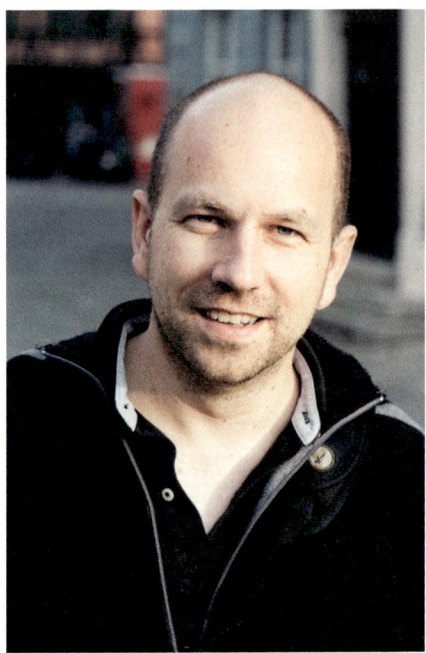

Fig. 238: With "dumb" mechanical adapters, **exposing with adapted lenses** is limited to modes A and M, and metering always takes place at the set working aperture. No matter which aperture you set, EXIF data will always show f/1. For this street portrait, I attached a Helios 44M-4 lens to my X-E2 using a Novoflex M42 adapter.

TIP 134	Focusing with mechanically adapted lenses

Mechanically adapted lenses can only be focused manually. Here are a few tips to make things easier for you:

- Set your camera to manual focus. This makes sure that MF assistants such as Focus Check, focus peaking, and digital split image are available.

- The electronic distance and depth-of-field (DOF) scale of your camera is useless in concert with mechanically adapted lenses. Instead, you must rely on analog scales and markers that may be engraved in the barrel of your adapted lens. Remember that the DOF scale on your lens is probably less conservative than what you're used to from the electronic scale in your camera. The analog scale doesn't guarantee pixel-sharp results at 100% image magnification. Instead, it will more likely resemble the FILM FORMAT BASIS option of the electronic DOF scale.

■ The most important tool for focusing with adapted lenses is the magnifier tool. You can usually activate it by pressing the rear command dial (if you didn't change its default Fn button assignment). Turn the rear command dial to cycle between the available magnifications. Don't forget: instead of focusing and recomposing, it's better to select a focus frame position that covers the part of the image you want to be in focus.

■ Use focus peaking or digital split image. You can cycle between these MF assistants and the standard view by pressing and holding the rear command dial. The magnifier tool can be combined with focus peaking and digital split image. However, in concert with digital split image, only one magnification level is available.

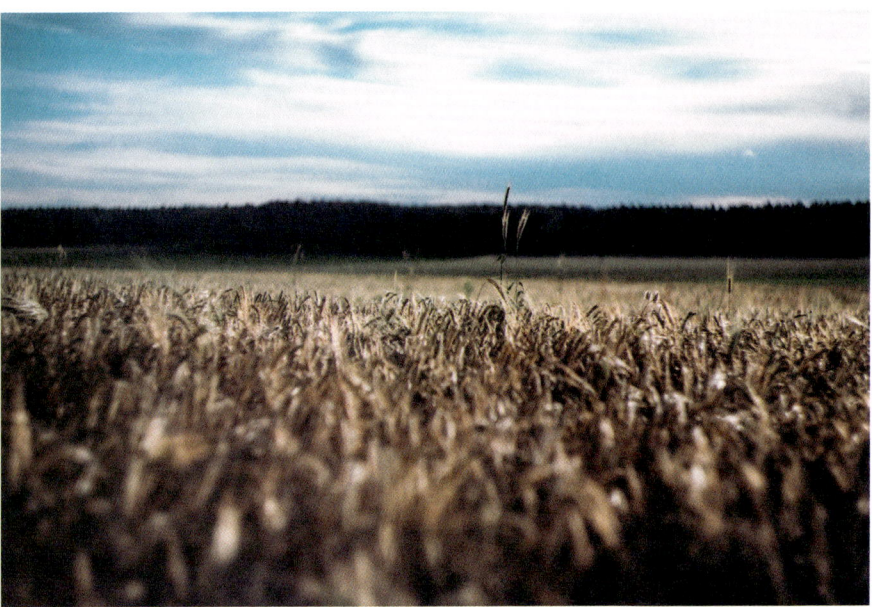

Fig. 239: **Focusing mechanically adapted lenses** can be tricky. My preferred method for pinpoint manual focus is focus peaking in concert with the magnifier tool. This example was shot with a Helios 44M-4 lens that was adapted to my X-E1 using a Lens Turbo II focal reducer.

■ The magnifier tool and MF assistants work best at wide-open aperture, when the DOF is as small as possible. However, some lenses exhibit focus shift, meaning the focus plane shifts when the lens is stopped down. The increased DOF from stopping down the lens may not be sufficient to compensate for the focus shift, so your carefully focused shot will end up out of focus when the aperture is closed. If you are using a lens with pronounced focus shift, it's better to focus with the actual working aperture instead of the wide-open aperture. Please note that focus shift isn't a matter of price—even a few high-end lenses from Leica and Zeiss exhibit it quite prominently.

| Fujifilm M-mount and H-mount adapters | TIP 135 |

Fuji's own M-mount adapter is a little bit different from conventional adapters:

- The adapter features electronic XF lens contacts to identify itself to the camera. However, there's no transmission of any lens data since the adapter doesn't know which M-type lens has been attached or what distance and aperture has been set. Sadly, the electronic contacts also make the inner adapter tube thinner than normal, so not all M-type lenses are physically compatible with it. To be certain, you can download a list of compatible and incompatible lenses [135]. Fuji also encloses a template with its M adapter that you can use to find out if your M lens measures up with the adapter.

- Pressing the function button on the adapter directly opens the camera's adapter menu.

- The camera's adapter menu offers a few additional functions when a Fuji M-mount adapter is attached. In addition to entering the focal length, you can also enter correction values for lens distortion, color shading, and vignetting. Those corrections only affect the JPEGs during RAW conversion with the built-in or external RAW converters. As usual, the corrections are burned into the RAW file metadata where they can be interpreted by RAW conversion software. However, color-shade data is currently only processed by the camera's built-in converter. For each adapted lens, you must find out the right correction values for yourself before you can enter them. There aren't any reference lists you can use that I know of.

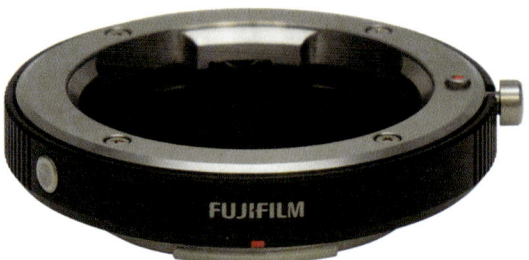

Fig. 240: Fujifilm's own **M-mount adapter** features electronic contacts and a function button that opens the camera's adapter menu.

Similar to the M-mount adapter, Fujifilm also offers their
own H-mount adapter to use H lenses from Hasselblad and
Fujifilm on a GFX camera. The FUJIFILM H-MOUNT ADAPTER
G is an electronic adapter that allows you to control the lens
aperture and built-in leaf shutter in the adapted lens with
your GFX. As of December 2018, there was still no autofocus
support, though. A list with compatible lenses is available
online [136].

   With the H-mount adapter, the lens aperture can be
changed using the command dial on the camera body. The
built-in leaf shutter in the lenses allows a maximum flash
sync speed of 1/800s without HSS/FP. Since the adapter is
equipped with electrical contacts that can communicate
with the camera body and the lens, it saves and applies cor-
rectional data for each adapted lens. The H-mount adapter
can be used in exposure modes **A** (aperture priority) and
M (manual mode).

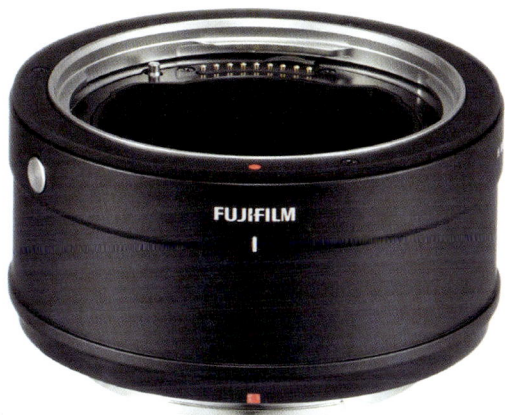

Fig. 241: Fujifilm's **H-mount adapter** communicates with Hassel-blad/Fujifilm H lenses via electronic contacts and features digital lens corrections as well as electronic aperture and leaf shutter control.

Quality considerations	TIP 136

In the age of pixel peeping, some classic lenses from the analog film age may have issues with high-resolution digital sensors. It's not about the price: While certain expensive Leica lenses may be outright disappointing when used on a digital system camera, some really cheap old lenses can deliver excellent results.

How can we explain that? The lens design plays a major role: Some compact lenses (typically for M-mount cameras) feature a symmetrical design that tends to be more problematic with digital sensors than telecentric SLR designs.

Also note that most adapted lenses are intended for full-frame [137] cameras. Attached to an X-mount camera with its smaller APS-C [138] sensor (23.7 x 15.6 mm), the original format of the lens is cropped. If you could extend the size of Fuji's older 16 MP APS-C sensors to full-frame (36 x 24 mm), their resolution would be 36 megapixels, just like the Nikon D810 or Sony A7R. There aren't that many older full-frame lenses that can fully use this kind of resolution, and with the current 24 MP and 26 MP APS-C sensors, the demands are even higher.

However, many older lenses offer something else: character. Because maximum sharpness and resolution weren't as important back then as they are today, the designers of legacy lenses could put their priorities elsewhere: for example, by designing lenses that provide outstanding bokeh [139].

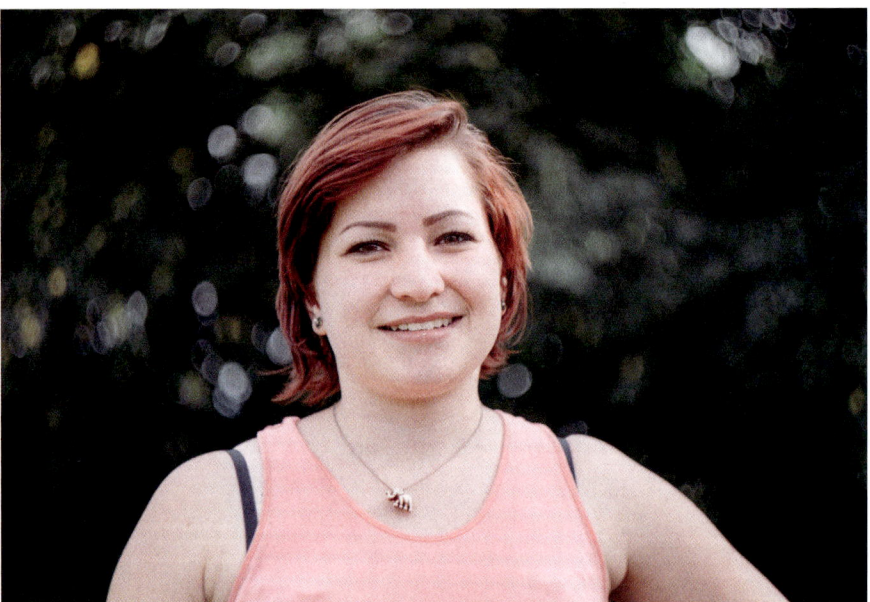

Fig. 242: Good or interesting legacy lenses don't have to be expensive: this shot was taken with a Russian **Helios 44M-4,** a 58mmF2 lens with an M42 screw-mount. You can often find this lens online for less than 25 dollars. For this example, I connected the lens with a Metabones Speed Booster Ultra focal reducer to my X-E2S.

Adapting full-frame (35mm format) lenses to the GFX can lead to similar issues. Luckily, most full-frame lenses are capable to illuminate the large sensor area of the GFX, however at the cost of more vignetting and possibly increased softness near the edges. Of course, you can always crop the image later, or you can set the GFX to 35mm crop mode right away. In crop mode, the GFX will only expose the full-frame portion of its larger sensor and behave like a 24×36mm camera. The live view, RAW files, and JPEGs will adjust accordingly, so you'll get smaller RAWs and JPEGs, too.

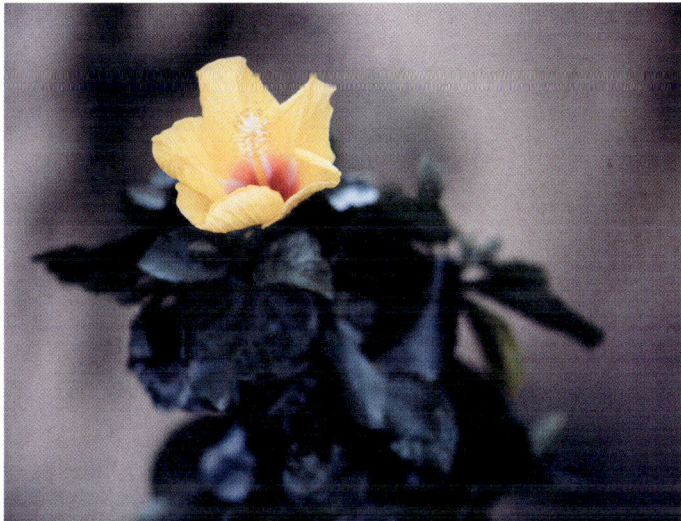

Fig. 243: Adapting "full-frame" lenses is popular among GFX users, because most legacy lenses (especially those with a focal length of 50mm and more) can illuminate the larger 44×33mm sensor without much vignetting. For this example, I attached a Zeiss T* Sonnar 2.8/180 MM via a mechanical Yashica/Contax-to-G-mount adapter and shot with the full GFX sensor area. Optionally, you can also use the GFX in crop mode, which covers the center 24×36mm section of the sensor and makes the GFX behave like a full-frame camera.

Speed Booster: miracle or trick?	TIP 137

Speed Booster and Speed Booster Ultra from Metabones are special adapters for X-mount cameras. They convert the focal lengths of full-frame lenses (35mm format) to their APS-C equivalents. This means that the adapted lens covers the same angle of view on your X-mount camera as it would on a full-frame camera.

Take my *Zeiss Sonnar T* 2.8/180 MM* as an example. It's a classic telephoto lens with a Contax/Yashica full-frame mount. Adapting this lens to any X-mount camera *without* Speed Booster causes the results to look like images taken with a 270mmF4.2 lens on a full-frame camera. That's because there is a crop factor of 1.5 between full-frame and APS-C.

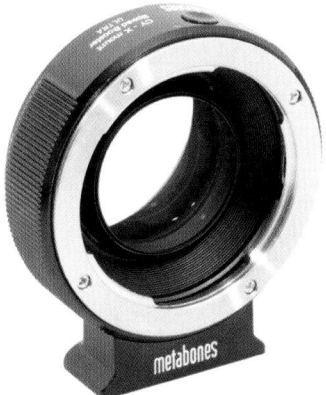

Fig. 244: Metabones **Speed Booster Ultra** with Contax mount.

Of course, many users of full-frame lenses would like to use them on their APS-C camera, yet keep the angle of view and depth of field intact. Speed Booster can do that for you because it reduces the focal length of the adapted lens by a factor of 0.71. With Speed Booster, my 2.8/180mm full-frame Sonnar turns into a 2/128mm APS-C lens. Enter 128mm as the focal length in the MOUNT ADAPTOR SETTING > LENS REGISTRATION menu of your camera.

Is there a price to pay? Well, yes, since Speed Booster isn't cheap. With regards to image quality, the MTF [140] of the new lens is actually improved, but there's a chance of vignetting when Speed Booster is used to adapt fast lenses. That said, the newer Speed Booster Ultra improves vignetting issues that were problematic with the original Speed Booster. In any case, it's better than knock-off products such as Lens Turbo II.

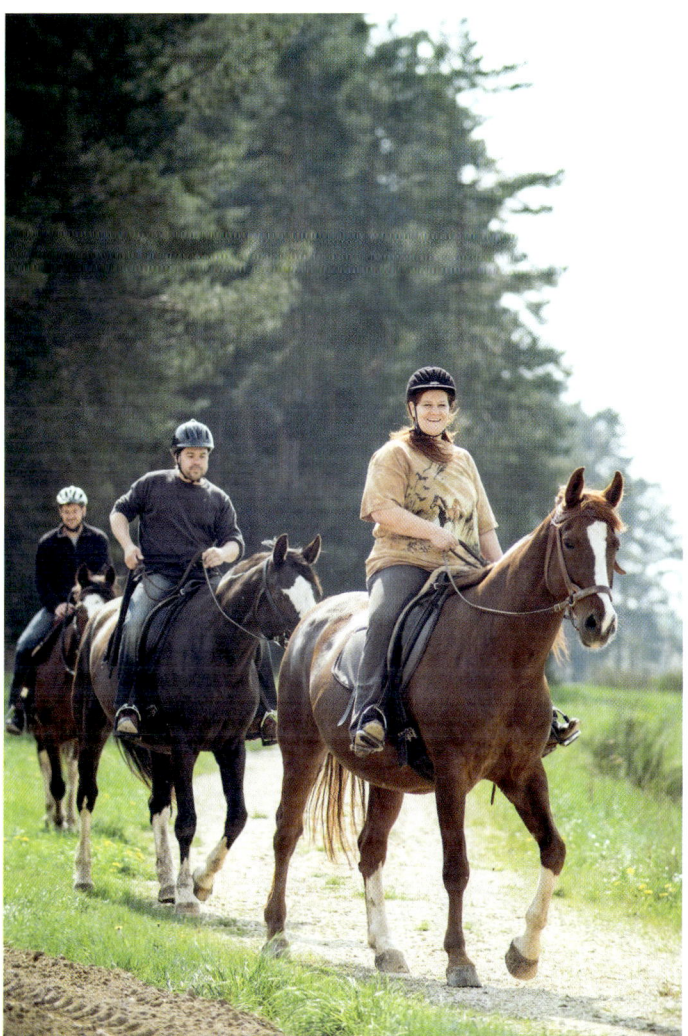

Fig. 245: This example was taken with the Contax version of **Speed Booster** and a Zeiss Sonnar T* 2.8/180 MM on an X-E1.

Speed Booster increases the speed (or maximum aperture) of a lens by about one stop, so you can use faster shutter speeds or lower ISO settings. For example, let's assume you need ISO 800 to shoot a scene with your full-frame DSLR at f/2.8 (wide open) with a 180mm lens and 1/1000s. On the X-mount, Speed Booster turns this lens into a 128mmF2 lens with the same angle of view. Shooting wide open (now f/2) at 1/1000s, you can drop the ISO to 400. Since full-frame sensors tend to offer an ISO advantage of about one stop over APS-C, the results from both cameras should be equivalent, because the APS-C sensor can compensate its smaller size by applying 1 EV less ISO amplification.

Speed Booster is available for several classic mounts, such as Canon FD, Nikon G, Contax/Yashica (Zeiss), Minolta MD, Contarex, ALPA, and Leica R. Sadly, there is no Speed Booster for Leica M, because an M adapter would be too thin to house the necessary optics. An announcement from Metabones competitor Kipon to build a really thin APS-C focal reducer for Leica M lenses also didn't materialize.

GFX users certainly don't need a Speed Booster to adapt full-frame lenses. They can either attach full-frame (35mm format) lenses "as is" with a mechanical or smart adapter, or use an optical format converter like the Laowa Magic Format Converter (MFC) [141]. It's basically a teleconverter that projects the smaller full-frame image circle on the larger image circle of the GFX.

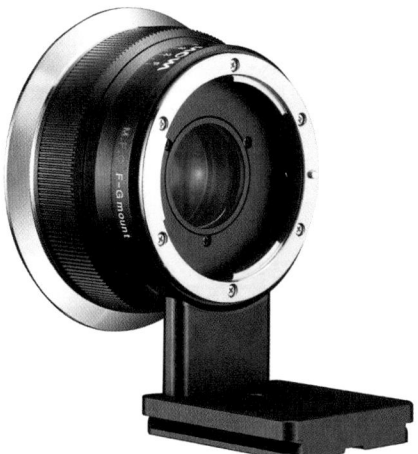

Fig. 246: The **Laowa MFC** from Venus Optics is a teleconverter that blows up the image circle of an adapted full-frame (35mm format) lens to cover the 44×33mm sensor in the GFX.

As of December 2018, the Laowa MFC was available in versions for Nikon F/G and Canon EF lenses. The latter adapter offers no electronic aperture control, so you are probably better off using one of the EF-to-G-mount smart adapters without image circle conversion. Many full-frame EF lenses cover the full GFX image circle, anyway.

Electronic smart adapters	TIP 138

Electronic smart adapters have been designed for modern third-party lenses like the Canon EF system. These lenses have electronic contacts and communicate with the camera body to offer functions such as autofocus, electronic aperture control, and optical image stabilization (OIS). They are also getting their power from the camera body.

Connecting modern EF lenses on the X-mount or G-mount with a simple mechanical (a.k.a. dumb) adapter turns out to be a frustrating experience: you cannot change the aperture while the lens is attached to the Fuji camera; there's no autofocus; the OIS doesn't work; and there is no EXIF data transmission to the camera.

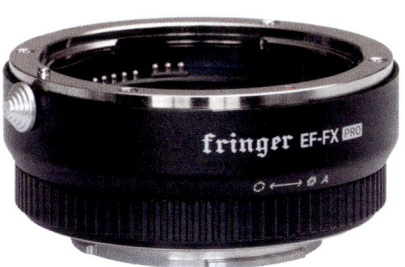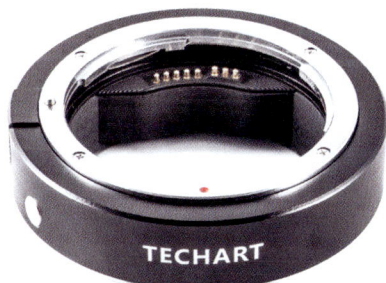

Fig. 247: The **Fringer EF-FX** was one of the first EF-to-XF smart adapters. You can also get the EF-FX Pro version (pictured on the left) with an integrated electronic aperture ring. A popular EF lens adapter for the GFX is the **Techart EF-GFX** (right).

The solution: use an electronic smart adapter. The majority of smart adapters is for Canon EF (and other EF-compatible) lenses, but you can also find an adapter to connect Contax 645 medium-format lenses to the GFX [142]. A smart adapter for current Nikon DSLR lenses might also be on the horizon.

An ideal smart adapter should meet the following criteria:

- Full electronic aperture control.

- Autofocus support (PDAF/CDAF, AF-S, AF-C, face detection, video, etc.).

- Support for built-in optical image stabilizers (OIS) in adapted lenses.

- Support for IBIS (X-H1, GFX 100) with adapted lenses that don't have built-in OIS.

- EXIF data transmission and recording (focal length, aperture, adapted lens model, serial number, etc.).

- Digital lens correction data transmission and conversion (chromatic aberrations, distortion, vignetting).

- Compatible with most or all lenses of the adapted system, including popular third-party offerings like Sigma or Tamron EF lenses.

- Frequent firmware updates to improve and maintain compatibility. New firmware updates should be easy to install from macOS and Windows computers. Alternatively, there should be support for adapter firmware upgrades via the lens firmware upgrade procedure of X series cameras.

Smart adapters are available from vendors like Fringer, Steelsring, Kipon, Viltrox, Techart, or Fotodiox. Kipon and Viltrox also offer EF-to-FX adapters with built-in focal length reducers (like the Speed Booster) to project the full image circle of the adapted full-frame lens on the smaller APS-C sensor of the X-mount camera.

2.8 WIRELESS REMOTE CONTROL AND TETHERING

Fuji's own Camera Remote app works with wireless iOS and Android devices, and it allows you to remotely control your camera by providing a live view image and a touch-screen interface to set the focus point, change exposure parameters, and release the shutter.

Using the Camera Remote app	TIP 139

Camera Remote allows you to control Wi-Fi enabled X cameras from an Android or iOS device running Fuji's Cam Remote app. To use Camera Remote, you must first download and install the free Cam Remote app on your smartphone or tablet. You can find download links, instructions, and additional information online [143].

*Important: Make sure you use the **Cam Remote App** and not the older **Camera App**.*

Here's how Camera Remote works with iOS devices (it shouldn't be much different for Android users):

- Select SHOOTING MENU > (SHOOTING SETTING >) WIRE-LESS COMMUNICATION on your camera. It now enters wireless mode and emits a Wi-Fi signal.

- Hook up your smartphone's or tablet's Wi-Fi with the camera's Wi-Fi network. Each camera comes with a unique network name that you can customize in SET UP > CONNECTION SETTING > WIRELESS SETTINGS > GENERAL SETTINGS > NAME.

- Open the Cam Remote app and select Remote Control. The mobile device will now assume control over the camera and display a live view image along with options

to adjust shutter speed, aperture or exposure compensation. There's also a virtual shutter button and a small
shooting menu that allows you to adjust parameters like
ISO, film simulation, white balance, macro, flash mode,
or self-timer.

■ To autofocus on a specific part of the live view image,
double-tap on it with your finger. Focus will be confirmed
with a green rectangle. If no focus lock can be established,
the rectangle will appear in red.

■ Adjust your exposure parameters as required. The brightness of the live view will change accordingly. Please note
that there's no live histogram.

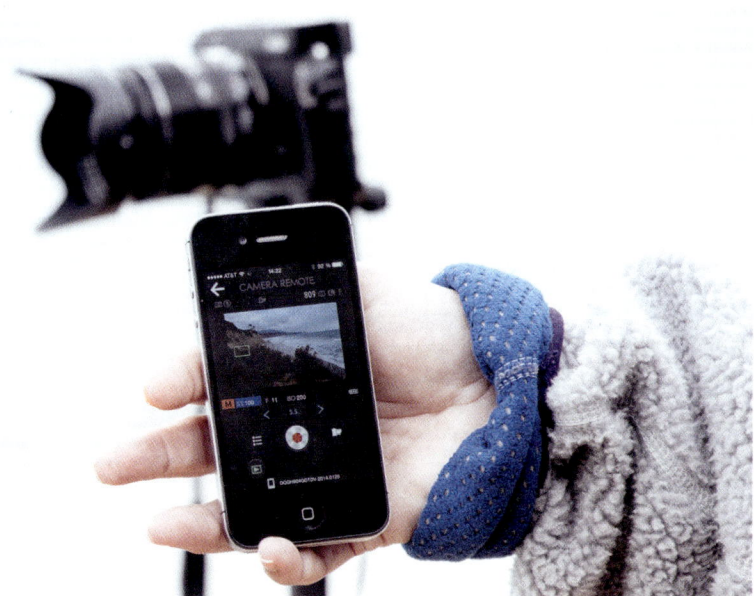

Fig. 248: **Camera Remote** offers a simple interface to control your
camera with a smartphone or tablet. To autofocus, double-tap on a
specific part of the WYSIWYG live view and wait for the green confirmation rectangle to appear. Sadly, there is no live histogram, and
you can't magnify the live view. There is a rudimentary shooting
menu, a virtual shutter button, and a playback button that allows
you to review images and transfer JPEGs to your mobile device.

Here are a few things you might want to know about Camera Remote:

■ Fuji's Camera Remote app allows you to adjust exposure parameters (aperture, shutter speed, ISO, exposure compensation), but you can't remotely change the camera's exposure mode. This means that you must manually set the camera to either **P**, **A**, **S**, or **M** mode *before* you select WIRELESS COMMUNICATION in the camera menu. To change the exposure mode during remote shooting, you must first disconnect Camera Remote, make the desired changes in the camera, and then start over with a new connection.

■ There's no electronic level indicator and no live histogram in the Camera Remote live view on your mobile device.

■ You can change several shooting parameters from within the Camera Remote app (ISO, film simulation, white balance preset, macro, flash mode, self-timer), but other parameters (such as dynamic range or Auto-ISO minimum shutter speed) must be preset in the camera before entering wireless communication mode.

■ There is no bulb functionality in Camera Remote, so your maximum exposure time is limited to the extent of the T setting. If you need more, better use a conventional (tethered or wireless) remote shutter release.

■ Some cameras also allow you to shoot HD video (but not 4K) with Camera Remote.

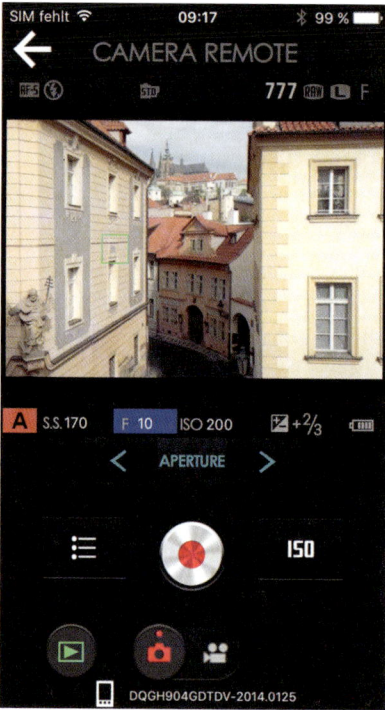

Fig. 249: Changing exposure parameters affects the **WYSIWYG live view**. The live view in Camera Remote always reflects the currently selected film simulation and JPEG parameters. If the camera offers this feature in its own live view, there is also a preview of manually selected DR settings (DR200%, DR400%).

A few more tips and hints:

- I use Camera Remote mostly in manual exposure mode **M**; I feel that this is the most convenient and efficient way to adjust shooting parameters. Changing a parameter (shutter speed, aperture, ISO) immediately adjusts the live view brightness.

- iOS users may be annoyed by the need to frequently reconnect the smartphone to the camera's Wi-Fi network, since the connection must be dropped and reestablished for every mode or parameter change made in the camera. This can be particularly cumbersome at home, where the iOS device is automatically reconnecting with your home network as soon as the camera has been disconnected. This has become easier with newer Bluetooth-enabled X cameras, because the app can automatically initiate a Wi-Fi connection between the smartphone and a Bluetooth-paired camera as needed.

■ Some users may suffer from connection losses caused by interfering networks that are transmitting on the same Wi-Fi channel as the camera. Sadly, there is currently no way to change the camera's transmission channel.

■ To transfer JPEGs from the camera to your mobile device with full resolution, make sure to select SET UP > CONNECTION SETTING > WIRELESS SETTINGS > RESIZE IMAGE FOR SMARTPHONE > OFF. Otherwise, the transferred images will be downsized to 3 megapixels.

■ Manual DR expansion settings (DR200%, DR400%) are reflected in the Camera Remote live view (as long as your camera supports DR expansion simulation in its own live view). The same applies to JPEG parameters such as contrast (HIGHLIGHT TONE, SHADOW TONE) or white balance settings. In manual mode **M**, the Camera Remote live view will also respect any settings made in SET UP > SCREEN SET-UP > PREVIEW EXP./WB IN MANUAL MODE.

Besides remote controlling [144] the camera, the Camera Remote app offers additional functions that allow you to transfer JPEGs from the camera to your mobile device (one by one [145] or in groups [146]) and to copy GPS location data [147] from your smartphone or tablet to the camera.

If you are using an X series camera with built-in Bluetooth, location data and the current time can automatically be synchronized from your smartphone. Bluetooth-enabled cameras can also benefit from a simple remote shutter release function [148], and there's the possibility to automatically obtain and install camera firmware updates [149]. To use Bluetooth with Camera Remote, make sure to pair the camera with your smartphone or tablet [150].

TIP 140	Streaming the live view via HDMI

The X-T2 and all other X cameras that were released after summer 2016 offer HDMI live-streaming, meaning that the contents of the live view (electronic viewfinder or LCD) can be transmitted to a monitor, TV, or beamer via the camera's HDMI output. All you have to do is connect the camera's Micro-HDMI jack to a suitable monitor with a digital input (HDMI, DVI, etc.). Real-time streaming will start automatically once the connection is established.

This is a useful feature for workshops, product demonstrations or professional productions, where customers can watch on a monitor what the photographer is seeing in the live view.

You can also use the HDMI live view output to connect the camera to an HD frame-grabber which is in turn connected to your computer. With this setup, you can make video recordings and screenshots of the live view.

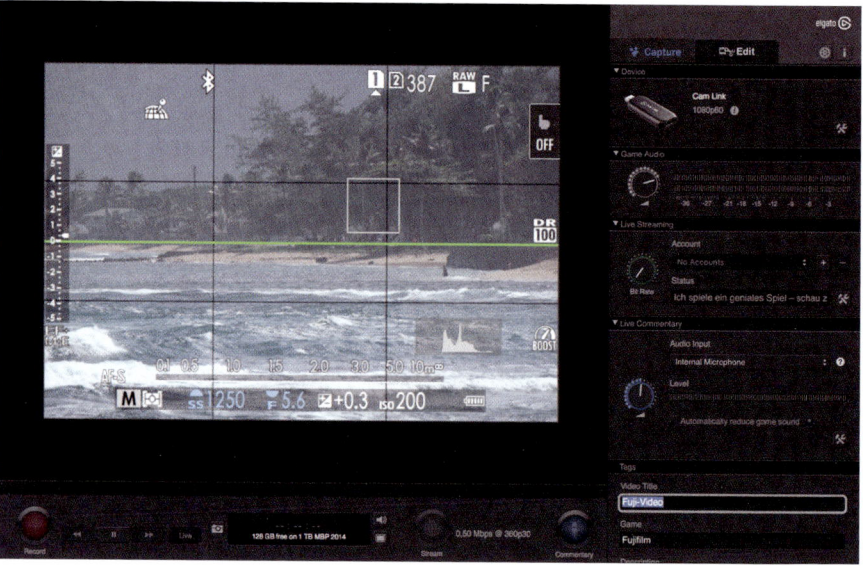

Fig. 250: The camera screenshots in this book were created by streaming the live view's HDMI output to my MacBook Pro, where I used **Elgato Cam Link** [151] with Game Capture HD software to capture screenshots. You can also use this hard- and software to create 60 fps HD video recordings of your camera's live view.

Tethered shooting via USB or Wi-Fi	TIP 141

Tethered shooting involves controlling the camera via a computer that is connected (tethered) to the camera via an USB cable or a Wi-Fi connection. As of December 2018, tethering was available in the X-T1/2/3, X-H1, X-Pro2, and GFX cameras.

In order to use USB tethering, you must select either USB TETHER SHOOTING AUTO or USB TETHER SHOOTING FIXED in the SET UP > CONNECTION SETTING > PC CONNECTION MODE menu. That way, the camera is either recognizing (AUTO) or even forcing (FIXED) a computer connection via USB, yielding control to compatible tethering software on the computer. For Wi-Fi tethering [152], select WIRELESS TETHER SHOOTING FIXED.

Speaking of compatible software, there is a table on the Fujifilm website that displays what's available for each X camera model [153]. There's also an online manual explaining different software options [154]: HS-V5 for Windows, Fujifilm X Acquire, the Fujifilm Tether Shooting Plug-in for Lightroom/ACR, and the Fujifilm Tether Shooting Plug-in Pro for Lightroom/ACR.

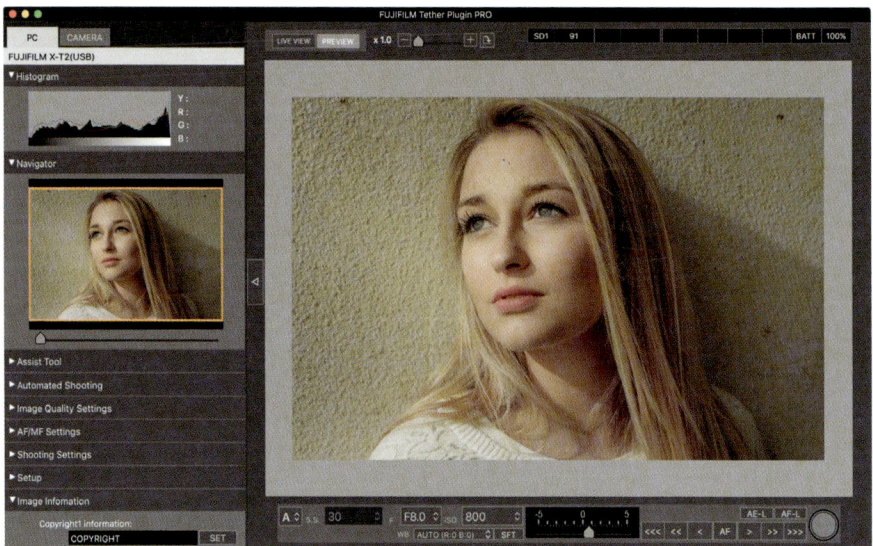

Fig. 251: The **Tether Shooting Plug-in Pro for Adobe Lightroom** includes a live view image and comprehensive control over the camera. Features include color histograms, focus stacking, expanded bracketing and the possibility to enter copyright information. You can also save and load full camera configurations.

I do not recommend buying **HS-V5** for Windows. It's an outdated software with a terrible user interface and limited functionality in concert with more recent X camera models [155].

Fujifilm X Acquire [156] is a simple freebie app for macOS and Windows that saves images to a hot folder from where other apps can obtain them. It also allows you to backup and restore full camera settings on your Mac or PC.

The **Fujifilm Tether Shooting Plug-in** [157] and **Tether Shooting Plug-in Pro** [158] are plug-ins for Adobe Lightroom/ACR. The Pro version offers shooting with a remote live view and remote control over most of the camera's settings.

In addition to that, **Capture One Pro** [159] now also adds direct tethering support thanks to the partnership between Fujifilm and PhaseOne that was revealed at Photokina 2018.

2.9 ANYTHING ELSE?

Hopefully, this book could answer many of your questions that went beyond the manual of your camera. However, this isn't the end: you can read my X-Pert Corner blog, participate in Fuji X forums, or join one of my Fuji X Secrets workshops.

Forums, blogs, magazines, and workshops	TIP 142

- High-resolution versions of many images in this book are available on Flickr [160].

- At Fuji X Secrets [161], you will find articles and reviews covering specific features, new firmware, and new products for the X series.

- My free X-Pert Corner blog [162] covers a variety of topics about the Fujifilm X series. You will find everything from service articles that go beyond this book to "First Look" previews of cameras and lenses.

- There are several online forums that focus on Fujifilm's X series: The Original Fuji X Forum [163]; The Ultimate Fuji X Forum [164]; and the Fuji X Series Forum [165].

- I am a regular contributor of gear-related articles in *FUJI-LOVE* [166], a great monthly magazine for all things Fuji X.

- Books, blogs, and forums are great, but what about a more personal touch? My site, Fuji X Secrets [167], offers a series of advanced workshops for Fuji X series users. My workshops cover topics that are similar to those in this book, but on a more in-depth and comprehensive level, including practical demonstrations and plenty of sample images. We work in small groups, and our delegates set the agenda. It's everything you always wanted to know about X but were afraid to ask.

ONLINE REFERENCES

Websites are not run by Rocky Nook, and are subject to change without our knowledge.

If necessary, we will update these references. For an updated version of this reference list, please download the available document at:

http://www.rockynook.com/fuji-x-secrets-online-references/

[1]   http://www.fujifilm.com/support/digital_cameras/manuals/
[2]   https://www.nitecorelights.com/products/fx1-travel-charger-for-fujifilm-np-w126-np-w126s-batteries
[3]   http://digital-cameras.support.fujifilm.com/app/answers/detail/a_id/20151/p/8453
[4]   http://www.fujifilm.com/support/digital_cameras/software/
[5]   http://digital-cameras.support.fujifilm.com/app/answers/detail/a_id/19061/kw/firmware/p/43/c/1524
[6]   http://digital-cameras.support.fujifilm.com/app/answers/detail/a_id/18998/kw/firmware/p/43/c/1524
[7]   http://digital-cameras.support.fujifilm.com/app/answers/detail/a_id/18997/kw/firmware/p/43/c/1524
[8]   http://app.fujifilm-dsc.com/en/camera_remote/index.html
[9]   http://app.fujifilm-dsc.com/en/camera_remote/fw_update.html
[10] http://www.fujifilm.com/products/digital_cameras/x/fujifilm_x_t2/features/page_06.html
[11] https://visibledust.com/products/sensor-cleaning-swabs-mxd-100-green-medium-format-30-33-mm-for-leica-s2-12-per-pack/
[12] https://en.wikipedia.org/wiki/Live_preview
[13] https://en.wikipedia.org/wiki/crop_factor
[14] https://en.wikipedia.org/wiki/image_stabilization
[15] https://en.wikipedia.org/wiki/motion_blur
[16] https://en.wikipedia.org/wiki/panning_(camera)
[17] https://en.wikipedia.org/wiki/circle_of_confusion
[18] http://www.cambridgeincolour.com/tutorials/diffraction-photography.htm
[19] https://en.wikipedia.org/wiki/deconvolution
[20] https://en.wikipedia.org/wiki/vignetting
[21] https://en.wikipedia.org/wiki/distortion_(options)
[22] https://en.wikipedia.org/wiki/chromatic_aberration
[23] https://en.wikipedia.org/wiki/exif

[24]   http://www.fujifilm.com/products/digital_cameras/accessories/
       pdf/mcex_01.pdf

[25]   http://www.fujifilm.com/products/digital_cameras/accessories/
       pdf/mcex_02.pdf

[26]   https://wordpress.lensrentals/blog/2012/05-testing-for-a-decen-
       tered-lens-an-old-technique-gets-a-makeover/

[27]   https://onzesi.de/technik/dezentrierung.php

[28]   http://translate.google.com/translate?sl=de&tl=en&js=y&prev=_t
       &hl=de&ie=UTF-8&u=http%3A%2F%2Fwww.onzesi.de%2Ftechnik
       %2Fdezentrierung.php&edit-text=

[29]   http://app.fujifilm-dsc.com/en/camera_remote/index.html

[30]   http://app.fujifilm-dsc.com/en/camera_remote/guide05.html

[31]   http://app.fujifilm-dsc.com/en/camera_remote/guide04.html

[32]   https://en.wikipedia.org/wiki/exif

[33]   https://en.wikipedia.org/wiki/dark-frame_subtraction

[34]   https://en.wikipedia.org/wiki/raw-image-format

[35]   https://en.wikipedia.org/wiki/jpeg

[36]   https://en.wikipedia.org/wiki/wysiwyg

[37]   https://en.wikipedia.org/wiki/live_preview

[38]   https://en.wikipedia.org/wiki/zone_system

[39]   http://www.cambridgeincolour.com/tutorials/histograms1.htm

[40]   http://www.cambridgeincolour.com/tutorials/histograms2.htm

[41]   https://en.wikipedia.org/wiki/depth_of_field

[42]   https://en.wikipedia.org/wiki/motion_blur

[43]   https://en.wikipedia.org/wiki/aperture_priority

[44]   https://en.wikipedia.org/wiki/aperture

[45]   https://en.wikipedia.org/wiki/depth_of_field

[46]   http://www.cambridgeincolour.com/tutorials/diffraction-photog-
       raphy.htm

[47]   https://en.wikipedia.org/wiki/shutter_priority

[48]   https://en.wikipedia.org/wiki/shutter_speed

[49]   https://en.wikipedia.org/wiki/motion_blur

[50]   https://en.wikipedia.org/wiki/panning_(camera)

[51]   https://en.wikipedia.org/wiki/long-exposure_photography

[52]   http://www.cambridgeincolour.com/tutorials/camera-shake.htm

[53]   https://en.wikipedia.org/wiki/image_stabilization

[54]   https://en.wikipedia.org/wiki/crop_factor

[55]   http://www.techradar.com/how-to/photography-video-capture/
       cameras/program-mode-explained-how-to-creatively-shift-
       aperture-and-shutter-speed-1321042

[56]   https://en.wikipedia.org/wiki/bracketing

[57]   https://en.wikipedia.org/wiki/dark-frame_subtraction

[58]   https://en.wikipedia.org/wiki/neutral-density_filter

[59]   http://en.wikipedia.org/wiki/film_speed#Digital_camera_ISO_
       speed_and_exposure_index

[60]   https://www.flickr.com/gp/ricopfirstinger/k38hti

[61]   http://www.diyphotography.net/lighting-high-key-and-low-key/
[62]   https://en.wikipedia.org/wiki/high-dynamic-range_imaging
[63]   https://en.wikipedia.org/wiki/rolling_shutter
[64]   http://www.fujifilm.com/products/digital_cameras/x/fujifilm_x_
       h1/features/page_05.htlm
[65]   http://digital-photography-school.com/the-problem-with-the-
       focus-recompose-method/
[66]   https://fujifilm-x.com/af/en/
[67]   https://en.wikipedia.org/wiki/hyperfocal_distance
[68]   https://en.wikipedia.org/wiki/circle_of_confusion
[69]   https://www.youtube.com/watch?v=7FR3l6S12JA
[70]   https://www.youtube.com/watch?v=rnkib7fz8s8
[71]   http://www.cambridgeincolour.com/tutorials/hyperfocal-
       distance.htm
[72]   http://www.fujifilm.com/products/digital_cameras/accessories/
       pdf/mcex_01.pdf
[73]   http://www.fujifilm.com/products/digital_cameras/accessories/
       pdf/mcex_02.pdf
[74]   https://en.wikipedia.org/wiki/depth_of_field
[75]   http://www.cambridgeincolour.com/tutorials/diffraction-photog-
       raphy.htm
[76]   https://photography.tutsplus.com/tutorials/how-to-calculate-the-
       sharpest-aperture-for-any-lens--cms-25153
[77]   https://en.wikipedia.org/wiki/focus_stacking
[78]   https://www.heliconsoft.com/heliconsoft-products/helicon-
       focus/
[79]   https://en.wikipedia.org/wiki/panning_(camera)
[80]   http://www.cambridgeincolour.com/tutorials/white-balance.htm
[81]   https://en.wikipedia.org/wiki/exif
[82]   https://en.wikipedia.org/wiki/gray_card
[83]   http://www.fujifilm.com/support/digital_cameras/software/
       application/
[84]   https://en.wikipedia.org/wiki/contrast_(vision)
[85]   https://en.wikipedia.org/wiki/colorfulness
[86]   https://en.wikipedia.org/wiki/color_space
[87]   https://en.wikipedia.org/wiki/srgb
[88]   https://en.wikipedia.org/wiki/adobe_rgb_color_space
[89]   https://en.wikipedia.org/wiki/gamut
[90]   http://www.fujifilm.com/support/digital_cameras/software/
       application/
[91]   http://fujifilm-x.com/en-us/stories/fujifilm-x-raw-studio-
       features-users-guide/
[92]   https://silkypix.isl.co.jp/en/
[93]   http://www.fujifilm.com/support/digital_cameras/software/
       myfinepix_studio/rfc/
[94]   https://www.adobe.com/products/photoshop-lightroom.html

[95]   https://www.phaseone.com/en/imaging _software.aspx
[96]   https://www.phaseone.com/en/Capture-One/Capture-One-Fuji
       film.aspx
[97]   https://www.phaseone.com/en/Online-Store.aspx
[98]   http://www.iridientdigital.com
[99]   http://www.picturecode.com
[100] https://www.iridientdigital.com/products/xtransformer.html
[101] https://en.wikipedia.org/wiki/exif
[102] http://en.wikipedia.org/wiki/through-the-lens_meter-
       ing#Through_the_lens_flash_metering
[103] https://en.wikipedia.org/wiki/neutral-density_filter
[104] http://www.godox.com/EN/Products_Witstro_Pocket_Flash_
       AD200.html
[105] http://www.godox.com/EN/Products_Remote_Control_X1TF_
       TTL_Wireless_Flash_Trigger.html
[106] https://en.wikipedia.org/wiki/flash_synchronization
[107] https://en.wikipedia.org/wiki/neutral-density_filter
[108] http://www.godox.com/EN/Products_Camera_Flash_Wit-
       stro_AD600_Powerfou&Portable_Flash.html
[109] http://www.phot-r.com/p-120bw.html
[110] http://www.godox.com/EN/Products_Remote_Control_XproF_
       TTL_Wireless_Flash_Trigger.html
[111] http://www.godox.com/EN/Products_Camera_Flash_TT600.html
[112] https://en.wikipedia.org/wiki/red-eye_effect
[113] https://en.wikipedia.org/wiki/catch_light
[114] http://www.metz-mecatech.de/en/lighting/flash-units/system-
       flash-units/mecablitz-m400/data-sheet/mecablitz-m400-fujifilm.
       html
[115] http://www.godox.com/EN/Products_Remote_Control_X1TF_
       TTL_Wireless_Flash_Trigger.html
[116] http://www.godox.com/EN/Products_Camera_Flash_TT600.html
[117] http://www.godox.com/EN/Products_Witstro_Pocket_Flash_
       AD200.html
[118] http://www.godox.com/EN/Products_Witstro_H200R_Round_
       Flash_Head.html
[119] https://www.fomito.shop/products/godox-ad-l-witsro-series-
       outdoor-flash-accessories-led-changeable-head-for-ad200
[120] http://www.godox.com/EN/Products_Camera_Flash_Witstro_
       Powerfou&Portable_Flash_Accessories.html
[121] http://www.godox.com/EN/Products_Witstro_EC200_Extension_
       Head.html
[122] http://www.godox.com/EN/Products_S_type_Speedlite_Bracket.
       html
[123] https://www.fomito.shop/products/godox-ad-b2-ad200-dual-
       power-flash-head-s-type-double-lamp-holder

[124] http://www.godox.com/EN/Products_Camera_Flash_Witstro_ Powerfou&Portable_Flash_Accessories.html

[125] https://petapixel.com/2018/07/11/godox-demystified-a-complete-guide-to-x-series-flash-gear/

[126] http://flashhavoc.com/godox-flash-system-overview/

[127] http://www.godox.com/EN/Products_Camera_Flash_TT685F.html

[128] https://rockynook.com/shop/photography/one-flash/?ref=21

[129] https://rockynook.com/shop/photography/the-flash-book/?ref=21

[130] https://rockynook.com/shop/photography/the-photographers-guide-to-posing/?ref=21

[131] http://strobist.blogspot.com

[132] https://passionphotographyexperience.com/

[133] https://www.morethanwords.be/

[134] https://en.wikipedia.org/wiki/teleconverter

[135] https://www.fujifilm.com/products/digital_cameras/accessories/ lens/mount/fujifilm_m_mount_adapter/compatibility_chart/ index.html

[136] http://www.fujifilm.com/support/digital_cameras/compatibility/ mountadapter/

[137] https://en.wikipedia.org/wiki/135_film

[138] https://en.wikipedia.org/wiki/aps-c

[139] https://en.wikipedia.org/wiki/bokeh

[140] https://en.wikipedia.org/wiki/optical_transfer_function

[141] https://www.venuslens.net/product/laowa-magic-format-converter-mfc/

[142] https://www.fringeradapter.com/#for-gfx50s

[143] http://app.fujifilm-dsc.com/en/camera_remote/index.html

[144] http://app.fujifilm-dsc.com/en/camera_remote/guide05.html

[145] http://app.fujifilm-dsc.com/en/camera_remote/guide01.html

[146] http://app.fujifilm-dsc.com/en/camera_remote/guide03.html

[147] http://app.fujifilm-dsc.com/en/camera_remote/guide02.html

[148] http://app.fujifilm-dsc.com/en/camera_remote/guide04.html

[149] http://app.fujifilm-dsc.com/en/camera_remote/fw_update.html

[150] http://app.fujifilm-dsc.com/en/camera_remote/index.html# connect

[151] https://www.elgato.com/en/gaming/cam-link

[152] http://app.fujifilm-dsc.com/en/tether/tether_wireless.html

[153] http://digital-cameras.support.fujifilm.com/app/answers/ detail/a_id/19878/

[154] http://app.fujifilm-dsc.com/en/tether/index.html

[155] http://www.fujifilm.com/support/digital_cameras/software/ hsv5/win/

[156] https://fujifilm-x.com/en-gb/stories/fujifilm-x-acquire-features-users-guide/

[157] http://www.fujifilm.com/products/digital_cameras/accessories/ others/#soft

[158] https://fujifilm-x.com/global/stories/fujifilm-tether-plug-in-pro-features/
[159] https://www.phaseone.com/fujifilm
[160] https://www.flickr.com/gp/ricopfirstinger/K38Hti
[161] https://fuji-x-secrets.net/
[162] http://www.fujirumors.com/category/x-pert/
[163] http://www.fujix-forum.com/
[164] http://www.fuji-x-forum.com/
[165] http://www.fujixseries.com/
[166] https://fujilove.com/
[167] https://fuji-x-secrets.net/

INDEX